SCOTT FORESMAN

Art

TEXAS TEACHER'S EDITION
Grade 4

Robyn Montana Turner, Ph.D.
Program Author

TEXAS EDITION

PEARSON

Scott Foresman

Editorial Offices: Glenview, Illinois • Parsippany, New Jersey • New York, New York

Sales Offices: Parsippany, New Jersey • Duluth, Georgia • Glenview, Illinois • Coppell, Texas • Ontario, California • Mesa, Arizona

ISBN: 0-328-08052-7
Copyright © 2005, Pearson Education, Inc.
All Rights Reserved. Printed in the United States of America. This publication is protected by Copyright, and permission should be obtained from the publisher prior to any prohibited reproduction, storage in a retrieval system, or transmission in any form by any means, electronic, mechanical, photocopying, recording, or likewise. For information regarding permission(s), write to: Permissions Department, Scott Foresman, 1900 East Lake Avenue, Glenview, Illinois 60025.

1 2 3 4 5 6 7 8 9 10 V064 13 12 11 10 09 08 07 06 05 04

Authors

PROGRAM AUTHORS

Robyn Montana Turner, Ph.D.

Kindergarten through Grade 6, Austin, Texas An acclaimed elementary visual arts textbook author, Dr. Turner's visual arts teaching experience spans from pre-kindergarten through graduate school. Most recently, she directed the Visual Arts Student Teacher Program at the University of Texas at Austin. Dr. Turner also conceptualizes and writes trade books for children and young adults. Her award-winning artist biographies, *Portraits of Women Artists for Children*, are featured in libraries and classrooms nationally. Her visual account of the history and culture of Texas, *Texas Traditions: The Culture of the Lone Star State*, received the Teddy Award, the state's highest honor for a children's book. Her academic publications include a chapter in the National Art Education Association anthology *Gender Issues in Art Education*, as well as contributions to the NAEA Journal *Studies in Art Education*.

Rebecca Brooks, Ph.D.

Grades 7 and 8, Austin, Texas A visual arts and art education professor and graduate advisor in the Department of Art and Art History at the University of Texas at Austin, Dr. Brooks is a nationally successful textbook author, lecturer, and researcher, focusing on the development and implementation of interdisciplinary curricula at the elementary, secondary, and college levels. The recipient of two prestigious Foxworth Fellowships from the College of Fine Arts, she received the Texas Art Education Association's Art Educator of the Year for Higher Education (1990) and the National Art Education Association's Art Educator of the Year, Western Division (1991). Currently, the former middle school art teacher remains an active liaison between the public schools and the university as Coordinator of Student Field Experiences in Art.

CONTRIBUTING AUTHORS

James Clarke, M.Ed.
Grades 6 through 8, Houston, Texas

Executive Director of the Texas Coalition for Quality Arts Education, Mr. Clarke is a successful arts educator, author, consultant, editor, and speaker. The former National Art Education Association and Texas Art Education Association President has won many NAEA honors, including the Marion Quinn Dix Award for Outstanding Leadership. He was on the National Coordinating Board for America's National Standards for Arts Education and a spokesman at the National Education Goals hearings in the 1990s.

Sara A. Chapman, Ed.D.
Grades 6 through 8, Houston, Texas

Coordinator of the Visual Arts Program for Alief Independent School District in Houston, Ms. Chapman is a successful middle school textbook author who has taught all levels of art education, including university course work. Currently Western Region Vice President of the National Art Education Association, she also served as President of the Texas Art Education Association and NAEA. She chaired the Texas Fine Arts Standards Visual Arts team and is a cadre member of the state's Center for Educator Development in the Fine Arts.

Consultants & Reviewers

PROGRAM CONSULTANTS

Christopher Adejumo, Ph.D.
Associate Professor, Visual Art Studies
University of Texas, Austin, TX

Doug Blandy, Ph.D.
Professor and Director, Arts and Administration
Program, Institute for Community Arts and Studies
University of Oregon, Eugene, OR

Rebecca Brooks, Ph.D.
Professor, Department of Art and Art History
University of Texas, Austin, TX

Sara A. Chapman, Ed.D.
Coordinator, Visual Arts Program
Alief Independent School District, Houston, TX

James Clarke, M.Ed.
Executive Director, Texas Coalition for Quality Arts
Education, Houston, TX

Georgia Collins, Ph.D.
Professor Emeritus, College of Fine Arts
University of Kentucky, Lexington, KY

Deborah Cooper, M.Ed.
Coordinating Director of Arts Education,
Curriculum and Instruction
Charlotte-Mecklenburg Schools, Charlotte, NC

Sandra M. Epps, Ph.D.
Multicultural Art Education Consultant
New York, NY

Mary Jo Gardere, B.S.
Multi-Arts Specialist, Eladio Martinez Learning Center
Dallas, TX

Carlos G. Gómez, MFA
Professor of Fine Art, University of Texas at Brownsville
and Texas Southmost College, Brownsville, TX

Kristina Lamour, MFA
Assistant Professor, The Art Institute of Boston
at Lesley University, Boston, MA

Melinda M. Mayer, Ph.D.
Assistant Professor, School of Visual Arts
University of North Texas, Denton, TX

Robyn Montana Turner, Ph.D.
Author, Austin, TX

CRITIC READERS

Celeste Anderson
Roosevelt Elementary School, Nampa, ID

Mary Jo Birkholz
Wilson Elementary School, Janesville, WI

Mary Jane Cahalan
Mitzi Bond Elementary School, El Paso, TX

Cindy Collar
Cloverleaf Elementary School, Cartersville, GA

Yvonne Days
St. Louis Public Schools, St. Louis, MO

Shirley Dickey
Creative Art Magnet School, Houston, TX

Ray Durkee
Charlotte Performing Arts Center, Punta Gorda, FL

Sue Flores-Minick
Bryker Woods Elementary School, Austin, TX

Denise Jennings
Fulton County Schools, Atlanta, GA

Alicia Lewis
Stevens Elementary School, Houston, TX

James Miller
Margo Elementary School, Weslaco, TX

Marta Olson
Seattle Public Schools, Seattle, WA

Judy Preble
Florence Avenue School, Irvington, NJ

Tonya Roberson
Oleson Elementary School, Houston, TX

Andrew Southwick
Edgewood Independent School District, San Antonio, TX

Nita Ulaszek
Audelia Creek Elementary School, Dallas, TX

Tessie Varthas
Office of Creative and Public Art, Philadelphia, PA

Penelope Venola
Spurgeon Intermediate School, Santa Ana, CA

Elizabeth Willett
Art Specialist, Fort Worth, TX

STUDIO REVIEWERS

Judy Abbott
Art Educator, Allison Elementary School
Austin Independent School District, Austin, TX

Lin Altman
Art Educator, Cedar Creek Elementary School
Eanes Independent School District, Austin, TX

Geral T. Butler
Retired Art Educator, Heritage High School
Lynchburg City Schools, Lynchburg, VA

Dale Case
Elementary Principal, Fox Meadow Elementary School
Nettleton School District, Jonesboro, AR

Deborah McLouth
Art Educator, Zavala Elementary School
Austin Independent School District, Austin, TX

Patricia Newman
Art Educator, Saint Francis Xavier School
Archdiocese of Chicago, La Grange, IL

Nancy Sass
Art Educator, Cambridge Elementary School, Alamo
Heights Independent School District, San Antonio, TX

Sue Spiva Telle
Art Educator, Woodridge Elementary School, Alamo
Heights Independent School District, San Antonio, TX

Cari Washburn
Art Educator, Great Oaks Elementary School, Round
Rock Independent School District, Round Rock, TX

Materials that inspire!

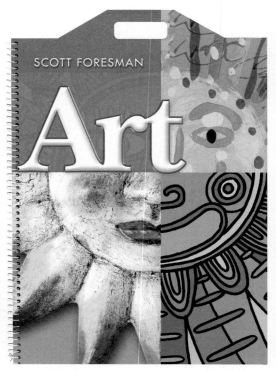

Teacher's Edition: Grade 3

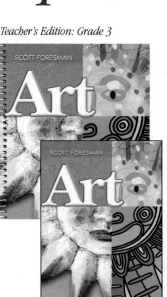

STUDENT EDITION
Grades 1 through 8

- Places fine art and engaging text in students' hands

- Explores wide range of styles and media

- Exposes students to art and artists in every lesson

BIG BOOK
Kindergarten through Grade 5

- Student book pages on a larger scale

- Suitable for whole-class instruction

- Great display for center or small-group activities

Student Edition: Grade 3   *Big Book: Grade 3*

TEXAS TEACHER'S EDITION
Kindergarten through Grade 8

- Detailed overviews for flexible and easy planning

- Cross-curricular links to core disciplines

- Varied assessment options

FINE ART TRANSPARENCIES
Grades 1 through 8

- More than 1,000 images; most of the fine artworks in the program

- Ideal for Feldman Model and compare/contrast discussions

FINE ART PRINTS*
Kindergarten through Grade 8

- Laminated 18" × 24" prints

- Instruction and activities in English and in Spanish on the back

- Set A features artworks for Unit Openers and Unit Reviews

- Set B includes artworks for the Look and Compare activity

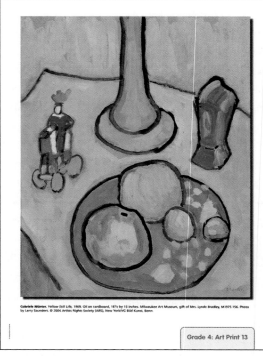

Gabriele Münter. *Yellow Still Life,* 1909. Oil on cardboard, 16½ by 13 inches, Milwaukee Art Museum, gift of Mrs. Lynde Bradley, M1975.156. Photo by Larry Saunders. © 2004 Artists Rights Society (ARS), New York/VG Bild-Kunst, Bonn

Grade 4: Art Print 13

Fine Art Print: Grade 4

INSTRUCTIONAL PRINTS*
Kindergarten through Grade 8

• Fourteen colorful classroom posters with English and Spanish instruction on the back. Includes one poster for each element of art and principle of design and one classroom safety poster, available in English and in Spanish

• Grade-level sets: Kindergarten through Grade 2, Grade 3 through Grade 5, and Grade 6 through Grade 8

UNIT-BY-UNIT RESOURCES*
Kindergarten through Grade 8

• Blackline masters in English and Spanish for family letters, vocabulary, activities, games

• Unit tests and assessments in English and Spanish

TIME LINE OF ART HISTORY

• A large format, full-color time line that spans Old Stone Age through the Modern World

• Features a wide variety of media and genres

MASTER INDEX

• Comprehensive reference to simplify planning

• Cross references all fine art, artists, techniques, media, themes, and more for Grades K–8

TAKS WORKBOOK AND ANSWER KEY*
Grades 1 through 8

• Integrated reading and writing activities for each unit to strengthen language arts skills

• Fiction and non-fiction passages with multiple-choice questions

• Writing exercises include writing prompts and graphic organizers

• Workbook and Answer Key available in English and in Spanish

Overview

Turn on the power of visual literacy!

Art is a powerful language that ignites

imaginations and helps students to acquire

critical thinking and communication skills.

Scott Foresman Art integrates classroom

instruction, hands-on activities, and literacy-

building experiences to turn on the power

of art for all students. Scott Foresman Art

focuses on the Elements of Art and the

Principles of Design, the basic tools artists

use to communicate their ideas.

Teach the basics of art

LESSONS Teach students how to explore, appreciate, and analyze the visual world and develop their artistic perception by introducing:

The Elements of Art

Line, Color, Value, Shape, Texture, Form, and Space

The Principles of Design

Balance, Rhythm, Pattern, Variety, Proportion, Emphasis, and Unity

Create art experiences

STUDIOS Involve students in the creative art process and give them an opportunity to practice the **Elements of Art** and the **Principles of Design** with age-appropriate art media and techniques. Use the Quick Studio shortcuts when time or resources are limited.

Total coverage of the
ART TEKS and **4 ART STRANDS:**
**Perception, Creative
Expression/Performance,
Historical and Cultural Heritage,**
and **Response/Evaluation**

Build literacy through art

ENRICHMENT FEATURES Develop students' higher order thinking skills using the **Unit Opener, Look and Compare,** and **Artist at Work** or **Meet the Artist** features.

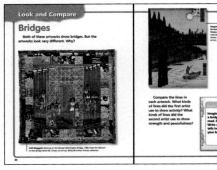

Grade 3: Look and Compare

Grade 3: Artist at Work

Assess what students learn

ASSESSMENT FEATURES
Monitor students' understanding and their development of visual literacy through hands-on **Portfolio Project** activities and written and oral responses in the **Unit Review**.

Flexible Organization

Each unit offers at least 6 Lessons, 6 Studios, Enrichment Features, and Assessment Features so you can customize curriculum.

Introduce *and motivate with engaging Fine Art in the* **Unit Opener**

> Teach **Lesson 1**
> Create *in* **Studio 1**

> Teach **Lesson 2**
> Create *in* **Studio 2**

> Teach **Lesson 3**
> Create *in* **Studio 3**

Enrich *with features like* **Look and Compare** *and* **Artist at Work** *or* **Meet the Artist**

> Teach **Lesson 4**
> Create *in* **Studio 4**

> Teach **Lesson 5**
> Create *in* **Studio 5**

> Teach **Lesson 6**
> Create *in* **Studio 6**

Enrich *with features like* **Look and Compare** *and* **Artist at Work** *or* **Meet the Artist**

Assess *with the* **Portfolio Project** *to artistically demonstrate understanding*

Assess *with the* **Unit Review** *through written and oral responses*

Teach the basics of art

Texas Essential Knowledge and Skills (TEKS)

Discover at a glance how lesson skills correlate to the TEKS.

3-Step Lesson Plan

Get students thinking like artists with easy-to-follow, structured instruction.

Transparency 3-18a

Vincent van Gogh. *The Café Terrace du Place du Forum Arles, at Night*, 1888. Oil on canvas, 31½ by 25½ inches. Rijksmuseum Kröller-Müller, Otterlo, Netherlands.

© Pearson Scott Foresman

Fine Art Transparencies

Provide large visual models for class discussions. Transparency size is 5.5" × 8.5".

Lesson 1

At a Glance

Objectives

- Identify and describe lines in artworks.
- Describe, analyze, interpret, and judge artworks.

Materials

- **Fine Art Transparency**
- jump rope
- Sketchbook Journal

Vocabulary

line, media

FA TEKS 3.1B Identify art elements such as color, texture, form, line, space, and value and art principles such as emphasis, pattern, rhythm, balance, proportion, and unity in artworks

FA TEKS 3.4B Apply simple criteria to identify main ideas in original artworks, portfolios, and exhibitions by peers and major artists

① Introduce

Place a jump rope on the floor. Stretch it tight so that it creates a straight line. Then let students use the rope to demonstrate lines that curve, bend, wave, zigzag, or spiral.

Next, have students look for lines in objects and artworks found in the classroom. Point out broad, straight lines in an artwork or on a student's shirt. Compare those to fine, straight lines found on a sheet of notebook paper. Then have students identify other types of lines in natural and human-made objects that they see in the classroom.

18

Grade 3: Teacher's Edition

Lesson 1

Line

A **line** is a continuous mark on a surface. Most lines are created by a pen, a pencil, or a brush. Find thick, thin, and wavy lines in this painting.

Vincent van Gogh. *The Café Terrace on the Place du Forum Arles, at Night*, 1888. Oil on canvas, 31½ by 25½ inches. Rijksmuseum Kröller-Müller, Otterlo, Netherlands.

18

🎨 Art Background

Art History During the Impressionist era, artists attempted to show light as we see it outdoors. They used thick brushstrokes and vivid colors. Although his brushwork shows the influence of the Impressionists, Vincent van Gogh developed his own style that emphasized swirling brushstrokes and intense colors.

ESL Notes

Have students take turns drawing each kind of line on the board. Ask them yes and no questions about each line. Or give them directives that call for a nonverbal response. For example, **Is this a straight line?** or **This is a wavy line. Draw another wavy line.**

ESL TEKS 3.1H Infer meaning by making associations of utterances

Types of Lines

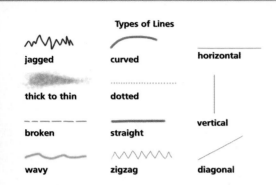

jagged   curved   horizontal

thick to thin   dotted

broken   straight   vertical

wavy   zigzag   diagonal

Horizontal lines show a peaceful scene. Vertical lines suggest strength. Diagonal lines bring motion and energy to an artwork. Find these three kinds of lines in Van Gogh's painting.

Artists use different **media** to create artworks. Van Gogh chose oil paints as his medium. Other media are pencils, paints, chalk, clay, and crayons.

Sketchbook Journal

Draw a special place you know, such as a park, restaurant, or playground. Use different kinds of lines and name them.

19

Curriculum Connection

Science Have students look for lines on animals. Explain that lines and colors on animals can help protect them from predators and disguise them from prey. The brightly colored stripes on a snake warn others to stay away because the snake might be venomous. The lines on a tiger make it more difficult to detect in the wild. Have students use reference sources to find pictures of animals whose markings show examples of curved, dotted, straight, wavy, or zigzag lines.

TAKS (Gr. 5) Sci Obj. 2 Understand life science
Sci TEKS 3.9A Observe and identify characteristics among species

2 Teach

Have students read page 18 and the credit line. Tell students that one way to identify the main idea in an artwork is to describe the setting. Ask:

- **What do you see in this painting?** (people eating at an outside café) DESCRIBE
- **What art tools and media did Van Gogh use?** (paintbrushes, oil paints) ANALYZE

After students read page 19, demonstrate how a line can be made by moving an art tool across a surface. Review different kinds of lines, then ask:

- **What kinds of lines did the artist use to make objects appear rough and bumpy?** (curved, broken) ANALYZE
- **How would the painting be different if the artist had shown the café during the day instead of at night?** (Possible response: It would have had brighter colors and more people.) INTERPRET
- **Which lines are the most interesting to you? Why?** (Possible response: curved lines in the sidewalk; because Van Gogh used a simple curved line to show a rocky surface) JUDGE

Sketchbook Journal Tell students to experiment with different media to see which ones work best for creating each kind of line.

3 Close

After students complete their sketches, have them label the different types of lines they used.

Assessment Play a game of Eye Spy. Have students take turns giving clues about lines in objects to help classmates guess the objects.

NVAS (K–4) **#1** Understanding and applying media, techniques, and processes
NVAS (K–4) **#2** Using knowledge of structures and functions
NVAS (K–4) **#4** Understanding the visual arts in relation to history and cultures

Unit 1 *Art All Around You*   **19**

The Feldman Model

Use an easy four-step process
DESCRIBE, ANALYZE, INTERPRET, JUDGE
to guide students' responses to visual art and develop higher order thinking skills.

Sketchbook Journal

Provide an opportunity for students to record ideas and demonstrate understanding of art concepts.

Curriculum Connection

Introduce activities that help students relate art to other disciplines.

Assessment Opportunity

Evaluate student understanding of content and correlate to national standards.

Texas Assessment of Knowledge and Skills

Identify activities that correlate to TEKS and TAKS Objectives.

Create art experiences

Studio 1

At a Glance

Objectives
- Express ideas by drawing favorite foods.
- Demonstrate different techniques for drawing.
- Evaluate original artworks by self and peers.

Materials
- pencils, pens, crayons, water-based markers, drawing paper
- Rubric 1 from **Unit-by-Unit Resources**

FA TEKS 3.2A Create artworks based on personal observations and experiences
FA TEKS 3.2C Produce drawings, paintings, prints, constructions, ceramics, and fiberart, using a variety of art materials appropriately.
FA TEKS 3.4A Identify general intent and expressive qualities in personal artworks

① Introduce

Review types of lines. Have students use their own experiences to describe types of lines and give examples.

Then have students brainstorm a list of favorite foods. Tell them they can use their experiences with food to create an artwork. Ask:

- **What favorite foods are part of a well-balanced meal?**
- **What do these foods look like?**
- **What kinds of lines will you use to show each food item?**

Technique Tip

Offer easy ideas for using art tools so students can connect the process with their results.

3-Step Studio

Empower students to think and act like artists by presenting the creative process in simple terms.

Meeting Individual Needs

Include all students in studio experiences by adapting to individual needs.

Quick Studio

Offer a quick alternative to the full studio using easy-to-find materials.

Studio 1

Draw Lines

What are your favorite foods? Do you like tacos best or colorful salads? Follow these steps to draw them.

1 Draw a large plate shape. Decorate the edge with many kinds of lines.

2 Draw a glass and a drink. Add your favorite foods to the plate.

Technique Tip

Use the tip of the marker to make thin lines and dots. Use the side of the marker to make thick lines.

20

Meeting Individual Needs

Inclusion Some students with physical disabilities may not be able to draw the pictures as shown. Provide a drawn plate where students can add lines to the edge. Allow students to look through magazines to find foods for their plates. You may want to assign partners who can help cut and paste pictures.

Quick Studio

Have students draw two food items on a white, paper plate. Remind them to use a variety of lines in their drawings.

20

Grade 3: Teacher's Edition

 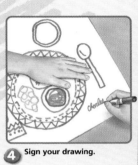

3 Add a fork, spoon, and napkin. Decorate the napkin with lines.

4 Sign your drawing.

21

Think Like an Artist

Imagine that you had shown only one type of line. How would that change your drawing?

Fine Arts Connection

Music There are many kinds of lines in music. Sing together "Row, Row, Row Your Boat." Point out the place in the song in which the notes form a diagonal line as they go down the scale. (Life is but a dream) Draw these notes on the board, pointing out the line. Then sing the notes again.

Life is but a dream.

Sing other familiar songs, such as "Make New Friends" or "This Old Man." Listen for notes that form a diagonal or horizontal line. If possible, let students play the notes on a piano, xylophone, or with bells.

FA TEKS 3.2A Sing or play a classroom instrument
FA TEKS 3.5C Describe relationships between music and other subjects

② Create

Have students read the directions on pages 20–21. Then distribute materials.

- Have students draw a circle inside the plate to indicate the inside edge of the border.
- Remind students to think about the shapes of their favorite foods. Help them name the kinds of lines they should use.
- As they add details to their drawings, remind them that the fork goes on the left and the spoon goes to the right of the plate.
- Encourage students to use their best handwriting.

Technique Tip Show students ways to hold a marker to draw thick or thin lines. If using a crayon, students can remove the paper and draw with the side to make broad lines.

③ Close

Have students identify their general intent and then reflect on their work by answering the *Think Like an Artist* question. (Possible response: Using only one type of line would make my drawing boring.)

Encourage students to share their work with classmates. Have them name the different kinds of lines they see in each other's drawings.

Ongoing Assessment

If . . . students have difficulty drawing light and thin lines,

then . . . suggest that they decrease the pressure applied to the art tool as they draw.

See page 18 from **Unit-by-Unit Resources** for a rubric to assess this studio.

NVAS (K–4) #1 Understanding and applying media, techniques, and processes
NVAS (K–4) #2 Using knowledge of structures and functions
NVAS (K–4) #6 Making connections between visual arts and other disciplines

Unit 1 *Art All Around You*   **21**

Studio Instruction

Engage students in the creative process using detailed, step-by-step instructions that are right on the student page.

Ongoing Assessment

Use exclusive "If . . . then" tip to intervene instantly and help students if they experience difficulty.

Rubric

Use specific criteria to analyze and evaluate student artworks.

Fine Art TAKS

Connect the art curriculum to other artistic forms and to Texas Fine Art TEKS.

Build literacy through art

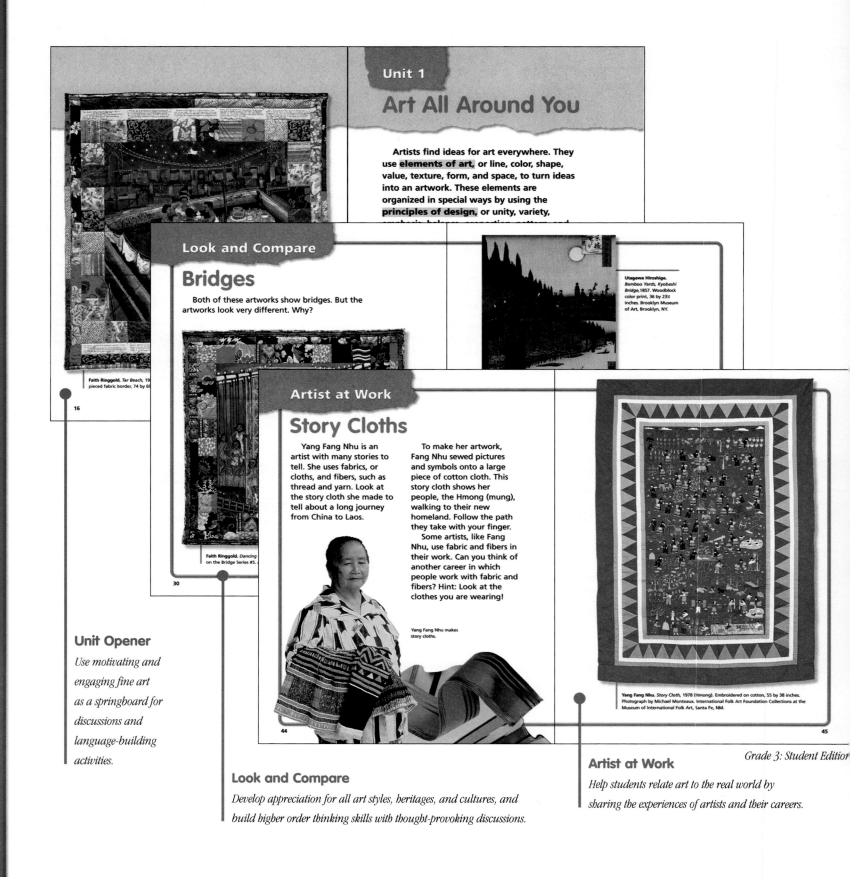

Unit 1
Art All Around You

Artists find ideas for art everywhere. They use **elements of art,** or line, color, shape, value, texture, form, and space, to turn ideas into an artwork. These elements are organized in special ways by using the **principles of design,** or unity, variety,

Faith Ringgold. *Tar Beach*, 19 pieced fabric border, 74 by 69

16

Look and Compare
Bridges

Both of these artworks show bridges. But the artworks look very different. Why?

Utagawa Hiroshige. *Bamboo Yards, Kyobashi Bridge,*1857. Woodblock color print, 36 by 23½ inches. Brooklyn Museum of Art, Brooklyn, NY.

Faith Ringgold. *Dancing on the Bridge Series #5.*

30

Artist at Work
Story Cloths

Yang Fang Nhu is an artist with many stories to tell. She uses fabrics, or cloths, and fibers, such as thread and yarn. Look at the story cloth she made to tell about a long journey from China to Laos.

To make her artwork, Fang Nhu sewed pictures and symbols onto a large piece of cotton cloth. This story cloth shows her people, the Hmong (mung), walking to their new homeland. Follow the path they take with your finger.

Some artists, like Fang Nhu, use fabric and fibers in their work. Can you think of another career in which people work with fabric and fibers? Hint: Look at the clothes you are wearing!

Yang Fang Nhu makes story cloths.

44

Yang Fang Nhu. *Story Cloth*, 1978 (Hmong). Embroidered on cotton, 55 by 38 inches. Photograph by Michael Monteaux. International Folk Art Foundation Collections at the Museum of International Folk Art, Santa Fe, NM.

45

Grade 3: Student Edition

Unit Opener
Use motivating and engaging fine art as a springboard for discussions and language-building activities.

Look and Compare
Develop appreciation for all art styles, heritages, and cultures, and build higher order thinking skills with thought-provoking discussions.

Artist at Work
Help students relate art to the real world by sharing the experiences of artists and their careers.

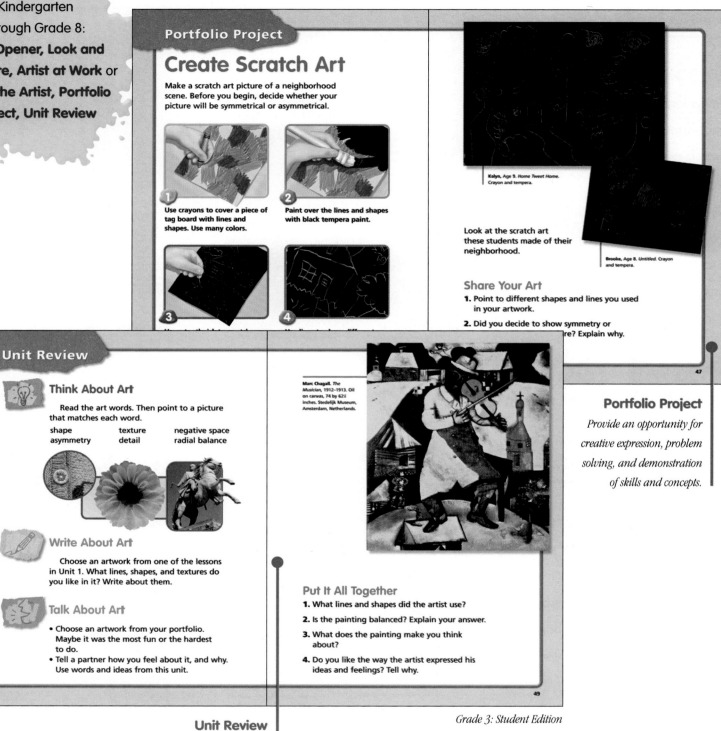

Kindergarten through Grade 8: **Unit Opener, Look and Compare, Artist at Work** or **Meet the Artist, Portfolio Project, Unit Review**

Portfolio Project

Create Scratch Art

Make a scratch art picture of a neighborhood scene. Before you begin, decide whether your picture will be symmetrical or asymmetrical.

1 Use crayons to cover a piece of tag board with lines and shapes. Use many colors.

2 Paint over the lines and shapes with black tempera paint.

3

4

Kalyn, Age 9. *Home Tweet Home.* Crayon and tempera.

Brooke, Age 8. *Untitled.* Crayon and tempera.

Look at the scratch art these students made of their neighborhood.

Share Your Art

1. Point to different shapes and lines you used in your artwork.

2. Did you decide to show symmetry or ...re? Explain why.

47

Unit Review

Think About Art

Read the art words. Then point to a picture that matches each word.

shape   texture   negative space
asymmetry   detail   radial balance

Write About Art

Choose an artwork from one of the lessons in Unit 1. What lines, shapes, and textures do you like in it? Write about them.

Talk About Art

• Choose an artwork from your portfolio. Maybe it was the most fun or the hardest to do.
• Tell a partner how you feel about it, and why. Use words and ideas from this unit.

48

Marc Chagall. *The Musician,* 1912–1913. Oil on canvas, 74 by 62½ inches. Stedelijk Museum, Amsterdam, Netherlands.

Put It All Together

1. What lines and shapes did the artist use?
2. Is the painting balanced? Explain your answer.
3. What does the painting make you think about?
4. Do you like the way the artist expressed his ideas and feelings? Tell why.

49

Portfolio Project
Provide an opportunity for creative expression, problem solving, and demonstration of skills and concepts.

Grade 3: Student Edition

Unit Review
Monitor students' development of visual literacy with a variety of written and oral assessments. **Think, Write,** *and* **Talk About Art** *activities and* **Put It All Together** *give all students an opportunity to demonstrate what they've learned.*

Teach the basics of art

LESSONS Teach students how to explore, appreciate, and analyze the visual world and develop their artistic perception by introducing:

The Elements of Art
Line, Color, Value, Shape, Texture, Form, and Space

The Principles of Design
Balance, Rhythm, Pattern, Variety, Proportion, Emphasis, and Unity

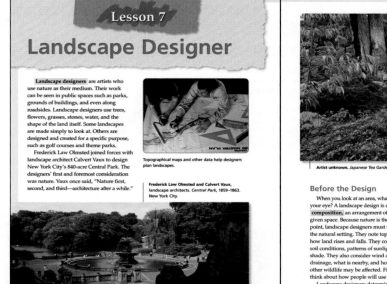

Lesson 7
Landscape Designer

Landscape designers are artists who use nature as their medium. Their work can be seen in public spaces such as parks, grounds of buildings, and even along roadsides. Landscape designers use trees, flowers, grasses, stones, water, and the shape of the land itself. Some landscapes are made simply to look at. Others are designed and created for a specific purpose, such as golf courses and theme parks.

Frederick Law Olmsted joined forces with landscape architect Calvert Vaux to design New York City's 840-acre Central Park. The designers' first and foremost consideration was nature. Vaux once said, "Nature first, second, and third—architecture after a while."

Topographical maps and other data help designers plan landscapes.

Frederick Law Olmsted and Calvert Vaux, landscape architects. *Central Park*, 1859–1863. New York City.

Artist unknown. *Japanese Tea Garden*. Golden Gate Park, San Francisco, CA.

Before the Design

When you look at an area, what appeals to your eye? A landscape design is a **visual composition**, an arrangement of objects in a given space. Because nature is the starting point, landscape designers must work with the natural setting. They note topography, or how land rises and falls. They consider the soil conditions, patterns of sunlight and shade. They also consider wind direction, drainage, what is nearby, and how birds or other wildlife may be affected. Finally, they think about how people will use the space.

Landscape designers determine which plants will grow in a specific climate. They often plan water features, such as ponds and fountains, and how these will work with the surroundings and overall design. The designer then formalizes the plan on paper.

Sketchbook Journal

Look carefully at physical features of landscape designs in your community. Draw a few of these spaces from a bird's-eye view. Take notes on how the design is laid out and balanced and whether it works with the natural environment.

280

281

Grade 7: Student Edition, Careers in Art Unit

Create art experiences

STUDIOS Involve students in the creative art process and give them an opportunity to practice the **Elements of Art** and the **Principles of Design** with age-appropriate art media and techniques. Use the Quick Studio shortcuts when time or resources are limited.

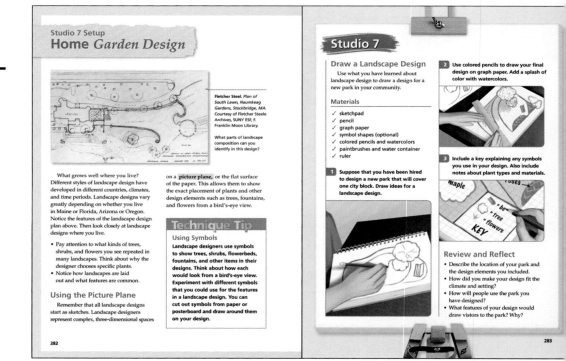

Studio 7 Setup
Home *Garden Design*

Fletcher Steel. *Plan of South Lawn, Naumkeag Gardens, Stockbridge, MA.* Courtesy of Fletcher Steele Archives, SUNY ESF, F. Franklin Moon Library.

What parts of landscape composition can you identify in this design?

What grows well where you live? Different styles of landscape design have developed in different countries, climates, and time periods. Landscape designs vary greatly depending on whether you live in Maine or Florida, Arizona or Oregon. Notice the features of the landscape design plan above. Then look closely at landscape designs where you live.

- Pay attention to what kinds of trees, shrubs, and flowers you see repeated in many landscapes. Think about why the designer chooses specific plants.
- Notice how landscapes are laid out and what features are common.

Using the Picture Plane

Remember that all landscape designs start as sketches. Landscape designers represent complex, three-dimensional spaces on a **picture plane**, or the flat surface of the paper. This allows them to show the exact placement of plants and other design elements such as trees, fountains, and flowers from a bird's-eye view.

Technique Tip

Using Symbols
Landscape designers use symbols to show trees, shrubs, flowerbeds, fountains, and other items in their designs. Think about how each would look from a bird's-eye view. Experiment with different symbols that you could use for the features in a landscape design. You can cut out symbols from paper or posterboard and draw around them on your design.

Studio 7

Draw a Landscape Design
Use what you have learned about landscape design to draw a design for a new park in your community.

Materials
✓ sketchpad
✓ pencil
✓ graph paper
✓ symbol shapes (optional)
✓ colored pencils and watercolors
✓ paintbrushes and water container
✓ ruler

1. **Suppose that you have been hired to design a new park that will cover one city block. Draw ideas for a landscape design.**

2. Use colored pencils to draw your final design on graph paper. Add a splash of color with watercolors.

3. Include a key explaining any symbols you use in your design. Also include notes about plant types and materials.

Review and Reflect
- Describe the location of your park and the design elements you included.
- How did you make your design fit the climate and setting?
- How will people use the park you have designed?
- What features of your design would draw visitors to the park? Why?

282

283

Grade 7: Student Edition, Careers in Art Unit

T14

Build literacy through art

ENRICHMENT FEATURES

Develop students' higher order thinking skills using the **Unit Opener, Look and Compare,** and **Artist at Work** or **Meet the Artist** features.

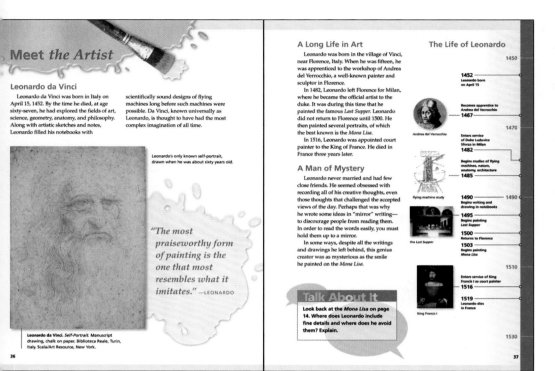

Grade 7: Student Edition

Assess what students learn

ASSESSMENT FEATURES

Monitor students' understanding and their development of visual literacy through hands-on **Portfolio Project** activities and written and oral responses in the **Unit Review**.

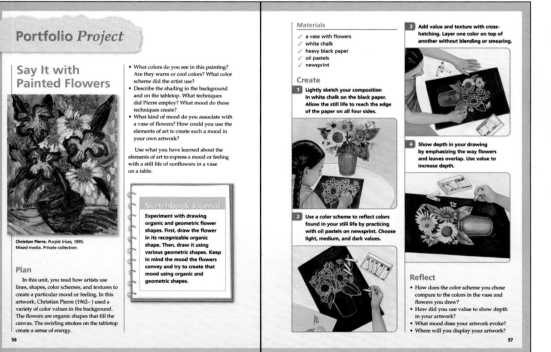

Grade 8: Student Edition

Contents

Unit 1

Art in Your World 16

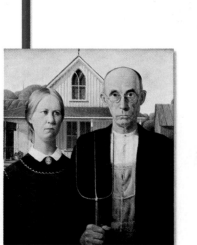

Grant Wood.
American Gothic,
1930.

Unit 2

Cultural Expressions 50

Frida Kahlo. *Long LIve Life (Viva la vida),* 1954.

1

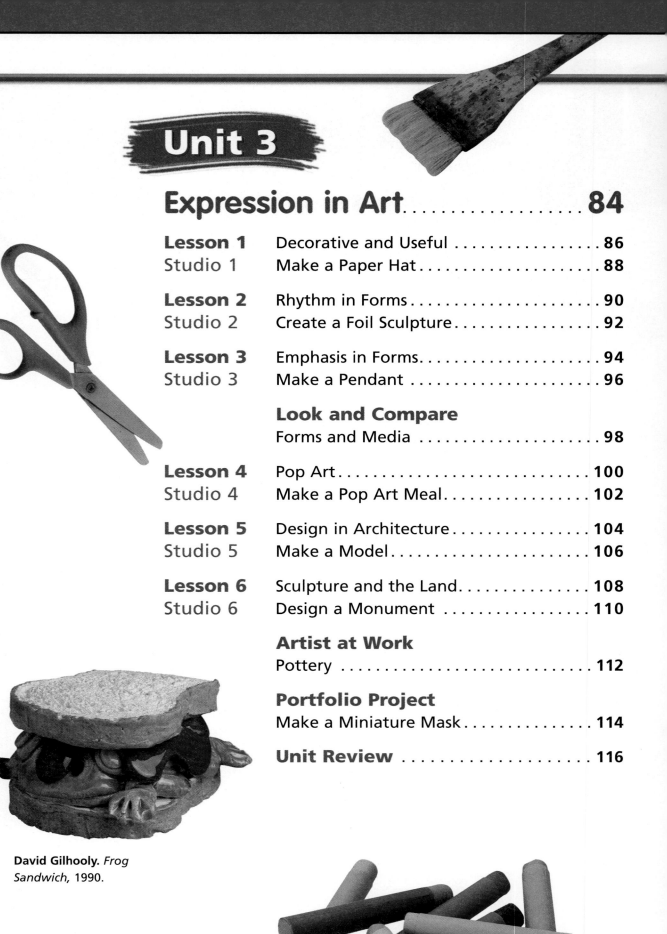

Unit 3

Expression in Art 84

David Gilhooly. *Frog Sandwich,* 1990.

Unit 4

Creative Expression 118

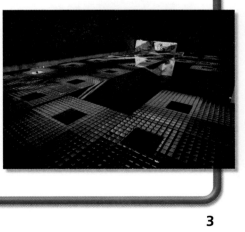

Thana Lauhakaikal.
Celebration,
1983–1985.

3

Unit 5

Art, Old and New 152

Artist unknown.
Ribbon Glass Cup,
ca. A.D. 1st century.

4

Unit 6

An Assortment of Art..........186

David Moctezuma.
Alebreje, 2003.

Start with Art

Start with Art

At a Glance

Objectives

- Identify art as a form of expression and a way to communicate ideas.
- Understand that art is everywhere in the environment.
- Generate ideas for art.

FA TEKS 4.1A Communicate ideas about self, family, school, and community, using sensory knowledge and life experiences

Introduce

Ask students what they think of when they think of art. (Answers will vary.) Point out that art is more than a painting or a sculpture. Jewelry can be artwork. Buildings, vases, and photographs can be artwork.

Explain to students that artists combine their sensory knowledge—how things look, feel, sound, and so on—with their life experiences to create all kinds of artworks that communicate ideas about themselves, their families, or their schools and communities. Have students describe different artworks they have seen at home, in school, or in the community. Ask: **What ideas was the artist trying to express?**

Call on students to name the art material that the student in the photograph is holding. (clay) Ask students if they know what this material is used to make. (sculptures, pots, etc.) Ask: **What objects have you made from clay?**

What is art? Is it a beautiful painting? Is it a colorful garden? Is it a sparkling item of jewelry? Art is all these things and so much more.

Art is everywhere. You can experience art every day. It is also important to understand art.

Ask yourself these questions.
Who makes art?
What is art?
Where is art made?
Why do artists make art?
How do artists make art?

These questions can help you learn about art. They can also help you form conclusions about what you see.

This book explores these questions and more. It talks about the nature of art. It also shows you how to create your own artworks.

6

🖱 Technology Connection

Take a Virtual Tour Many major art museums have Web sites that offer virtual tours, galleries, or exhibitions. Search the Internet or direct students to the virtual exhibitions at the National Gallery of Art Web site. **(http://www.nga.gov/exhibitions/webtours.htm)** Always assess Internet sites beforehand to make sure they are appropriate for your students.

Tech TEKS 4.5A Acquire information including text, audio, video and graphics

You are an artist. Look for art all around you. You may find new ways to express your ideas and feelings.

Vincent van Gogh. *Irises,* 1889.
Oil on canvas, 28 by 36⅝ inches.
The J. Paul Getty Museum,
Los Angeles.

Look in your kitchen for artworks. What other artworks can you find in your home?

Artist unknown.
Gold Stag,
6th-5th century B.C.
Republic of Tuva, Russia.

7

Explore

Have students look at the artworks on page 7. Ask students what they see when they look at Vincent van Gogh's artwork. (blue and white irises in the foreground; orange flowers in the background) Point out that Van Gogh used bright colors to capture the cheerful mood of the flowers.

Now ask students to look at the kitchen items. Point out that not all art is found in museums. Common everyday objects can show a variety of forms, textures, and colors. Have students compare these everyday items to more conventional artworks, such as sculptures or paintings. Explain to students that art is all around them.

Direct students' attention to the golden stag. Tell students that this artwork was found in a tomb in Russia. It was once part of a man's headpiece, a type of hat. Point out that art made for special occasions or ceremonies often provides clues about what the people in a culture value. Ask: **What animals are important in our culture?**

Close

Have students use their own words to tell what art *is* and what art *includes*.

NVAS (K–4) #4 Understanding the visual arts in relation to history and cultures

👫👫 **Meeting Individual Needs**

Extend Have students take turns selecting objects in the classroom and, without naming the object, have them describe how it looks, feels, sounds, and smells. Call on volunteers to name the object. Then ask: **How might you convey these details in an artwork?**

Your Art Words

At a Glance

Objectives

• Identify the elements of art and the principles of design.

Vocabulary

line, space, form, texture, shape, value, color, emphasis, proportion, variety, pattern, rhythm, balance, unity

FA TEKS 4.1B Choose appropriate vocabulary to discuss the use of art elements such as color, texture, form, line, space, and value and art principles such as emphasis, pattern, rhythm, balance, proportion, and unity

Introduce

After students read pages 8 and 9, explain that choosing appropriate vocabulary helps us talk about and understand art. Note that throughout the book, important art words such as these are boldfaced and highlighted in yellow.

Help students access their prior knowledge about these words by creating a two-column graphic organizer on a transparency. Write the elements and principles on the left side of the chart. Leave room for student comments on the right side. Say each word, then ask students what they know or think they know about the word. Write their responses in the right column. Students may provide an example, such as *blue* for *color*. Or they may provide a definition.

To understand art, it is important to understand the language of art. Your book contains many art words. They are shown in **yellow.** These words help artists talk about art.

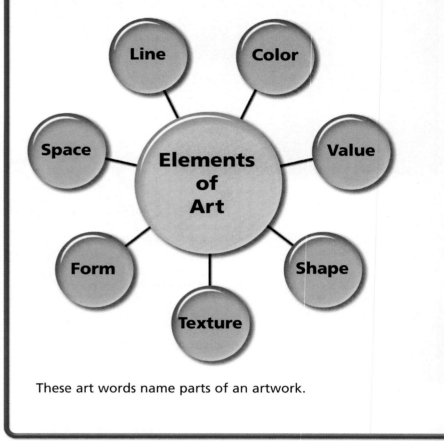

These art words name parts of an artwork.

8

 Notes

Help students understand the difference between *color* and *value* by bringing to class several objects of the same color, such as red apples, red cherries, and red tomatoes. Point out that, though we call all of the objects red, each one actually shows a different value of red. Some are dark red, others are medium red, and others are light red. Have students point out which have darker values and which have lighter values.

ESL TEKS 4.5F Clarify and support spoken ideas with evidence, elaborations, and examples

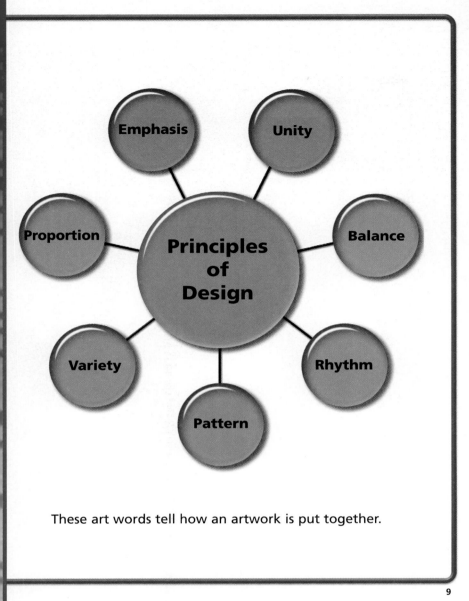

Principles of Design

- Emphasis
- Unity
- Proportion
- Balance
- Variety
- Rhythm
- Pattern

These art words tell how an artwork is put together.

9

Explore

Model for students how to identify the elements of art and the principles of design. Display an **Art Print** and point out each of the elements of art and principles of design in the artwork. Or, refer to the artworks on page 7. Ask students to comment on the artworks. Guide them to use art vocabulary by asking the following questions.

- **What shapes do you see in the Van Gogh painting? Describe them. Where might you see these shapes in the environment?**
- **Point to the lines in *Gold Stag.* How would this artwork change if the artist only used straight lines?**
- **List several words to describe the different textures of the kitchen items. What clues does the photograph give you about how these items feel?**

Close

Ask students to name or point out objects in the classroom that relate to each element of art and principle of design.

NVAS (K–4) #2 Using knowledge of structures and functions

👥 Meeting Individual Needs

Reteach If students have difficulty with any of the words, model a way to think about the word. For example, say: **Look at the space in this room. Name something that is near you. Name something farther away. What is in between?** (space)

Visit a Museum

Objectives

• Explore the role of art museums.

• Understand different jobs at an art museum.

Vocabulary

art museums, curator, docents

FA TEKS 4.3A Identify simple main ideas expressed in art

FA TEKS 4.4B Interpret ideas and moods in original artworks, portfolios, and exhibitions by peers and others

Introduce

After students read pages 10 and 11, explain that art museums are places where people can view art exhibitions. An art exhibition is a showing of several or many artworks in one location. An exhibition might also be in a gallery, a restaurant, an office building, or even in a classroom. Point out that art exhibitions may include art created by professional artists, by students at a school, or by people who belong to a club.

Invite students who have visited an art exhibition to share their experiences. Ask: **What did you notice about viewing art in person? How was it different from seeing art in a textbook?** (Possible responses: The colors are more vivid in person; you can see the texture of the paint or other media; you can view the artwork in its original size.

William H. Johnson. *Chalet in the Mountains*, ca. 1938. Oil on burlap, 28½ by 35¼ inches. Smithsonian American Art Museum, Washington, D.C.

10

 Career Research

Guest Speaker Invite a curator or docent to be a guest speaker in your classroom. Ask the speaker to be prepared to talk about his or her job and the role art museums have in our society. Have students prepare questions for the speaker ahead of time.

Field Trip Take students on a field trip to see an art exhibition. If there is not a local museum, consider taking students to an alternative exhibition space, such as an office or public building.

Visit a Museum

Art museums are places that collect and display artworks. You can see artworks like this at an art museum.

Many people work in art museums. One such person is the curator. A **curator** is an art expert who collects and takes care of artworks. The curator also decides where to place the artworks.

Another person you may see at an art museum is a docent. **Docents** greet visitors and show them around the museum. They also provide information about the art and artists. They can answer questions to help you better understand the art.

What questions would you ask about this artwork?

11

Gallery Options

Student Art Exhibition Save student artworks during the school year to mount a student art exhibition. Solicit two volunteers to serve as curators of the exhibition and several others to serve as docents. Instruct students to submit three artworks each to the curators.

Display the artworks in the space you have chosen, and invite other classes, teachers, and parents to the exhibition. Have students ask themselves questions, such as the bulleted questions shown on this page, to identify the ideas and moods of the exhibit.

Explore

Tell students that artists express ideas and moods in their artworks. For example, an artist might express the idea of natural beauty by taking a photograph of a maple tree. Explain to students that they can use questions such as the following to identify simple main ideas and moods expressed in original artworks, portfolios, and exhibitions by peers and others.

- **What is the title of this artwork?**
- **What part of the artwork catches my attention first?**
- **What story does the artwork tell?**
- **How does the artwork make me feel?**

Museum Etiquette

Tell students to follow these rules when viewing an art exhibition.

- Talk softly so you do not disturb others.
- Never touch an artwork.
- Do not walk in front of someone who is viewing an artwork.
- Do not photograph artworks; flash photography can damage artworks.

Close

Ask students to explain what a museum is and why museums are special and important places.

NVAS (K–4) #5 Reflecting upon and assessing the characteristics and merits of their work and the work of others

Art Tools

At a Glance

Objectives

- Understand how to use a variety of art tools.
- Assemble a portfolio.

Materials

- Various art materials as shown on Student Edition page 12
- poster board, markers, tape
- construction paper and/or fabric scraps

FA TEKS 4.2C Invent ways to produce artworks and to explore photographic imagery, using a variety of art media and materials

FA TEKS 4.4A Describe intent and form conclusions about personal artworks

Introduce

Display the art tools pictured on page 12. Add any other tools that are available to you. Model for students how to use a variety of art media and materials. For example, show the different effects one can create with different paintbrushes. Or, challenge each student to use a crayon, colored pencil, or oil pastel and make a mark that is different from the marks made by all other classmates.

Allow students to touch and explore the tools. Have them group tools according to the type of artwork they would be used to make. Encourage students to consider how they would use these tools to create an original artwork of their own.

Art Tools

Artists use tools to make their artworks. Different types of tools are used to create different types of art. Think about some of the art tools you would like to explore as you make your own artwork.

Chalk pastels and artists' pencils can be used for drawing.

Artists often experiment with many types of paintbrushes and other tools when painting.

These tools are used to make beautiful mosaic designs.

Ink, paint, sponges, and a roller called a brayer, are tools used in printmaking.

When artists make clay sculptures, they use some of these tools.

Photography is the art of taking pictures. The most important tools for photography are a camera and film.

12

 Home Connection

Have students look around their homes for art tools they might already have, such as paintbrushes, different types of paper, or yarn. Encourage them to make artworks at home and bring them to school to share with the class.

Make a Portfolio

Artists often keep their artworks in a portfolio. You can store your flat artwork in a portfolio too. Follow these steps to make a portfolio. Use it to share your artworks with others.

1 Use two sheets of poster board. Write your name across the top of one sheet.

2 Place one sheet over the other. Be sure your name is on the front.

3 Tape the bottom and sides of your portfolio.

4 Use colored markers to decorate your portfolio.

13

Explore

Make a Portfolio Have students review the steps on page 13. Then direct them to create their own portfolios. Explain to students that they will use their new portfolios to store and protect artworks.

Tell students to add original images or designs to their portfolios with various materials. Encourage them to experiment with as many of the art tools shown on page 12 as possible.

Analyze Portfolios Tell students that they can use their portfolios to see how their artwork changes or develops over time. Explain that by analyzing their own artworks, they can improve their skills and apply those skills to future artworks.

Guide students to form conclusions about their artwork. Say: **One way to form conclusions about artwork is to analyze its expressive qualities. Take a close look at your portfolio design and describe what makes it unique. Did you show interesting lines, shapes, or colors? How do these features help tell the story of your design?**

Call on volunteers to present their designs to the class and form conclusions about its expressive qualities.

Close

Have students choose a favorite art tool and explain or demonstrate how to use it. Ask students to describe how they would use the tool to create an artwork for their portfolio.

NVAS (K–4) #1 Understanding and applying media, techniques, and processes

NVAS (K–4) #3 Choosing and evaluating a range of subject matter, symbols, and ideas

NVAS (K–4) #5 Reflecting upon and assessing the characteristics and merits of their work and the work of others

---

👥 Meeting Individual Needs

Inclusion You may find that many students do not have the fine-motor skills to manipulate many of the art tools listed. Provide opportunities throughout the year for students to practice manipulating different art tools and materials. You will note that many students will be able to handle the art tools much more effectively by the end of the year.

Sketchbook Journal

At a Glance

Objectives

- Create a personal Sketchbook Journal.
- Develop and organize ideas from the environment.

Materials

- drawing paper, construction paper
- markers or other media, stapler

FA TEKS 4.1A Communicate ideas about self, family, school, and community, using sensory knowledge and life experiences

FA TEKS 4.2A Integrate a variety of ideas about self, life events, family, and community in original artworks

FA TEKS 4.4A Describe intent and form conclusions about personal artworks

Introduce

Explain to students that their Sketchbook Journals should include both writing and drawings. Lead them to see that they can use their Sketchbook Journals to write down their impressions of artists and artworks, as well as of their own surroundings. They can also plan original artworks by recording their ideas and making sketches.

Explain that by making notes and drawings, students will be able to describe their intentions for personal artworks. Demonstrate this concept by jotting down your own notes and sketches for an artwork on an overhead transparency. Then share these ideas with the class and describe the artwork you intend to create.

Ask a volunteer to read the steps on page 15 aloud. Call on students to describe their intentions for their Sketchbook Journal designs.

Make a Sketchbook Journal

Many artists plan by drawing sketches. Sketches can help them remember what they have seen or imagined. Artists also record their thoughts and feelings with their sketches.

A sketchbook is a special tool. In it, artists can draw, paint, and even write their ideas. Later, they can use their sketches as a starting place for a larger artwork.

Look at this sketch by Pablo Picasso. Do you make sketches like this?

Pablo Picasso. *Don Quijote*, 1955. Pen and Ink sketch. Private collection.

14

 Notes

Tell students to record new art vocabulary in their Sketchbook Journals. They should write the word, its pronunciation, and its definition. Direct students to show at least one example for each word as well. For example, beside the word *shape*, students could draw a circle.

ESL TEKS 4.5G Employ content are vocabulary words in context

Follow these steps to make a Sketchbook Journal.

1 Fold eight sheets of drawing paper in half.

2 Staple the sheets together along the fold.

3 Fold and staple a construction paper cover.

4 Decorate the cover. Write your name on it.

15

🚹👦👧 Meeting Individual Needs

Extend Offer students alternative approaches to creating their Sketchbook Journals. For example, they could bind their journals with yarn woven through holes. Or, they could cover a piece of cardboard with fabric or textured paper.

Explore

Tell students that artists pay attention to all of their senses when recording observations and experiences, not just their sense of sight. Explain that Sketchbook Journal entries about how something smells, tastes, sounds, or feels can help students communicate ideas in artworks. Demonstrate this concept by recalling a memorable event that you attended, such as a family reunion. Describe to students all of the sensory details that you can recall about the event. Point out how you could use these details to convey ideas in an artwork.

Ask students to recall a special occasion, such as a family celebration. What did they see? What sounds did they hear? What aromas did they smell? What did the food taste like? What did the clothes they were wearing feel like? Have students describe how they could integrate these ideas about family in an artwork. Allow time for them to sketch ideas in their Sketchbook Journals.

Close

Have students display their Sketchbook Journals for their classmates. Remind students to be respectful of other people's artworks, both in terms of handling it and in terms of commenting on its qualities.

NVAS (K–4) #3 Choosing and evaluating a range of subject matter, symbols, and ideas

Unit 1 Overview

Inspiration for art is everywhere, in both natural and human-made environments. Artists take ideas from their environment and turn them into artworks. They may create a realistic view or convey a new view to others. In this unit, students will explore how artists observe and interpret the world around them.

	Unit Opener, p. 16	Lesson 1, p. 18 Line / Studio 1, p. 20 Design a New School	Lesson 2, p. 22 See and Imagine Lines / Studio 2, p. 24 Make Lines	Lesson 3, p. 26 Shape / Studio 3, p. 28 Create a Shape Collage	Look and Compare, p. 30 Churches
Artworks	Claude Monet. (Detail) *Waterlilies: Green Reflections*, 1916–1923.	Grant Wood. *American Gothic*, 1930.	Henri Rousseau. *Les joueurs de football (The Football Players)*, 1908.	Marianne von Werefkin. *The Washerwomen*, 1908–1909.	Claude Monet. *Rouen Cathedral*, 1894. Georgia O'Keeffe. *Ranchos Church–Taos*, 1930.
Vocabulary	elements of art, principles of design	line, horizontal, vertical, diagonal	subject, details, actual line, implied lines	shape, geometric shapes, organic shapes	
Materials	• **Art Print 1** • **Fine Art Transparency** • **Instructional Prints**	• **Fine Art Transparency** • bags • common classroom items, such as pencils, rulers, glue bottles, and balls • Sketchbook Journal • pencils, pens, crayons, water-based markers • drawing paper	• **Fine Art Transparency** • rubber ball • Sketchbook Journal • colored construction paper • white glue • string, scissors ⚠, crayons	• **Fine Art Transparency** • Sketchbook Journal • drawing paper, colored construction paper • pencil, glue sticks • tempera paints and paintbrushes or water-based markers	• **Art Prints 1, 2, 3** • **Fine Art Transparency**
Connections	**Home Connection** views from home **Bookshelf** *Zin! Zin! Zin! A Violin!* by Lloyd Moss, illustrated by Marjorie Priceman, Simon & Schuster, 1995	**Curriculum Connection** Science: types of lines in nature **ESL Notes** **Fine Arts Connection** Theatre: types of lines on stage **Meeting Individual Needs** Inclusion	**Curriculum Connection** Physical Education: games in other countries **ESL Notes** **Fine Arts Connection** Dance: actual and implied lines in dance **Meeting Individual Needs** Reteach, Extend	**Curriculum Connection** Math: shape patterns **ESL Notes** **Fine Arts Connection** Music: shapes in musical instruments **Meeting Individual Needs** Extend	**Reading Strategy** Compare and contrast
Assessment Opportunities		Visual Culture Rubric 1 from **Unit-by-Unit Resources** Ongoing Assessment	Informal Assessment Rubric 1 from **Unit-by-Unit Resources** Ongoing Assessment	Informal Assessment Rubric 1 from **Unit-by-Unit Resources** Ongoing Assessment	

Lesson 4, p. 32 **Texture** **Studio 4, p. 34** **Rub Textures**	Lesson 5 p. 36 **Space and Distance** **Studio 5, p. 38** **Make a Nature Scene**	Lesson 6, p. 40 **Artists See Spaces** **Studio 6, p. 42** **Draw a Cover Design**	**Artist at Work, p. 44** **Cake Designs**	**Portfolio Project, p. 46** **Make an Etching**	**Unit Review, p. 48**
Frank Romero. *Scamp in the Snow,* 1995.	**Clara McDonald Williamson.** *The Old Chisholm Trail,* 1952.	**Rupert García.** *Maguey de la Vida,* 1973.	Cake by Toba Garrett.		**Gabriele Münter.** *The Russian House (Das-Russen-Haus),* 1931.
texture, tactile texture, visual texture	space, foreground, background, middle ground, overlap	positive space, negative space, composition			
• **Fine Art Transparency** • objects with different textures • Sketchbook Journal • pictures or slides of city skylines (optional) • drawing paper or newsprint • pencils, crayons, oil pastels • various textured objects, such as green kitchen "scrubby," sandpaper, corduroy, bubble wrap, or corrugated cardboard • tempera paint thinned with water (1:3 paint to water ratio) and wide paintbrushes	• **Fine Art Transparency** • Sketchbook Journal • drawing paper, pencils • three crayons of different colors for each student	• **Fine Art Transparency** • construction paper • newsprint, poster board, heavy colored paper, or colored construction paper • pencils, crayons, or oil pastels	• finger paint • resealable bags	• 9" × 12" white drawing paper • crayons or oil pastels (light colors and black) • toothpicks ⚠, paper clips, craft sticks ⚠ • Sketchbook Journal	• **Art Print 4** • **Fine Art Transparency**
Technology Scanning textures **ESL Notes** **Fine Arts Connection** Music: texture in music **Meeting Individual Needs** Inclusion	**Curriculum Connection** Social Studies: art as a record of historical events **ESL Notes** **Fine Arts Connection** Theatre: space in stage design **Meeting Individual Needs** Reteach, Extend	**Curriculum Connection** Social Studies: regional climate and plants **ESL Notes** **Fine Arts Connection** Dance: positive and negative space in dance **Meeting Individual Needs** Extend	**Career Research** Cake designers **Reading Strategy** Identify details	**Gallery Options** Classroom museum **Meeting Individual Needs** Reteach, Extend	
Visual Culture Rubric 1 from **Unit-by-Unit Resources** Ongoing Assessment	Informal Assessment Rubric 1 from **Unit-by-Unit Resources** Ongoing Assessment	Informal Assessment Rubric 1 from **Unit-by-Unit Resources** Ongoing Assessment		Rubric 1 from **Unit-by-Unit Resources**	**Unit-by-Unit Resources** Vocabulary Worksheets, pp. 11–14 Unit 1 Test, pp. 19–22

Unit 1

Claude Monet. (Detail) *Waterlilies: Green Reflections,* 1916–1923. Detail of the far left side, Room 1. Musée de l'Orangerie, Paris, France.

16

Introduce the Unit

Ask a volunteer to read the title of Unit 1. Tell students that they will learn that art is a part of their world. Have students look around the classroom. Then ask them to share some of the things they observe, guiding them to use descriptive language.

Explain that many artists get their inspiration from what they see around them or from the environment in which they live. Ask: **What objects, people, plants, or animals in your everyday environment might inspire you to create art?** (Answers will vary.)

Ask students to look through artworks in this unit. Have them discuss their favorites. Encourage students to talk about what they think may have inspired some of these artworks. (Possible responses: where the artist lived; the artists' personal experiences)

Art Background

Waterlilies: Green Reflections Claude Monet based his *Waterlilies* series on an actual pond he built across the road from his house in France. He spent almost thirty years painting and meditating in his water garden, creating many versions of *Waterlilies.* He, like other Impressionists, frequently painted outside rather than in a studio to observe how light and color appeared and changed throughout the day and over time.

Home Connection

Have students look out a window of their home and draw what they see. Encourage them to think about the time of day and current season as they draw.

16

Unit 1

Art in Your World

Artists take inspiration from their environments. They create artworks using line, shape, color, value, texture, form, and space. These are the **elements of art.** The **principles of design,** or unity, variety, emphasis, balance, proportion, pattern, and rhythm, help artists to communicate feelings and ideas. How did Monet communicate his feelings in *Waterlilies*?

Meet the Artist

Artist Claude Monet belonged to a group of painters called Impressionists. Monet often painted outdoors. He is well known for his colorful paintings of water lilies. For many years, Monet had problems with his sight, yet he continued to paint. You will see another painting by Monet later in this unit.

Claude Monet. *Self-Portrait,* 1917.

17

 Bookshelf

Discuss Unit Concepts

Have students read page 17 and look at the painting. Point out the credit line. Tell students that this line gives information about the artwork, such as the artist's name, the title of the artwork, the date it was completed, the medium used, and the artwork's current owner or location.

Next, have students describe what they see in the artwork. Discuss how the soft shapes and colors communicate a peaceful feeling. Ask: **How do you feel when you look at this artwork?** (Possible responses: calm, happy, relaxed)

As you introduce each element of art and principle of design in Unit 1, you may wish to display the **Instructional Prints.** A print is provided for each element and principle.

In addition, **Art Prints 1–4** and **Transparencies** are available for fine art in the unit.

Meet the Artist

Claude Monet (1840–1926) Monet spent his childhood observing the sea and the rapidly shifting Normandy weather on the coast of France, where he lived. These experiences shaped his unique vision of nature. Throughout his life, Monet searched for ways to record his impressions of nature. Using artworks in series, such as with *Waterlilies,* Monet explored how to show the same subject under different light and weather conditions, striving to paint what he saw "in the face of the most fugitive effects."

NVAS (K–4) #4 Understanding the visual arts in relation to history and cultures

NVAS (K–4) #5 Reflecting upon and assessing the characteristics and merits of their work and the work of others

Lesson 1

At a Glance

Objectives
- Identify and describe lines in artworks.
- Describe, analyze, interpret, and judge artworks.

Materials
- **Fine Art Transparency**
- bags
- common classroom items, such as pencils, rulers, glue bottles, and balls
- Sketchbook Journal

Vocabulary
line, horizontal, vertical, diagonal

FA TEKS 4.1B Choose appropriate vocabulary to discuss the use of art elements such as color, texture, form, line, space, and value and art principles such as emphasis, pattern, rhythm, balance, proportion, and unity

FA TEKS 4.3C Identify the roles of art in American society

❶ Introduce

Have students work in groups. Give each group a bag filled with common objects, such as a pencil, a ball, and a notebook. In turn, invite students to reach inside the bag, choose an object, and describe its lines and shape without looking. Have students guess what the object is and then reveal it to the group. Continue until all students have had a chance to play the game.

Then send the groups on a scavenger hunt to look for items with interesting lines. You may want to point out some examples, such as diagonal lines in a shirt, horizontal lines in floor tiles, and vertical lines in a bookshelf. Have students record their findings in a list or as sketches. Discuss them as a class.

18

Lesson 1

Line

If you move your pencil point along a surface, you form a **line.** A line in an artwork is a continuous mark made on a surface by a tool. Artists use lines in their artworks to express many ideas.

Grant Wood. *American Gothic,* 1930. Oil on beaver board, 29¾ by 25 inches. The Art Institute of Chicago and VAGA, New York. Friends of American Art Collection, image © 1996 The Art Institute of Chicago, 1930.934. All rights reserved. Photograph © 1996, The Art Institute of Chicago.

18

🎨 Art Background

American Gothic Grant Wood's (1892–1942) painting, *American Gothic,* depicts a dour farmer and his daughter standing in front of a farmhouse. The models for the painting were actually Wood's sister and the family's dentist. Since its creation in 1930, advertisers and cartoonists have comically duplicated this pair, who seem to represent archetypal American characters.

ESL Notes

Draw the lines from page 19 on the left side of the board and list each line's name on the right. As you say the name, have volunteers repeat it and point to the correct drawing and word.

ESL TEKS 4.27A Use active listening comprehension

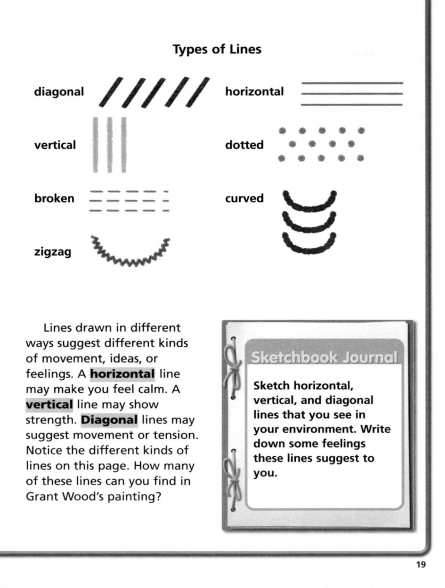

Types of Lines

diagonal

horizontal

vertical

dotted

broken

curved

zigzag

Lines drawn in different ways suggest different kinds of movement, ideas, or feelings. A **horizontal** line may make you feel calm. A **vertical** line may show strength. **Diagonal** lines may suggest movement or tension. Notice the different kinds of lines on this page. How many of these lines can you find in Grant Wood's painting?

Sketchbook Journal

Sketch horizontal, vertical, and diagonal lines that you see in your environment. Write down some feelings these lines suggest to you.

19

② Teach

Have students read page 18 and the credit line. Ask:

- **What objects do you see in this painting?** (Possible response: pitchfork, house, windows, eyeglasses) DESCRIBE
- **How big are the people compared to other elements in the painting?** (the people are much bigger) ANALYZE

After students have read page 19, review the different kinds of lines with them. Demonstrate how a line can be made by moving an art tool across a surface. Point out that vertical lines run up and down; horizontal lines run across; and diagonal lines start at a slant. Have them identify the different types of lines in Grant Wood's painting. Ask:

- **What words do you think of as you look at the vertical lines in the painting?** (Possible response: strong, tall, thin) INTERPRET
- **Which lines interest you the most? Why?** (Possible response: zigzag line of the woman's collar; the rest are too serious) JUDGE

Sketchbook Journal Have students draw and label three of the other lines they see on page 19. Encourage them to use different media to make these lines.

③ Close

After students have completed their drawings, discuss which media were most useful for making each kind of line.

Visual Culture Invite students to look for lines on buildings, on television, in video games, and so forth. Discuss their observations.

🧩 Curriculum Connection

Science Have students look at prepared slides of plants or bugs under a microscope or project them onto an overhead. Tell students to look for different types of lines on the slide. Then have them make quick sketches of the lines they observed and label them.

Studio 1

At a Glance

Objectives

- Express ideas by drawing lines in an original artwork.
- Evaluate original artworks by self and peers.

Materials

- pencils, pens, crayons, water-based markers
- drawing paper
- Rubric 1 from **Unit-by-Unit Resources**

FA TEKS 4.2A Integrate a variety of ideas about self, life events, family, and community in original artworks

FA TEKS 4.2B Design original artworks

FA TEKS 4.4A Describe intent and form conclusions about personal artworks

 Introduce

Model communicating ideas using sensory knowledge by looking for and pointing out examples of lines in your school. Then have students brainstorm features to include in a drawing of a school. Ask:

- **How many floors will the school have?**
- **Describe the windows and doors.**
- **What do you intend the lines in your drawing to show about your school?**

Design a New School

What features would you include in the perfect school? Think about what you want in the building, and then follow these steps.

1 **Imagine either the inside or the outside of your new school.**

2 **Draw your school design.**

Technique Tip

Try using a dull pencil and a sharp pencil to create different effects with your lines.

20

Meeting Individual Needs

Inclusion Consider working with an occupational therapist for suggestions on how to adapt drawing instruments for students who have physical disabilities.

Quick Studio

Have students draw the front entrance to their school. Ask them to include vertical, broken, dotted, curved, or zigzag lines.

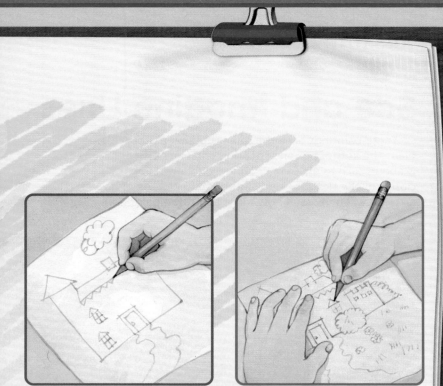

3 As you draw, use a variety of lines. How many kinds can you include?

4 Add some finishing touches to your drawing.

Think Like an Artist

Describe the different lines you used in your drawing. What does each kind communicate?

21

Fine Arts Connection

Theatre Have students visit your school's stage or the stage of a local theatre. Invite them to observe the stage from the point of view of the audience, of an actor on stage, and from behind the scenes. Point out the horizontal, vertical, and diagonal lines of the stage from different points of view. Then have students choose a point of view and draw the stage from that position, using different kinds of lines.

FA TEKS 4.5B Define and discuss aspects of formal theatre

❷ Create

Have students read the directions on pages 20–21. Then distribute materials.

- Have students choose an interior or exterior design.
- Tell students to look around their school for ideas and inspiration. Invite them to communicate those ideas in their drawings.
- Direct students to the examples on page 19.
- Challenge students to use unusual lines, such as broken, dotted, and zigzag.

Technique Tip Students can also create thicker lines with crayons by peeling the paper off and using the crayon's side to draw.

❸ Close

Have students form conclusions about their artworks by answering the *Think Like an Artist* question. (Possible response: I used vertical lines on the school to show strength and curvy lines on the flag to show movement.)

Ongoing Assessment

If . . . students have trouble getting started for fear of making mistakes,

then . . . demonstrate how to lightly draw the outlines of large shapes and focus on adding details later.

See page 18 from **Unit-by-Unit Resources** for a rubric to assess this studio.

NVAS (K–4) #1 Understanding and applying media, techniques, and processes

NVAS (K–4) #3 Choosing and evaluating a range of subject matter, symbols and ideas

NVAS (K–4) #5 Reflecting upon and assessing the characteristics and merits of their work and the work of others

Lesson 2

At a Glance

Objectives

- Identify and describe actual and implied lines in artworks.
- Identify subjects and details in artworks.
- Describe, analyze, interpret, and judge artworks.

Materials

- **Fine Art Transparency**
- rubber ball
- Sketchbook Journal

Vocabulary

subject, details, actual line, implied lines

FA TEKS 4.1B Choose appropriate vocabulary to discuss the use of art elements such as color, texture, form, line, space, and value and art principles such as emphasis, pattern, rhythm, balance, proportion, and unity

FA TEKS 4.4B Interpret ideas and moods in original artworks, portfolios, and exhibitions by peers and others

1 Introduce

Have two volunteers throw and bounce a small rubber ball back and forth in front of the class. Tell students that the paths the ball takes between the students' hands and the floor are examples of implied lines. Ask students to point out other implied lines in this scenario. (Possible response: between the students' eyes and the ball.)

Also ask students to imagine that an artist has made a painting of the two ball throwers. Ask them what the subject of this painting would be. (Possible response: two fourth-graders playing) Have them identify details in the scenario, such as what the students are wearing, how far away they are from each other, and what lies behind them.

Lesson 2

See and Imagine Lines

These paintings have the same subject—a group of men. The **subject** of an artwork is what the artwork is about, such as an animal, object, or scene. Look closely at the **details.** Studying these small parts of an artwork will help you know more about the painting.

Henri Rousseau. *Les joueurs de football (The Football Players),* 1908. Oil on canvas, 39½ by 31⅛ inches. The Solomon R. Guggenheim Museum, New York. © The Solomon R. Guggenheim Foundation, New York (FN 60.1583). Photograph by David Heald.

22

 **Art Background**

About the Artist French painter Henri Rousseau (1844–1910) was a self-taught artist who did not begin to paint seriously until he was in his forties. Many critics of his time called his work technically clumsy, but today he is considered the first major artist to paint in the Naïve style. This style is characterized by simple images created by artists with little or no formal training in art.

About the Artist Japanese artist Katsushika Hokusai (1760–1849) was a painter, wood engraver, and print designer. He may have produced as many as thirty thousand book illustrations and color prints. During his career, Hokusai also used more than fifty different names.

Katsushika Hokusai. *Six Master Poets*, Edo period (Tokugawa). Ink and color on paper, 13 by 22 inches. The Freer Gallery of Art, Smithsonian Institution, Washington, D.C.

Artists use two kinds of lines. Look at the stripes on the shirts of Rousseau's football players. A line you can see is called an **actual line.** Lines that are imagined but not actually seen are **implied lines.** With your fingers, follow a line from the eyes of one poet to another in the artwork by Hokusai. You can imagine the line, but you cannot see it. Describe other actual and implied lines in both paintings.

Sketchbook Journal

Think about a game or activity that you enjoy. Make a sketch, including both actual and implied lines. Each kind of line is important to your sketch. Write down why this is so.

23

Curriculum Connection

Physical Education Discuss the game that is depicted in Rousseau's painting. Ask students if it looks like the game of football that is played in the United States. Tell them the game is actually rugby and that in other countries, "football" sometimes refers to soccer. If possible, have students toss footballs, soccer balls, and rugby balls or play a game from their Sketchbook Journal.
PE TEKS 4.3A Describe and select physical activities

ESL Notes

Refer students to the artwork *Six Master Poets.* As you point out the implied and actual lines, ask students to describe each line.
ESL TEKS 4.9E Study word meanings systematically

② Teach

Have students read pages 22 and 23. Direct students to the painting on page 23. Ask:

- **Where do you see curved lines?** (Possible response: people's robes, the positions of their bodies, hats) DESCRIBE

Point out the actual lines in Hokusai's painting, including the outlines of the poets' robes. Have students use their fingers to follow the implied lines between the eyes of the poets. Then ask:

- **What kind of lines are most of the actual lines in Hokusai's drawing?** (curved) ANALYZE
- **How do the implied lines in Hokusai's artwork show relationships among the poets?** (Possible response: they show who is interested in whom) INTERPRET
- **If you were to draw six master poets, what details would you include that Hokusai did not?** (Possible response: books and pens) JUDGE

Then ask students to look at Rousseau's painting on page 22. Have them point out and describe the actual and implied lines they see. (Possible responses: actual lines on the clothing and fence, implied line in the path of the ball)

Sketchbook Journal Have students brainstorm a list of games and activities before they begin drawing.

③ Close

Have students describe the actual and implied lines in each other's artwork.

Assessment Have students work with a partner to identify the subjects and details in each other's drawings.

NVAS (K–4) #2 Using knowledge of structures and functions
NVAS (K–4) #4 Understanding the visual arts in relation to history and cultures
NVAS (K–4) #6 Making connections between visual arts and other disciplines

Studio 2

At a Glance

Objectives

- Express ideas by drawing actual and implied lines.
- Evaluate original artworks by self and peers.

Materials

- colored construction paper
- white glue
- string, scissors ⚠, crayons
- Rubric 1 from **Unit-by-Unit Resources**

FA TEKS 4.2B Design original artworks

FA TEKS 4.2C Invent ways to produce artworks and to explore photographic imagery, using a variety of art media and materials

FA TEKS 4.4A Describe intent and form conclusions about personal artworks

FA TEKS 4.4B Interpret ideas and moods in original artworks, portfolios, and exhibitions by peers and others

① Introduce

Review actual and implied lines. Have students describe examples of these lines in the classroom. Review vertical, horizontal, diagonal, curved, straight, zigzag, broken, dotted, and continuous lines.

Have students describe what they intend their designs to show. Remind them that their designs do not have to create a recognizable form. Ask:

- **Will you use lines to make random shapes?**
- **Will you design a recognizable object, such as a car or a building?**
- **What kinds of lines will you include?**

Quick Studio

Have students draw a house in pencil and go over a few lines with crayon. Have them erase the pencil to create implied lines.

Studio 2
Make Lines

Follow these steps to experiment with both actual and implied lines.

① Draw a design on colored paper using glue. Leave some open spaces.

② Cut strings and lay them along the glue lines.

Technique Tip

Leave some glue lines uncovered where a viewer could imagine implied lines that connect one string to another.

24

👫👫 Meeting Individual Needs

Reteach Cut strings of different colors and lengths ahead of time and give each student five strings. Instruct them to make a design and include a diagonal line, a vertical line, and a curved line. Make sure that they include at least one implied line.

Extend Instruct students to create a landscape involving actual and implied lines. Have them use either the string and glue or crayons and paper to make their artwork.

3 Repeat the same design on another sheet of paper, but use crayons.

4 Have a friend locate actual and implied lines in both artworks.

Think Like an Artist

Did your friend see the same implied lines that you did? Explain why or why not.

 Fine Arts Connection

Dance Have students view a video of people line dancing. Point out the actual lines people form as they dance in step and the implied lines between dancers. Have students work in small groups to create their own simple line dances. Have each group perform its dance while others watch for actual and implied lines.

PE TEKS 4.1I Perform basic folk dance steps

2 Create

Have students read pages 24–25. Then distribute materials.

• Have students decide what designs they want to make with the glue.
• Encourage students to choose a variety of colors of string for their design.
• Remind students to use their string artworks as guides for their crayon drawings.
• After listening to their friend's comments, have students share their design ideas and show the implied lines in their artwork.

Technique Tip Have students use paintbrushes or toothpicks to extend glue lines.

3 Close

Have students reflect on their designs by answering the *Think Like an Artist* question on page 25. (Answers will vary.)

As students identify the actual and implied lines in each other's artwork, ask them to name the kinds of lines they see. Remind them to use respectful language when discussing each other's work.

Ongoing Assessment

If . . . students have difficulty keeping the glued string from sticking to their fingers,

then . . . have them use a craft stick to press the string into the glue and provide wet napkins for cleaning their fingers.

See page 18 from **Unit-by-Unit Resources** for a rubric to assess this studio.

NVAS (K–4) #1 Understanding and applying media, techniques, and processes

NVAS (K–4) #3 Choosing and evaluating a range of subject matter, symbols, and ideas

NVAS (K–4) #5 Reflecting upon and assessing the characteristics and merits of their work and the work of others

Lesson 3

At a Glance

Objectives

- Identify and describe organic and geometric shapes in artworks.
- Describe, analyze, interpret, and judge artworks.

Materials

- **Fine Art Transparency**
- Sketchbook Journal

Vocabulary

shape, geometric shapes, organic shapes

FA TEKS 4.1B Choose appropriate vocabulary to discuss the use of art elements such as color, texture, form, line, space, and value and art principles such as emphasis, pattern, rhythm, balance, proportion, and unity

FA TEKS 4.4B Interpret ideas and moods in original artworks, portfolios, and exhibitions by peers and others

①Introduce

Divide the class into five groups: circles, squares, triangles, stars, and blobs. Have each group search the classroom for items representing their shapes.

Write the headings "geometric shapes" and "organic shapes" on the board. As each group presents their findings, write them under the appropriate heading.

Then ask students to brainstorm other examples of their represented shapes. Encourage them to think of shapes found in nature and human-made shapes to add to the lists.

Shape

What shapes do you notice in this painting? A **shape** in a painting is a flat area, such as a circle or square. It has height and width but not depth.

Marianne von Werefkin. *The Washerwomen*, 1908–1909. Tempera on paper mounted on board, 20 by 25 inches. Städtische Galerie im Lenbachhaus, Munich, Germany.

26

Art Background

About the Artist Marianne von Werefkin (1860–1938) was born in Tula, Russia. Her mother, who was an artist, encouraged her to draw from an early age. Although she permanently injured the thumb and index finger of her right hand in a hunting accident in 1888, she pursued a career as an artist, creating large oil paintings in dark colors.

ESL Notes

Gather objects that have organic shapes. Give students time to touch and explore each object. Have them describe each object with one or two words.

ESL TEKS 4.31F Describe how color, shape, and line influence the message

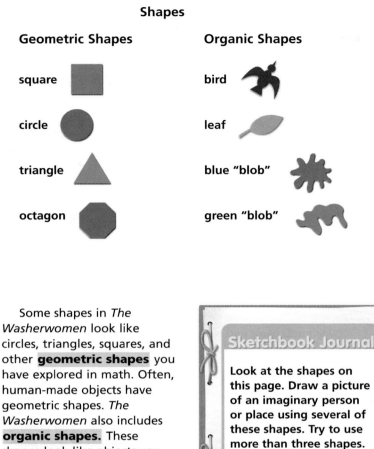

Shapes

Geometric Shapes

square

circle

triangle

octagon

Organic Shapes

bird

leaf

blue "blob"

green "blob"

Some shapes in *The Washerwomen* look like circles, triangles, squares, and other **geometric shapes** you have explored in math. Often, human-made objects have geometric shapes. *The Washerwomen* also includes **organic shapes.** These shapes look like objects you see in nature, such as clouds or puddles. What geometric and organic shapes can you find in the painting?

Sketchbook Journal

Look at the shapes on this page. Draw a picture of an imaginary person or place using several of these shapes. Try to use more than three shapes.

27

Curriculum Connection

Math Using the overhead projector, show a series of geometric shapes that forms a pattern. Include parallelograms and trapezoids, as well as circles, rectangles, and triangles. Have students identify the pattern shown and continue it in their Sketchbook Journal. Proceed with new patterns, or allow volunteers to create a pattern and have the class complete it.

TAKS Math Obj. 2 Understand patterns and relationships
Math TEKS 4.7 Analyze and describe patterns

② Teach

Have students read page 26. Ask:

- **Where do you see continuous lines in the painting?** (Possible response: around the baskets and the woman's face) DESCRIBE
- **Which geometric shapes occur most frequently in the painting?** (Possible response: ovals, rectangles) ANALYZE

After students read page 27, explain that most geometric shapes have straight edges and distinct lines, while organic shapes are more free-form. Then have students point out the geometric and organic shapes in *The Washerwomen*. (Possible responses: geometric—circles, rectangles, triangles; organic—people, tree, clouds, flowers) Ask:

- **What feelings or ideas do the organic shapes convey?** (Possible response: a sense of calm and purpose) INTERPRET
- **Do you find the artist's use of geometric shapes appealing? Why or why not?** (Possible response: No, they distract the viewer too much.) JUDGE

Sketchbook Journal Have students add additional details by using more shapes. For example, if students drew a person, encourage them to create a landscape background.

③ Close

Make sure that students have included at least three different shapes in their drawings. Have them identify the shapes they used and name them aloud.

Assessment Have small groups share drawings and tell which shape they like best in each other's artworks.

NVAS (K–4) #2 Using knowledge of structures and functions
NVAS (K–4) #5 Reflecting upon and assessing the characteristics and merits of their work and the work of others
NVAS (K–4) #6 Making connections between visual arts and other disciplines

Studio 3

At a Glance

Objectives

• Express ideas by creating a collage using organic and geometric shapes.
• Evaluate original artworks by self and peers.

Materials

• drawing paper, colored construction paper
• pencil, glue sticks
• tempera paints and paintbrushes or water-based markers
• Rubric 1 from **Unit-by-Unit Resources**

FA TEKS 4.2B Design original artworks

FA TEKS 4.2C Invent ways to produce artworks and to explore photographic imagery, using a variety of art media and materials

FA TEKS 4.4A Describe intent and form conclusions about personal artworks

①Introduce

Review organic and geometric shapes. Explain that a collage is an artwork created by arranging and gluing pictures, photographs, paper, fabric, or other materials onto a flat surface.

Have students brainstorm ideas about an activity they like to do with their family. Model an example by saying: **Every summer, my family gathers at the lake for a family reunion. This event would make a good subject for a collage.** Explain to students that they will be integrating their own ideas about a family activity into their collages. Ask:

• **Is the scene outdoors or indoors?**
• **What family members did you include in your scene?**
• **What kinds of shapes will you use to create the collage?**

Quick Studio

Have students make a viewfinder by cutting a hole in the middle of a sheet of paper. Draw any shapes seen through the hole.

Create a Shape Collage

Imagine a scene from a familiar environment. Show the scene in a collage of shapes.

1 Draw some organic and geometric shapes for your scene.

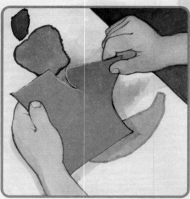

2 Tear similar shapes from colored paper.

Technique Tip

Add interest by varying the edges of your paper. Tear to make rough edges. For a smooth edge, fold paper first, and tear on the fold.

28

Meeting Individual Needs

Extend Have students tear a variety of organic shapes from different types of paper. Without first making a sketch, have students create a collage that demonstrates an interesting design. After gluing the shapes, invite students to use markers to define them or to create details on their collage. Have students reflect on the similarities and differences between their artworks.

28

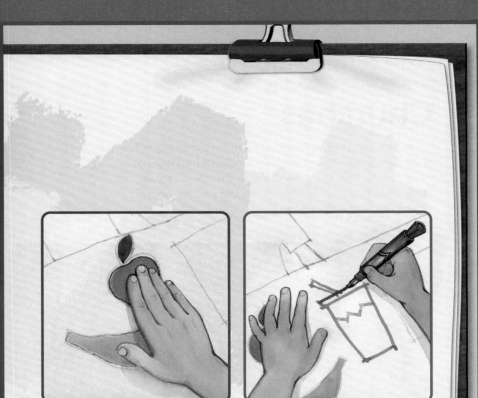

3 Glue the torn paper shapes into place on your sketch.

4 Draw or paint more shapes to complete your collage.

Think Like an Artist

Did your organic and geometric shapes turn out the way you planned? Would you make any changes? Why or why not?

 Fine Arts Connection

Music Display photographs of musical instruments or, if possible, have students bring in musical instruments that they play. Explain that most musical instruments feature both organic and geometric shapes. You may want to point out the shapes in a guitar as an example. Have students draw musical instruments, keeping in mind the various shapes they see.

FA TEKS 4.5D Identify connections between music and other fine arts

2 Create

Have students read the directions on pages 28–29. Then distribute materials.

• Remind students to take a moment to plan their design. Draw a variety of shapes on the chalkboard to model Step 1.
• Have students select a variety of colors and types of paper for their shapes.
• Have students try out different arrangements.
• Encourage variety and review the different kinds of lines and shapes.

Technique Tip Have students draw around the shapes and then carefully tear along the lines.

3 Close

Have students describe their intentions and then form conclusions about their work by answering the *Think Like an Artist* questions. (Possible response: Yes. But I would change some of the geometric shapes to organic shapes.)

Ask students to share their collages with a small group. Invite them to describe the family activity shown in their artwork. Call on volunteers to name the geometric and organic shapes in the collage.

Ongoing Assessment

If . . . students have difficulty choosing shapes,

then . . . suggest that they use ovals for faces, crescents for the moon, and trapezoids for people's bodies.

See page 18 from **Unit-by-Unit Resources** for a rubric to assess this studio.

NVAS (K–4) #1 Understanding and applying media, techniques, and processes

NVAS (K–4) #3 Choosing and evaluating a range of subject matter, symbols and ideas

NVAS (K–4) #5 Reflecting upon and assessing the characteristics and merits of their work and the work of others

Look and Compare

Look and Compare

At a Glance

Objectives

- Compare and contrast artworks that show churches.
- Analyze the influences of culture in artworks.
- Respond to and make judgments about artworks.

Materials

- **Art Prints 1, 2, 3**
- **Fine Art Transparency**

FA TEKS 4.3A Identify simple main ideas expressed in art

FA TEKS 4.3B Compare and contrast selected artworks from a variety of cultural settings

Explore

Display **Art Print 1,** *Waterlilies: Green Reflections.* Help students recall this artwork by Claude Monet from page 16. As students look at the two artworks on pages 30 and 31, ask them to predict which one was also created by Monet, and give reasons for their answer. (Possible response: *Rouen Cathedral;* the credit line tells the artist's name; the soft colors are similar)

Discuss

Explain that artworks often have a simple main idea. Point out that the main idea in both of these paintings is a church.

After students read pages 30 and 31, have them discuss the actual and implied lines each artist used. Invite volunteers to identify the strong horizontal and vertical lines in O'Keeffe's painting. Explain that these lines help create a sense of strength and peacefulness. Students can contrast this with the many broken lines, curves, and edges in Monet's painting.

30

Churches

Artists can choose from many different subjects for their paintings. Monet sometimes chose buildings as his subjects. This painting shows a church in France. How does this church differ from the one by Georgia O'Keeffe on the next page?

Claude Monet. *Rouen Cathedral,* 1894. Oil on canvas, 39¼ by 25⅞ inches. The Metropolitan Museum of Art, New York.

30

🎨 Art Background

Rouen Cathedral Claude Monet's paintings of the great Gothic Rouen Cathedral are an attempt to record the passage of time. Monet was fascinated with how light, through the day, changed the appearance and colors of objects. In *Rouen Cathedral,* Monet used short brushstrokes to represent the movement of light on the ancient stones.

Ranchos Church—Taos Georgia O'Keeffe painted many images of the San Francisco de Assis Church in Taos, New Mexico. *Ranchos Church—Taos* reflects O'Keeffe's unique style, which can be described as a mixture of symbolism, abstraction, and photography. The painting also exemplifies O'Keeffe's use of muted colors and thin but exquisite application of oil paint.

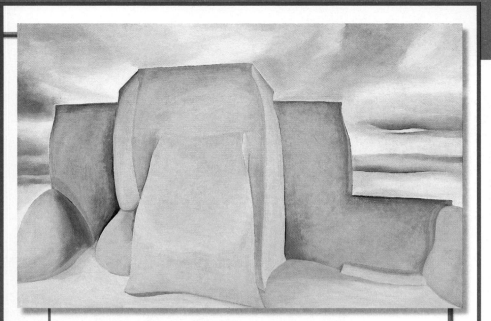

Georgia O'Keeffe. *Ranchos Church–Taos*, 1930. Oil on canvas, 24¼ by 36 inches. Courtesy of Amon Carter Museum, Ft. Worth, Texas. © 1997 The Georgia O'Keeffe Foundation/Artists Rights Society (ARS), New York.

Georgia O'Keeffe created this painting of an adobe church in New Mexico.

Think about how these paintings are alike and how they are different. How many different kinds of lines can you find? Are the shapes organic or geometric? Explain your answer.

Research

The Impressionist painters were named after Monet's painting, *Impression: Sunrise*. Find it in an art book or encyclopedia.

31

Reading Strategy

Compare and Contrast Remind students that to compare two things, they look for ways in which the things are similar. To contrast two things, they look for differences between them. Have students reread the paragraph on page 30. Ask them if the question at the end is asking them to compare or contrast. (contrast) Tell them that they will often be asked to find both similarities and differences at the same time. Remind them that they can use lists to brainstorm their ideas and then organize the ideas in a graphic organizer.

TAKS Rdg. Obj. 4 Apply critical thinking
ELA TEKS 4.11D Make connections in response to texts

Apply

Draw a Venn diagram like the one below. Tell students that this graphic organizer is a good way to show how two artworks are the same and how they are different.

Guide students as they look for differences by suggesting that they focus on lines, shapes, and details in the two artworks. Possible responses are shown in blue.

Paintings of Churches

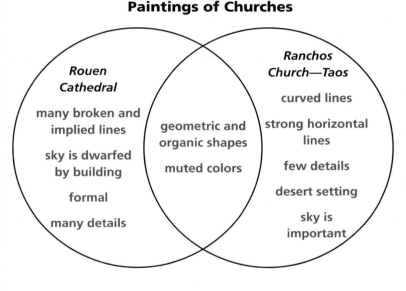

Rouen Cathedral

many broken and implied lines

sky is dwarfed by building

formal

many details

geometric and organic shapes

muted colors

Ranchos Church—Taos

curved lines

strong horizontal lines

few details

desert setting

sky is important

Close

Have students think back to the Monet painting from the beginning of the unit. Ask them how that painting is different from *Rouen Cathedral*. (Possible response: One is about nature and the other is about a building) Then invite them to learn more about Monet's work by conducting research.

Research Have students find other Impressionist paintings and ask them what these paintings have in common. (Possible response: they feature bright colors and blurred, broken lines)

NVAS (K–4) #4 Understanding the visual arts in relation to history and culture
NVAS (K–4) #5 Reflecting upon and assessing the characteristics and merits of their work and the work of others

Lesson 4

At a Glance

Objectives

- Identify and describe texture in artworks.
- Describe, analyze, interpret, and judge artworks.

Materials

- **Fine Art Transparency**
- objects with different textures
- Sketchbook Journal
- pictures or slides of city skylines (optional)

Vocabulary

texture, tactile texture, visual texture

FA TEKS 4.1B Choose appropriate vocabulary to discuss the use of art elements such as color, texture, form, line, space, and value and art principles such as emphasis, pattern, rhythm, balance, proportion, and unity

FA TEKS 4.4B Interpret ideas and moods in original artworks, portfolios, and exhibitions by peers and others

❶ Introduce

Collect objects with different textures, such as an apple, a pineapple, a rock, a stick, and a piece of cloth. Ask students to describe the actual texture of the object. Write the words they use to describe texture on the board under the heading "Tactile Texture."

Explain that they just identified tactile texture, which is sometimes called actual texture. Tell students that in artworks, there is also visual, or simulated, texture, which is the way the object's surface appears to the eye.

Have students describe the visual texture of the objects you brought in. They may use words such as *shiny, dull,* and *rough.* Write those words on the board under "Visual Texture."

Lesson 4

Texture

When you touch a surface or an object, it might feel smooth, bumpy, soft, hard, or sticky. The way a surface or object feels is its **texture.** Texture is an element of art.

Frank Romero. *Scamp in the Snow,* 1995. Oil on paper, 17 by 24 inches. Courtesy of Frank Romero.

 **Art Background**

Art and Culture Born in East Los Angeles, California, in 1941, Frank Romero finds inspiration for his paintings, sculptures, and murals in his Hispanic roots. His bold artworks show the influence of folk art from Mexico and the American Southwest. Romero is a founding member of *Los Four,* a group of artists dedicated to promoting art and social activism in the Latino community.

ESL Notes

Provide students with several objects, each having a different texture. As students touch each object, name the texture and have students repeat it.

ESL TEKS 4.5G Employ content area vocabulary in context
ESL TEKS 4.27A Use active listening comprehension

These glasses show visual texture.

If you touched a real cat you could feel its **tactile texture.** Many artworks show **visual texture.** This is texture that you see rather than feel.

The visual texture of the glasses in the photograph is shiny. If you could touch the glasses, their tactile texture would be smooth. What textures do you see in *Scamp in the Snow?*

Sketchbook Journal

Draw a variety of geometric shapes. Fill them with textures, such as rough, pebbly, and lumpy. Use your imagination to add more textures to your drawing.

33

Technology

Scanning Textures Have students gather and scan examples of textures from magazine advertisements into a computer. You can also have them download examples of textures from textile and carpet Web sites. If possible, have them save these textures for future use in a collage or other project. Suggest that students write ideas in their Sketchbook Journals on ways they can use the textures in an artwork.

Tech TEKS 4.2A Use a variety of input devises

② Teach

Have students read page 32 and the credit line. Ask:

- **What details do you see in this artwork?** (Possible response: snowflakes, stripes on the cat, whiskers, claws) DESCRIBE
- **Do the textures on the cat look the same or different than the textures of the snow?** (different) ANALYZE

After students read page 33, discuss the textures in Romero's painting. Students may say that the snow appears bumpy and the cat looks soft. Explain that they have identified the painting's visual texture. Then ask:

- **How would the mood of the painting be different if the snow appeared to be shiny?** (Possible response: the subject would not seem as calm) INTERPRET
- **Would you want to pet this cat? Why?** (Possible response: yes; it looks friendly) JUDGE

Sketchbook Journal Take students outside to find a variety of textures to draw. You could also have them look through magazines for texture ideas.

③ Close

After students finish their drawings, have them ask themselves if they used a variety of textures. Ask them to note the textures they like the best.

Visual Culture Have students think about a cityscape, or show them pictures of cities. Invite them to describe the different visual textures they notice in the buildings. For example, some skyscrapers appear smooth and shiny while other buildings may look rough or bumpy.

NVAS (K–4) #1 Understanding and applying media, techniques, and processes

NVAS (K–4) #3 Choosing and evaluating a range of subject matter, symbols, and ideas

NVAS (K–4) #5 Reflecting upon and assessing the characteristics and merits of their work and the work of others

Studio 4

At a Glance

Objectives

- Express ideas by creating texture rubbings.
- Evaluate original artworks by self and peers.

Materials

- drawing paper or newsprint
- pencils, crayons, oil pastels
- various textured objects, such as green kitchen "scrubby," sandpaper, corduroy, bubble wrap, or corrugated cardboard
- tempera paint thinned with water (1:3 paint to water ratio) and wide paintbrushes
- Rubric 1 from **Unit-by-Unit Resources**

FA TEKS 4.2B Design original artworks
FA TEKS 4.4A Describe intent and form conclusions about personal artworks

❶ Introduce

Review tactile and visual texture. Ask students to name some textures in the natural world. Then have students brainstorm ideas for the type of animal they wish to draw and its environment. Ask:

- **Where does the animal live—in a house, a jungle, or a desert?**
- **What objects or plants will you show?**
- **How will you show the texture of the animal's coat?**

Quick Studio

Have students cut shapes from different texture rubbings and arrange them to depict a familiar plant, animal, or object.

Studio 4

Rub Textures

Use a mix of shapes and textures to make a texture rubbing.

① **Draw your favorite animal on the paper.**

② **Add large shapes that might appear in the animal's environment.**

Technique Tip

Make test rubbings of different textures on scrap paper before adding them to your picture.

🧍🧍🧍 Meeting Individual Needs

Inclusion This lesson can be adapted for students not yet creating representational images. Have these students do a finger painting. Then incorporate texture by stamping or rubbing the wet paint with sponges, sandpaper, and other textured materials.

 3 Rub crayons over a different texture for each part of the picture.

4 Cover the entire picture with one color of thinned tempera.

Think Like an Artist

If you could do the project again, what would you do differently? How did the rubbing help to describe your animal?

Fine Arts Connection

Music In music, texture refers to the layering of sounds to create a thick or thin quality. Songs with more layers have a thicker texture. Layers can be added by introducing more voices or instruments playing at the same time. Have students listen to different pieces of music, some with vocals and some without. Then have them discuss the musical textures that they hear.

FA TEKS 4.1A Categorize a variety of musical sounds
FA TEKS 4.1B Use standard terminology in explaining music
FA TEKS 4.5D Identify connections between music and other fine art

② Create

Have students read pages 34–35. Then distribute materials.

- Allow students time to explore the different textures of the materials distributed.
- Remind students of the ideas they brainstormed.
- Have students experiment with the amount of pressure to use when rubbing with the crayon.
- Protect work surfaces with newsprint or reusable table covers.

Technique Tip Tell students that different kinds of paper will change their texture rubbings.

③ Close

Have students describe their intentions and then form conclusions about their artworks by answering the *Think Like an Artist* questions on page 35. (Possible responses: I would use different textures in smaller areas for a more interesting look. My animal looks furry.)

Have students share their work with classmates.

Model positive comments as they describe their visual textures, lines, and shapes.

Ongoing Assessment

If . . . students have trouble finding a variety of textures,

then . . . distribute prefabricated textures available from art catalogs.

See page 18 from **Unit-by-Unit Resources** for a rubric to assess this studio.

NVAS (K–4) #1 Understanding and applying media, techniques, and processes
NVAS (K–4) #3 Choosing and evaluating a range of subject matter, symbols and ideas
NVAS (K–4) #5 Reflecting upon and assessing the characteristics and merits of their work and the work of others

Lesson 5

Lesson 5

Space and Distance

Look around and notice how objects that are far away appear smaller than those that are close. To show this in artworks, many artists use **space**, the area within and around shapes. This element helps artists show distance in artworks.

Clara McDonald Williamson. *The Old Chisholm Trail*, 1952. Oil on panel, 24 by 36½ inches. The Roland P. Murdock Collection, Wichita Art Museum, Wichita, Kansas.

At a Glance

Objectives

- Identify and describe space and distance in artworks.
- Describe, analyze, interpret, and judge artworks.

Materials

- **Fine Art Transparency**
- Sketchbook Journal

Vocabulary

space, foreground, background, middle ground, overlap

FA TEKS 4.1B Choose appropriate vocabulary to discuss the use of art elements such as color, texture, form, line, space, and value and art principles such as emphasis, pattern, rhythm, balance, proportion, and unity

FA TEKS 4.3C Identify roles of art in American society

FA TEKS 4.4B Interpret ideas and moods in original artworks, portfolios, and exhibitions by peers and others

❶ Introduce

Take students outside and direct their attention to a fixed point in the distance more than one hundred yards away. Have students name things they can see in the distance, up close, and in between. Explain that one way artists define space in their artworks is to create backgrounds, foregrounds, and middle grounds to show the illusion of distance.

Point out particular objects, such as cars, trees, or buildings. Have students observe how the object appears in the space around it. Discuss how objects that are far away appear smaller than ones that are up close.

🎨 Art Background

Art History Williamson's painting tells the story of cattle drives on the Chisholm Trail, a trail that extended from San Antonio, Texas, to Abilene, Kansas. The trail was named for Jesse Chisholm, a Native American trader who blazed the trail in a wagon in the mid-1800s. From 1867 to 1884, ranchers used the Chisholm Trail to drive cattle from Texas to railroad lines in Kansas and other states.

ESL Notes

Show students photographs that clearly show backgrounds, middle grounds, and foregrounds. As you say each term, have students repeat it and point to the corresponding part.

ESL TEKS 4.27A Use active listening comprehension
ESL TEKS 4.27F Infer meaning

Objects in the foreground of the picture appear larger than those in the background.

What objects in this photograph seem closer to the viewer? The part of an artwork that seems nearest is the **foreground. Background** is the part that seems farthest away. **Middle ground** is the area in between. Point to objects in the painting and photograph that are in the foreground, middle ground, or background. Notice how the cattle in the foreground cover, or **overlap,** one another.

Sketchbook Journal

Think of a view you have seen outdoors. Draw a sketch of it, showing objects that overlap. Show foreground, middle ground, and background.

37

2 Teach

Have students read page 36 and the credit line. Ask:

- **What do you see in this painting?** (Possible response: cows, cowboys, trees, mountains, a river, sky, fields) DESCRIBE
- **Where are the smallest objects in the painting?** (near the top, in the background) ANALYZE

After students read page 37, point out the background, middle ground, and foreground of the painting and show students where objects overlap. Discuss how the objects in the foreground seem closer because they are bigger and at the bottom of the painting. Then have students name objects in each section of the painting and ask:

- **Why do you think the artist included mountains in the painting?** (Possible response: to show distance) INTERPRET
- **What are your thoughts about this painting?** (Possible response: it conveys a lot of information about cattle drives) JUDGE

Sketchbook Journal If possible, provide pictures of various outdoor scenes that students can use for references. Point out any objects in the foreground, middle ground, and background, as well as any overlapping objects.

3 Close

After students make their drawings, have them check to make sure some objects overlap. Some students may wish to add details.

Assessment Display some student drawings and have the class identify the foreground, background, and middle ground in each artwork. Clarify any questions about these terms.

Curriculum Connection

Have students look again at *The Old Chisholm Trail* on page 36. Ask them to identify the subject of this painting. Explain that artworks such as this tell about events in American history, in this case, the birth of the cattle industry in Texas. Point out that art plays an important role in American society as a record of historical events.

Have students look through their Social Studies books to find other examples of paintings or drawings that depict historical events or specific periods in American history. Then have them work in small groups to discuss how the artwork tells the story of the event or time. As students view these artworks, have them use the words foreground, middle ground, and background in their discussions.

SS TEKS 4.4B Explain growth and development of cattle industry
SS TEKS 4.5A Identify the impact of various issues and events of life in Texas

NVAS (K–4) #2 Using knowledge of structures and functions
NVAS (K–4) #4 Understanding the visual arts in relation to history and cultures
NVAS (K–4) #5 Reflecting upon and assessing the characteristics and merits of their work and the work of others
NVAS (K–4) #6 Making connections between visual arts and other

Studio 5

Make a Nature Scene

Make some objects appear farther away than others in a nature scene.

1 Draw a scene that has foreground, middle ground, and background.

2 Choose different colors for the foreground, middle ground, and background.

Technique Tip

Overlap small objects in the background first. Make objects gradually larger in the middle ground and foreground.

38

At a Glance

Objectives

- Express ideas by drawing a scene showing distance and space.
- Evaluate original artworks by self and peers.

Materials

- drawing paper, pencils
- 3 crayons of different colors for each student
- Rubric 1 from **Unit-by-Unit Resources**

FA TEKS 4.2B Design original artworks
FA TEKS 4.3C Identify the roles of art in American society

1 Introduce

Review foreground, middle ground, background, and overlapping. Have students look out a window and use the first three terms to describe the scene they see. Then have students brainstorm objects to include in their own outdoor scenes. Ask:

- **What people, plants, or animals will appear in the foreground?**
- **What will the people or animals be doing?**
- **What landforms, such as mountains or plateaus, will appear in the background?**

Quick Studio

Have students draw a farm scene. Have them show one example of overlapping and add details to the objects in the foreground.

Meeting Individual Needs

Reteach Have students make sketches of objects in the foreground before making the drawing. Remind them that they can change their minds about what to include.

Extend Have students work in small groups to make an outdoor scene into a mural on butcher paper. Have them add color to the scene with tempera paints after they draw it in pencil.

38

③ Overlap objects to show depth.

④ Add details to the objects in the foreground.

Think Like an Artist
Ask a friend to identify the foreground, middle ground, and background of your drawing.

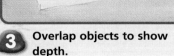 **Fine Arts Connection**

Theatre Tell students that stage designers and directors throughout history have sought ways to overcome the limitations of space and distance imposed by the stage. For example, the Shakespearean stage had three parts in which action could take place: outdoor scenes were played on a forestage or runway that jutted into the audience; indoor scenes took place on a traditional inner stage further back; and other scenes took place on a balcony.

To illustrate how theatre and film designers create the illusion of space today, show clips from an approved classroom video. Then have students point out background, middle ground, and foreground in different scenes.

FA TEKS 4.4A Explain theatre as a reflection of life
FA TEKS 4.4B Identify the role of live theatre in American society

② Create

Have students read pages 38–39. Then distribute materials.

- Have students consider the ideas they brainstormed at the beginning of this lesson.
- Tell students to use lighter colors to show the background and darker colors for objects in the foreground.
- Suggest that students draw the overlapping objects in pencil and then color them.
- Have students look for implied and actual lines in their artwork.

Technique Tip To practice drawing overlapping objects, have students line up three or four objects on their desks, one in front of the other. Ask them to draw what they see.

③ Close

Have students reflect on their artworks using the *Think Like an Artist* activity. (Answers will vary.) Point out where students effectively use overlapping.

Ongoing Assessment

If . . . students have difficulty imagining an outdoor scene,

then . . . provide them with copies of photographs or magazine images showing natural scenes.

See page 18 from **Unit-by-Unit Resources** for a rubric to assess this studio.

NVAS (K–4) #1 Understanding and applying media, techniques, and processes
NVAS (K–4) #3 Choosing and evaluating a range of subject matter, symbols, and ideas
NVAS (K–4) #5 Reflecting upon and assessing the characteristics and merits of their work and the work of others

Lesson 6

At a Glance

Objectives

- Identify and describe positive and negative space in artworks.
- Describe, analyze, interpret, and judge artworks.

Materials

- **Fine Art Transparency**
- construction paper

Vocabulary

positive space, negative space, composition

FA TEKS 4.1A Communicate ideas about self, family, school, and community, using sensory knowledge and life experiences

FA TEKS 4.1B Choose appropriate vocabulary to discuss the use of art elements such as color, texture, form, line, space, and value and art principles such as emphasis, pattern, rhythm, balance, proportion, and unity

FA TEKS 4.4B Interpret ideas and moods in original artworks, portfolios, and exhibitions by peers and others

❶ Introduce

Before class, create several construction-paper cutouts of common objects, such as a key, leaf, spoon, or hand. Arrange the cutouts on a large sheet of paper, and have students look at the positive and negative spaces. Discuss how both the negative and positive spaces make up the composition.

Explain that the space taken up by the object is the positive space and the area around the object is the negative space. If you wish, have students transfer the outline of one of the objects on to paper. Have them color in the positive space.

Ask students where else they notice strong positive and negative spaces. Mention that the positive space usually attracts your eye first.

40

Lesson 6

Artists See Spaces

People see spaces in artworks in different ways. In the artwork on this page, most people see the leaf shape first. This area is called **positive space.** The area around the positive space is called **negative space.**

Rupert García. *Maguey de la Vida,* 1973. Color screenprint, 18⅞ by 24⅞ inches. Fine Arts Museums of San Francisco, gift of Mr. and Mrs. Robert Marcus, 1990.1.116.

40

🎨 Art Background

Maguey de la Vida American artist Rupert García (1941–) created this stark image of the maguey, a desert plant originally from Mexico. Maguey plants are also found throughout the Southwest and in the Philippines. Sporting thick, fleshy leaves, they can adapt to many different kinds of climate and do not require much rainfall.

ESL Notes

Display artwork showing obvious positive and negative spaces. Point to and name the spaces in each artwork, and have students repeat the terms.

ESL TEKS 4.27A Use active listening comprehension
ESL TEKS 4.27F Infer meanings

What attracts your eye in this image?

Negative space serves as contrast. It helps you see the positive space. Both positive and negative spaces are parts of the **composition,** or the whole artwork.

Point to the positive space in the picture on this page. Positive space has outlines, edges, or colors that attract your eye. Now look at the negative space in García's artwork. How did he make the positive space stand out?

Art in My World

Find a family photo. It might be of your last birthday or from a family trip. Identify the positive and negative space in the picture.

Curriculum Connection

Social Studies Have students describe the climate of their region and research plants that grow there. For example, the climate of the Southwest is generally hot and dry. Desert cacti, such as the saguaro, grow there. Have students draw one of these plants, showing positive and negative space.

SS TEKS 4.7B Describe a variety of regions in Texas

② Teach

Have students read pages 40 and 41. Ask:

- **Do you see organic or geometric shapes in this artwork?** (organic) DESCRIBE
- **How is the subject of the artwork emphasized?** (It is large and there are few details.) ANALYZE

Point out to students how Garcia used color to make the positive space stand out. The red and orange of the negative space contrast sharply with the green of the positive space. Then ask:

- **How would Garcia's artwork be different if he had included details?** (It would be more difficult to see the positive space.) INTERPRET
- **What do you think about the maguey after viewing Garcia's artwork?** (Possible response: it is a strong plant) JUDGE

Art in My World Model communicating ideas using life experiences by holding up a photograph of your family and telling a story. Then identify positive and negative space in the photograph. Have students repeat with their family photos.

③ Close

Have students discuss positive and negative spaces in the layout of the classroom.

Assessment Display an object such as a vase against a plain backdrop. Have students draw only the boundary of the negative space around the object. Point out that by drawing the negative space, they also drew the positive space.

NVAS (K–4) #2 Using knowledge of structures and functions

NVAS (K–4) #5 Reflecting upon and assessing the characteristics and merits of their work and the work of others

Studio 6

At a Glance

Objectives

- Express ideas by showing positive and negative space in a drawing.
- Evaluate original artworks by self and peers.

Materials

- newsprint, poster board, heavy colored paper, or colored construction paper
- pencils, crayons, or oil pastels
- Rubric 1 from **Unit-by-Unit Resources**

FA TEKS 4.2B Design original artworks

FA TEKS 4.2C Invent ways to produce artworks and to explore photographic imagery, using a variety of art media and materials

FA TEKS 4.4A Describe intent and form conclusions about personal artworks

① Introduce

Review positive and negative space. Have students describe positive and negative space in artworks they have already created.

Tell students that the purpose of a CD or DVD design is to tell something about the music or the movie. Ask:

- **What instruments, musicians, or actors will be involved?**
- **What objects will represent the songs or movie?**
- **What kinds of shapes will you use to show positive and negative space?**

Quick Studio

Have students draw a silhouette of a familiar object using two colors to highlight the positive and negative spaces.

Studio 6
Draw a Cover Design

Plan a composition for a CD or DVD cover. How will you show positive and negative space? Follow these steps.

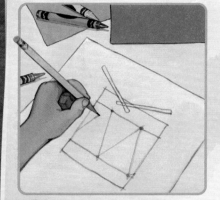

1 Use a pencil to draw the main shape or image for your CD or DVD cover.

2 Use swirly lines to make interesting shapes on another sheet of paper.

Technique Tip

Choose colors to help you show positive space. Choose other colors to help you show negative space.

Meeting Individual Needs

Extend Have students create several folds in a sheet of white paper. Using scissors, have students make a series of cutouts in the folded paper, being careful not to completely cut away the fold. Ask students to open their paper and observe the images created. Invite them to mount this paper onto a sheet of black construction paper. Then ask students to discuss how the shapes show positive and negative space.

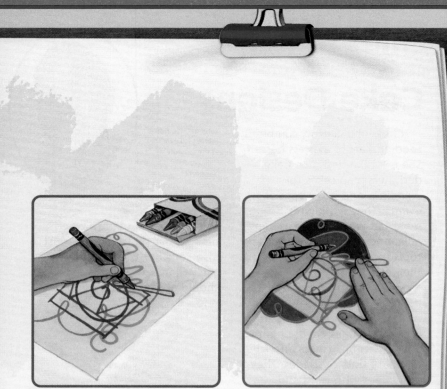

③ **Draw the main shape or image for your cover.**

④ **Color in dark shapes next to light ones to make a visual puzzle.**

Think Like an Artist

Do you think your cover design will make people want to buy the CD or DVD? Why or why not?

43

 Fine Arts Connection

Dance Tell students that dance choreographers also must think about positive and negative space when they choreograph, or design, dances. They need to determine how the dancers on stage appear to the audience and consider props, backdrops, and the number of people on stage at a time. Have the class watch a live or recorded dance performance and discuss how space is used.

PE TEKS 4.2B Identify ways movement concepts can be used to refine movement skills

② Create

Have students read pages 42–43. Then distribute materials.

- Provide students with paper that is larger than the actual 5-by-5-inch dimensions of a CD.
- Encourage students to add many swirling, intersecting lines to their drawing.
- Have students center their image on the page.
- Have students experiment with blending two colors together to create different shades.

Technique Tip Help students choose colors that contrast sharply, such as red and green, blue and yellow, or orange and violet.

③ Close

Have students think about the purpose of a CD or DVD design and then answer the *Think Like an Artist* question to form conclusions about their artworks. (Possible response: Yes; I used interesting shapes and lines to catch people's eye.)

Ongoing Assessment

If . . . students have difficulty thinking of cover ideas,

then . . . have them bring a favorite CD or DVD cover to class for inspiration.

See page 18 from **Unit-by-Unit Resources** for a rubric to assess this studio.

NVAS (K–4) #1 Understanding and applying media, techniques, and processes

NVAS (K–4) #3 Choosing and evaluating a range of subject matter, symbols and ideas

NVAS (K–4) #5 Reflecting upon and assessing the characteristics and merits of their work and the work of others

At a Glance

Objectives

- Read about a career in art.
- Identify the use of art in everyday life.
- Relate art to personal experience.

Materials

- **Fine Art Transparency**
- finger paint
- resealable bags

FA TEKS 4.3C Identify the roles of art in American society

Explore

Tell students that professional cake designers use precise tools in their work. Bakers at home can use simpler tools to make their cakes look special. Give each student a small resealable bag. Put a few spoonfuls of finger paint in each bag and then cut off the tip of one corner. Demonstrate by squeezing a bag gently to make lines and shapes on cardboard. Then have students experiment with their bags.

Discuss

Have students read pages 44–45. Ask:

- **Name some special events for which a cake designer might make cakes.** (Possible response: weddings, birthdays, graduations)
- **What kinds of lines do you see in the cake on page 45?** (vertical, horizontal, curved)
- **What shapes and textures would you use to design a cake?** (Answers will vary.)
- **Would you want to be a cake designer? Why or why not?** (Answers will vary.)

Artist at Work

Cake Designs

Chef Toba Garrett combines food and art to express herself. She is a cake designer. Cake designers plan cakes for weddings and other special events. They work with materials we eat, such as eggs, milk, and sugar. They also use tools to help them add icing to their cakes.

Toba Garrett, right, teaches cake design at the Institute of Culinary Education in New York.

Icing is made from sugar. It can be thin, thick, fluffy, or firm. Cake designers use icing almost like painters use paints. They often mix colors into icing to create tints or shades. They draw lines with icing and experiment with shapes.

Garrett begins her cake designs with a pencil and sketchbook. She considers color, line, and texture when making her sketches. She must also consider the ingredients she will use. A great cake should always taste as good as it looks.

Cake designers use tools such as this spatula and icing bag to add texture to their cakes.

44

Career Research

Take students to a culinary school or a bakery where cake designers work. Have students observe the cake designer designing a cake. You may want to have students prepare questions to ask the designer. Encourage students to ask about:

- tools used to make designs
- how to train to become a cake designer
- where to get ideas for cake designs

What colors, lines, and textures has Garrett added to this cake?

45

Apply

Have students work in groups to identify details about what cake designers do. Display a graphic organizer like the one below. Fill in the word web together as students share their ideas.

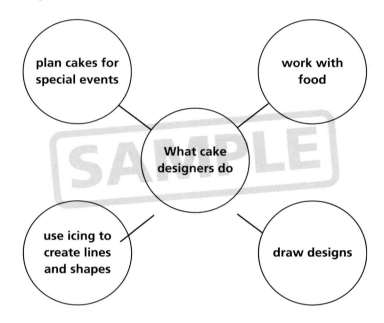

plan cakes for special events

work with food

What cake designers do

use icing to create lines and shapes

draw designs

Then have each group write 3–5 interview questions they would like to ask a cake designer. If possible, have a local cake designer visit and answer students' questions, or arrange to have students write their questions in the form of letters to send to local bakers.

Close

Have the class discuss the interview questions they wrote. Ask them what they have learned about art through this lesson on cake designers. (Possible response: Cake designers have to use a variety of lines, shapes, and textures to create unique designs for their cakes.)

NVAS (K–4) #5 Reflecting upon and assessing the characteristics and merits of their work and the work of others

NVAS (K–4) #6 Making connections between visual arts and other disciplines

Reading Strategy

Identify Details Review identifying details with students and remind them that details support the main idea. Tell students that the main idea of this reading is how cake designers combine food and art. Have students reread page 44 and find details that support the main idea. Have them use a word web to record their ideas. Discuss their answers as a class.

TAKS Rdg. Obj. 3 Use strategies to analyze tests
  ELA TEKS 4.10F Determine how ideas are supported with details
  ELA TEKS 4.10G Summarize text to organize ideas
  ELA TEKS 4.10L Represent text information in different ways
  ELA TEKS 4.13H Use compiled information to direct questions
  ELA TEKS 4.21A Frame questions to direct research

Portfolio Project

Portfolio Project

Make an Etching

Show your interest in a hobby or sport. Use what you know about line, shape, texture, and space.

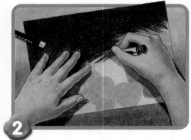

1 Color many shapes with bright oil pastels. Press hard and fill the whole paper.

2 Color over the paper again with black crayon or oil pastel. Press hard.

3 Use a toothpick to draw objects. Include foreground, middle ground, and background.

4 Use a craft stick and other tools to scratch away the negative space.

46

At a Glance

Objectives

• Develop and organize ideas from the environment.
• Demonstrate knowledge about line, shape, texture, and space.
• Evaluate original artworks by self and peers.

Materials

• 9″ × 12″ white drawing paper
• crayons or oil pastels (light colors and black)
• toothpicks ⚠, paper clips, craft sticks ⚠
• Sketchbook Journal
• Rubric 1 from **Unit-by-Unit Resources**

FA TEKS 4.2B Design original artworks

FA TEKS 4.2C Invent ways to produce artworks and to explore photographic imagery, using a variety of art media and materials

FA TEKS 4.4A Describe intent and form conclusions about personal artworks

FA TEKS 4.4B Interpret ideas and moods in original artworks, portfolios, and exhibitions by peers and others.

Plan

Instruct students to read page 46. Then ask:

• **What equipment or tools are used in your sport or hobby?** (Responses will vary.)

Have students think about the lines, shapes, textures, and spaces they will use in their etchings. Ask them to brainstorm what they want to show, and have them look through their Sketchbook Journal for ideas.

Quick Project

Using crayons, have students make four solid bands of color. Color over the bands with a black crayon. Scratch an abstract design.

👥👥 Meeting Individual Needs

Reteach If students are using oil pastels, encourage them to experiment by mixing them to create different colors.

Extend Have students use a variety of tools to scratch their designs, such as safety scissors, clothespins, or sticks. Discuss which tools worked best for creating different kinds of shapes and lines.

Gavin, Age 9. *Tubing at the Lake.* Crayon.

Morgan, Age 9. *Fishing.* Crayon.

Look at how these students etched scenes showing their favorite hobbies or sports.

Share Your Art

1. What kinds of lines and shapes did you use? What kinds of texture?

2. Where are the foreground, middle ground, and background in your artwork?

47

Gallery Options

Classroom Museum Explain that a museum is a place where artworks are displayed for the enjoyment and education of its visitors. Tell students that most of the artworks in this unit are housed in museums. Help them make a classroom museum by mounting or matting their artwork on brightly colored construction paper or matte board. Create kiosks to view their artworks by painting large cardboard boxes. Invite students and adults to visit the museum.

Create

Provide students with heavy paper to withstand the thick application of media and the scratching away of color. Have students read page 46. Then guide them to complete the project:

- Have students cover all the white space on the paper completely.
- Be sure students have applied thick layers of light or bright colors when drawing their organic and geometric shapes.
- Warn students to take care when using toothpicks and paper clips, as they are sharp.
- Encourage students to use a variety of tools to make lines, shapes, and spaces. To correct a mark, have students color over it with black crayon or pastel.

Close

Point out that the student art on page 47 is from the portfolios of other fourth-graders. Ask:

- **What lines, shapes, spaces, and textures do you see?** (Possible response: curved lines for water, circle for tube, background of trees, bumpy texture in waves)
- **How are these artworks similar to your own? How are they different?** (Possible response: We both used a lot of colors. I put in less details.)

Invite students to share their artworks with other students. Then use the *Share Your Art* questions to help students form conclusions about their own artwork. (1. Possible responses: diagonal and zigzag lines; lots of rectangles; the dots and wavy lines show texture. 2. Answers will vary.)

See page 18 from **Unit-by-Unit Resources** for a rubric to assess this project.

NVAS (K–4) #1 Understanding and applying media, techniques, and processes

NVAS (K–4) #3 Choosing and evaluating a range of subject matter, symbols and ideas

Unit 1 Review

At a Glance

Objectives

- Relate art terms to the environment.
- Identify subjects and details in artworks.
- Identify line, shape, space, and texture in artworks.
- Describe, analyze, interpret, and judge an artwork.

Materials

- **Art Print 4**
- **Fine Art Transparency**

FA TEKS 4.1B Choose appropriate vocabulary to discuss the use of art elements such as color, texture, form, line, space, and value and art principles such as emphasis, pattern, rhythm, balance, proportion, and unity

FA TEKS 4.4A Describe intent and form conclusions about personal artworks

FA TEKS 4.4B Interpret ideas and moods in original artworks, portfolios, and exhibitions by peers and others

Think About Art

Possible responses:

background (Point to farm.)
diagonal line (Point to roofs.)
foreground (Point to horses.)
geometric shape (Point to doors.)
horizontal line (Point to fences.)
negative space (Point to sky beyond houses.)
organic shape (Point to horses.)
subject (Point to chair.)
texture (Point to rug under chair.)

Write About Art

Before students write, ask:

- **What shapes do you see around you? Write adjectives to describe them.** (Possible responses: hard, square, cool)
- **Which textures really make an impression on you? Why?** (Possible response: the fuzzy texture of the rug, because it makes the room warmer)

48

Unit Review

Think About Art

Read the art words. Then point to a picture that matches each word. Explain how the picture illustrates what the word means.

background	geometric shape	organic shape
diagonal line	horizontal line	subject
foreground	negative space	texture

Write About Art

Look around your immediate environment. How do the lines, shapes, and textures affect how people might feel in that place? Write about them.

Talk About Art

- Look through your portfolio.
- Choose an artwork that best shows a variety of lines and shapes.
- Tell a friend about the lines and shapes.
- Explain what you used to make this artwork.

 **Assessment Options**

Options for assessing the students appear in the **Unit-by-Unit Resources.**

Use the **Vocabulary Worksheets** on pages 11–14 for an informal assessment of Unit 1 vocabulary.

Use the **Unit 1 Test** on pages 19–22 to assess students' mastery of unit and vocabulary concepts.

Gabriele Münter. *The Russian House (Das Russen-Haus)*, 1931. Oil on canvas, 16¾ by 22½ inches. Städtische Galerie im Lenbachhaus, Munich, Germany.

Put It All Together

1. Describe the subject of the painting. What elements of art did the artist use to show the subject?

2. How did the artist show foreground, middle ground, and background? How did she show positive and negative space?

3. What do you think the person in the window is looking at? What does this painting remind you of?

4. Tell about your favorite parts of this painting. Explain why you like them.

49

Talk About Art

Prompt students to use words such as *line, implied line, shape, texture, visual texture,* and *detail* to talk about their artworks. Have students describe their intent and form conclusions about the artwork they choose to share.

Put It All Together

Use the questions on page 49 to help students evaluate the artwork. Possible responses:

1. The painting shows a house with rocks, trees, and bushes around it. The artist used lines, shapes, textures, and space. DESCRIBE

2. She overlapped shapes. The larger tree in the foreground overlaps the house in the middle ground; the house overlaps the trees in the background. She used a contrast in colors to show the house as positive space; the sky creates negative space. ANALYZE

3. Possible responses: The grounds surrounding the house or perhaps a visitor who has arrived; a relative's house. INTERPRET

4. Possible response: The trees because they seem full and peaceful. JUDGE

Unit 2 Overview

The world is home to many different cultures. Art helps preserve a culture by providing visual records of it. In this unit students will explore how artists make visual records of their own cultures. They will discover how the different styles of artists reflect their cultures, and they will create artworks that represent their own backgrounds.

	Unit Opener, p. 50	Lesson 1, p. 52 **Color** Studio 1, p. 54 **Paint a Rainbow**	Lesson 2, p. 56 **Color Schemes** Studio 2, p. 58 **Draw with Colors**	Lesson 3, p. 60 **Landmarks and Color** Studio 3, p. 62 **Paint a Landmark**	Look and Compare, p. 64 **Community Scenes**
Artworks	**Jacob Lawrence.** *"In a Free Government, the security of civil rights must be the same as that for religious rights...." (the words of James Madison),* 1976.	**Auguste Macke.** *Geraniums Before Blue Mountain,* date unknown.	**Frida Kahlo.** *Long Live Life (Viva la vida),* 1954.	**Paul Cézanne.** *Mont Sainte-Victoire Seen from the Bibemus Quarry,* ca. 1897.	**Jacob Lawrence.** *The Library,* 1960. **Richard Estes.** *Helene's Florist,* 1971.
Vocabulary		colors, primary colors, secondary color, intermediate color	color scheme, cool colors, warm colors, analogous, complementary	color values, tint, shade, neutral colors	
Materials	• Art Print 5 • Fine Art Transparency • Instructional Prints	• **Fine Art Transparency** • Sketchbook Journal • colored construction paper • **Instructional Print** (optional) • tempera paints (red, yellow, blue, and white only) and paintbrushes • mixing trays, water containers, paper towels • large drawing paper	• **Fine Art Transparency** • Sketchbook Journal • magazine advertisements • oil pastels, drawing paper	• **Fine Art Transparency** • colored typing paper • folder • 11-by-17-inch drawing paper • tempera paints, paintbrushes • mixing trays	• **Art Prints 5, 6, 7** • **Fine Art Transparency** • pencils, crayons, water-based markers, or oil pastels • Sketchbook Journal
Connections	**Home Connection** objects that represent their culture **Bookshelf** *Story Painter: The Life of Jacob Lawrence* by John Duggleby, illustrated by Jacob Lawrence, Chronicle Books, 1998	**Technology** Digital color mixing **ESL Notes** **Fine Arts Connection** Music: color and mood **Meeting Individual Needs** Extend	**Curriculum Connection** Science: color schemes of birds **ESL Notes** **Fine Arts Connection** Theatre: color and light to create mood **Meeting Individual Needs** Inclusion	**Curriculum Connection** Social Studies: famous landmarks **ESL Notes** **Fine Arts Connection** Dance: color values in costumes **Meeting Individual Needs** Reteach, Extend	**Reading Strategy** Activate prior knowledge
Assessment Opportunities		Informal Assessment Rubric 2 from **Unit-by-Unit Resources** Ongoing Assessment	Visual Culture Rubric 2 from **Unit-by-Unit Resources** Ongoing Assessment	Informal Assessment Rubric 2 from **Unit-by-Unit Resources** Ongoing Assessment	

Lesson 4, p. 66 **Balance** Studio 4, p. 68 **Design Stained Glass**	Lesson 5 p. 70 **Pattern** Studio 5, p. 72 **Design a Quilt**	Lesson 6, p. 74 **Prints** Studio 6, p. 76 **Make a Print**	Artist at Work, p. 78 **Printmaking**	Portfolio Project, p. 80 **Make Gadget Prints**	Unit Review, p. 82
 Georgia O'Keeffe. *Evening Star, III,* 1917.	 **Artist unknown, possibly Gertrude Knappenberger.** *The Centennial Quilt,* date unknown.	 **Max Weber.** *Rabbi Reading,* 1919.	 **Annemaree Rea.** *Hide,* 2003.		 **Henri Rousseau.** *Tropical Storm with a Tiger (Surprise),* 1891.
balance, symmetrical balance, asymmetrical balance, radial balance	patterns, quilts, quilt block, symbols	print, print block, relief print, brayer			
• **Fine Art Transparency** • balance scale and counting chips • Sketchbook Journal • photographs of famous buildings (optional) • black construction paper, colored tissue paper • cardboard circle • pencils and old paintbrushes • safety scissors ⚠ • water-thinned glue or starch • waxed paper or newspaper	• **Fine Art Transparency** • colored pencils or crayons • Sketchbook Journal • quilt (optional) • pencils, construction paper • safety scissors ⚠, glue	• **Fine Art Transparency** • Sketchbook Journal • water-based inkpad or printers' ink • clean plastic foam meat trays • pencils or markers • tempera paints, dish soap • brayers and plastic trays • drawing paper	• **Fine Art Transparency** • a potato • inkpad and butcher paper • other printmaking materials • printed items such as greeting cards, wallpaper, or fabric swatches (optional)	• gadgets (parts of machines, such as nuts, bolts, washers, cogs, belts, etc.) • black construction paper, neon tempera paints • chalk pastels, sponges (optional)	• **Art Print 8** • **Fine Art Transparency**
Curriculum Connection Physical Education: balance **ESL Notes** **Fine Arts Connection** Dance: balance in dance **Meeting Individual Needs** Reteach, Extend	**Curriculum Connection** Math: numerical and geometric patterns **ESL Notes** **Fine Arts Connection** Music: patterns in songs **Meeting Individual Needs** Inclusion	**Curriculum Connection** Social Studies: cultural leaders **ESL Notes** **Fine Arts Connection** Theatre: skits featuring leaders **Meeting Individual Needs** Reteach, Extend	**Career Research** Printmakers **Reading Strategy** Relate to personal experience	**Gallery Options** Digital gallery **Meeting Individual Needs** Extend	
Visual Culture Rubric 2 from **Unit-by-Unit Resources** Ongoing Assessment	Visual Culture Rubric 2 from **Unit-by-Unit Resources** Ongoing Assessment	Visual Culture Rubric 2 from **Unit-by-Unit Resources** Ongoing Assessment		Rubric 2 from **Unit-by-Unit Resources**	**Unit-by-Unit Resources** Vocabulary Worksheets, pp. 29–32 Unit 2 Test, pp. 37–40

Unit 2

At a Glance

Objectives

- Identify cultural expression in artworks.
- Relate art to personal experiences.
- Respond to and make judgments about artworks.

Materials

- **Art Print 5**
- **Fine Art Transparency**

FA TEKS 4.1A Communicate ideas about self, family, school, and community, using sensory knowledge and life experiences

FA TEKS 4.3A Identify simple main ideas expressed in art

FA TEKS 4.4B Interpret ideas and moods in original artworks, portfolios, and exhibitions by peers and others

Introduce the Unit

Ask a volunteer to read the title of Unit 2. Tell students that they will learn that art can be an expression of ones' culture.

Tell students that *culture* is a term that describes a shared set of customs, beliefs, attitudes, values, and goals among members of a racial, religious, or social group. Have students talk about how their cultures help define who they are. Then discuss aspects of their own cultures, such as the foods they eat, the clothing they wear, and the holidays they celebrate. Ask: **What food item would you draw to represent your culture?** (Answers will vary.)

Have students look through the artworks in this unit and notice the different colors and styles used by the artists. Tell them that in this unit, they will learn about how artists create artworks to reflect the culture of people from particular times and places. Then explain that they will create artworks to represent aspects of themselves.

Jacob Lawrence. *"In a Free Government, the security of civil rights must be the same as that for religious rights. . . ."* (the words of James Madison), 1976. Opaque watercolor and pencil on paper, mounted on fiberboard, 30 by 22⅛ inches. Gift of the Container Corporation of America. National Museum of American Art, Smithsonian Institution, Washington, D.C./Art Resource, New York. Courtesy of the artist and Francine Seders Gallery, Seattle, Washington.

50

Art Background

In a Free Government . . . This painting was part of the Container Corporation of America's advertising campaign called "Great Ideas." The artworks in this series were titled with thought-provoking quotations and appeared in popular magazines. The corporation's founder, William Paepcke, recognized the strong impact businesses had on American culture. He hoped the artwork in the advertisements would spark ideas and discussion to improve society.

Home Connection

Tell students to look around their home and list five objects that represent their culture. Then have them bring in one of these objects to share with the class.

Unit 2

Cultural Expressions

Earth is home to many cultures. Artists make visual records of these cultures. Their artworks may show landmarks or community leaders. Others show ideas about food, clothing, or shelter that make a culture special. What visual records of your culture would you like to show?

Meet the Artist

Jacob Lawrence's art tells the history and culture of twentieth-century African Americans. Lawrence began making art with only a few poster paints. He once said, "Limiting yourself . . . forces you to be more inventive." He later created some groups of paintings that tell stories of African American families. Watch for another artwork by Lawrence later in this unit.

Jacob Lawrence. *Self-Portrait*, 1977.

51

Bookshelf

Story Painter: The Life of Jacob Lawrence
by John Duggleby, illustrated by Jacob Lawrence
Chronicle Books, 1998

Encourage students to read more about Lawrence's life and view more of his artworks in *Story Painter: The Life of Jacob Lawrence*. This lively biography tells how Lawrence developed as an artist, as it recounts the cultural and historical influences that shaped him.

Discuss Unit Concepts

Have students look at the painting and read page 51. Discuss the quotation and explain that James Madison (1751–1836), the fourth President of the United States, is considered to be the Father of the U.S. Constitution.

Next point out the details in the painting, such as the toolbox, the bowl of fruit, the newspaper showing the Capitol, and the eagle in the window. Explain that looking closely at details can help you interpret ideas about artworks. Ask: **How do you think these details add to the main idea of this painting?** (Possible response: Reading, family, the pursuit of freedom, and hard work are important parts of the culture Lawrence shows.)

As you introduce each element of art and principle of design in Unit 2, you may wish to display the **Instructional Prints.** A print is provided for each element and principle.

In addition, **Art Prints 5–8** and **Transparencies** are available for fine art in the unit.

Meet the Artist

Jacob Lawrence (1917–2000) showed his first artwork at the age of eighteen. His early works drew on his experiences growing up in Harlem during the 1930s. Throughout his career, he sought to dispel racial stereotypes while illuminating the struggles of African Americans against violence, poverty, and discrimination. His sixty-panel masterwork, *The Migration of the Negro*, shows the movement of millions of African Americans from the rural South to northern cities after World War I. He was the first African American artist to be embraced by the American art establishment.

NVAS (K–4) #4 Understanding the visual arts in relation to history and culture

NVAS (K–4) #5 Reflecting upon and assessing the characteristics and merits of their work and the work of others

Lesson 1

At a Glance

Objectives

- Identify and describe colors in artworks.
- Describe, analyze, interpret, and judge artworks.

Materials

- **Fine Art Transparency**
- Sketchbook Journal
- colored construction paper
- **Instructional Print** (optional)

Vocabulary

colors, primary colors, secondary color, intermediate color

FA TEKS 4.1B Choose appropriate vocabulary to discuss the use of art elements such as color, texture, form, line, space, and value and art principles such as emphasis, pattern, rhythm, balance, proportion, and unity

FA TEKS 4.4B Interpret ideas and moods in original artworks, portfolios, and exhibitions by peers and others

① Introduce

Have students write down the name of their favorite color. Then have them share their choice with the class. As they do so, point out whether the color is primary, secondary, or intermediate. Explain these terms as you refer students to a color wheel. You may want to use the **Instructional Print.**

Have students form groups based on the category in which their color fits. Then have students identify primary, secondary, and intermediate colors in other classroom objects, such as furniture, art tools, and posters. Tell them that they will be learning about how artists use color to express ideas.

Color

Colors, or hues, help artists of every culture express their thoughts and feelings. Point to red and blue on the color wheel on page 53. Where do you see these hues in *Geraniums Before Blue Mountain?*

Auguste Macke. *Geraniums Before Blue Mountain,* date unknown. Oil on canvas, 20½ by 25½ inches. Milwaukee Art Museum. Gift of Mrs. Harry Lynde Bradley.

52

 Art Background

About the Artist Auguste Macke (1887–1914) was a German painter, but his style was more akin to the French painters of his time. He visited Paris several times from 1907–1912 and became acquainted with the work of the late-Impressionists, Fauvists, and Cubists. Synthesizing, or combining, these styles, he created his own Expressionistic way of painting, using bold colors to convey feelings.

ESL Notes

Using the color wheel as a guide, have students find three objects: one that is a primary color, another a secondary color, and the third an intermediate color. Have students write the name of each color and then say it.

ESL TEKS 4.1C Understand major ideas in spoken messages

Color Wheel

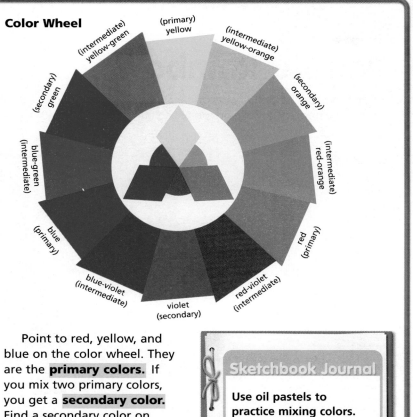

Point to red, yellow, and blue on the color wheel. They are the **primary colors.** If you mix two primary colors, you get a **secondary color.** Find a secondary color on the color wheel. To make an **intermediate color,** mix a primary color and a secondary color. Look again at Macke's painting. What intermediate colors do you see? Choose one. What hues did Macke mix to get that color?

Sketchbook Journal

Use oil pastels to practice mixing colors. Make some secondary and intermediate hues. Blend colors together with a tissue.

🐭 Technology

Digital Color Mixing Have students use a software program, such as ClarisWorks®, to explore color mixing on a computer. Using the Draw mode, have them create overlapping shapes of different colors. Then have them experiment with the transparency and opaque options from the Options menu. Tell them to save their experiments or print them out and place them in their portfolios.

Tech TEKS 4.2A Use a variety of input devices
Tech TEKS 4.7A Use software programs to enhance learning experiences

② Teach

Have students read pages 52–53 and look at the painting. Discuss the colors Macke used, pointing out the reds in the flowers and flowerpots and the blues in the mountain, sky, and house. Guide students to see how the liveliness of the red flowers stands out against the peacefulness of the blue background. Ask:

- **What is the subject of the painting?** (a country scene; a mountain and geraniums) DESCRIBE
- **Which color is used the most in the background?** (blue) ANALYZE
- **Why do you think Macke used red in the foreground?** (Possible response: to emphasize the flowers) INTERPRET
- **What is your favorite color in the painting? What mood does it convey?** (Possible response: violet, because it seems soothing) JUDGE

Extend discussion by asking students to talk about what ideas the artist may have been trying to convey by choosing these colors.

Sketchbook Journal Tell students to mix colors by putting one on top of another. Tell them that they can also blend colors with their fingers. If using fingers, remind students to clean their fingers before starting new blends.

③ Close

Have students label the secondary and intermediate hues they made.

Assessment Place students in small groups of three to five. Give each group a stack of different colored construction paper. Have groups sort the stacks into primary, secondary, and intermediate colors.

NVAS (K–4) #2 Using knowledge of structures and functions
NVAS (K–4) #5 Reflecting upon and assessing the characteristics and merits of their work and the work of others
NVAS (K–4) #6 Making connections between visual arts and other disciplines

Studio 1

At a Glance

Objectives

- Express ideas by using primary, secondary, and intermediate colors.
- Evaluate original artworks by self and peers.

Materials

- tempera paints (red, yellow, blue, and white only) and paintbrushes
- mixing trays, water containers, paper towels
- large drawing paper
- Rubric 2 from **Unit-by-Unit Resources**

FA TEKS 4.2A Integrate a variety of ideas about self, life events, family, and community in original artworks

FA TEKS 4.2B Design original artworks

FA TEKS 4.2C Invent ways to produce artworks and to explore photographic imagery, using a variety of art media and materials

FA TEKS 4.4A Describe intent and form conclusions about personal artworks

1 Introduce

Review primary, secondary, and intermediate colors with students. Have them identify these types of colors in the clothing they are wearing. Tell students that a rainbow is an arc of light separated into bands of color that sometimes appears after a rainstorm. Ask how many students have seen a rainbow and have them share their experiences. Tell them that by using a variety of primary, secondary, and intermediate colors, they can capture their own personal experience of a rainbow.

Engage students in a brief discussion about what they intend to show in their rainbow paintings. Ask:

- **Where on the page will you put your rainbow?**
- **What details would you like to include in the foreground?**

Studio 1

Paint a Rainbow

Paint a rainbow of primary, secondary, and intermediate colors. Use primary colors and white as your tools.

1 **Mix white paint with blue. Brush it over your paper to show the sky.**

2 **Mix paints to make secondary and intermediate colors.**

Technique Tip

To make violet, start with some white paint. Add a dab of blue. Then add a dab of red. Mix the paints together.

54

Meeting Individual Needs

Extend Have students use the white paint to experiment with making tints. Tell them to put some white paint in a tray and then add a dot of colored paint and mix the two together. They can keep adding the colored paint until they get the tint they want. Point out that the more color they add, the darker the tint will be. Have them add details to their paintings using tints.

Quick Studio

Have students draw a rainbow using crayons. Have them use a variety of primary, secondary, and intermediate hues.

3 Use primary, secondary, and intermediate colors to paint a rainbow.

4 Add details to your painting. Use colors from your rainbow.

Think Like an Artist

What did you learn about mixing colors?
Explain how you made a secondary color.
Describe how you made an intermediate color.

Fine Arts Connection

Music Both music and color can inspire different moods. Play a song without lyrics for students, such as "Almost Blue" by Laura Crema, and have them discuss what color they think of when they hear the piece. Then have them describe the mood of the music, or the way it makes them feel.

Discuss connections between music, color, and mood. Play other songs and invite students to describe the mood of each piece. Then associate it with a color.

FA TEKS 4.5D Identify connections between music and other fine arts

② Create

Tell students to read pages 54–55. Then distribute materials.

- Have students mix water and tempera paint at a ratio of 10:1 to achieve a thin, smooth paint.
- Encourage students to use a variety of secondary and intermediate colors in the color wheel.
- Remind students to clean their paintbrushes when switching colors by dipping them in water and then blotting them on a paper towel.
- Tell students that they can use the tip of the brush to make thin lines when adding details.

Technique Tip Palettes for mixing paints can be made from a variety of materials, such as clean polystyrene egg cartons, muffin tins, or plastic lids.

③ Close

Have students reflect on their artwork by answering the *Think Like an Artist* question on page 55. (Two primary colors get a secondary color. A primary and secondary color make an intermediate color. White makes colors lighter.)

Invite students to discuss how their rainbows express ideas about themselves.

Ongoing Assessment

If . . . students have difficulty mixing colors,

then . . . have them add the second color one small dot at a time.

See page 36 from **Unit-by-Unit Resource** for a rubric to assess this studio.

NVAS (K–4) #1 Understanding and applying media, techniques, and processes

NVAS (K–4) #3 Choosing and evaluating a range of subject matter, symbols, and ideas

NVAS (K–4) #5 Reflecting upon and assessing the characteristics and merits of their work and the work of others

Lesson 2

At a Glance

Objectives

- Identify and describe color schemes in artworks.
- Describe, analyze, interpret, and judge artworks.

Materials

- **Fine Art Transparency**
- Sketchbook Journal
- magazine advertisements

Vocabulary

color scheme, cool colors, warm colors, analogous, complementary

FA TEKS 4.1B Choose appropriate vocabulary to discuss the use of art elements such as color, texture, form, line, space, and value and art principles such as emphasis, pattern, rhythm, balance, proportion, and unity

FA TEKS 4.4B Interpret ideas and moods in original artworks, portfolios, and exhibitions by peers and others.

①Introduce

Have a volunteer come to the front of the classroom and identify the colors he or she is wearing. Then point out whether the colors are warm or cool, explaining these terms.

Tell students they will be learning about color schemes. Describe the colors in the volunteer's outfit as complementary or analogous and explain these terms to students. Use a color wheel to show examples of each. Invite students to point out other complementary and analogous color schemes in the room or outside.

Lesson 2

Color Schemes

Frida Kahlo used a **color scheme,** or plan for combining colors, to paint *Long Live Life*. What message do you think the artist wanted to send with her choice of colors?

Frida Kahlo. *Long Live Life (Viva la vida),* 1954. Oil on masonite, 20¼ by 28¼ inches. Reproduction authorized by the National Institute of Fine Arts and Literature, Mexico City, Mexico.

Art Background

About the Artist Mexican artist Frida Kahlo (1907–1954) began painting at the age of nineteen, while recovering from a bus accident that left her severely injured. Kahlo underwent more than thirty operations and drew on her painful experiences to create over two hundred vividly colored paintings, many of which are self-portraits. *Viva la Vida,* translated as *Long Live Life,* is her last painting.

ESL Notes

Pair students with an English-speaking partner and have the partner read the colors and the terms as the two look at the color wheel on page 53. Have the English-language learner repeat each term as it is read.

ESL TEKS 4.1C Understand major ideas in spoken messages
ESL TEKS 4.1D Distinguish and produce sounds and intonation patterns of English

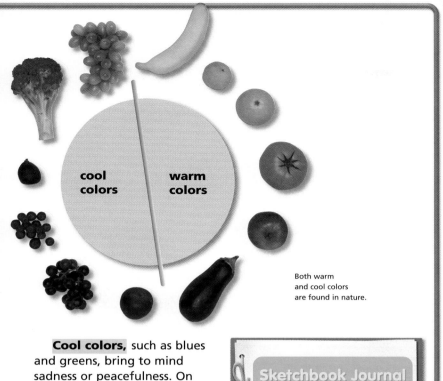

cool colors

warm colors

Both warm and cool colors are found in nature.

Cool colors, such as blues and greens, bring to mind sadness or peacefulness. On the other side of the color wheel are the **warm colors.** Yellows, oranges, and reds may show anger or excitement.

Find green and blue-green on the color wheel. They are **analogous,** or next to each other on the color wheel. **Complementary** colors are opposite each other on the color wheel.

Sketchbook Journal

Cut out colored shapes from magazines. Arrange them into different color schemes. Glue them down and label the groups. Tell about a mood each color group can create.

Curriculum Connection

Science Tell students that male birds often display brightly colored feathers to attract mates. Male peacocks, for example, possess iridescent blue and green feathers. Have students find photographs of colorful birds and point out whether their color schemes are analogous or complementary.

TAKS (Gr. 5) Sci. Obj. 1 Understand the nature of science
  Sci TEKS 4.2C Analyze and interpret information to construct reasonable explanations

② Teach

Have students read pages 56–57. Then ask:

• **Which colors did Kahlo use most?** (red, green, and blue) DESCRIBE
• **What is the effect of using these colors together?** (Possible response: It makes each color stand out.) ANALYZE

Discuss how Kahlo used both the warm color red and the cool colors blue and green. Point out that using red and green creates a complementary color scheme. Discuss the title. Then ask:

• **What mood do you think the artist is trying to convey by choosing these colors for this painting?** (Possible response: The title is carved into the red melon which shows warmth and life. The rind and background elicits a mood of peacefulness.) INTERPRET
• **Do you think *Long Live Life* is a good title for this painting? Why or why not?** (Possible response: Yes; it celebrates the beauty of everyday things.) JUDGE

Sketchbook Journal Have students make four different color schemes, each showing one of the following: warm colors, cool colors, analogous colors, and complementary colors.

③ Close

Have students present their color schemes, describing each as warm, cool, analogous, or complementary.

Visual Culture Have students work in small groups to find examples of different color schemes in magazine advertisements. Have each group present an advertisement and describe the color scheme. Ask the class: **What messages do those colors convey?**

NVAS (K–4) #2 Using knowledge of structures and functions
NVAS (K–4) #5 Reflecting upon and assessing the characteristics and merits of their work and the work of others
NVAS (K–4) #6 Making connections between visual arts and other disciplines

Unit 2 *Cultural Expressions* **57**

Studio 2

At a Glance

Objectives

- Express ideas by using color schemes in original artwork.
- Demonstrate the use of complementary colors in original artwork.
- Evaluate original artworks by self and peers.

Materials

- oil pastels, drawing paper
- Rubric 2 from **Unit-by-Unit Resources**

FA TEKS 4.1A Communicate ideas about self, family, school, and community, using sensory knowledge and life experiences

FA TEKS 4.2A Integrate a variety of ideas about self, life events, family, and community in original artworks

FA TEKS 4.2B Design original artworks

FA TEKS 4.2C Invent ways to produce artworks and to explore photographic imagery, using a variety of art media and materials

FA TEKS 4.4A Describe intent and form conclusions about personal artworks

1 Introduce

Review complementary colors. Then have students brainstorm ideas for the subject of their drawings. Point out that students can draw about an experience they've had to communicate ideas about themselves and the event. Ask:

- **What mood or feeling would you like to portray?**
- **What color symbolizes this mood or feeling?**
- **What is its complementary color?**
- **What will your drawing convey about an experience you have had?**

Quick Studio

Have students use colored pencils or crayons to draw a familiar kitchen object using only two complementary colors.

Studio 2

Draw with Colors

Draw a picture using two complementary colors. Follow the steps.

1 Choose a pair of complementary colors in oil pastels.

2 Think about a mood you want to create with the colors.

Technique Tip

Place complementary colors close together to make an area stand out. Separate the colors for a less bold effect in the background.

58

Meeting Individual Needs

Inclusion Using oil pastels may be difficult for some students. Consider having them use an instant camera to photograph objects with complementary color schemes. They could also look through magazines to identify and collect images that use complementary colors.

③ **Use your complementary colors to outline areas of the drawing.**

④ **Add dots, swirls, lines, and other kinds of marks to fill in your drawing.**

Think Like an Artist
Do you like the effects of the complementary colors? Explain.

59

Fine Arts Connection

Theatre Tell students that lighting designers enhance the sets for plays, films, and operas with light. By placing special filters over the lights, they can project different colors onto the stage. If possible, have the class visit a theatre and ask a lighting designer to talk about how he or she uses color and light to create mood and other effects.

FA TEKS 4.5B Define and discuss aspects of formal theatre

② Create

Have students read pages 58–59. Then distribute materials.

- Help students choose complementary colors by referring them to the color wheel on page 53.
- Encourage students to draw about an experience they have had that reflects their culture.
- Pressing down firmly with the oil pastel will create a more intense, brighter color.
- Remind students that they can peel back the paper and use the side of the pastel to make thicker lines and fill positive spaces.

Technique Tip If oil pastels are applied heavily, "crumbs" of color will form on the paper. Caution students on how to remove crumbs so as not to smudge their artworks.

③ Close

Have students form conclusions about their artwork to answer the *Think Like an Artist* question on page 59. (Yes. The use of complementary colors make the individual colors stand out.)

Then have students discuss how the colors, designs, or objects they showed conveys something about their culture.

Ongoing Assessment

If . . . students have difficulty choosing a subject to draw,

then . . . provide a variety of common objects for them to select a subject.

See page 36 from **Unit-by-Unit Resources** for a rubric to assess this studio.

NVAS (K–4) #1 Understanding and applying media, techniques, and processes
NVAS (K–4) #3 Choosing and evaluating a range of subject matter, symbols, and ideas

Lesson 3

At a Glance

Objectives

- Identify and describe color values in artworks.
- Describe, analyze, interpret, and judge artworks.

Materials

- **Fine Art Transparency**
- colored typing paper
- folder

Vocabulary

color values, tint, shade, neutral colors

FA TEKS 4.1A Communicate ideas about self, family, school, and community, using sensory knowledge and life experiences

FA TEKS 4.1B Choose appropriate vocabulary to discuss the use of art elements such as color, texture, form, line, space, and value and art principles such as emphasis, pattern, rhythm, balance, proportion, and unity

FA TEKS 4.3C Identify the roles of art in American society

FA TEKS 4.4B Interpret ideas and moods in original artworks, portfolios, and exhibitions by peers and others

 Introduce

Stand next to a window and hold a piece of colored typing paper in the light. Then have students observe what happens to it when you block the light with a folder. Ask them to describe how the color of the paper changes when it is in shadow.

Explain that they have identified color values. Color values refer to lighter and darker tints or shades of a color. White is the lightest value and black is the darkest. Say that tints and shades of the same hue can be made by adding white or black to it. Then have students go outside and find neutral colors in the school building and other structures.

Have students look and touch the structures. Engage them in a discussion by asking how the tints and shades change the color of the structure.

60

Lesson 3

Landmarks and Color

The painting on this page shows different **color values,** or lighter and darker colors. To show color values, artists make tints and shades. Adding a color to white makes a **tint.** To make a **shade,** add black to a color.

Paul Cézanne. *Mont Sainte-Victoire Seen from the Bibemus Quarry,* ca. 1897. Oil on canvas, 25½ by 31¼ inches. The Baltimore Museum of Art, Baltimore, MD.

60

Art Background

Art and Culture The peak of Mont Sainte-Victoire, a massive limestone mountain in France, attracted Paul Cézanne all his life. To him, the mountain represented a sculpture of sorts. He described his vision by saying, "The landscape becomes human, becomes a thinking, living being within me." His obsession with this natural landmark is evident in his monumental compositions of the site.

Art and Culture Mount Rushmore National Memorial in South Dakota features sixty-foot sculptures of the heads of four U.S. presidents: George Washington, Thomas Jefferson, Abraham Lincoln, and Theodore Roosevelt. It was built between 1927 and 1941.

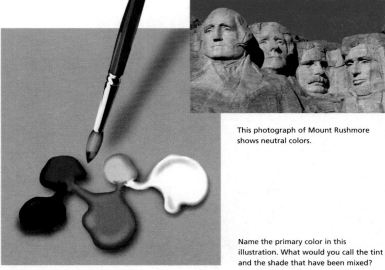

This photograph of Mount Rushmore shows neutral colors.

Name the primary color in this illustration. What would you call the tint and the shade that have been mixed?

Black, white, and gray are **neutral colors.** Some artists use brown as a neutral color, too. Find the neutral colors in the photograph of Mount Rushmore.

The faces of the presidents appear realistic in this landmark. Some artists show fantasy images. These images do not appear real. Which landmarks in your community appear realistic?

Art in My World

Look at landmarks and buildings in your community. What color schemes do they show? Tell why the landmarks are there and what they mean.

61

Curriculum Connection

Social Studies Discuss how human-made landmarks reflect the culture of the region in which they are built. Make a list of famous landmarks found in the United States. Examples might include the Empire State Building, the Washington Monument, the St. Louis Gateway Arch, and San Francisco's Golden Gate Bridge. Have students discuss what these landmarks tell about the culture of the United States and the culture of the region.

SS TEKS 4.23C Express ideas orally based on research and experience

 Notes

Say the names of neutral colors. (black, white, gray, and brown) Have students repeat the color names and identify them in the classroom.

ESL TEKS 4.4A Connect experiences, information, insights, and ideas with those of others

② Teach

Have students look at the artworks and read pages 60–61. Tell them that a landmark can be any noticeable feature that identifies a place, such as a tree, a building, or a statue. Then ask them about the Cézanne painting:

- **What colors do you see in the painting?** (blues, oranges, white, gray, greens, black) DESCRIBE
- **What color scheme did the artist use? Explain.** (A complementary color scheme was used showing the orange in the rocks and the blue of the sky.) ANALYZE
- **What ideas about the mountain peak do you think the artist is trying to convey through this color scheme?** (Possible response: The neutral colors of the mountain peak stand out, showing its strength and permanence.) INTERPRET
- **After viewing this painting, would you want to visit this location? Why or why not?** (Answers will vary.) JUDGE

Art in My World You may want to take the class to visit a landmark in your community. If the landmark is a building or statue, guide them to discuss its role in the community and how architects and sculptors used color values in their designs to support that role.

③ Close

As students view the landmark, have them point out neutral colors they see.

Assessment Have all the students wearing shirts of neutral colors gather together. Ask the class to arrange them in order from lightest to darkest values.

NVAS (K–4) #2 Using knowledge of structures and functions

NVAS (K–4) #4 Understanding the visual arts in relation to history and cultures

NVAS (K–4) #5 Reflecting upon and assessing the characteristics and merits of their work and the work of others

NVAS (K–4) #6 Making connections between visual arts and other disciplines

Studio 3

At a Glance

Objectives

- Express ideas by using tints, shades, and neutral colors in an original artwork.
- Evaluate original artworks by self and peers.

Materials

- 11-by-17-inch drawing paper
- tempera paints, paintbrushes
- mixing trays
- Rubric 2 from **Unit-by-Unit Resources**

FA TEKS 4.2A Integrate a variety of ideas about self, life events, family, and community in original artworks

FA TEKS 4.2B Design original artworks

FA TEKS 4.2C Invent ways to produce artworks and to explore photographic imagery, using a variety of art media and materials

FA TEKS 4.4A Describe intent and form conclusions about personal artworks

① Introduce

Review color value and neutral colors. Have students point out lighter and darker values of the same color in the classroom.

Have students brainstorm ideas for their paintings. Ask:

- **What historic buildings or geographic features stand out in your community?**
- **What colors are used in this landmark?**
- **What colors do you intend to use to make your fantasy landmark?**

Quick Studio

Using pencils or charcoal, have students make a value scale that shows gradual shading from lightest to darkest.

Studio 3
Paint a Landmark

Think of a landmark that represents your community. Now imagine your own version of the same landmark. Follow these steps to paint both.

1 Divide a sheet of paper in half with a pencil line.

2 Blend color values to show your imaginary landmark.

Technique Tip

To mix gray, add a dab of black to white. To mix brown, start with white. Add dabs of any two complementary colors.

Meeting Individual Needs

Reteach Have students use neutral colors to paint a landform, such as rolling hills, a rugged mountain, or a rocky shoreline.

Extend Have students research the landmark they painted. Ask them to write and illustrate a report about its history.

3 Paint your imaginary landmark on one side of the paper.

4 Now paint a realistic picture of your landmark using neutral colors.

Think Like an Artist

What does your landmark tell about your culture?

Fine Arts Connection

Dance Tell students that designers who create the costumes for dancers must also consider color values. They think about how colors work together and what color values will stand out on stage. Show a video of a ballet or modern dance performance and have students note the color values used in the costumes.

② Create

Tell students to read pages 62–63. Then distribute materials.

- Prepare the tempera paints. To mix powdered tempera, add water to small amounts of powder until it is the consistency of thick cream.
- Have students mix tints and shades of several colors. Remind them to use small dabs of paint when mixing. Allow time for them to practice mixing.
- Suggest that shades and tints can be used to create shadows.
- Remind students that black, white, browns, and tints and shades of gray are considered neutral colors.

Technique Tip Consider placing the paint in squeeze bottles. Students can then add drops of paint when mixing different color values.

③ Close

Ask students to form conclusions about their work by discussing the *Think Like an Artist* question on page 63. (Possible response: The Native American culture greatly influenced the artwork in my town.)

Ongoing Assessment

If . . . students have difficulty choosing a landmark,

then . . . show them pictures of local landmarks and explain their significance.

See page 36 from **Unit-by-Unit Resources** for a rubric to assess this studio.

NVAS (K–4) #1 Understanding and applying media, techniques, and processes

NVAS (K–4) #3 Choosing and evaluating a range of subject matter, symbols, and ideas

NVAS (K–4) #5 Reflecting upon and assessing the characteristics and merits of their work and the work of others

Look and Compare

At a Glance

Objectives

- Compare and contrast two artworks that show community scenes.
- Analyze the influences of culture in artworks.
- Respond to and make judgments about artworks.

Materials

- **Art Prints 5, 6, 7**
- **Fine Art Transparency**
- pencils, crayons, water-based markers, or oil pastels
- Sketchbook Journal

FA TEKS 4.1A Communicate ideas about self, family, school, and community, using sensory knowledge and life experiences

FA TEKS 4.3A Identify simple main ideas expressed in art

FA TEKS 4.3B Compare and contrast selected artworks from a variety of cultural settings

Explore

Display **Art Print 5** by Jacob Lawrence. Then display **Art Prints 6 and 7.** Have students predict which one was also created by Lawrence, and ask them to explain their choice. (*The Library;* the colors are similar, both show many types of lines.)

Discuss

Have students discuss ways these artists expressed similar main ideas. Explain that each artist portrayed everyday life in a community scene. Point out the broad brushstrokes in Lawrence's library scene. Have students identify the warm and cool colors that attract attention and have them notice the color values from white to black.

Students can contrast it with Estes' street scene, where touches of red and blue against a neutral background attract the viewer's eye. Shadows in this painting add to the realistic style.

64

Look and Compare

Community Scenes

Jacob Lawrence. *The Library,* 1960. Tempera on fiberboard, 24 by 29⅝ inches. Smithsonian American Art Museum, Washington, D.C.

Artists may show different parts of their communities in their artworks. Look at this painting of people in the library. Notice the flat shapes and bold colors. Who was the artist?

64

Art Background

The Library This painting is one of many that Lawrence made depicting life in Harlem, an area of New York City, during the 1930s. Using bright colors, geometric shapes, and flattened forms, Lawrence portrayed the lives, struggles, and aspirations of African Americans living in the city during the Depression.

Helene's Florist Like many of Richard Estes' (1932–) paintings, *Helene's Florist* shows his dedication to photorealism. Estes bases his paintings on photographs, creating a "reality" of multiple viewpoints. Note that you can see reflections in the window, the surface of the glass, and what is behind it.

Richard Estes. *Helene's Florist*, 1971. Oil on canvas, 48 by 72 inches. Toledo Museum of Art, Toledo, OH.

Now look at Richard Estes' flower shop. His details and colors make the sidewalk display look so real you can almost smell the flowers!

In what ways are these paintings alike? How are they different? How did each artist use color to get your attention?

Sketchbook Journal

Draw your own picture of a community scene. Use color to draw a viewer's eye to parts of your artwork. Add details that tell about your community.

Apply

As students compare and contrast the two paintings, you may want to have them complete a Venn diagram like the one below. Draw the diagram on the board and add their answers in the appropriate spaces.

As students look for differences between the two paintings, guide them to see the types of colors used, the way color values show contrast and shadow, and the shapes and lines presented. Possible answers are shown in blue.

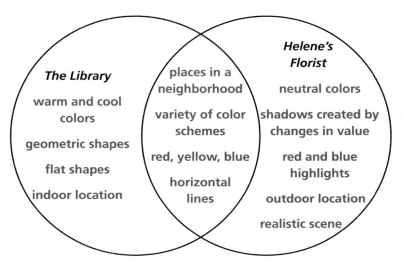

The Library
warm and cool colors
geometric shapes
flat shapes
indoor location

places in a neighborhood
variety of color schemes
red, yellow, blue
horizontal lines

Helene's Florist
neutral colors
shadows created by changes in value
red and blue highlights
outdoor location
realistic scene

Close

Ask students to describe the use of blue and brown in Lawrence's painting. How many tints and shades of these colors do they see? (at least three of each color) What mood do these colors create? (somber, peaceful mood)

Sketchbook Journal Tell students to add specific details to their scene that suggest sights, sounds, and smells. Have students write a caption describing their community scene. Display drawings with the captions.

NVAS (K–4) #4 Understanding the visual arts in relation to history and cultures

NVAS (K–4) #5 Reflecting upon and assessing the characteristics and merits of their work and the work of others

Reading Strategy

Activate Prior Knowledge Before reading the text, have students discuss shops and public buildings in their neighborhood or town.

As they name various locations, write them on the board, and have students describe what they look like from the outside, if they are usually busy, and what business or activities take place in or around the buildings.

Ask students to choose their favorite place and explain what makes it their favorite. Then have them read the text and look at the two paintings.

TAKS Rdg. Obj. 1 Understand written texts
    ELA TEKS 4.10A Use knowledge and experience to comprehend
    ELA TEKS 4.14A Compare text events with readers' experiences

Lesson 4

At a Glance

Objectives

- Identify and describe balance in artworks.
- Describe, analyze, interpret, and judge artworks.

Materials

- **Fine Art Transparency**
- balance scale and counting chips
- Sketchbook Journal
- photographs of famous buildings (optional)

Vocabulary

balance, symmetrical balance, asymmetrical balance, radial balance

FA TEKS 4.1B Choose appropriate vocabulary to discuss the use of art elements such as color, texture, form, line, space, and value and art principles such as emphasis, pattern, rhythm, balance, proportion, and unity

FA TEKS 4.3C Identify the roles of art in American society

FA TEKS 4.4B Interpret ideas and moods in original artworks, portfolios, and exhibitions by peers and others

①Introduce

Show students a balance scale. Invite a volunteer to place equal numbers of counting chips onto each side of the scale, and have the class observe the result. Explain that this is an example of symmetrical balance, with both sides being equal or about equal. Then place a few more chips on one side. Have the class observe the results.

Tell students that they will learn about balance in this lesson. Point out examples of symmetrical balance, such as in leaves. Show them examples of radial balance as in flowers. Then discuss asymmetrical balance, explaining how color, texture, shape, and other elements of art can create balance in a composition.

Lesson 4

Balance

Balance describes the way parts of an artwork are arranged. This principle of design helps make an artwork pleasing. Artists work with three types of balance.

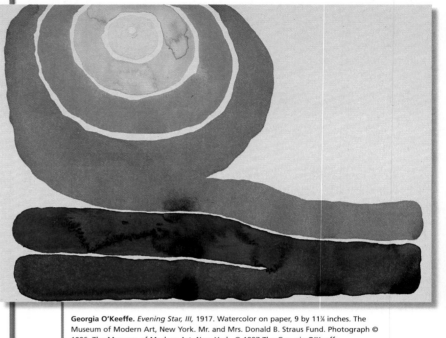

Georgia O'Keeffe. *Evening Star, III,* 1917. Watercolor on paper, 9 by 11⅞ inches. The Museum of Modern Art, New York. Mr. and Mrs. Donald B. Straus Fund. Photograph © 1996. The Museum of Modern Art, New York. © 1997 The Georgia O'Keeffe Foundation/Artists Rights Society (ARS), New York. Photograph © The Museum of Modern Art, New York.

Art Background

About the Artist Georgia O'Keeffe (1887–1986) was born in Wisconsin but lived most of her adult life in New York City and New Mexico. She is best known for her abstract paintings of natural forms, such as skulls, bones, flowers, shells, rocks, stars, mesas, and clouds.

Art History Rose windows were often found in Gothic churches built in the twelfth and thirteenth centuries. The large, circular windows were usually glazed with stained glass and had stone lines, called traceries, radiating from their centers to form intricate, petal-like patterns.

The picture of the butterfly shows **symmetrical balance.** Both sides are about the same. The painting by Georgia O'Keeffe shows **asymmetrical balance.** Each side is not the same, yet the artwork appears balanced and complete.

Now look at the stained-glass window. Its **radial balance** shows the lines, shapes, and colors coming from a center point. Point to an example of radial balance in the painting by O'Keeffe.

Look for examples of symmetry and asymmetry in your community. What type of balance will you show in your artworks?

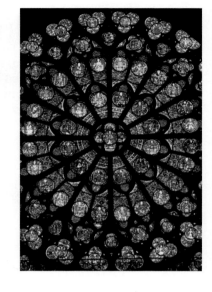

Examples of symmetry are found in art and in nature.

Sketchbook Journal

What type of balance does a horse's face show? Make some drawings. Then add a body and legs. Draw the surroundings. How is the whole drawing balanced?

67

Have students read pages 66–67. Ask:

- **Where do you see radial balance in O'Keeffe's painting?** (in the star or upper left corner) DESCRIBE
- **Which part of the painting most attracts your attention?** (the star) ANALYZE
- **Does this composition seem balanced to you? Why or why not?** (Possible response: Yes; the blue/green stripe offsets the weight of the star.) INTERPRET
- **What is the mood of this painting? Explain.** (Possible response: It is serene and cheerful due to the broad, colorful lines and the overall balance.) JUDGE

Discuss how O'Keeffe uses cool bands of color to create a grounding counterbalance to the star in the upper left corner. Then have students discuss the radial balance of the rose window.

Sketchbook Journal Encourage students to draw a horse's head from the front as well as the side view. Elicit responses to the question. (Front view is symmetrical; side view is asymmetrical.)

③ Close

Ask students to evaluate their drawing. Did adding the horse's body and legs affect the drawing's balance? (Possible response: Yes. Each side of the horse adds symmetrical balance to the drawing.)

Visual Culture Have students look at buildings in their neighborhood or show them photographs of famous buildings in the United States. Discuss how architects use symmetrical and asymmetrical balance in their designs. Have students identify different kinds of balance in the buildings.

Curriculum Connection

Physical Education Tell students that maintaining a sense of balance is important to physical health. Have them try various poses that require balance, such as standing on one foot with arms outstretched, or walking on a low balance beam. Then have students play a game in which balance is used, such as hopscotch.

PE TEKS 4.1E Perform sequences showing good body control

ESL Notes

Provide students with a piece of construction paper and a variety of geometric shapes. Name a type of balance and have students use the geometric shapes to create that balance on the paper background. Then have students name the type of balance they created.

ESL TEKS 4.4A Connect experiences, information, insights, and ideas with those of others

NVAS (K–4) #2 Using knowledge of structures and functions

NVAS (K–4) #4 Understanding the visual arts in relation to history and culture

NVAS (K–4) #5 Reflecting upon and assessing the characteristics and merits of their work and the work of others

NVAS (K–4) #6 Making connections between visual arts and other disciplines

Studio 4

At a Glance

Objectives

- Express ideas by using symmetrical and radial balance.
- Evaluate original artworks by self and peers.

Materials

- black construction paper, colored tissue paper
- cardboard circle
- pencils and old paintbrushes
- safety scissors ⚠
- water-thinned glue or starch
- waxed paper or newspaper
- Rubric 2 from **Unit-by-Unit Resources**

FA TEKS 4.2B Design original artworks

FA TEKS 4.2C Invent ways to produce artworks and to explore photographic imagery, using a variety of art media and materials

FA TEKS 4.4A Describe intent and form conclusions about personal artworks

❶ Introduce

Review balance. Have students point out examples of balance in the classroom. Have students discuss examples of stained-glass windows they have seen. Ask them where they have seen them and why they think the stained glass was chosen for a particular building.

Have students brainstorm ideas for their stained-glass windows. Ask:

- **What geometric shapes do you intend to use in the design?**
- **What warm colors will you include?**
- **What cool colors will you use?**

Quick Studio

Have students make snowflakes using circles of white paper. Have them fold the circles three times and then cut along the folds.

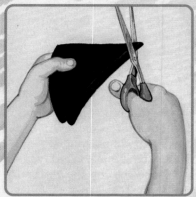

Studio 4

Design Stained Glass

Artists have used color and the design principle of balance to make beautiful stained-glass windows for centuries. Now you can design one, too.

1. Cut a large circle from black construction paper.

2. Fold the circle in half, then in half again, and then once more. Cut off the tip.

Technique Tip

Overlap different colors of tissue paper sheets to add color variety to your window.

68

🚶🚶🚶🚶 Meeting Individual Needs

Reteach To simplify the design, students could fold their circles twice rather than three times. The folds will also be easier to cut through.

Extend Place students in small groups and invite each group to build a cardboard house in which they can feature their windows.

3 Snip small shapes along the folds. Open the circle. Spread thin glue over it.

4 Cut tissue paper and arrange it over the holes. Brush thin glue all over.

Think Like an Artist

What kinds of balance does your window show? Are you satisfied with your design? Why or why not?

 Fine Arts Connection

Dance Tell students that dancers train themselves to develop a keen sense of balance so that their movements are graceful. Have a dancer or dance instructor visit the class and lead students through exercises or routines that enhance balance.

PE TEKS 4.1E Perform sequences showing good body control
PE TEKS 4.1I Perform basic folk dance steps

② Create

Have students read pages 68–69. Then distribute materials.

- Provide cardboard circles for students to draw around to ensure that their paper circles are symmetrical.
- Demonstrate how to triple-fold the circle and cut out shapes. Show students that the cut-out shapes become much larger when the circle is opened.
- Before students spread glue on their shapes, have them place the circle on waxed paper or newspaper.
- Encourage students to create patterns of color as they arrange their tissue paper.

Technique Tip Before students start the studio, you may want to precut the tissue paper into small pieces to save time.

③ Close

Have students form conclusions about their artworks by answering the *Think Like an Artist* questions on page 69. (Possible responses: It shows radial balance; I would like to have shown more details.)

Ongoing Assessment

If . . . students have difficulty cutting their shapes,

then . . . have them tear shapes along the folds.

See page 36 from **Unit-by-Unit Resources** for a rubric to assess this studio.

NVAS (K–4) #1 Understanding and applying media, techniques, and processes
NVAS (K–4) #3 Choosing and evaluating a range of subject matter, symbols, and ideas
NVAS (K–4) #5 Reflecting upon and assessing the characteristics and merits of their work and the work of others

Lesson 5

At a Glance

Objectives

- Identify and describe patterns in artworks.
- Describe, analyze, interpret, and judge artworks.

Materials

- **Fine Art Transparency**
- colored pencils or crayons
- Sketchbook Journal
- quilt (optional)

Vocabulary

patterns, quilts, quilt block, symbols

FA TEKS 4.1B Choose appropriate vocabulary to discuss the use of art elements such as color, texture, form, line, space, and value and art principles such as emphasis, pattern, rhythm, balance, proportion, and unity

FA TEKS 4.3A Identify simple main ideas expressed in art

FA TEKS 4.3C Identify the roles of art in American society

FA TEKS 4.4B Interpret ideas and moods in original artworks, portfolios, and exhibitions by peers and others

 Introduce

Write the following letters on the board:

x x x o x x x o x x x o x x x o.

Ask students what letter comes next. (x) Tell them that they can guess, because the letters form a pattern.

If practical, bring in a quilt and have students view and touch it. Tell them that sometimes artists use patterns in functional artworks, such as quilts and rugs. Point out how the quilt blocks form parts of the pattern. Note the symbols the artist used in the quilt. Have students name some other symbols and draw them on the board.

Then engage students in a discussion about patterns they have seen in rugs and quilts at different times or places in their lives. Make a list of interesting patterns they may have noticed in them.

Lesson 5

Pattern

What patterns do you see in these artworks? **Patterns,** or repeated colors, lines, and shapes, add interest to the design. What do you think the title of this quilt means?

Artist unknown, possibly Gertrude Knappenberger. *The Centennial Quilt*, date unknown. Cotton with cotton embroidery, 84 by 74 inches. Collection of the Museum of American Folk Art, NY. Gift of Rhea Goodman, 1979.9.1.

 Art Background

Art and Culture Quilting is a technique in which two layers of fabric are sewn together by rows of stitching, usually over an interior layer. It has long been used for clothing and coverings in Northern Europe, China, the Middle East, and North Africa. In the United States, quilting flourished during the 1800s, when different forms of quilts were popularized.

ESL Notes

Give students pattern blocks and have them experiment with making different visual forms showing repetition. Ask students to briefly describe the patterns they formed.

ESL TEKS 4.5G Employ English content area vocabulary words in context

Patterns and symbols can turn functional objects into artworks.

Some artworks have a function, or purpose. Rugs and **quilts** are examples of functional art. Hand-stitched quilts were often made as group projects. Each person might plan and sew one **quilt block,** or square.

Quilts and rugs often include **symbols,** shapes or pictures that represent ideas and values. What might the symbols in these patterns mean?

Sketchbook Journal

Draw a pattern design for an object you can use, such as a dish or a bedspread. Include symbols that hold special meaning for you. Add color to your pattern design.

71

2 Teach

Have students read pages 70–71. Discuss the title and explain that it indicates the quilt was made to celebrate the one-hundredth birthday of the United States. Ask:

• **What shapes or symbols do you see repeated in this quilt?** (hearts, flowers, triangles, leaves) DESCRIBE

• **What types of balance do you see in this quilt?** (radial and symmetrical) ANALYZE

• **What ideas about the United States do you think the symbols and patterns represent?** (Possible response: The hearts symbolize love; the flowers represent growth.) INTERPRET

• **What part of the quilt is most interesting to you? Why?** (Possible response: the center, because the patterns of squares and triangles are interesting) JUDGE

You may want to ask similar questions about the rug on page 71.

Sketchbook Journal Have students go outside and draw some small sketches of patterns they observe in nature and in human-made objects.

3 Close

Have students share their designs and interpret the meaning of the symbols in each other's artworks.

Visual Culture Tell students that some people collect quilts. Explain that most collectors would probably agree on the importance of preserving the story and history of the quilt. Have students work in small groups to find examples of quilts on the Web. Then invite each group to choose one quilt and share its story.

NVAS (K–4) #2 Using knowledge of structures and functions

NVAS (K–4) #4 Understanding the visual arts in relation to history and cultures

NVAS (K–4) #5 Reflecting upon and assessing the characteristics and merits of their work and the work of others

NVAS (K–4) #6 Making connections between visual arts and other disciplines

Curriculum Connection

Math Have students practice making generalizations from numerical and geometric patterns. Write the following pattern on the board: 2, 4, 8, 16, 32, 64. Have students say what number comes next and how they know. (128; each number is doubled to get the next) Continue with other numerical patterns.

TAKS Math Obj. 2 Understand patterns and relationships
Math TEKS 4.7 Analyze and describe patterns

Studio 5

At a Glance

Objectives

- Express ideas by using patterns.
- Evaluate original artworks by self and peers.

Materials

- pencils, construction paper
- safety scissors ⚠, glue
- Rubric 2 from **Unit-by-Unit Resources**

FA TEKS 4.2A Integrate a variety of ideas about self, life events, family, and community in original artworks

FA TEKS 4.2B Design original artworks

FA TEKS 4.2C Invent ways to produce artworks and to explore photographic imagery, using a variety of art media and materials

① Introduce

Review patterns and symbols. Have students describe quilts they have seen and discuss how the quilts were used.

Then guide students to discuss people, events, or things in school that are important to them and list them on the board. Have them select a theme from the board.

Tell students they will be making a class quilt out of paper. Brainstorm ideas for the quilt block designs by asking:

- **What shapes and symbols relate to the theme?**
- **What colors will you use to make your shapes stand out?**

Quick Studio

Have students fold a piece of paper into quarters. In each quarter, have them draw different patterns of geometric shapes.

Studio 5

Design a Quilt

Choose a theme for a class quilt. Then plan your own quilt block of geometric shapes with two classmates.

① Choose geometric shapes to illustrate your theme. Make sketches of them.

② Plan a design. Draw the shapes on colored paper.

Technique Tip

Choose simple patterns or symbols that relate to the quilt theme. Avoid images that have too many details.

72

🚶 Meeting Individual Needs

Inclusion Consider having students with visual impairments use textured materials to make their shapes or provide raised shapes with which to make a pattern.

③ Cut out your shapes. Glue them in place on the quilt block.

④ Add the group blocks to a bulletin-board display of the class quilt.

Think Like an Artist
Describe the symbols on each quilt block. Tell what they mean.

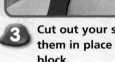 **Fine Arts Connection**

Music Tell students that songs contain patterns which are formed by the repetition of sounds or the repetition of parts of the song. For example, many songs feature a refrain, or section of a song that is sung the same way every time. Play a song with a noticeable refrain, such as "Oh, Susanna," and have students sing along with it.

FA TEKS 4.1C Identify music forms presented aurally
FA TEKS 4.3B Incorporate basic rhythmic patterns in musical compositions

② Create

Have students read pages 72–73. Then distribute materials.

• Help students choose shapes and symbols that illustrate the theme. For example, if the theme is the class field trip to the planetarium, they could show the sun, moon, or stars.
• As students draw their designs, remind them to repeat shapes somewhere in the design.
• Provide students with equally sized pieces of paper (suggest 11-by-11-inch squares) for their quilt blocks.
• Help students arrange and attach the quilt blocks on a bulletin board.

Technique Tip Have each group use only one shape or symbol to create a pattern. Encourage them to use color to enhance the pattern they make.

③ Close

Have students reflect on their artwork by completing the *Think Like an Artist* activity on page 73. (Answers will vary.)

Ongoing Assessment

If . . . students have difficulty drawing shapes in a pattern,

then . . . have them use a ruler or a stencil to guide their drawings.

See page 36 from **Unit-by-Unit Resources** for a rubric to assess this studio.

NVAS (K–4) #1 Understanding and applying media, techniques, and processes
NVAS (K–4) #3 Choosing and evaluating a range of subject matter, symbols, and ideas
NVAS (K–4) #5 Reflecting upon and assessing the characteristics and merits of their work and the work of others

Lesson 6

At a Glance

Objectives

- Identify and describe the printmaking process.
- Describe, analyze, interpret, and judge artworks.

Materials

- **Fine Art Transparency**
- Sketchbook Journal
- water-based inkpad or printers' ink

Vocabulary

print, print block, relief print, brayer

FA TEKS 4.1B Choose appropriate vocabulary to discuss the use of art elements such as color, texture, form, line, space, and value and art principles such as emphasis, pattern, rhythm, balance, proportion, and unity

FA TEKS 4.3B Compare and contrast selected artworks from a variety of cultural settings

FA TEKS 4.4B Interpret ideas and moods in original artworks, portfolios, and exhibitions by peers and others

❶ Introduce

Press your thumb into the inkpad and make a thumbprint. Explain that each person's thumbprint is unique to them. Then have students make thumbprints in their Sketchbook Journals. Have them point out the lines and swirls that were transferred on the page. Explain that they just made a print. Remind them that prints are created when you coat something with wet ink and press it onto another flat surface. Point out that multiple copies of a print can be made by re-inking and repeating the process. Have students experiment by re-inking their thumbs and making more prints.

Tell students to look at the prints in this lesson. Explain that prints like these are made by carving a design on a block. Then discuss the materials that can be used to make print blocks, such as wood, plastic foam trays, and clay.

Prints

The artworks on these pages are prints. Both prints show cultural leaders or public figures. To make a **print,** artists apply ink to a surface, or **print block.** Then they press paper onto the print block. Or, they press the print block onto paper.

Max Weber. *Rabbi Reading,* 1919. Woodcut, printed in color, composition, 4⅜ by 1¹³⁄₁₆ inches. The Museum of Modern Art, New York. Gift of Abby Aldrich Rockefeller. Photograph © 1996. The Museum of Modern Art, New York.

🎨 Art Background

About the Artist Max Weber (1881–1961) was born in Russia to Orthodox Jewish parents. He emigrated with his family to New York City in 1891. His Expressionistic, warmly colored artworks depict subjects ranging from urban scenes to fantastical stories from the Talmud, a collection of Jewish writings.

Art History Andy Warhol (1928–1987) was one of the foremost practitioners of Pop Art, which emerged in the United States and Great Britain in the mid-1950s. Ironic and often shocking, early Pop Art drew on images of mass production, such as advertisements, comic strips, and celebrity icons, to portray consumerist culture.

Andy Warhol. *Moonwalk,* 1987. Screenprint, 38 by 38 inches. Courtesy of Ronald Feldman Fine Arts, New York. © 1997 Andy Warhol Foundation for the Visual Arts/Ronald Feldman Fine Arts/ARS, New York. Photograph by D. James Dee.

To make a **relief print,** artists carve a design into a print block. Then they use a **brayer,** a rubber roller, to apply ink to the raised or uncarved surface. Finally, they press the block onto paper.

Read the credit lines for the prints on these two pages. What two cultures are represented? What do you think the prints show you about the beliefs of these cultures?

Sketchbook Journal

What symbols are part of your family or culture? Draw a sketch for a relief print that shows what is important in your culture. Explain the meaning of the symbols to a friend.

75

Curriculum Connection

Social Studies Place students in small groups and give each group a photograph or portrait of a cultural leader. Have students work together to describe what they see in the portrait and find biographical information about the leader. Invite each group to present their findings. As a class, discuss what qualities these leaders have in common.
SS TEKS 4.19B Identify leadership qualities of state and local leaders, past and present

 Notes

Gather together the materials for making prints, including print blocks, a brayer, ink or paint, and a finished relief print. Hold up one item at a time, name it, and have students repeat the name.
ESL TEKS 4.4A Connect, experiences, information, insights, and ideas with those of others

② Teach

Have students read pages 74–75. Explain that prints of leaders often offer clues about the ideas and beliefs of a culture. Tell them that Weber's print reflects Jewish culture, as it shows a rabbi, a leader of a Jewish congregation. Ask them the following questions about *Rabbi Reading:*

• **What neutral and secondary colors do you see?** (neutral: browns, tans, black, white; secondary: green, violet) DESCRIBE

• **Which object stands out the most to you? Why?** (Possible response: the book, because it is bright blue) ANALYZE

• **How would you describe the rabbi's expression?** (Possible response: serious) INTERPRET

• **What ideas does the print tell you about the culture?** (Possible response: Reading and religion are important to the culture.) JUDGE

Discuss how Warhol's print reflects the culture of a modern United States and ask students similar questions about *Moonwalk.*

Sketchbook Journal Help students brainstorm ideas by having them think about things they see and do every day. Encourage them to use a variety of lines and textures in their sketches.

③ Close

Have students share how their drawing reflects something important to their family or culture.

Visual Culture Have students find information about the printing process for newspapers and magazines. Take them to visit a print shop or printing press of a local publication.

NVAS (K–4) #1 Understanding and applying media, techniques, and processes

NVAS (K–4) #3 Choosing and evaluating a range of subject matter, symbols, and ideas

NVAS (K–4) #5 Reflecting upon and assessing the characteristics and merits of their work and the work of others

Studio 6

At a Glance

Objectives

- Express ideas by creating a relief print.
- Demonstrate the printmaking process when creating a print.
- Evaluate original artworks by self and peers.

Materials

- clean plastic foam meat trays
- pencils or markers
- tempera paints, dish soap
- brayers and plastic trays
- drawing paper
- Rubric 2 from **Unit-by-Unit Resources**

FA TEKS 4.2A Integrate a variety of ideas about self, life events, family, and community in original artworks

FA TEKS 4.2B Design original artworks

FA TEKS 4.2C Invent ways to produce artworks and to explore photographic imagery, using a variety of art media and materials

FA TEKS 4.4A Describe intent and form conclusions about personal artworks

❶ Introduce

Review how to make prints. Then point out examples of cultural leaders or symbols in your community.

Have students brainstorm ideas for their prints. Ask:

- **What cultural leaders or symbols of leadership are important in your community?**
- **What images come to mind when you think of these people or symbols?**
- **What kinds of lines, textures, and colors will you use to show your leader or symbol?**

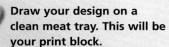

Studio 6
Make a Print

Think of a leader or a symbol of leadership in your culture. Follow these steps to make a relief print.

1 Draw your design on a clean meat tray. This will be your print block.

2 Mix tempera with a bit of dish soap. Roll the paint evenly on your print block.

Technique Tip

Do not put too much paint on the brayer or on the print block. The paint should *not* fill in the lines you carved.

76

Meeting Individual Needs

Reteach Have students use oil pastels or crayons to draw a picture of a cultural leader on drawing paper. Then have them print a patterned border around the picture by using printing blocks made from plastic foam or cardboard.

Extend Have students write a paragraph explaining some of the accomplishments of the leader they chose. Tell them to include reasons why they admire this leader.

Quick Studio

Have students cut a shape from cardboard. Attach a masking tape handle. Dip the shape into paint, press onto paper, and lift to make a print.

3 Place a clean sheet of paper on top of your design. Rub it gently with your hands.

4 Slowly pull the print. Let it dry completely.

Think Like an Artist

How does the color you used help show your cultural leader or symbol?

Fine Arts Connection

Theatre Place students in groups of four to six. Have each group choose one of the leaders they depicted in their prints and create a skit featuring that leader. Tell them to assign one person to be the leader and the others to play supporting roles. Then have each group perform their skits as other students guess the name of the leader.

FA TEKS 4.2C Develop characters and assume roles in short improvised scenes
FA TEKS 4.4A Explain theatre as a reflection of life

2 Create

Tell students to read pages 76–77. Then distribute materials.

- Tell students that some markers will eat away plastic foam and remove larger areas of negative space.
- Mixing soap into the tempera paint will enable it to adhere to the surface better. You may wish to premix and place it in squeeze bottles for student use.
- Have a volunteer distribute 12-by-14-inch drawing-paper rectangles to each student.
- Have students place their prints in a designated drying area.

Technique Tip Have students roll the brayer back and forth in the paint to coat it evenly. Then have them roll the brayer both horizontally and vertically to apply the paint to the block.

3 Close

Have students reflect on and form conclusions about their artwork by answering the *Think Like an Artist* question on page 77. (Possible response: I used red because it is powerful.)

Ongoing Assessment

If . . . students have trouble choosing a leader to portray,

then . . . assign them a subject, such as the school principal.

See page 36 from **Unit-by-Unit Resources** for a rubric to assess this studio.

NVAS (K–4) #1 Understanding and applying media, techniques, and processes

NVAS (K–4) #3 Choosing and evaluating a range of subject matter, symbols, and ideas

NVAS (K–4) #5 Reflecting upon and assessing the characteristics and merits of their work and the work of others

Artist at Work

Artist at Work

At a Glance

Objectives

- Read about a career in art.
- Identify the use of art in everyday life
- Relate art to personal experiences.

Materials

- **Fine Art Transparency**
- a potato
- inkpad and butcher paper
- other printmaking materials
- printed items such as greeting cards, wallpaper, or fabric swatches (optional)

FA TEKS 4.3C Identify the roles of art in American society

Explore

Demonstrate how to make a print by cutting a potato in half and carving a simple design into the white part. Press the potato onto an inkpad, and then onto paper several times. Then discuss with students the different products made by printmaking, such as greeting cards and fabrics.

Discuss

Have students read pages 78–79. Explain that printmakers make editions, or more than one of the same image, using the same printing method every time. Direct students to look at the artwork on page 79. Ask:

- **What object is repeated to create a pattern in *Hide*?** (a bird)
- **What colors stand out the most to you?** (Possible response: the red of the birds and the yellow of the dress)
- **What images would you include in a print? Where would you get your ideas?** (Answers will vary.)

78

Printmaking

Annemaree Rea is a printmaker. Artists who specialize in making prints may use many different materials and nearly any subject for their artworks. Rea might get an idea for a print from almost anything, even trash! A picture from a children's book may become the subject of one of her prints. Whatever the subject though, the final print is her own work.

Rea uses many printmaking techniques. One is relief printing. The printmaker carves an image into a block using special tools. Then she places paper or fabric over the top and uses a heavy press to transfer the image from the block to the paper or fabric.

Some of Rea's prints become greeting cards. Other prints may hang in art galleries for people to buy. Rea does not try to sell all of her artworks, though. She trades some with other artists whose work she likes.

Rea takes pleasure from the sense of order that comes from making multiple copies. Also, she says, "When you make a print, you're making a little piece of you for the whole world to see—a hundred times!"

Printmaker
Annemaree Rea
at work

78

 Career Research

Explain to students that before computers, a form of printing was used to create newspapers, magazines, and books. Printmaking of this type is very important in American history.

Have students research Ben Franklin and his career as a skilled printer. Invite them to find out how he used his printing press to bring news to early Americans in his most famous publications, *The Pennsylvania Gazette* and *Poor Richard's Almanack*.

Annemaree Rea.
No Added Hormones,
2003. Linocut.

Annemaree Rea. *Run*, 2002. Collagraph.

Annemaree Rea.
Hide, 2003. Inkjet
study for four-color
lithography.

79

Reading Strategy

Relate to Personal Experience Tell students that the products of printmaking are all around them. After students read page 78, have them think of places where they have seen prints. (Possible responses: on clothing, wallpaper, tablecloths, furniture fabric, and wrapping paper) Then have them reread the passage. Answer any questions they have about printmaking.

TAKS Rdg. Obj. 1 Understand written texts
ELA TEKS 4.10A Use knowledge and experience to comprehend

Apply

Tell students that they are going to create their own wrapping paper. Ask them to brainstorm design elements, such as the kinds of colors to use, shapes or symbols to include, and patterns to create. Have students add these ideas to the following graphic organizer.

Design Elements	Details of Design
Color	• warm or cool colors • primary colors
Shapes and symbols	• hearts, stars, balloons
Patterns	• repeated shapes, colors • mirrored images

Provide students with printmaking materials and large sheets of butcher paper. Have them create their planned design.

Close

Have students share their wrapping paper with the class. Review the graphic organizers and have students reflect on how their plan helped them in creating their design. Then ask: **What does your wrapping paper design tell about you?** (Possible response: It shows my favorite colors; it shows symbols that represent my interests.)

NVAS (K–4) #5 Reflecting upon and assessing the characteristics and merits of their work and the work of others

NVAS (K–4) #6 Making connections between visual arts and other disciplines

Portfolio Project

Portfolio Project

At a Glance

Objectives

- Develop and organize ideas from the environment.
- Demonstrate knowledge about color, balance, and pattern.
- Evaluate original artworks by self and peers.

Materials

- gadgets (parts of machines, such as nuts, bolts, washers, cogs, belts, etc.)
- black construction paper, neon tempera paints
- chalk pastels, sponges (optional)
- Rubric 2 from **Unit-by-Unit Resources**

FA TEKS 4.2B Design original artworks

FA TEKS 4.2C Invent ways to produce artworks and to explore photographic imagery, using a variety of art media and materials

FA TEKS 4.4A Describe intent and form conclusions about personal artworks

FA TEKS 4.4B Interpret ideas and moods in original artworks, portfolios, and exhibitions by peers and others

Make Gadget Prints

What kinds of designs can you make with gadgets? Use gadgets and your imagination to make prints.

1 Plan a real or imaginary design. Choose some gadgets to use in your print.

2 Dip the gadgets into neon tempera paint and press them onto your paper.

3 Overlap some of the shapes. Create symmetrical or asymmetrical balance.

4 Let it dry. Then use chalk pastels to fill in with a variety of lines and shapes.

80

Plan

Have students read page 80 and ask:

- **What gadgets would make interesting shapes?**
- **Which shapes will look good together?**
- **What kinds of colors do you intend to use in your print?**

Have students brainstorm ideas for their designs. Ask them to look at the prints on pages 74, 75, and 79 and think about the color schemes, patterns, and type of balance they will use.

Quick Project

Have students make prints using tempera paints and found objects, such as discarded buttons and paper clips.

👥 Meeting Individual Needs

Extend If gadgets are not readily available, have students make prints using objects that might be thrown away, such as cardboard tubes, corks, plastic lids, and spools. Have students research the use of recycled products in the creation of art.

Rachel, Age 10. *Flamingo Land.*
Tempera and chalk pastels.

What type of balance did these students show? Do you see any patterns?

Elizabeth, Age 9. *X.* Tempera and chalk pastels.

Share Your Art

1. Identify the gadgets you used in your print.

2. Explain the type of balance your print shows.

81

Gallery Options

Digital Gallery Have students create their own digital gallery using software such as Kid Pix® or ClarisWorks®. Encourage students to scan their favorite artworks from Unit 2 to make a digital gallery. Show these artworks in a digital slide show.

Create

Before students begin the project, collect and display gadgets. Have students read page 80 again and follow the steps to make their prints.

- Remind students to use all sides of the gadgets to make designs.
- Help students choose warm and cool colors and tell them to think about their color schemes. Remind them that the same gadget can be used many times to create a pattern.
- Remind students to clean the gadgets between color changes. Consider placing a sponge in each dish of paint for students to use as a printing pad, which will reduce drips.
- Show students how to blend colors of chalk pastels by putting one on top of another. Explain that the pastels can enhance symmetrical or asymmetrical balance.

Close

Point out the student portfolio art on page 81 and discuss ideas shown in each artwork. Then ask:

- **What warm and cool colors do you see?** (warm: pink flamingos, yellow sun; cool: blue sky, green grass)
- **What shapes are repeated in patterns?** (circles, *x*'s, lines, cloud shapes)
- **How are these prints similar to your own?** (Answers will vary.)

Have students share their prints and answer the *Share Your Art* questions on page 81 to form conclusions about their artwork. Ask them what the gadgets they used tell them about their culture.

See page 36 from **Unit-by-Unit Resources** for a rubric to assess this project.

NVAS (K–4) #1 Understanding and applying media, techniques, and processes

NVAS (K–4) #3 Choosing and evaluating a range of subject matter, symbols, and ideas

NVAS (K–4) #5 Reflecting upon and assessing the characteristics and merits of their work and the work of others

Unit 2 Review

At a Glance

Objectives

- Relate art terms to the environment.
- Identify color, balance, and pattern in artworks.
- Describe, analyze, interpret, and judge an artwork.

Materials

- **Art Print 8**
- **Fine Art Transparency**

FA TEKS 4.1B Choose appropriate vocabulary to discuss the use of art elements such as color, texture, form, line, space, and value and art principles such as emphasis, pattern, rhythm, balance, proportion, and unity

FA TEKS 4.4A Describe intent and form conclusions about personal artworks

FA TEKS 4.4B Interpret ideas and moods in original artworks, portfolios, and exhibitions by peers and others

Think About Art

Possible responses:

primary color (Point to red flower.)
warm and cool colors (Point to red flowers, blue background.)
tint (Point to flower background.)
shade (Point to leaves.)
balance (Point to the arrangement of plates.)
pattern (Point to plate borders.)

Write About Art

Before students write, ask:

- **Which warm, cool, and neutral colors are used?** (Possible response: orange, pink, blue-green, white)
- **What adjectives come to mind when you think of this place?** (Possible response: happy, safe, warm)

Unit Review

Think About Art

Read the art words. Then explain how either picture relates to each term.

primary color	tint	balance
warm and cool colors	shade	pattern

Write About Art

What color scheme is used in a place where you spend a lot of time? What message do you think the color scheme sends to anyone entering this place? Write about your special place.

Talk About Art

- Look through your portfolio.
- Choose an artwork that you especially like.
- Tell someone how you made it. Talk about decisions you made about color and balance.
- What might someone learn about your culture from this artwork?

82

Assessment Options

Options for assessing students appear in the **Unit-by-Unit Resources.**

- Use the **Vocabulary Worksheets** on pages 29–32 for an informal assessment of Unit 2 vocabulary.
- Use the **Unit 2 Test** on pages 37–40 to assess students' mastery of unit vocabulary and concepts.

Henri Rousseau. *Tropical Storm with a Tiger (Surprise)*, 1891. Oil on canvas, 51⅛ by 31⅜ inches. Trustees, National Gallery, London.

Put It All Together

1. What color scheme did Rousseau use?

2. What type of balance does this artwork show? Explain.

3. What mood does this painting express?

4. The title suggests that the artist wanted to send the viewer a message about storminess and surprise. Was he successful? Explain.

83

Talk About Art

Encourage students to use words such as *color scheme, values, patterns,* and *balance* to form conclusions about their artwork. Then have them tell whether the finished artwork matches their intended design.

Put It All Together

Use the questions on page 83 to evaluate the artwork. Possible responses follow.

1. Rousseau used complementary colors in the reds and greens and analogous ones in the greens and yellow-greens. DESCRIBE
2. asymmetrical balance, the sides are not exactly alike ANALYZE
3. excitement, fearfulness INTERPRET
4. Yes; the painting's colors and patterns convey a sense of surprise and excitement about the storm. JUDGE

NVAS (K–4) #1 Understanding and applying media, techniques, and processes
NVAS (K–4) #2 Using knowledge of structures and functions
NVAS (K–4) #5 Reflecting upon and assessing the characteristics and merits of their work and the work of others

 Art Background

Art History The French painter Henri Rousseau (1844–1910) is considered an exemplar of the modern Naïve artist. During the early 1900s, established painters and critics began to embrace paintings by artists like Rousseau who lacked formal training and whose works exhibited a fresh departure from conventional art production. Usually working in isolation, Naïve painters have often produced artworks admired for their psychological perspective and attention to detail.

Unit 3 Overview

In this unit students will explore three-dimensional artworks. Three-dimensional artworks can include sculptures, assemblages, pottery, or even jewelry. Students will also create their own 3-D artworks in the studios.

	Unit Opener, p. 84	Lesson 1, p. 86 **Decorative and Useful** Studio 1, p. 88 **Make a Paper Hat**	Lesson 2, p. 90 **Rhythm in Forms** Studio 2, p. 92 **Create a Foil Sculpture**	Lesson 3, p. 94 **Emphasis in Forms** Studio 3, p. 96 **Make a Pendant**	Look and Compare, p. 98 **Forms and Media**
Artworks	**Louise Nevelson.** *Royal Tide I,* 1960.	**Artist unknown,** Bamana culture. *Antelope Headdress,* late 19th–early 20th century.	**Artist unknown.** *Nataraja: Siva as King of Dance,* 11th century.	**Dale Chihuly.** *Red Ikebana Flower,* 2001.	**Louise Nevelson.** *Dawn's Wedding Chapel I,* 1959. **Nancy Graves.** *Tarot,* 1984.
Vocabulary	forms, three-dimensional	decorative artworks, functional artworks, headgear, masks	rhythm, media, medium	emphasis, center of interest, jewelry	
Materials	• **Art Print 9** • **Fine Art Transparency** • **Instructional Prints** • three-dimensional artwork, such as a sculpture, a mask, or jewelry	• **Fine Art Transparency** • student-provided hats • Sketchbook Journal • drawing and heavy-stock paper • pencils, safety scissors ⚠, staplers ⚠, glue • decorative items, such as sequins, feathers, doilies, pipe cleaners, tissue paper, ribbon	• **Fine Art Transparency** • Sketchbook Journal • comics from the Sunday newspaper • pipe cleaners or wire ⚠ • aluminum foil, cut into 1-by-4-inch strips • glue, heavy cardboard, foam, or wood	• **Fine Art Transparency** • jewelry catalogues and advertisements • Sketchbook Journal • classroom or library books • drawing paper and pencils, copper foil • water-based markers, hole punch, heavy cord	• **Art Prints 9, 10, 11** • **Fine Art Transparency** • colored pencils or crayons • Sketchbook Journal
Connections	**Home Connection** functional forms at home **Bookshelf** *I Carve Stone* by Joan Fine and Thomas Y. Crowell, 1988	**Curriculum Connection** Social Studies: the Cherokee **ESL Notes** **Fine Arts Connection** Theatre: character masks or hats **Meeting Individual Needs** Extend	**Curriculum Connection** Physical Education/Health: movement and rhythm **ESL Notes** **Fine Arts Connection** Music: rhythm **Meeting Individual Needs** Inclusion	**Curriculum Connection** Social Studies: Native American jewelry **ESL Notes** **Fine Arts Connection** Dance: lead roles **Meeting Individual Needs** Reteach	**Reading Strategy** Set a purpose for reading
Assessment Opportunities		Informal Assessment Rubric 3 from **Unit-by-Unit Resources** Ongoing Assessment	Visual Culture Rubric 3 from **Unit-by-Unit Resources** Ongoing Assessment	Informal Assessment Rubric 3 from **Unit-by-Unit Resources** Ongoing Assessment	

Lesson 4, p. 100 **Pop Art** Studio 4, p. 102 **Make a Pop Art Meal**	Lesson 5 p. 104 **Design in Architecture** Studio 5, p. 106 **Make a Model**	Lesson 6, p. 108 **Sculpture and the Land** Studio 6, p. 110 **Design a Monument**	Artist at Work, p. 112 **Pottery**	Portfolio Project, p. 114 **Make a Miniature Mask**	Unit Review, p. 116
 Claes Oldenburg. *Pastry Case, I*, 1961–1962.	 Exterior of the Pantheon, Rome, Italy.	 **Andy Goldsworthy.** *Sand Brought to an Edge to Catch the Light*, August, 1991.	 **Les Orenstein.** *Stoneware Pitcher*, 2002.		 **Ant Farm (Charles L. Lord, Hudson Marquez, Doug Michels).** *Cadillac Ranch,* 1974.
Pop Art, ceramic, clay, glaze	architecture, architects, model	outdoor spaces, monuments			
• **Fine Art Transparency** • Sketchbook Journal • food advertisements	• **Fine Art Transparency** • photographs or slides of buildings	• **Fine Art Transparency** • pencils	• **Fine Art Transparency** • a ceramic mug, bowl, or vase (optional)	• sheets of newsprint • tissue paper in different colors • blender, water, scoops or plastic cups • 8-by-10-inch window screen sheets, flat pans • paper towels, sponges • small balloons, hole punch, glue • decorative objects, such as raffia, yarn, beads	• **Art Print 12** • **Fine Art Transparency**
• self-hardening or ceramic clay • clay tools, plastic forks, paper clips, toothbrushes, and toothpicks ⚠ • water containers, kiln, if using ceramic clay • acrylic paints or ceramic glaze and paintbrushes, butter paper	• graph paper or drawing paper, cardboard or construction paper, heavy-stock paper • rulers, pencils, water-based markers • safety scissors ⚠ • found objects (buttons, shells, fabric scraps) • transparent tape or glue sticks	• drawing and construction paper, colored pencils, glue • paper forms, such as paper towel rolls • found objects, such as scraps of paper, old keys and jewelry, and paper clips • scissors ⚠, cardboard or wood • natural found objects, such as leaves, rocks, and sticks (optional)			
Curriculum Connection Health: healthy meal **ESL Notes**	**Curriculum Connection** Math: measure dimensions **ESL Notes**	**Technology** Search the Web **ESL Notes**	**Career Research** Pottery production **Reading Strategy** Activate prior knowledge	**Gallery Options** Library gallery **Meeting Individual Needs** Inclusion	
Fine Arts Connection Music: pop music **Meeting Individual Needs** Reteach, Extend	**Fine Arts Connection** Theatre: design features **Meeting Individual Needs** Inclusion	**Fine Arts Connection** Dance: ceremonial dance **Meeting Individual Needs** Extend			
Visual Culture Rubric 3 from **Unit-by-Unit Resources** Ongoing Assessment	Informal Assessment Rubric 3 from **Unit-by-Unit Resources** Ongoing Assessment	Visual Culture Rubric 3 from **Unit-by-Unit Resources** Ongoing Assessment		Rubric 3 from **Unit-by-Unit Resources**	**Unit-by-Unit Resources** Vocabulary Worksheets, pp. 47–50 Unit 3 Test, pp. 55–58

Unit 3

At a Glance

Objectives

• Identify expression in artworks.
• Relate art to personal experiences.
• Respond to and make judgments about artworks.

Materials

• **Art Print 9**
• **Fine Art Transparency**
• three-dimensional artwork, such as a sculpture, a mask, or jewelry

Vocabulary

forms, three-dimensional

FA TEKS 4.1A Communicate ideas about self, family, school, and community, using sensory knowledge and life experiences

FA TEKS 4.1B Choose appropriate vocabulary to discuss the use of art elements such as color, texture, form, line, space, and value and art principles such as emphasis, pattern, rhythm, balance, proportion, and unity

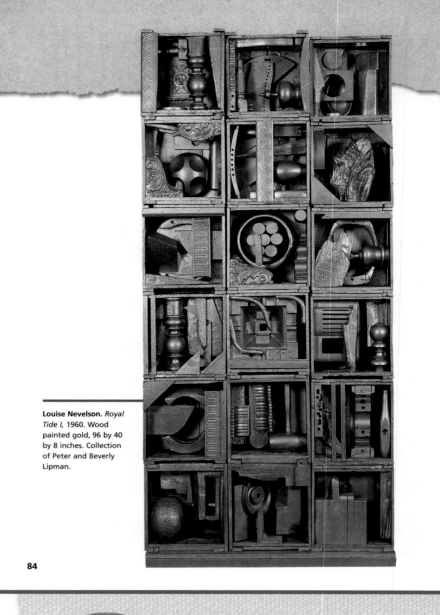

Louise Nevelson. *Royal Tide I,* 1960. Wood painted gold, 96 by 40 by 8 inches. Collection of Peter and Beverly Lipman.

84

Introduce the Unit

Show students examples of a form, or three-dimensional artwork, such as a sculpture, a mask, or jewelry. If possible, pass the item around so that students can feel the form.

Tell students that three-dimensional artworks are not flat, but have height, width, and depth. Ask: **What examples of three-dimensional artwork have you seen? Describe them.** (Responses will vary.)

Have students take a tour in and around the school, looking for three-dimensional artworks. Be sure to point out the structure of the school itself.

Explain that in this unit, students will learn about how artists create forms that express thoughts and feelings. Tell them that they will use elements of art and principles of design to create their own three-dimensional artworks.

Art Background

Royal Tide I Louise Nevelson was an assemblage artist. Assemblage involves finding things not normally intended for artwork and putting them together into something new.

As in *Royal Tide I,* Nevelson collected and arranged objects, such as furniture legs, spindles, moldings, and other bric-a-brac, into stacked boxes. Then she painted the boxes and objects with a single color as in the gold of this artwork, creating mysterious free-standing wall structures.

Home Connection

Have students find functional forms in their homes, such as bowls, cups, or vases. Invite them to photograph or draw the objects and then describe what thoughts or feelings the forms convey to them.

Unit 3

Expression in Art

Artists express their thoughts and feelings through their work. Some artworks make people laugh or cry. Others make people ask questions. Many artists express themselves by making **forms.** These **three-dimensional** artworks have height, width, and depth. Forms may be delicate necklaces or huge public buildings. What three-dimensional artworks have you seen?

Meet the Artist

At an early age, sculptor Louise Nevelson was asked what she wanted to do when she grew up. "I'm going to be an artist," she replied. Then she added, "No, I'm going to be a sculptor. I don't want color to help me." Indeed, Nevelson's artworks are mostly collections of found objects painted a single color—black, white, or gold.

85

Bookshelf

I Carve Stone
by Joan Fine and Thomas Y. Crowell, 1988

In this book, sculptor and teacher Joan Fine describes the process of carving a sculpture from a 350-pound block of marble. Read the book to students as you show the photographs of Fine using various tools, such as chisels, grinders, and buffers to shape the stone.

Fine says, "Carving is slow, strenuous work. It is like taking a long, wondrous, and difficult journey, searching for the beauty hidden deep inside the stone."

Discuss Unit Concepts

Have students read page 85 and look at the sculpture on page 84. Explain that Nevelson used objects she found to make her sculpture.

Point out that the artist communicated ideas about herself using sensory knowledge (the way the sculpture feels and the way the objects look together) and life experiences (using familiar objects that, when placed together, give meaning to the piece).

Lead students in a discussion about how their own sensory knowledge and life experiences can be a way of communicating their ideas through art.

Have volunteers identify familiar objects within the sculpture. Ask: **What patterns do you see repeated?** (Possible response: chair legs are used throughout) **What objects could you use to make a form?** (Accept all responses.)

As you introduce each principle of design in Unit 3, you may wish to display the **Instructional Prints.** A print is provided for each principle.

In addition, **Art Prints 9–12** and **Transparencies** are available for fine art in the unit.

Meet the Artist

Louise Nevelson (1899–1988) Born in Kiev, Ukraine, Louise Nevelson grew up in Rockland, Maine, and lived in New York City from 1920 onward. Her early works of the 1930s were influenced by Cubism and Surrealism, as well as African, American Indian, and Pre-Columbian art.

Although she worked in relative obscurity and poverty for many years, she gained recognition for her monochromatic wooden box wall sculptures during the late 1950s. She used scraps of wood found littering the streets of New York City to create these abstract sculptures.

NVAS (K–4) #5 Reflecting upon and assessing the characteristics and merits of their work and the work of others

Lesson 1

At a Glance

Objectives

- Identify and describe decorative and functional artworks.
- Describe, analyze, interpret, and judge artworks.

Materials

- **Fine Art Transparency**
- student-provided hats
- Sketchbook Journal

Vocabulary

decorative artworks, functional artworks, headgear, masks

FA TEKS 4.1B Choose appropriate vocabulary to discuss the use of art elements such as color, texture, form, line, space, and value and art principles such as emphasis, pattern, rhythm, balance, proportion, and unity

FA TEKS 4.4B Interpret ideas and moods in original artworks, portfolios, and exhibitions by peers and others

① Introduce

Invite students to bring in a favorite hat or cap from home. Have volunteers share their hats, telling where they came from and describing their uses. Then hold up a hat of your own and point out the colors, lines, textures, and symbols you see. Ask students to identify the colors, textures, and symbols on their hats.

Explain that hats are examples of functional artwork, meaning they have a purpose, such as shielding the sun from your face. Point out that they are also decorative, because they add beauty or interest to the wearer.

Tell students that masks and headgear are other forms of decorative and functional artwork. Have them predict what purposes headgear and masks might have.

86

Lesson 1

Decorative and Useful

Artists create **decorative artworks** to add interest and beauty to surroundings. A painting that hangs on a wall is an example. Other artworks may have a function, or purpose, and are known as **functional artworks.** Often, functional art, such as furniture or clothing, is also decorative.

Artist unknown, Bamana culture. *Antelope Headdress,* late 19th–early 20th century. Wood. North Carolina Museum of Art, Raliegh, NC.

86

Art Background

Art and Culture The Bamana people who created the artwork on page 86 are from the Republic of Mali, a country in central-western Africa. Although it is very poor, Mali has a rich cultural tradition.

Contemporary Malian artists draw on this rich history, adding archetypes, such as tourists with cameras and anthropologists with notebooks, to traditional forms.

Art and Culture *Kifwebe* masks were made by the Songe and Luba peoples of Central Africa. Probably originating in the early 1900s, the masks combine human and animal features and are symbolically colored red, white, and black.

Artist unknown, African. *Kifwebe Mask*, date unknown. Wood fiber, pigments and feathers, 14⅛ by 8⅛ inches. © Royal Museum of Central Africa, Tervuren, Belgium.

In many cultures, people wear **headgear,** or hats. These artworks have different purposes. Some hats may be worn as protection from the weather. Others are worn as ceremonial dress.

Masks, another type of three-dimensional artwork, are often worn during cultural ceremonies. Sometimes masks and headgear are worn together.

Sketchbook Journal

Let the objects on these pages inspire you. Draw yourself wearing an imaginative mask. What headgear might you add to your drawing?

87

2 Teach

Have students read page 86 and the credit line. Ask the following questions about the headdress:

- **What material is used to make this headdress?** (wood) DESCRIBE
- **What design principles does the artist use? Explain.** (a pattern of small shapes along the antelope's back; symmetrical balance throughout) ANALYZE

After students have read page 87, tell them that the *Antelope Headdress* is a type of headgear and that it is both decorative and functional. Point out that it would likely have been worn in a ceremonial dance. Then ask:

- **What moods or messages do you think this headdress conveys when it is worn?** (Possible response: fierceness and grace) INTERPRET
- **Where would you wear this headdress? Why?** (Answers will vary.) JUDGE

Now ask similar questions as students look at the mask on page 87.

Sketchbook Journal Encourage students to use a variety of lines, shapes, and textures as they draw their masks. Suggest that students also use symmetry.

3 Close

After students complete their drawings, have them describe what the purpose of the mask would be and what mood it conveys.

Assessment Hold up a three-dimensional classroom object, such as a pencil holder or backpack. Ask students to name its function and discuss whether or not it is decorative.

NVAS (K–4) #2 Using knowledge of structures and functions

NVAS (K–4) #4 Understanding the visual arts in relation to history and cultures

NVAS (K–4) #5 Reflecting upon and assessing the characteristics and merits of their work and the work of others

NVAS (K–4) #6 Making connections between visual arts and other disciplines

Curriculum Connection

Social Studies Have students research the native homeland of the Cherokee people. Invite them to find photographs and drawings of traditional clothing and masks worn by the Cherokee people who lived in the region before the "Trail of Tears."

Then find examples of masks and artworks created by the many modern-day Cherokee who formed an organization called Qualla.

SS TEKS 4.1A Identify Native-American groups before European exploration

 **Notes**

Have students work with an English-speaking partner to find and name three examples of functional artworks in the classroom.

ESL TEKS 4.4A Connect experiences with those of others

Studio 1

At a Glance

Objectives

- Express ideas by creating a three-dimensional paper hat.
- Demonstrate an understanding of decorative and functional artworks.
- Evaluate original artworks by self and peers.

Materials

- drawing and heavy-stock paper
- pencils, safety scissors ⓢ, staplers ⓢ, glue
- decorative items, such as sequins, feathers, doilies, pipe cleaners, tissue paper, ribbon
- Rubric 3 from **Unit-by-Unit Resources**

FA TEKS 4.2A Integrate a variety of ideas about self, life events, family, and community in original artworks
FA TEKS 4.2B Design original artworks
FA TEKS 4.2C Invent ways to produce artworks and to explore photographic imagery, using a variety of art media and materials
FA TEKS 4.4A Describe intent and form conclusions about personal artworks

① Introduce

Review forms. Have students describe forms in the classroom and say whether they are decorative, functional, or both.

Tell students they will make hats for special occasions, such as a birthday or graduation. Then have students brainstorm ideas. Ask:

- **What are some special life events for which people wear hats?**
- **Will your hat serve a function? If so, what will it be?**
- **What textures, forms, and colors will you include?**

Studio 1

Make a Paper Hat

Design a three-dimensional paper hat to express your mood. Make it decorative, functional, or both.

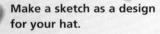

1 Make a sketch as a design for your hat.

2 Gather lightweight materials as decorations for surface texture.

Technique Tip

Arrange objects, such as bottle caps, buttons, and sequins, as a decorative surface texture for your hat.

88

🧍🧍🧍🧍 Meeting Individual Needs

Extend Have students experiment with making different forms for their hats. To make a crown, have them draw a zigzag line along the long side of a sheet of paper, cut it out, and glue or staple it to make a loop. Challenge them to make a square or cylindrical hat.

Quick Studio

Have students make masks using brown paper bags and markers. Help them cut out holes for the eyes, nose, and mouth.

3 Cut out a large circle. Slit to center. Staple into a cone.

4 Glue on the decorations. Wear your hat for a celebration!

Think Like an Artist

How might you use or display your paper hat? Would you describe it as functional, decorative or both? Explain your answer.

89

Fine Arts Connection

Theatre Organize students into small groups. Help each group choose or write a simple play to perform. Invite group members to create masks or hats for each character. Then have groups perform their plays for the class while wearing the headgear or masks.

FA TEKS 4.3D Interact with others in dramatizations

② Create

Have students look at the drawings and read pages 88–89. Then distribute materials.

- Have students look at the decorative items and other materials to spark design ideas.
- Help students choose items to create color schemes and textures that will suit the purpose of their hats.
- Encourage students to create a circle large enough to fit on top of the head, approximately 12 inches in diameter.
- Have students put their hats in a designated drying area so the glue can dry completely.

Technique Tip Have students practice arranging decorative objects on a flat piece of paper to help them decide how to decorate their paper hats.

③ Close

Have students form conclusions about their artworks by answering the *Think Like an Artist* questions on page 89. (Possible response: My hat is a celebration hat and will be worn any time I celebrate. It will be both functional and decorative because it is both comfortable and pretty.)

Ongoing Assessment

If . . . students have difficulty stapling the circles to make cones,

then . . . suggest they use tape to secure the circle shape into a cone.

See page 54 from **Unit-by-Unit Resources** for a rubric to assess this studio.

NVAS (K–4) #1 Understanding and applying media, techniques, and processes

NVAS (K–4) #3 Choosing and evaluating a range of subject matter, symbols, and ideas

NVAS (K–4) #5 Reflecting upon and assessing the characteristics and merits of their work and the work of others

Lesson 2

At a Glance

Objectives

- Identify and describe rhythm in artworks.
- Describe, analyze, interpret, and judge artworks.

Materials

- **Fine Art Transparency**
- Sketchbook Journal
- comics from the Sunday newspaper

Vocabulary

rhythm, media, medium

FA TEKS 4.1B Choose appropriate vocabulary to discuss the use of art elements such as color, texture, form, line, space, and value and art principles such as emphasis, pattern, rhythm, balance, proportion, and unity

FA TEKS 4.4B Interpret ideas and moods in original artworks, portfolios, and exhibitions by peers and others

❶ Introduce

Draw a wave pattern on the board. Have students discuss how the drawing shows movement. Then invite them to pantomime with their hands the motion or action of the wave.

Explain that rhythm in artwork refers to a sense of visual movement created by the repetition of one or more elements of art, such as lines, colors, shapes, or forms. Point out the flames repeated in the sculpture on page 90 as an example.

Then have students look for examples of visual rhythm in the classroom. Discuss the media used to make each of the examples and how a medium affects the way rhythm is shown.

90

Rhythm in Forms

Artists show movement, or **rhythm,** in artworks such as this one. Notice the elements of art that seem to move. Flickering flame shapes on the circle lead the eye around it. Even the toes appear to move. Where else do you see rhythm?

Artist unknown. *Nataraja: Siva as King of Dance.* South India, Chola Period, 11th century. Bronze, height 44½ inches. © The Cleveland Museum of Art, 1996, purchase from the J. H. Wade Fund, 1930.331.

How do the arms in this form suggest movement?

90

Art Background

Art and Culture Shiva, or Siva, is one of the main deities of Hinduism. A complex god, he is known as both destroyer and restorer. The dancer Nataraja is one of his many forms. Here he is shown four-armed; bearing drums, trident, or club; and dancing on one foot atop a demon.

Art History *Roller Skating* is a bronze sculpture. An alloy of copper, tin, and other metals, bronze is ideal for casting artworks, as it is readily melted and flows into molds. The Egyptians, Greeks, and Romans used bronze to make statues, utensils, armor, and other items.

Abastenia St. Leger Eberle. *Roller Skating*, ca. 1906. Bronze, 12¹³⁄₁₆ by 11¼ by 6½ inches. Photograph © 1996 Whitney Museum of American Art, New York. Gift of Gertrude Vanderbilt Whitney. Photograph by Geoffrey Clements.

Artists may choose from a variety of materials, or **media,** to create artworks. Look at the credit lines to see what **medium** each of these artists used. Some types of media are clay, fabric, paint, and charcoal. How do the media in these sculptures help create a sense of rhythm?

Sketchbook Journal

Draw some flames, waves, trees, or other natural forms that show movement. Practice showing visual rhythm in a variety of ways using lines, shapes, and colors.

91

② Teach

Have students read pages 90–91 and the credit lines of both artworks. Direct students to the sculpture on page 90 and ask:

- **What media has been used to make the sculpture?** (bronze) DESCRIBE
- **Where do you see rhythm in the artwork?** (the flickering flames on the circle and along his shoulders, the crown on Shiva's head) ANALYZE
- **Why do you think the artist used bronze instead of fabric to create this artwork?** (Possible response: The rhythm is easier to see using bronze.) INTERPRET
- **What is your impression of Shiva from looking at this artwork?** (Possible response: He is lively, full of energy.) JUDGE

Ask similar questions about *Roller Skating.* Have students interpret the mood the artist conveys in *Roller Skating.* (joyful) Then, as a class, discuss how the use of bronze as the medium in both sculptures creates rhythm by enabling the artists to make hard forms with curved lines and details.

Sketchbook Journal Tell students to practice using different media to see which ones work best to create various kinds of rhythm.

③ Close

After students complete their drawings, have them identify rhythm in each others' drawings.

Visual Culture Have students find examples of rhythm or visual movement in comic strips. Discuss the ways in which artists use lines, shapes, and colors to show movement.

NVAS (K–4) #2 Using knowledge of structures and functions

NVAS (K–4) #4 Understanding the visual arts in relation to history and cultures

NVAS (K–4) #5 Reflecting upon and assessing the characteristics and merits of their work and the work of others

NVAS (K–4) #6 Making connections between visual arts and other disciplines

Curriculum Connection

Physical Education/Health Have students experience movement and rhythm by teaching them a simple jump-rope rhyme, such as "Miss Mary Mack," or "Teddy Bear." These and other popular rhymes can be found in books or on the Internet. Then give each student a jump rope and have them recite the rhymes while jumping.

PE TEKS 4.1F Demonstrate body control

 Notes

Provide students with several pictures showing visual movement. Identify the areas where movement is shown and say: **This shows movement (rhythm).** Then ask students to find other examples and name where they see rhythm.

ESL TEKS 4.1C Understand major ideas in spoken messages

Studio 2

At a Glance

Objectives

- Express ideas by showing movement in an original artwork.
- Evaluate original artworks by self and peers.

Materials

- pipe cleaners or wire  ⓢ
- aluminum foil, cut into 1-by-4-inch strips
- glue, heavy cardboard, foam, or wood
- Rubric 3 from **Unit-by-Unit Resources**

❶ Introduce

Review rhythm, movement, and media. Have students list as many different types of media as they can remember.

Have students describe what they intend to create as they brainstorm ideas for their sculptures. Ask:

- **What is your favorite sport to play?**
- **What activities or sports do you like to watch (dancing, ice skating, skiing)?**
- **What movements are involved in this sport or activity?**

Then have students discuss ways they can integrate these ideas about themselves into their artworks.

Studio 2

Create a Foil Sculpture

What kind of movement do you enjoy most? Is it kicking a soccer ball or skateboarding down a hill? Make a form that shows movement.

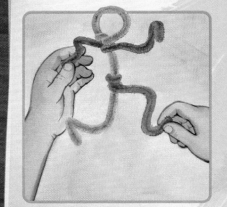

1 Build an armature, or frame, to show a figure in motion.

2 Wrap strips of aluminum foil around the frame of your form.

Technique Tip

Draw a sketch of the motion you want your figure to express or show. Refer to your sketch as you make the armature.

92

Meeting Individual Needs

Inclusion Show the class artworks or photographs featuring people with disabilities engaged in sports or active pursuits. Discuss how these images portray the many capabilities of people with physical limitations. Encourage students to model their sculptures on these images and consider having an artist with disabilities talk to the class about his or her artwork and process.

Quick Studio

Have students draw a figure running or swimming using pencils or crayons. Tell them to repeat lines to show rhythm.

3 **Wrap and shape the foil to cover the entire form.**

4 **Attach the sculpture to a sturdy base of cardboard, wood, or foam.**

Think Like an Artist

Have a friend act out the motion shown in your sculpture. Compare the lines of the rhythm with those of your artwork.

93

 Fine Arts Connection

Music Tell students that in music, rhythm refers to the repeated pattern of beats in a song. Invite students to follow as you clap out various rhythms. Next, play a recording of a song with discernible rhythm, such as one that features drums. Have students listen for the rhythm and clap along. Then give students various rhythm instruments to play along with the beat of the music.

Extend the activity by having students create a pattern of lines on paper. The patterns should show the rhythm created by the instruments.

FA TEKS 4.3B Incorporate basic rhythm patterns in musical compositions

2 Create

Have students look at the pictures and read the directions on pages 92–93. Then distribute materials.

- Explain that an armature is a frame that is used to hold up a sculpture.
- Show students how to bunch or crinkle the foil to make it stick.
- Show how foil can be layered to make parts of the sculpture thicker. Have them use smaller strips for hands, feet, and other details.
- Help students attach their sculptures to a base by using small dabs of glue and pressing the sculpture down lightly.

Technique Tip Suggest that students use repeated elements to show motion, such as curved lines coming off a ball. Tell them that in their sculptures, these elements may be implied.

3 Close

Have students interpret ideas in their peers' artworks by completing the *Think Like an Artist* activity on page 93.

Ongoing Assessment

If . . . students have difficulty showing movement,

then . . . show them how to reposition arms and legs to show the desired effect.

See page 54 from **Unit-by-Unit Resources** for a rubric to assess this studio.

NVAS (K–4) #1 Understanding and applying media, techniques, and processes

NVAS (K–4) #3 Choosing and evaluating a range of subject matter, symbols, and ideas

NVAS (K–4) #5 Reflecting upon and assessing the characteristics and merits of their work and the work of others

Lesson 3

At a Glance

Objectives
- Identify and describe emphasis and center of interest in artworks.
- Describe, analyze, interpret, and judge artworks.

Materials
- **Fine Art Transparency**
- jewelry catalogues and advertisements
- Sketchbook Journal
- classroom or library books

Vocabulary
emphasis, center of interest, jewelry

FA TEKS 4.1B Choose appropriate vocabulary to discuss the use of art elements such as color, texture, form, line, space, and value and art principles such as emphasis, pattern, rhythm, balance, proportion, and unity

FA TEKS 4.3C Identify the roles of art in American society

FA TEKS 4.4B Interpret ideas and moods in original artworks, portfolios, and exhibitions by peers and others

① Introduce

Show students an advertisement for jewelry and talk about the role of jewelry in American society. Talk about who wears jewelry and why. Then ask students what attracts their eye in the piece. Tell them that what they notice first in an artwork is its center of interest and that it is created by emphasis.

Explain that emphasis can be created by color, size, placement, or shape. Have students look at other examples of jewelry and point out the centers of interest they see. Then have students look back at some of the artworks they have studied in previous units. Ask them to identify the centers of interest in those artworks and discuss ways the artists created emphasis.

Lesson 3

Emphasis in Forms

Dale Chihuly wanted one part of his artwork to stand out. He created **emphasis** with color. The bright color draws your eye to the pink flower-like form. This is the artwork's **center of interest.**

Dale Chihuly. *Red Ikebana Flower,* 2001. Blown glass, length 14 inches. Collection of the artist.

Chihuly used color to create emphasis. Other artists might use size, placement, or shape.

94

Art Background

About the Artist A native of Tacoma, Washington, Dale Chihuly (1941–) has contributed significantly to the development of glassblowing as a contemporary art form. His glass creations are known for their vibrant colors and remarkable patterns, textures, and undulating shapes.

In 2002, he worked with an architect to create the *Chihuly Bridge of Glass,* a five-hundred-foot-long bridge covered with glass sculptures in Tacoma.

Art History The crescent-shaped center of interest in the squash blossom necklace is believed to have been inspired by ornaments worn by the Spanish and Mexicans who came to the Southwest. The Navajo incorporated ideas from these cultures into their design and created a unique, harmonious piece of art.

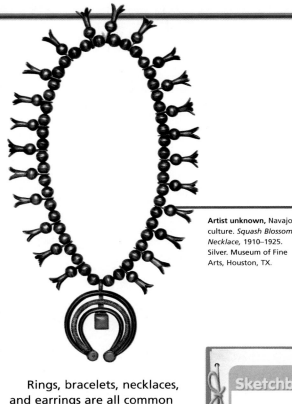

Artist unknown, Navajo
culture. *Squash Blossom
Necklace,* 1910–1925.
Silver. Museum of Fine
Arts, Houston, TX.

Rings, bracelets, necklaces, and earrings are all common forms of **jewelry.** Often jewelry is made of precious metals and gems. Many items of jewelry are designed with a center of interest. Point to the center of interest in the squash blossom necklace.

Would you say that jewelry is decorative, functional, or both? Explain.

Sketchbook Journal

Draw a Native American design for a necklace you might like to wear. How will you show a center of interest? Will you use line, shape, color, or another art element to help you?

Curriculum Connection

Social Studies Have students work in small groups to find images of Native American jewelry on the Web or in books you provide. Specifically students can focus on jewelry created by the Navajo people. Have them draw sketches based on the images and find out what kind of media were used to make the jewelry.

 Notes

Display jewelry or other artworks and have students point to the center of interest in each. Have them repeat: **This is the center of interest.**

ESL TEKS 4.4C Employ content area vocabulary words in context

② Teach

Have students read pages 94–95 and look at Chihuly's artwork. Ask:

- **What colors do you see in the sculpture?** (reddish pink, orange, pale green) DESCRIBE
- **How does the color used for the flower create emphasis?** (The reddish pink stands out and attracts your eye.) ANALYZE

Review the lines, organic shapes, and warm and cool colors. Ask:

- **What other elements of art are used to create emphasis?** (Possible response: organic shapes; curved lines) ANALYZE
- **How would the artwork be different if he had used a cool color in the flowerlike form?** (Possible response: The emphasis would not be as strong.) INTERPRET
- **If you had to give this form a title what would it be?** (Answers will vary.) JUDGE

Discuss how jewelry is decorative and may also be functional, as when it is worn in ceremonies. Ask students to compare the role jewelry plays in American and other societies. Then ask similar questions about the necklace on page 95.

Sketchbook Journal Help students choose elements of art to show emphasis.

③ Close

After students complete their designs, have them explain how they created centers of interest.

Assessment Set up a small exhibition of artwork from this unit or previous units. Ask students to describe how the artists used emphasis to convey their ideas.

NVAS (K–4) #2 Using knowledge of structures and functions

NVAS (K–4) #4 Understanding the visual arts in relation to history and cultures

NVAS (K–4) #6 Making connections between visual arts and other disciplines

Studio 3

At a Glance

Objectives

- Express ideas by showing emphasis in an original artwork.
- Demonstrate the use of texture, shape, and size to create emphasis.
- Evaluate original artworks by self and peers.

Materials

- drawing paper and pencils, copper foil
- water-based markers, hole punch, heavy cord
- Rubric 3 from **Unit-by-Unit Resources**

FA TEKS 4.2B Design original artworks

FA TEKS 4.2C Invent ways to produce artworks and to explore photographic imagery, using a variety of art media and materials

FA TEKS 4.4A Describe intent and form conclusions about personal artworks

① Introduce

Review emphasis and center of interest. Have students note emphasis in posters or artworks around the classroom.

Have students brainstorm ideas for their pendants. Ask:

- **What animal, plant, or symbol will you include?**
- **Where will the center of interest be?**
- **What colors, textures, and shapes will you use to create emphasis?**

Studio 3

Make a Pendant

Create a foil pendant that shows emphasis. Then make the pendant into a necklace.

1 Sketch a pendant design that expresses a special interest. Show emphasis.

2 Place the design on top of the copper foil. Go over the lines with a dull pencil.

Technique Tip

Show emphasis by making one area more detailed or bold in color. Make your shape unusual in size.

96

👥 Meeting Individual Needs

Reteach Have students use markers or tempera paint to create their pendant on cardboard or heavy paper instead of using the copper foil. Have students fold aluminum foil around the edges of their pendant to add a shiny texture.

Quick Studio

Have students draw a design for a watch using markers or crayons. Guide them to show emphasis using color, shape, or size.

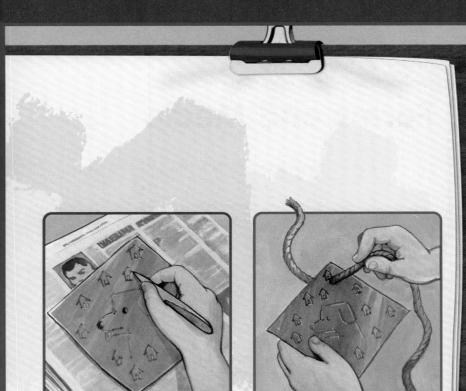

3 Use tools to create a repeating pattern for the background.

4 Punch a hole in the pendant and string a heavy cord through it.

Think Like an Artist
How did you use lines and shapes to show emphasis?

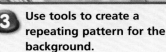 **Fine Arts Connection**

Dance Tell students that in some dance performances, certain dancers are selected to perform lead roles. These dancers create a center of interest by being the ones that the audience watches most closely.

Show students a video of a ballet performance and have them identify the leads. Discuss how the dancers' costuming and positioning creates emphasis among the other dancers.

PE TEKS 4.2B Identify ways movement concepts can be used to refine movement skills

❷ Create

Have students look at the drawings and read the instructions on pages 96–97. Ask them to describe their intentions before beginning the project. Then distribute materials.

- Have students show emphasis by using texture or shape to attract attention or by making the center of interest the largest part of the design.
- Have them use a dull pencil or a craft stick to transfer their drawings.
- Have them use the pencil's eraser or another soft object, so that the impressions are not as pronounced.
- You may want to cut cords ahead of time.

Technique Tip Before students punch a hole in the foil, have them use markers to add color and emphasis to their pendants.

❸ Close

Have students form conclusions about their pendant designs by answering the *Think Like an Artist* question on page 97. (Possible response: The lines radiate from the center of interest to show emphasis.)

Ongoing Assessment

If . . . students have difficulty holding the paper as they transfer the image,

then . . . attach the paper to the foil with a paper clip.

See page 54 from **Unit-by-Unit Resources** for a rubric to assess this studio.

NVAS (K–4) #1 Understanding and applying media, techniques, and processes

NVAS (K–4) #3 Choosing and evaluating a range of subject matter, symbols, and ideas

NVAS (K–4) #5 Reflecting upon and assessing the characteristics and merits of their work and the work of others

Look and Compare

Look and Compare

Forms and Media

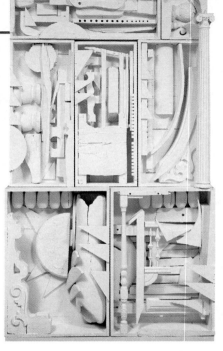

Louise Nevelson. *Dawn's Wedding Chapel I,* 1959. Wood painted white, 90 by 51 by 6 inches. Courtesy of the Estate of Louise Nevelson. The Pace Gallery, New York. Photograph by Bill Jacobson.

These two artworks show some of the different choices sculptors make about form, media, shape, and color. These choices help the artists express themselves.

98

At a Glance

Objectives

• Compare and contrast two artworks that use found objects.
• Respond to and make judgments about artworks.

Materials

• **Art Prints 9, 10, 11**
• **Fine Art Transparency**
• colored pencils or crayons
• Sketchbook Journal

FA TEKS 4.3A Identify simple main ideas expressed in art

FA TEKS 4.4B Interpret ideas and moods in original artworks, portfolios, and exhibitions by peers and others

Explore

Display **Art Print 9,** *Royal Tide I,* and have students recall this artwork by Louise Nevelson from page 84. Then, as they look at the two artworks on pages 98 and 99, ask them to predict which one was also created by Nevelson and give reasons for their answers. (Possible response: *Dawn's Wedding Chapel I;* both artworks are one color and use boxes and furniture pieces.)

Discuss

After students have read pages 98–99, have them discuss the forms, media, and colors each artist used. Point out that Nevelson creates a sense of calm by using wooden objects and only the color white.

Students can contrast the sense of excitement created by Graves' use of bright colors. Have students notice that using different metal objects also enhances the lively mood of the piece.

Art Background

Dawn's Wedding Chapel I In this sculpture, Nevelson used her familiar style of assembling wooden objects into boxes. She chose to paint this artwork white, which creates a sense of unity and coherence. The design and color evoke the traditional wedding elements, such as white lace, wedding cakes, and bridal gowns.

Tarot Nancy Graves' (1940–1995) approach to art merged a variety of disciplines, including the natural sciences, history, and cultural studies. Her eclectic background led to the creation of interesting and unusual artworks, such as the brightly painted, bronze sculpture titled *Tarot.*

You saw another sculpture by Louise Nevelson on page 84. Both she and sculptor Nancy Graves often used everyday objects in their artworks.

Compare these two artworks. How have the artists' choices of media, color, and shape contributed to the mood of each sculpture? Which one would you prefer to have in your room? Why?

Sketchbook Journal

Sketch a sculpture you would like to create. Express a mood through your sketch. Make notes about the colors and media you would use to make the sculpture.

Nancy Graves. *Tarot,* 1984. Bronze with polychrome patina and enamel, 88 by 49 by 20 inches. Courtesy of Knoedler & Company, New York. © 1998 Nancy Graves Foundation/ Licensed by VAGA, New York.

99

Reading Strategy

Set a Purpose for Reading Before students read pages 98–99, have them set a purpose for reading. Tell them that the Look and Compare feature guides them to compare and contrast two artworks by different artists.

Ask them what their purpose might be for reading the lesson and looking at the artworks. They may say their purpose is to become informed about the artists and how they are similar and different.

TAKS Rdg. Obj. 4 Apply critical thinking
ELA TEKS 4.10B Establish and adjust purposes for reading

Apply

Draw a Venn diagram such as the one below on the board. Tell students that this graphic organizer is a good way to show how two artworks are the same and different.

Complete the middle section as students suggest ways the artworks are similar. Then have students note differences in media, color, form, and mood while recording their responses in the circles. Possible responses are shown in blue.

Sculptures Using Found Objects

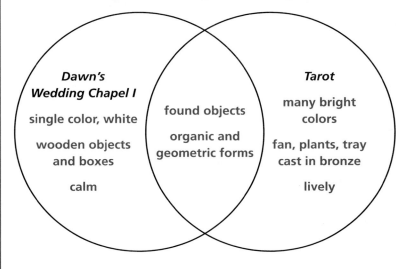

Dawn's Wedding Chapel I

single color, white

wooden objects and boxes

calm

found objects

organic and geometric forms

Tarot

many bright colors

fan, plants, tray cast in bronze

lively

Close

Ask students what these artists have taught them about using everyday objects in their artworks. (Possible response: You can use anything!)

Sketchbook Journal Tell students they will interpret the mood in each other's sketches. Model with a sample artwork. Say: **This artwork makes me feel energetic because of its zigzag lines, repeating geometric shapes, and bright colors.** Ask partners to describe the mood of each other's artworks for the class.

NVAS (K–4) #5 Reflecting upon and assessing the characteristics and merits of their work and the work of others

Lesson 4

At a Glance

Objectives

- Identify and describe artworks made in the Pop Art style.
- Describe, analyze, interpret, and judge artworks.

Materials

- **Fine Art Transparency**
- Sketchbook Journal
- food advertisements

Vocabulary

Pop Art, ceramic, clay, glaze

FA TEKS 4.1A Communicate ideas about self, family, and community, using sensory knowledge and life experiences
FA TEKS 4.3C Identify the roles of art in American society
FA TEKS 4.4B Interpret ideas and moods in original artworks, portfolios, and exhibitions by peers and others

① Introduce

Have students brainstorm a list of their favorite foods and record their ideas. Then have the class describe three items from the list, noting their colors, forms, and textures.

Tell students that this lesson features artworks with food as their subject. Explain that artists who work in the Pop Art style make artworks of familiar objects, such as food, soup cans, celebrity images, and cartoons. Explain that Pop Artists often depict a humorous or playful mood in their subjects in order to present a fresh look at common objects in our society. Have students share their thoughts about the food in these artworks based on their experiences. Then ask them to describe the role the artworks have, if any, in providing them with new ideas about the objects.

Tell students that Gilhooly's sculpture is ceramic and painted with colorful glazes. Ask students to relate times they have worked with clay.

100

Lesson 4

Pop Art

Do these sculptures make you hungry? Watch out! You could chip a tooth if you took a bite. Read the credit line to discover the medium the artist used. These food forms are made in a style called **Pop Art,** which began in the 1950s.

Claes Oldenburg. *Pastry Case, I,* 1961–1962. Enamel paint on nine plaster sculptures in glass case, 20¾ by 30⅛ by 14¾ inches. The Sidney and Harriet Janis Collection, The Museum of Modern Art, New York.

Pop artists like Claes Oldenberg use everyday objects such as food, soup cans, typewriters, and boxes of steel wool as subjects for their artworks.

Art Background

About the Artist Claes Oldenburg (1929–) is a Swedish-born American sculptor, draftsperson, printmaker, and performance artist. He is best known for his permanently installed monumental sculptures of everyday objects, such as *Giant Trowel, Screwarch,* and *Clothespin.* In 1962, he created a series of *Happenings,* experimental events involving sound, movement, objects, and people.

About the Artist During the 1960s, David Gilhooly (1943–) was a primary figure in California's Funk Art movement, creating humorous, anti-consumerist ceramic sculptures, including many sculptures of frogs wearing food and frogs as historical personages.

David Gilhooly. *Frog Sandwich,* 1990. Ceramic, 2½ by 4½ by 4 inches. Collection of Fenton Fine Arts, Fort Worth, TX. Photograph by David Wharton.

Ceramic artworks like *Frog Sandwich* are made from clay. **Clay** is a soft, moist medium dug from the ground. After the form is shaped, the artist fires it in a kiln, or special oven. After the object cools, the artist paints it with glaze. **Glaze** is a mix of water and minerals that produce different colors. Then the clay object is fired again.

What mood do you think these sculptors tried to create?

Sketchbook Journal

Draw a picture of yourself eating your favorite food. How will you show the color and texture of the food in your drawing? How might you add humor to it?

101

Have students read pages 100–101 and look at the sculptures. Tell them that Oldenburg's artwork was part of *The Store,* an actual store he rented and stocked with his sculptures of food, clothing, and other items in 1960. Have them look at *Pastry Case I* and ask:

- **What objects do you see in the pastry case?** (pie, banana split, cakes, sundaes, candy apple, pastry, cookies) DESCRIBE
- **Which item stands out the most to you? Why?** (Possible response: the pastry on the bottom shelf, because it is so large) ANALYZE
- **What mood do you think Oldenburg intended to create?** (Possible response: fun, humorous) INTERPRET
- **Would you want to eat the foods in *Pastry Case I*? Why or why not?** (Possible response: No; they look too shiny.) JUDGE

Now have students answer similar questions about Gilhooly's humorous sculpture.

Sketchbook Journal Encourage students to be imaginative by telling them that the food item can be fanciful and unrealistic like the frog sandwich or very large like the pastry.

3 Close

Have partners share their drawings and discuss how each provides new ideas about common objects.

Visual Culture Have students research the "tricks of the trade" that advertisers use to make food items look more appealing. Then have students look for examples in magazines with food advertisements.

Curriculum Connection

Health Have students find out what types of food constitute a healthy diet for a fourth grader. Then have them use this information to create a healthy meal. Invite students to create a menu featuring their chosen meal. Have students include the food's nutritional information and add sketches of the finished meal to the menu.
Health TEKS 4.1A Identify benefits of major nutrients
Health TEKS 4.1B Identify information on menus and food labels

 **Notes**

Provide students with pieces of clay. Invite them to manipulate the clay and form it into food items from their culture. Encourage them to use one-word descriptions, such as *soft, cold,* and *wet,* to explain the feeling of the clay.
ESL TEKS 4.4A Connect experiences with those of others
ESL TEKS 4.5G Employ content area vocabulary words in context

NVAS (K–4) #2 Using knowledge of structures and functions

NVAS (K–4) #5 Reflecting upon and assessing the characteristics and merits of their work and the work of others

NVAS (K–4) #6 Making connections between visual arts and other disciplines

Studio 4

At a Glance

Objectives

- Express ideas using ceramics in an original artwork.
- Demonstrate the slab, pinch, and coil methods for molding clay.
- Evaluate original artworks by self and peers.

Materials

- self-hardening or ceramic clay
- clay tools, plastic forks, paper clips, toothbrushes, and toothpicks ⚠
- water containers, kiln, if using ceramic clay
- acrylic paints or ceramic glaze and paintbrushes, butcher paper
- Rubric 3 from **Unit-by-Unit Resources**

FA TEKS 4.2A Integrate a variety of ideas about self, life events, family, and community in original artworks

FA TEKS 4.2B Design original artworks

FA TEKS 4.2C Invent ways to produce artworks and to explore photographic imagery, using a variety of art media and materials

FA TEKS 4.4A Describe intent and form conclusions about personal artworks

Studio 4
Make a Pop Art Meal

What favorite food would you like to bring to a meal? Make a sculpture of that food.

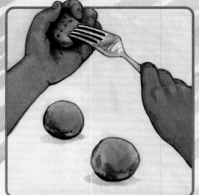

1. Use your fingers or tools to mold a type of food from clay.

2. Add designs to the surface or apply small pieces for details. Let it dry.

Technique Tip

Use kitchen tools and other gadgets to create the texture of your food.

102

① Introduce

Review Pop Art and the process of making ceramics. Then share a story with students about a favorite meal your family likes to eat. Explain what makes it a family favorite, describing its sight, smell, and taste.

Have students tell about a favorite meal they share with their family. Then have them brainstorm ideas by asking:

- **What is a food your family often eats?**
- **Which colors, textures, and forms will you use to make your food sculpture?**

Quick Studio

Have students make sculptures of a fruit using a self-hardening clay or polymer clay that you can bake in a regular oven.

🏃 Meeting Individual Needs

Reteach Have students work in small groups. Ask each group to create a slice of pizza from clay. Put the slices together to create a class pizza.

Extend Have students use clay to make serving dishes, utensils, candle holders, glasses, and other pieces for a complete table setting. Encourage students to set a table using their serving items and food pieces.

3 Paint your sculpture with glazes or acrylic paints.

4 Make a table setting with some friends. Present the food you made.

Think Like an Artist

How did you use shapes, forms, textures, and colors to make your Pop Art food look almost real?

Fine Arts Connection

Music Tell students that *pop music* refers to music that is popular with the general public. Ask them to name some current pop songs. You may want to play some recordings of approved pop songs from different decades, having students compare the similarities and differences in musical taste over several generations.

FA TEKS 4.5A Identify music representing diverse genres, styles, periods, and cultures

② Create

Have students look at the pictures and read the steps on pages 102–103. Then distribute materials.

- Review with students the slab, coil, and pinch methods for molding clay.
- Show students how to make slip, a mixture of clay and water that acts like glue when joining scored pieces of clay.
- If using ceramic clay, allow clay to become bone dry, then fire the pieces before applying glaze.
- Have students decorate a large piece of butcher paper to make a tablecloth.

Technique Tip Instruct students on how to use the tools safely to make various lines, textures, and patterns in clay.

③ Close

Have students form conclusions about their sculptures by answering the *Think Like an Artist* question on page 103. (Answers will vary.)

Ongoing Assessment

If . . . students have difficulty making slabs,

then . . . show them how to use a rolling pin to roll the clay out from the center toward the edges.

See page 54 from **Unit-by-Unit Resources** for a rubric to assess this studio.

NVAS (K–4) **#1** Understanding and applying media, techniques, and processes

NVAS (K–4) **#3** Choosing and evaluating a range of subject matter, symbols, and ideas

NVAS (K–4) **#5** Reflecting upon and assessing the characteristics and merits of their work and the work of others

Lesson 5

At a Glance

Objectives

- Identify and describe design in architecture.
- Describe, analyze, interpret, and judge artworks.

Materials

- **Fine Art Transparency**
- photographs or slides of buildings

Vocabulary

architecture, architects, model

FA TEKS 4.1A Communicate ideas about self, family, school, and community, using sensory knowledge and life experiences

① Introduce

Take the class outside and point out nearby buildings, including the school building. Ask students to describe the forms they see, such as cubes, cylinders, and spheres.

Tell students that when architects design buildings they think about the purpose of the structure and each of its rooms. Then they determine which forms and sizes suit each purpose. Explain that architects communicate ideas about communities using what they see, hear, or feel around them. Have students describe buildings in their community and tell whether they match the sights, sounds, and textures nearby.

Take students to different rooms in your school, such as the gym or the cafeteria. Talk about experiences the class has had in each room, then call on students to tell their own stories. Identify the forms used to design the space, and discuss how the forms suit the purposes of the room. Point out that sometimes architects build models to show how a completed building will look.

Lesson 5

Design in Architecture

The art of designing buildings is called **architecture.** Artists who design buildings are called **architects.** They make plans for homes, schools, stores, museums, and other structures. As they plan, architects use forms such as cubes, cylinders, pyramids, and cones. These forms give height, width, and depth to the structures.

Exterior of the Pantheon, Rome, Italy.

104

🎨 Art Background

Art History The Pantheon is the best preserved major structure of ancient Rome and an important building in architectural history. Originally built in 27 B.C. as a temple dedicated to Roman gods, it was later destroyed and then rebuilt by the emperor Hadrian between A.D. 118 and 128.

The huge circular building is made of concrete and faced with brick. A dome measuring 142 feet in diameter tops the structure, and the building is fronted by a porch with Corinthian columns. With the exception of a few decorative embellishments, the Pantheon exists today in its original form.

ESL Notes

Draw each of the forms from page 105 on the board. Point to and name each object as students repeat.

ESL TEKS 4.4A Connect experiences with those of others

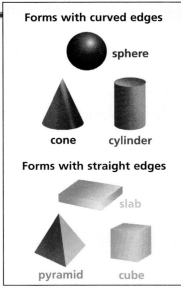

Forms with curved edges

sphere

cone   cylinder

Forms with straight edges

slab

pyramid   cube

Where do you see these forms in the Pantheon?

The Pantheon has influenced the design of many other buildings around the world.

An architect asks many questions to plan a building. How will the building be used? Where will it be located? Next, the architect makes a floor plan, or map, of the rooms. Often the architect will make a three-dimensional **model** to show how the structure will look. Finally, the architect makes a drawing, or blueprint. Builders use this drawing to construct the building.

Art in My World

Look around your community. What forms are included in the design of the public buildings? Find out when the buildings were built. Who designed them?

105

Curriculum Connection

Math Have students work in small groups and provide each group with a measuring tape. Assign groups to different rooms in the school and have them measure the length of the walls.

Invite one student from each group to record the dimensions of the room as the measurements are taken. Then help students to calculate the perimeter of their room. Point out the different sizes of the rooms and discuss how the size of the room fits with its purpose.

TAKS Math Obj. 4 Understand measurement
  Math TEKS 4.12 Apply measurement concepts

---

② Teach

Have students read pages 104–105 and look at the photographs of the Pantheon. Ask:

- **What shapes and forms do you see in the photograph on page 104?** (Possible response: triangle, cylinders, rectangles) DESCRIBE
- **How does the Pantheon compare with other important buildings you may have seen?** (Possible response: It has columns and a large dome.) ANALYZE
- **What adjective would you use to describe the Pantheon? Why?** (Possible response: strong; because it has lasted so many years) INTERPRET
- **Would you want to live in the Pantheon? Why or why not?** (Possible response: No; it seems like it would be cold.) JUDGE

Continue the discussion by asking students what forms and shapes they see in the second photograph on page 105.

Art in My World Contact a local historical society and ask for information regarding the architectual background of buildings in your community. Share these resources with students. Then share an experience you've had in a community building, such as jury duty, and invite students to tell stories of their own.

③ Close

Have volunteers present their findings on different buildings to the class.

Assessment Show photographs or slides of different buildings. Have students point out and name the different forms they observe.

NVAS (K–4) #2 Using knowledge of structures and functions
NVAS (K–4) #4 Understanding the visual arts in relation to history and cultures

Studio 5

At a Glance

Objectives

- Express design ideas for an art center.
- Demonstrate using a floor plan to design a three-dimensional model.
- Evaluate original artworks by self and peers.

Materials

- graph paper or drawing paper, cardboard or construction paper, heavy-stock paper
- rulers, pencils, water-based markers
- safety scissors ⓢ
- found objects (buttons, shells, fabric scraps)
- transparent tape or glue sticks
- Rubric 3 from **Unit-by-Unit Resources**

FA TEKS 4.2A Integrate a variety of ideas about self, life events, family, and community in original artworks

FA TEKS 4.2B Design original artworks

FA TEKS 4.2C Invent ways to produce artworks and to explore photographic imagery, using a variety of art media and materials

FA TEKS 4.4A Describe intent and form conclusions about personal artworks

Studio 5
Make a Model

Work with a group to design a model of an art center for the future. Plan together how people might use different areas of the art center.

1 **Get some ideas from buildings of the past.**

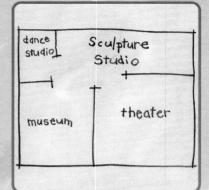

2 **Make a floor plan. Then decide what shape the outside will take.**

Technique Tip

Add pencil or marker details before you put the building parts together. It is easier to add fine details when the pieces are lying flat.

106

1 Introduce

Review architecture and have students recall what architects do. Ask students to describe why models are useful and discuss any models they may have seen.

Have students brainstorm ideas for a community art center. Explain that they will work in groups to integrate their ideas. Ask:

- **What types of activities will take place in your art center?**
- **How many rooms will it have?**
- **What geometric forms will you use for each room?**

Quick Studio

Have students create a model of a building from shoeboxes or other small containers. Add details with markers or construction paper.

Meeting Individual Needs

Inclusion As students design their models, invite them to consider issues of access for students in wheelchairs or with physical disabilities. For example, have them design the building so that people in wheelchairs would be able to maneuver all the spaces. Have the class discuss different features, such as ramps or elevators, that architects use to create access for all people.

3 Create forms from heavy paper or found objects. Glue or tape the forms together.

4 Place the museum model on a base. Add details to the outdoor spaces.

Think Like an Artist

Does your three-dimensional model look like your two-dimensional sketches or floor plan? How are they alike and different?

Fine Arts Connection

Theatre Take students to visit the theatre of a local high school or a community theatre. Point out the design features, such as the shape of the main room, the placement of the seats, and the location of the stage.

Then invite an architect knowledgeable in theatre design to explain what considerations are necessary to create productive performance spaces. Have students ask questions about how architects design theatres so that everyone in the audience can see and hear the event.

FA TEKS 4.1A Relate sensory and emotional responses to theatre

② Create

Have students look at the pictures and read pages 106–107. Then distribute materials.

- Tell students to design rooms with different purposes. Encourage them to use forms, such as cones, cylinders, and pyramids.
- Tell students that a floor plan is an arrangement of rooms in a building as seen from above.
- To save time, pre-cut different sized circles and squares from tagboard or construction paper for students to use.
- Attach the models to bases using tape or glue. Have them add features, such as paths and fountains, made from found objects.

Technique Tip Remind students to add details, such as windows and doors.

③ Close

Have students tell whether their models match their original intent by answering the *Think Like an Artist* questions on page 107. (Possible response: It looks the same because the model has the same rooms as the plan. It is different because the model has height and depth.)

Ongoing Assessment

If . . . students have difficulty making forms,

then . . . create examples of several different forms for students to use as a model.

See page 54 from **Unit-by-Unit Resources** for a rubric to assess this studio.

NVAS (K–4) #1 Understanding and applying media, techniques, and processes

NVAS (K–4) #3 Choosing and evaluating a range of subject matter, symbols, and ideas

NVAS (K–4) #5 Reflecting upon and assessing the characteristics and merits of their work and the work of others

Lesson 6

At a Glance

Objectives

- Identify and describe structures for outdoor spaces including monuments.
- Describe, analyze, interpret, and judge artworks.

Materials

- **Fine Art Transparency**
- pencils

Vocabulary

outdoor spaces, monuments

FA TEKS 4.1A Communicate ideas about self, family, school, and community, using sensory knowledge and life experiences

FA TEKS 4.3A Identify simple main ideas expressed in art

FA TEKS 4.3C Identify the roles of art in American society

FA TEKS 4.4B Interpret ideas and moods in original artworks, portfolios, and exhibitions by peers and others

1 Introduce

Ask students if they have ever built a sand castle. Have them describe their sand sculpture and the tools they used to make it. Invite them to share details about their sculpting experiences that tell about themselves. Then take students outside. Tell them to work in small groups to use natural found items, such as sticks, rocks, dirt, or leaves, to create a simple sculpture.

Then explain that artists use many kinds of media to make structures for outdoor spaces. Some artists use the actual materials that make up the environment, such as dirt, sand, and snow. Others make monuments that are meant to last a long time. Explain that these monuments often honor historic people or events. Have students describe any monuments or other outdoor structures that they have seen. Guide the class to identify the main idea conveyed in these structures.

Sculpture and the Land

Some artists design structures for **outdoor spaces.** These may be large sculptures, such as the one below, made of soft materials that wash away. Other outdoor structures may be **monuments** that are built in memory of people or events.

Andy Goldsworthy. *Sand Brought to an Edge to Catch the Light,* August, 1991. Shore of Lake Michigan. © Andy Goldsworthy. Photograph courtesy of the artist.

Art Background

About the Artist English sculptor and photographer Andy Goldsworthy (1956–) uses natural materials, such as stones, leaves, and ice, to create his structures. He then photographs his "land art" before it disappears and becomes part of the Earth's cycles.

About the Artist American architect and sculptor Maya Lin (1959–) won a nationwide competition to design the Vietnam Veterans Memorial while she was still an undergraduate at Yale University. Her other large-scale artworks include the Civil Rights Memorial and *Groundswell.*

Maya Ying Lin. *Vietnam Veterans Memorial*, 1981. Black granite monument.

Names of Americans who died in the Vietnam War are carved on the monument.

Artist Andy Goldsworthy uses natural materials for his outdoor sculptures. The materials come from the area where he builds the sculpture. Some of his sculptures last only a few hours.

Maya Ying Lin designed the Vietnam Veterans Memorial. It seems a natural part of the land around it. The black granite walls resemble a scar in the earth. What do you think the artist was saying?

Art in My World

Look around for natural materials that you could use in an outdoor structure. Sketch what the structure might look like. What ideas will your structure convey?

109

Technology

Search the Web Give students instruction on how to use Internet search engines. Ask the school librarian for a list of approved search engines and a suggested list of online databases. Then help students search to find information about the structures in this lesson or another outdoor structure. Have them present their findings to the class.

Tech TEKS 4.4A Apply appropriate electronic search strategies
Tech TEKS 4.4B Select strategies to navigate and access information

ESL Notes

Find pictures of monuments from the students' countries of origin. Have students name the monument and then use appropriate art terms to describe shapes and features in the sculpture.

ESL TEKS 4.1A Determine purposes for listening
ESL TEKS 4.4A Connect experiences with those of others

② Teach

Have students read pages 108–109 and look at the artwork on page 108. Ask:

- **What kinds of lines do you see in Goldsworthy's structure?** (Possible response: curved, continuous) DESCRIBE
- **Would you describe the form as organic, geometric, or both? Explain.** (Possible response: Both, because the pyramidal form is geometric but it is curving like something organic.) ANALYZE
- **What ideas do you think the sculpture conveys?** (Possible response: nature and art can work together) INTERPRET
- **Do you think it is a good idea to build an outdoor structure out of sand? Why or why not?** (Possible response: No; it will not last.) JUDGE

Tell students that the Vietnam Veterans Memorial is made of black granite and that it lists all the names of Americans who died in the Vietnam War. Elicit student ideas about the role of this artwork in our country's society. Then ask questions about the monument similar to the ones listed above.

Art in My World Have students brainstorm a list of unusual media, such as leaves, rocks, and dirt.

③ Close

Tell students to give their designs one-sentence titles and explain the purpose of the structures.

Visual Culture Have the class discuss the purpose of other forms of art in the environment, such as skywriting and fireworks and the role they play in our society.

NVAS (K–4) #2 Using knowledge of structures and functions
NVAS (K–4) #4 Understanding the visual arts in relation to history and cultures
NVAS (K–4) #5 Reflecting upon and assessing the characteristics and merits of their work and the work of others
NVAS (K–4) #6 Making connections between visual arts and other disciplines

Studio 6

Studio 6
Design a Monument

At a Glance

Objectives

- Express ideas by designing and creating a model for a monument.
- Demonstrate the use of various forms.
- Evaluate original artworks by self and peers.

Materials

- drawing and construction paper, colored pencils, glue
- paper forms, such as paper towel rolls
- found objects, such as scraps of paper, old keys and jewelry, and paper clips
- scissors ⚠, cardboard or wood
- Rubric 3 from **Unit-by-Unit Resources**
- natural found objects, such as leaves, rocks, and sticks (optional)

FA TEKS 4.1A Communicate ideas about self, family, school, and community, using sensory knowledge and life experiences

FA TEKS 4.2B Design original artworks

FA TEKS 4.2C Invent ways to produce artworks and to explore photographic imagery, using a variety of art media and materials

Design a Monument

Brainstorm about some historic people and events. Then choose one as the subject of a monument.

1 Draw some designs that show your subject. Choose one.

2 Use paper or foam forms for the monument and its base.

Technique Tip

Score foam by running the sharp edge of scissors along a line you have drawn on the foam. Bend the foam on the line to break it.

110

① Introduce

Review monuments. Have volunteers describe monuments they have visited in their communities.

Have students brainstorm ideas for their models. Invite them to look through their Social Studies textbooks for historical events and famous people to commemorate. Ask:

- **What historic figures or events are important to your community?**
- **What current events would you like to honor?**

Quick Studio

Have students use construction paper and tape to create a paper cube. Create meaningful symbols for each side.

👥👥 Meeting Individual Needs

Extend Have students research the event or person they chose to honor in their monument. Then have them organize this information into an outline. Invite students to use the outline to plan a short oral report about their monument and its inspiration. Provide a time for students to make their presentations to the class.

110

3 Attach everyday objects. Then attach your monument to a base. Add details.

4 Write words for a plaque, or sign.

Fire Fighters are Important

Think Like an Artist

Discuss how your monument expresses the importance of the person or event.

111

 Fine Arts Connection

Dance Tell students that in many cultures, special dances are performed to commemorate certain social and historic events. Have students look for information on these types of dances.

You may also ask your school media director to assist you in locating a videotape of such a ceremonial dance. If possible, have a dance instructor familiar with these types of dances come to talk with students and lead them through the steps of a commemorative dance.

FA TEKS 4.1I Perform basic folk dance steps

2 Create

Have students read pages 110–111 to make a model of a monument. Then distribute materials.

- Have students experiment with different colors to express their ideas.
- Provide students with a variety of forms, such as foam balls and cylinders, paper boxes and rolls.
- Suggest that students use objects, such as leaves, grass, and rocks, to create the monument's environment.
- Remind students to focus on key words and phrases when choosing the caption.

Technique Tip Explain that scoring and bending the base will add height to it.

3 Close

To form conclusions about their artwork, have students discuss the *Think Like an Artist* statement on page 111. (Accept all answers.)

Ongoing Assessment

If . . . students have difficulty thinking of a subject for their monument,

then . . . suggest they look through newspaper articles to find an interesting current event.

See page 54 from **Unit-by-Unit Resources** for a rubric to assess this studio.

NVAS (K–4) **#1** Understanding and applying media, techniques, and processes

NVAS (K–4) **#3** Choosing and evaluating a range of subject matter, symbols, and ideas

NVAS (K–4) **#5** Reflecting upon and assessing the characteristics and merits of their work and the work of others

Artist at Work

At a Glance

Objectives

- Read about a career in art.
- Identify the use of art in everyday life.
- Relate art to personal experiences.

Materials

- **Fine Art Transparency**
- a ceramic mug, bowl, or vase (optional)

FA TEKS 4.3C Identify the roles of art in American society

Explore

Display a ceramic mug, vase, or bowl. Let students feel its weight and texture. Explain that a ceramist or potter made the piece by shaping clay, letting it dry, firing it in a kiln, then glazing it and firing it again. Ask students to discuss what they know about the process of making ceramics.

Discuss

Have students read pages 112–113 and look at the images. Ask:

- **Would you describe the pitcher as decorative, functional, or both? Why?** (Both; it is beautiful, but it also serves liquids.)
- **Where can ceramists find ideas for their artworks?** (the world around them; what they see that people need)
- **What skills do you think a ceramist needs?** (Possible responses: patience, design skills, knowledge of firing techniques)
- **How long have people worked as ceramists?** (for thousands of years)

Pottery

Les Orenstein is a grown-up, but he likes to play with clay. Of course, Orenstein works with clay for a living so it is all in a day's work. As a ceramist, Orenstein gets ideas from other potters. Some lived thousands of years ago; others are his friends today. Orenstein also gets ideas for his own artworks by observing his family and the world around him.

The artist tries to keep the principles of design in mind as he makes a pot or other ceramic artwork. Still, during the firing process, surprises occur. According to Orenstein, "There are different things that make a pot special—the color, the shape, the surface. You don't have control over all of them."

Orenstein finds satisfaction in keeping up a tradition that goes back thousands of years. He also likes the way his work combines so many elements of nature—earth, fire, and water.

Les Orenstein working at a potter's wheel in his studio

Career Research

Engage students in a discussion about the role of pottery in our country's society. Point out that many household items, such as bowls and plates, are often made from clay.

Have students research contemporary careers related to pottery production in the United States. Then have them look in books or search the Internet to learn the methods used by Native Americans to create pottery. Tell students to describe similarities and differences between the different productions.

Les Orenstein.
Stoneware Pitcher, 2002.
Private collection.

113

Apply

Have students brainstorm a list of ceramic objects
and their uses. On the board, write a table such as
the one below. Fill it in as students brainstorm
ideas. Possible responses are shown.

Objects	Purpose or Function
mugs or cups	to hold cocoa, tea, and other liquids
vases	to hold water and cut flowers
flower pots	to hold dirt and plants

Close

Review the completed table and ask:

- **Are these objects functional? What ceramic objects can you think of that are purely decorative?** (Possible response: Yes; Clay sculptures can be purely decorative.)
- **Why do you think clay is used for these common objects in our society?** (Possible responses: Wet clay can be molded into helpful forms; It is one of our natural resources.)

NVAS (K–4) #5 Reflecting upon and assessing the characteristics and merits of their work and the work of others

 Reading Strategy

Activate Prior Knowledge Tell students that they can
use what they already know to help them understand a
reading passage. Before reading pages 112–113, have
them discuss what they already know about the objects
ceramists make and the function of these products.
Record their ideas in a table.

TAKS Rdg. Obj. 1 Understand written texts
  ELA TEKS 4.10A Use knowledge and experience to comprehend

Portfolio Project

Portfolio Project

At a Glance

Objectives

- Develop and organize ideas from the environment.
- Demonstrate knowledge about forms, media, emphasis, and center of interest.
- Evaluate original artworks by self and peers.

Materials

- sheets of newsprint
- tissue paper in different colors
- blender, water, scoops or plastic cups
- 8-by-10-inch window screen sheets, flat pans
- paper towels, sponges
- small balloons, hole punch, glue
- decorative objects, such as raffia, yarn, beads
- Rubric 3 from **Unit-by-Unit Resources**

FA TEKS 4.2B Design original artworks

FA TEKS 4.2C Invent ways to produce artworks and to explore photographic imagery, using a variety of art media and materials

FA TEKS 4.4B Interpret ideas and moods in original artworks, portfolios, and exhibitions by peers and others

Make a Miniature Mask

Make a miniature mask to decorate your wall. Will your mask resemble a person, an animal, or a fantasy character?

1 Shred newsprint and tissue paper. Your teacher will blend with water.

2 Scoop the pulp onto a piece of screen and gently blot it with paper towels.

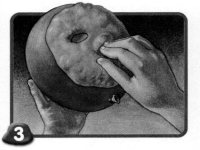

3 Place the damp pulp on a balloon. Add layers to build up features from the surface. Let it dry.

4 Remove the balloon. Paint your mask. Add decorative objects.

114

Plan

Have students read page 114. Ask:

- **What animal, person, or character would you like to portray?**
- **What feature will stand out the most?**

Ask them to think about where the center of interest will be in their mask. Have students think about the lines, forms, textures, and patterns they will use to show emphasis.

Have students look in books about masks to generate ideas.

Quick Project

Using construction paper and tape, have students make a portrait of an animal or creature on a clean, empty milk or water jug.

Meeting Individual Needs

Inclusion Some students may benefit from having a partner assist them with this project. Pair those students with a peer who can provide help with manipulating materials and following complicated instructions.

114

Emily, Age 9. *Mask of the Kiwi People*. Newsprint and tissue paper.

These masks were designed by other fourth-graders. How might they be used?

Gage, Age 9. *Mask of the Square Face*. Newsprint and tissue paper.

Share Your Art

1. Compare molding paper with molding clay.

2. What is successful about your miniature mask? Explain.

115

 Gallery Options

Library Gallery Ask the school librarian if you can display the masks along the wall of the library or in a glass case. Have students create display cards showing the titles of the masks, their names, and one sentence describing what the masks represent.

Then model how to interpret the mood of the class exhibition. Say: **Most of these masks show bright colors and exaggerated proportions which makes the overall mood lively and humorous.** Call on students to interpret the mood of the exhibition and explain their response.

Create

Prepare the work area ahead of time by gathering decorative items, setting up the blender, and laying window screens on top of flat pans.

Then pass out four or five sheets of newsprint and three sheets of analogously colored tissue paper per student. Display a color wheel and review analogous colors.

- Have students take turns bringing you their strips of paper. Blend each batch with half a blender full of water.
- If time allows, create different colored batches of blender paper and allow students to use a variety of colors in their mask.
- Let the masks dry for at least one day.
- Help students punch holes in the edges of the mask and string yarn through the holes.

Close

Point out the student art on page 115. Explain that these artworks come from the students' portfolios. Then ask:

- **How do these masks show emphasis?** (Possible response: Both masks emphasize the facial features by showing exaggerated proportions for the eyes and mouth.)
- **What moods does the student portfolio art convey?** (Possible response: Both show a playful mood because of the funny use of texture for hair.)

Use the *Share Your Art* questions on page 115 to help students form conclusions about their own artwork.

See page 54 from **Unit-by-Unit Resources** for a rubric to assess this project.

NVAS (K–4) #1 Understanding and applying media, techniques, and processes

NVAS (K–4) #3 Choosing and evaluating a range of subject matter, symbols, and ideas

NVAS (K–4) #5 Reflecting upon and assessing the characteristics and merits of their work and the work of others

Unit 3 Review

Unit Review

At a Glance

Objectives

- Relate art terms to the environment.
- Identify form, rhythm, media, emphasis, and center of interest in artworks.
- Describe, analyze, interpret, and judge an artwork.

Materials

- **Art Print 12**
- **Fine Art Transparency**

FA TEKS 4.1B Choose appropriate vocabulary to discuss the use of art elements such as color, texture, form, line, space, and value and art principles such as emphasis, pattern, rhythm, balance, proportion, and unity

FA TEKS 4.4B Interpret ideas and moods in original artworks, portfolios, and exhibitions by peers and others

Think About Art

Possible responses:

three-dimensional (Point to all three forms.)
functional art (Point to the Lincoln Memorial.)
center of interest (Point to the center of the bracelet and sun.)
monument (Point to Lincoln Memorial.)
decorative art (Point to the sun or the bracelet.)
rhythm (Point to the rays of the sun, the pillars of the memorial, or the repeated elements in the bracelet.)

Write About Art

Before students write, use the **Art Prints** and **Transparencies** to set up an exhibition of artworks from the unit. Then have students interpret the ideas and moods of the exhibition, noting the forms and media of each artwork.

Think About Art

Read the art words. Then explain how one or more of the pictures relates to each term.

three-dimensional   center of interest   decorative art
functional art   monument   rhythm

Write About Art

Write about how an artist's choice of form and media can help express an idea or feeling. Use artwork from this unit to explain your ideas.

Talk About Art

- Look through your portfolio.
- Choose the artwork that you think is most rhythmic or interesting in some way.
- Tell a classmate what you like about it.
- Use words such as *media, rhythm,* and *emphasis.*

Assessment Options

Options for assessing students appear in the **Unit-by-Unit Resources.**

- Use the **Vocabulary Worksheets** on pages 47–50 for an informal assessment of Unit 3 vocabulary.
- Use the **Unit 3 Test** on pages 55–58 to assess students' mastery of unit vocabulary and concepts.

Put It All Together

1. *Cadillac Ranch* is a monument in a large outdoor space in Texas. Describe the lines, shapes, and forms.

2. How are the forms alike? What effect does the unusual position of the cars create?

3. In what way is the sculpture's style similar to Pop Art? Do you think this sculpture is meant to be humorous or serious? Why?

4. If you could ask the artists of this sculpture a question, what would it be?

117

Art Background

Cadillac Ranch This monument lies just west of Amarillo in the Texas Panhandle. The artists, who called their collaboration *Ant Farm*, "planted" ten vintage Cadillac automobiles hood first into the sand in 1974. The ten Caddies (vintage 1949–1962) face west and are angled at the incline of the Great Pyramid at Giza, Egypt. The monument's image has been duplicated in many magazine covers and advertisements and was memorialized in song by popular recording artist Bruce Springsteen.

Talk About Art

Prompt students to use words such as *form, media, rhythm, emphasis,* and *center of interest* to describe the artwork.

Ask students to select a favorite artwork from a partner's portfolio. Model how to interpret ideas. Say: **This sculpture is a monument designed for firefighters. Its dramatic cylinder form and decorative detail tell me the artist believes firefighters are admirable.** Then have students interpret the ideas in each other's artworks.

Put It All Together

Use the questions on page 117 to help students interpret the ideas and mood of the artwork. Possible responses follow.

1. curved, continuous, and diagonal lines, rectangular shapes, "fin" forms, and boxy forms **DESCRIBE**

2. The forms are painted with similar colors, and they are at the same angle. The repetition of forms creates a sense of rhythm. **ANALYZE**

3. It is like Pop Art, because it uses an everyday product, the car, as its subject and media. I think it is meant to be humorous, because it is strange to bury cars in sand. **INTERPRET**

4. Why did you choose Cadillacs? **JUDGE**

NVAS (K–4) #1 Understanding and applying media, techniques, and processes

NVAS (K–4) #2 Using knowledge of structures and functions

NVAS (K–4) #5 Reflecting upon and assessing the characteristics and merits of their work and the work of others

Unit 4 Overview

Artists use artworks to express themselves. The artist may choose from a variety of media to represent a unique idea. Other artists, however, specialize in a particular media. In this unit, students will explore the effects of media on artworks.

	Unit Opener, p. 118	Lesson 1, p. 120 Collage Studio 1, p. 122 Make a Still-Life Collage	Lesson 2, p. 124 Unity and Variety Studio 2, p. 126 Draw with Oil Pastels	Lesson 3, p. 128 Photography Studio 3, p. 130 Make a Photograph	Look and Compare, p. 132 Outdoor Scenes
Artworks	Gabriele Münter. *Yellow Still Life,* 1909.	Henri Matisse. *The Snail,* 1953.	Jasper Johns. *Map,* 1961.	Annie Leibovitz. *Louise Bourgeois, Sculptor,* 1999.	Gabriele Münter. *Cliff Portion of Bornholm,* 1919. Georgia O'Keeffe. *Grey Hills,* 1941.
Vocabulary		collages, realistic, abstract, still life, theme	unity, variety	photography, still photography	
Materials	• **Art Print 13** • **Fine Art Transparency** • **Instructional Prints** • a sculpture, a painting, a sketch, a photograph, a collage, and jewelry	• **Fine Art Transparency** • photograph of a snail • 11" × 17" sheets of paper • old magazines, paper, and fabric scraps in a variety of textures and colors • scissors ⚠, glue	• **Fine Art Transparency** • Sketchbook Journal • 11" × 17" drawing paper • oil pastels; markers • maps, telephone books, bus schedules, and other familiar ordering systems (optional) • plastic knives ⚠ and tissues (optional)	• **Fine Art Transparency** • black and white photographs • newspapers and magazines • disposable cameras with black and white film • drawing paper, crayons or charcoal, poster board • acid-free tape or glue	• **Art Prints 13,14,15** • **Fine Art Transparency** • Sketchbook Journal
Connections	**Home Connection** family portraits **Bookshelf** *In Real Life: Six Women Photographers* by Leslie Sills, Holiday House, 2000	**Curriculum Connection** Math: angles **ESL Notes** **Fine Arts Connection** Theatre: theme in theatre **Meeting Individual Needs** Inclusion	**Curriculum Connection** Social Studies: maps **ESL Notes** **Fine Arts Connection** Music: unity and variety in music **Meeting Individual Needs** Extend	**Technology** Digital photography **ESL Notes** **Fine Arts Connection** Dance: expression in dance **Meeting Individual Needs** Extend	**Reading Strategy** Relate to personal experience
Assessment Opportunities		Informal Assessment Rubric 4 from **Unit-by-Unit Resources** Ongoing Assessment	Visual Culture Rubric 4 from **Unit-by-Unit Resources** Ongoing Assessment	Visual Culture Rubric 4 from **Unit-by-Unit Resources** Ongoing Assessment	

Lesson 4, p. 134 **Moving Pictures** Studio 4, p. 136 **Make a Zoetrope**	Lesson 5 p. 138 **Artists See Places** Studio 5, p. 140 **Draw a Landscape**	Lesson 6, p. 142 **Technology as Expression** Studio 6, p. 144 **Create an Installation**	Artist at Work, p. 146 **Photojournalism**	Portfolio Project, p. 148 **Make Abstract Art**	Unit Review, p. 150
 Nam June Paik. *Video Flag, Z,* 1985.	 **Paul Gauguin.** *Tahitian Landscape,* 1891.	 **Thana Lauhakaikul.** *Celebration,* 1983-1985.	 **Ralph Barrera.** *Central Texas Tornado,* 1997.		 **Dorothea Lange.** *Migrant Mother, Nipomo, California,* 1936.
animation, motion picture, video art	landscapes, Expressionist, abstract	technology, mixed-media, installation			
• **Fine Art Transparency** • animated cartoon clip • poster board and drawing paper • rulers, safety scissors ⚠ • pencils with erasers, colored pencils or water-based markers • tape, thumbtacks ⚠	• **Fine Art Transparency** • examples of landscapes • Sketchbook Journal • travel advertisements • 11" × 17" drawing paper • colored pencils • Sketchbook Journal	• **Fine Art Transparency** • dictionary • Sketchbook Journal • an assortment of found objects, such as sand, boxes, telephone wire, cellophane, maps, flashlights, strings of colored or white lights, cassette recorders, and other audio or video equipment	• **Fine Art Transparency** • newspaper or magazine photograph (optional)	• drawing paper and colored pencils or crayons • heavy paper stock and collage materials, such as colored construction paper, wallpaper, wrapping paper, tissue paper, old magazines, and fabric scraps	• **Art Print 16** • **Fine Art Transparency**
Curriculum Connection Physical Education/Health: health in the media **ESL Notes** **Fine Arts Connection** Music: music animation **Meeting Individual Needs** Reteach	**Curriculum Connection** Social Studies: geography and landscape **ESL Notes** **Fine Arts Connection** Theatre: designing outdoor sets **Meeting Individual Needs** Inclusion	**Curriculum Connection** Science: science technology and art **ESL Notes** **Fine Arts Connection** Music: music in installations **Meeting Individual Needs** Extend	**Career Research** Photojournalism **Reading Strategy** Set a purpose for reading	**Gallery Options** Restaurant gallery **Meeting Individual Needs** Reteach, Extend	
Informal Assessment Rubric 4 from **Unit-by-Unit Resources** Ongoing Assessment	Visual Culture Rubric 4 from **Unit-by-Unit Resources** Ongoing Assessment	Informal Assessment Rubric 4 from **Unit-by-Unit Resources** Ongoing Assessment		Rubric 4 from **Unit-by-Unit Resources**	**Unit-by-Unit Resources** Vocabulary Worksheet, pp. 65–68 Unit 4 Test, pp. 73–76

Unit 4

At a Glance

Objectives

- Identify how artists express ideas, thoughts, and feelings through artworks.
- Relate art to personal experiences.
- Respond to and make judgments about artworks.

Materials

- **Art Print 13**
- **Fine Art Transparency**
- a sculpture, a painting, a sketch, a photograph, a collage, and jewelry

FA TEKS 4.1A Communicate ideas about self, family, school, and community, using sensory knowledge and life experiences

FA TEKS 4.1B Choose appropriate vocabulary to discuss the use of art elements such as color, texture, form, line, space, and value and art principles such as emphasis, pattern, rhythm, balance, proportion, and unity

FA TEKS 4.4B Interpret ideas and moods in original artworks, portfolios, and exhibitions by peers and others

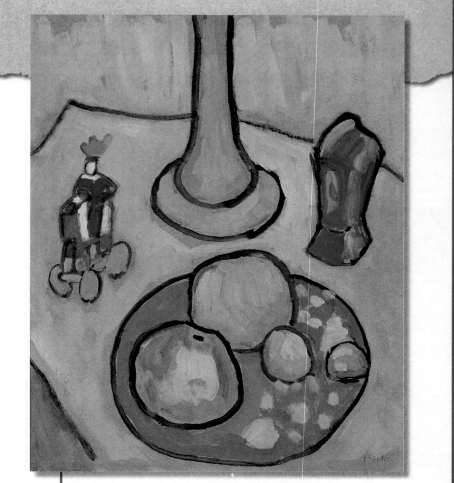

Gabriele Münter. *Yellow Still Life,* 1909. Oil on cardboard, 16½ by 13 inches. Millwaukee Art Museum, gift of Mrs. Lynde Bradley, M1975.1556. Photo by Larry Saunders.

118

Introduce the Unit

Display as many of the following items as possible: a sculpture, a painting, a sketch, a photograph, a collage, and jewelry. Ask students to name the different media used in each artwork.

Explain that artists use different media to communicate their ideas, thoughts, and feelings. Ask: **What are some ideas, thoughts, and feelings that you have communicated in your artworks?** (Accept all responses.)

Then ask a volunteer to read the title of Unit 4. Tell students that they will be expressing themselves by creating artworks that use a variety of media.

🎨 Art Background

Yellow Still Life This painting is one of many still lifes Münter made representing everyday objects in a highly stylized, flattened manner with an intensely expressive color scheme.

🏠 Home Connection

Model how to communicate ideas about family by sharing experiences your family has had, such as a time you celebrated or traveled together. Then ask students to look at home for photographs, paintings, or other portraits of family members. Have them choose one and write a paragraph saying what ideas, thoughts, or feelings they think the portrait communicates about a family experience.

Unit 4

Creative Expression

Artists express their ideas, thoughts, and feelings through their artworks. Some artists express themselves by exploring a variety of media. Others use a single medium and may experiment with different subjects. How do *you* express yourself through art?

Meet the Artist

Portraits of Gabriele Münter show the artist as a sweet, dainty woman. In fact, this artist was an important figure in the world of art. She played a large role in the rise of an art movement in Germany in the early twentieth century. Watch for another artwork by Münter later in this unit.

Wassily Kandinsky. *Lady (Portrait of Gabriele Münter)*, ca. 1910.

119

 Bookshelf

In Real Life: Six Women Photographers
by Leslie Sills
Holiday House, 2000

In this book, Sills tells the story and features the artwork of six pioneering photographers, including Imogen Cunningham and Dorothea Lange, who are featured in this unit. Read the biographies aloud and display the photographs to inspire students to pick up a camera and express themselves.

Discuss Unit Concepts

Have students read page 119 and look at Münter's painting. Point out the title and explain that a still life is a type of artwork that features an arrangement of different objects, such as fruit, plants, and bowls.

Remind students that artists communicate ideas about themselves using sensory knowledge, which guides them in arranging the look and feel of their composition. Have the class describe the look and feel of *Yellow Still Life.* Ask: **What colors, forms, and textures do you see in this still life?** (Possible response: bright colors; flattened forms; smooth, uniform texture) **What feelings or moods does this painting seem to express?** (Possible response: cheerful, energetic) Have students discuss how their own sensory knowledge can help them communicate ideas about themselves through art.

As you introduce each principle of design in Unit 4, you may wish to display the **Instructional Prints.** A print is provided for each principle.

In addition, **Art Prints 13–16** and **Transparencies** are available for fine art in the unit.

Meet the Artist

Gabriele Münter (1877–1962) was one of the major painters in the German Expressionist movement, which emphasized feelings and moods rather than depictions of objective reality. She helped to found the pioneering Expressionist groups New Artists' Association of Munich in 1909 and The Blue Rider in 1911.

NVAS (K–4) #5 Reflecting upon and assessing the characteristics and merits of their work and the work of others

Lesson 1

At a Glance

Objectives

- Identify and describe realistic and abstract artworks.
- Describe, analyze, interpret, and judge artworks.

Materials

- **Fine Art Transparency**
- photograph of a snail

Vocabulary

collages, realistic, abstract, still life, theme

FA TEKS 4.3A Identify simple main ideas expressed in art

FA TEKS 4.4B Interpret ideas and moods in original artworks, portfolios, and exhibitions by peers and others

❶ Introduce

Display a photograph of a snail. Have students compare the photograph with that of Matisse's snail on page 120. Discuss how Matisse's snail is not realistic but is recognizable.

Next, explain that a still life is an artwork made up of a collection of items that cannot move on their own. Ask students to identify objects in the classroom that could be included in a still life.

Then use library resources to create an exhibition of abstract artworks. Point out that students can look for familiar shapes and patterns to interpret ideas in the artworks. Explain that reading the titles in the credit lines can also provide clues. Call on students to share their interpretations with the class.

Collage

When Henri Matisse's eyesight began to fail, he put down his paintbrush. Then he picked up his scissors. He used them to create colorful **collages,** works made of torn or cut paper, fabric, or other materials.

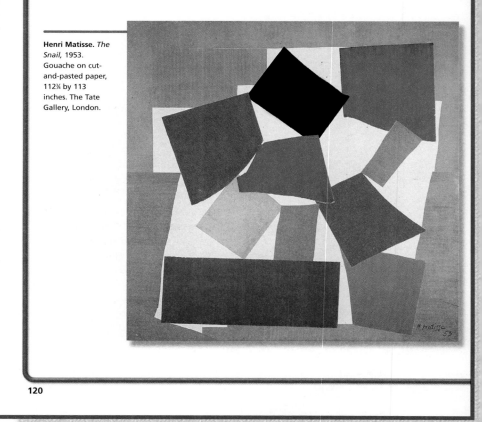

Henri Matisse. *The Snail,* 1953. Gouache on cut-and-pasted paper, 112¾ by 113 inches. The Tate Gallery, London.

120

🎨 Art Background

Art History Although French artist Henri Matisse (1869–1954) concluded his career by making paper cutouts, he began as the leader of Fauvism. Due to the brilliance of the colors they used and their raw expressiveness, artists of this movement were dubbed *les fauves,* which means "wild beasts" in French.

Art History Working with the French artist Georges Braque, Spanish artist Pablo Picasso (1881–1973) developed Cubism, a style in which multiple views of an object are represented in one artwork.

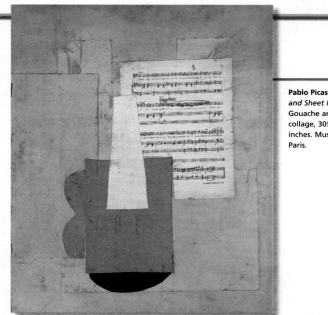

Pablo Picasso. *Violin and Sheet Music*, 1912. Gouache and paper collage, 30⅜ by 24¼ inches. Musée Picasso, Paris.

Matisse's collage is not a **realistic** view of a snail. It does not look real. Still, it does have a recognizable subject. Look for the spiral snail shape. An artwork that does not have a realistic subject is **abstract.**

Like Matisse, Picasso made collages. This **still life** shows objects that cannot move on their own. Each artwork has a **theme,** or artist's message about the subject.

Research

Pablo Picasso created some of the first collages and helped develop an art style known as Cubism. Research other art styles that show artists' expressions.

121

 **Curriculum Connection**

Math Have students identify right, acute, and obtuse angles in Matisse's artwork. Then have them identify these types of angles in the classroom.

TAKS Math Obj. 3 Understand geometry
   Math TEKS 4.8A Identify right, acute, and obtuse angles

ESL Notes

Pair students with native English speakers and have them read the lesson together. Clarify any terms by showing students more examples of the featured concepts.

ESL TEKS 4.10C(ii) Monitor comprehension

② Teach

Have students read pages 120–121 and look at *The Snail.* Ask:

• **What shapes do you see?** (trapezoids, rectangles, square) DESCRIBE
• **Which shape stands out the most to you? Why?** (Possible response: The blue rectangle, because it is the largest.) ANALYZE

Point out the spiral shape around the green center and note how the blue rectangle could be the snail's body. Tell students that one way to identify the main idea of an artwork is to determine what the artist wants to express about the subject. Ask:

• **What is the main idea expressed in this artwork?** (Possible response: The snail is a gentle, slow-moving creature.) INTERPRET
• **Do you think this artwork should be more realistic? Explain.** (Accept all responses.) JUDGE

Then ask similar questions about Picasso's artwork.

Research Ask the school librarian to guide students through ways of using various research tools, such as encyclopedias, art books, or the Internet. Then assist students in developing effective note-taking skills.

③ Close

After students research different art styles, have them share their findings with the class.

Assessment Have students work in small groups to collect materials they could use in making a collage.

NVAS (K–4) #2 Using knowledge of structures and functions
NVAS (K–4) #5 Reflecting upon and assessing the characteristics and merits of their work and the work of others
NVAS (K–4) #6 Making connections between visual arts and other disciplines

Studio 1

At a Glance

Objectives

- Express ideas by creating a still life.
- Demonstrate collage method when creating a still life.
- Evaluate original artworks by self and peers.

Materials

- 11" × 17" sheets of paper
- old magazines, paper, and fabric scraps in a variety of textures and colors
- scissors ⚠, glue
- Rubric 4 from **Unit-by-Unit Resources**

FA TEKS 4.2A Integrate a variety of ideas about self, life events, family, and community in original artworks

FA TEKS 4.2B Design original artworks

FA TEKS 4.2C Invent ways to produce artworks and to explore photographic imagery, using a variety of art media and materials

FA TEKS 4.4A Describe intent and form conclusions about personal artworks

❶ Introduce

Review still life, collage, and theme. Explain that choosing a subject and theme with personal meaning will help students communicate ideas about themselves in their artworks. Have students brainstorm ideas. Ask:

- **What foods, flowers, or other objects interest you?**
- **What theme or message fits with these items?**
- **What colors, shapes, and textures will you use to communicate ideas about yourself?**

Studio 1

Make a Still-Life Collage

Many artists create still-life images in the medium of collage.

1 Choose a subject and a theme for your collage.

2 Collect the shapes, textures, and colors you will use.

Technique Tip

As you prepare the paper bits for your collage, cut some with scissors. Tear others with your fingers.

🧍🧍🧍 Meeting Individual Needs

Inclusion Students with impaired vision will appreciate collage materials that are textured and materials that allow them to make high contrast images.

Quick Studio

Arrange a piece of fruit, a flower, and a cup. Have students create a collage using colored construction paper.

3 Prepare bits of paper. Arrange shapes and paper bits into a pleasing design.

4 Fill in the background with paper bits.

Think Like an Artist

Are you satisfied with your still-life collage? What might you do differently?

123

 Fine Arts Connection

Theatre Take students to a play or have them watch a video of one. Then have them work in small groups to design a poster for the play using collage. Tell them to think about the colors, shapes, and textures they will use to express the play's theme.

FA TEKS 4.4A Explain theatre as a reflection of life

② Create

Have students look at the pictures and read the directions on pages 122–123. Then distribute materials. Provide students with photographic imagery to include in their collages.

- Remind students to choose a theme that tells about themselves.
- Demonstrate how to explore photographic imagery. For example, show how bold lines can be added with markers or torn paper shapes can be glued onto the image to create rhythm.
- Remind students that repeated elements create rhythm.
- Tell them to use only a small amount of glue, so that the collage will not wrinkle.

Technique Tip Tell students tearing the paper will add texture to their collages.

③ Close

Have students form conclusions about their artwork by answering the *Think Like an Artist* questions on page 123. (Possible response: yes; use more textures and colors)

Ongoing Assessment

If . . . students have difficulty thinking of a subject,

then . . . provide them with a variety of objects to arrange and use as a model.

See page 72 from **Unit-by-Unit Resources** for a rubric to assess this studio.

NVAS (K–4) #1 Understanding and applying media, techniques, and processes

NVAS (K–4) #3 Choosing and evaluating a range of subject matter, symbols, and ideas

NVAS (K–4) #5 Reflecting upon and assessing the characteristics and merits of their work and the work of others

Lesson 2

At a Glance

Objectives

- Understand and define unity and variety in artworks.
- Describe, analyze, interpret, and judge artworks.

Materials

- **Fine Art Transparency**
- Sketchbook Journal

Vocabulary

unity, variety

FA TEKS 4.1A Communicate ideas about self, family, school, and community, using sensory knowledge and life experiences

FA TEKS 4.1B Choose appropriate vocabulary to discuss the use of art elements such as color, texture, form, line, space, and value and art principles such as emphasis, pattern, rhythm, balance, proportion, and unity

FA TEKS 4.4B Interpret ideas and moods in original artworks, portfolios, and exhibitions by peers and others

❶ Introduce

Display a still-life arrangement of classroom objects, such as books, pencils, pens, and paper. Model how to communicate ideas about school using sensory knowledge. Say: **These objects have different colors, forms, and textures, but they belong together because they are all items used at school.** Invite students to discuss how they can use sensory knowledge to convey ideas about school through their artworks. Have them collect classroom objects to create a still-life arrangement of their own.

Explain that in artwork, as in any grouping, unity and variety are important. Point out that unity involves elements that seem to belong together, and variety, or differences, add interest. Have students point out examples of unity and variety in their still-life arrangements.

124

Lesson 2

Unity and Variety

The similar lines, shapes, and colors of this map give it **unity.** These elements of art work together to create a feeling that the artwork is complete. However, all the lines, shapes, and colors are not exactly alike. In this way, the combination of elements provides **variety.**

Jasper Johns. *Map,* 1961. Oil on canvas, 78 by 128 inches. Museum of Modern Art, New York. ©2003 Jasper Johns/Licensed by VAGA, New York, NY.

124

Art Background

About the Artist American painter, sculptor, and printmaker, Jasper Johns (1930–) began his artistic career by painting American flags, maps, targets, numbers, and other recognizable subjects in series. Johns is considered a forerunner of American Pop Art.

About the Artist South Korean-born electronic-media pioneer, performance artist, musician, sculptor, and filmmaker Nam June Paik (1932–), is considered the father of video art. Since 1959 he has made assemblages from television sets, refashioning both the sets themselves and their broadcast images.

Nam June Paik. *Space Kid,* 1991. Video sculpture, 49 by 58 by 11 inches. Courtesy Carl Solway Gallery, Cincinnati, OH. Photo by Chris Gomien.

Nam June Paik's video sculpture is very different from Jasper Johns's painting. Yet both show unity and variety.

Think about Nam June Paik's use of line, shape, and color. How did he create unity? Do you see variety in the video sculpture? Tell what elements of art the artist used to create variety.

Sketchbook Journal

Design an artwork that could be titled either *Map 2* or *Space Kid 2*. Think of a medium that would suit your idea. Draw a plan that shows unity and variety.

② Teach

Have students read pages 124 and 125 and look at Johns' painting. Ask:

- **What colors do you see throughout the painting?** (blue, red, and yellow) DESCRIBE
- **Which colors provide variety?** (black, violet, and dusky pink) ANALYZE
- **Do you think the painting shows unity? Why or why not?** (Possible response: Yes; Unity is shown through the repetition of color, blurred lines, and scratchy visual texture.) INTERPRET
- **What do you like best about this artwork?** (Accept all responses.) JUDGE

Ask similar questions about Paik's artwork. Explain how the repetition of lines, colors, and video screens creates unity in *Space Kid.*

Sketchbook Journal Point out that one way to interpret ideas in an artwork is to identify the varied elements in a unified design. Explain that artists often want these elements to stand out and express something about the subject. Have students identify variety in each other's compositions to interpret ideas.

③ Close

After students have completed their plans, have them give their artworks descriptive titles.

Visual Culture Have students discuss places where they have seen or used a map, such as a bus terminal, nature park, zoo, or theme park. Discuss different map features and how designers highlight important information.

NVAS (K–4) #2 Using knowledge of structures and functions

NVAS (K–4) #5 Reflecting upon and assessing the characteristics and merits of their work and the work of others

NVAS (K–4) #6 Making connections between visual arts and other disciplines

Curriculum Connection

Social Studies Provide students with a variety of United States maps, including a satellite weather map and a topographic map. Have them discuss the different information each map provides and how that information is conveyed. Review legends, symbols, scales, and compass roses.

SS TEKS 4.6A Apply geographic tools to interpret maps

 Notes

Point out aspects of Johns' painting that show either unity or variety. For example, say: **The color yellow provides unity.** Have students repeat the sentence while pointing to a yellow element.

ESL TEKS 4.1C Understand major ideas in spoken messages

Studio 2

At a Glance

Objectives

- Express ideas by drawing with oil pastels.
- Demonstrate unity and variety in an artwork.
- Evaluate original artworks by self and peers.

Materials

- 11" × 17" drawing paper
- oil pastels; markers
- maps, telephone books, bus schedules, and other familiar ordering systems (optional)
- plastic knives ⚠ and tissues (optional)
- Rubric 4 from **Unit-by-Unit Resources**

FA TEKS 4.2B Design original artworks

FA TEKS 4.2C Invent ways to produce artworks and to explore photographic imagery, using a variety of art media and materials

FA TEKS 4.4A Describe intent and form conclusions about personal artworks

① Introduce

Explain to students that having a clear plan for an artwork can help them convey their ideas. Model how to describe intentions: Say: **In my next artwork, I want to create unity with a pattern of lines and show variety through color.** Have students describe their intentions. Ask:

- **Which organizational tools, such as dictionaries, telephone books, or address books, will you use?**
- **What kinds of lines and patterns do you intend to draw?**

Quick Studio

Have students draw an illustrated alphabet using colored pencils. Encourage them to show unity and variety in their illustrations.

Studio 2

Draw with Oil Pastels

Maps, telephone books, and bus schedules all share a theme of organization. Choose a familiar system that creates order as a subject for an oil pastel drawing.

① With an oil pastel, draw an object or system that creates order.

② Lightly draw only a few details to show how the system works.

Technique Tip

If you need to make a change, scrape oil pastel off the paper with a plastic knife, or draw over the area with another color.

126

Meeting Individual Needs

Extend Have students work in small groups to create a map mural. First assign or have groups choose a subject for their murals, such as a map of the school or their state.

Next have students work together to make sketches of the map, adding details such as legends and keys. Then have them make the map using tempera paints and long rolls of brown paper.

③ Color your drawing using oil pastels. Add words with markers.

④ Blend some colors. Then add a few more details.

Think Like an Artist

How does your artwork show unity and variety? Explain.

 Fine Arts Connection

Music Tell students that unity and variety are also important principles in music. Melody that occurs several times in a song can be called a theme, providing unity through repetition. Variation is music that is repeated, but changed in some important way.

Explain that musicians create variations by changing the tempo, dynamics, melody, rhythm, or timbre in a piece of music. Then have students listen to several music samples while you point out examples of unity and variety.

FA TEKS 4.1C Identify music forms presented aurally
FA TEKS 4.5D Identify connections between music and other fine arts

② Create

Have students look at the pictures and follow the steps on pages 126–127. Then distribute materials.

- Provide students with maps, schedules, or other organizing systems to help them gather ideas.
- Remind them that they should press lightly for a softer color and press firmly for a brighter color.
- Remind students that oil pastels do not work well when writing small letters or numbers.
- Tell students to blend colors by putting one on top of another.

Technique Tip When drawing over one color with another, tell students that the other color may dirty the end of their oil pastel. Rubbing the end with a paper towel will keep it clean and prevent the color from becoming muddied.

③ Close

Have students reflect on their drawings by answering the *Think Like an Artist* question. (Possible response: I used blue and red throughout for unity and added details for variety.)

Ongoing Assessment

If . . . students have difficulty conveying a system with order,

then . . . have them make a sample drawing to plan where elements of the design will be placed on the paper.

See page 72 from **Unit-by-Unit Resources** for a rubric to assess this studio.

NVAS (K–4) #1 Understanding and applying media, techniques, and processes

NVAS (K–4) #3 Choosing and evaluating a range of subject matter, symbols, and ideas

NVAS (K–4) #5 Reflecting upon and assessing the characteristics and merits of their work and the work of others

Lesson 3

Lesson 3

At a Glance

Objectives

- Identify and describe photography.
- Describe, analyze, interpret, and judge artworks.

Materials

- **Fine Art Transparency**
- black and white photographs
- newspapers and magazines

Vocabulary

photography, still photography

FA TEKS 4.1A Communicate ideas about self, family, school, and community, using sensory knowledge and life experiences

FA TEKS 4.3A Identify simple main ideas expressed in art

FA TEKS 4.4B Interpret ideas and moods in original artworks, portfolios, and exhibitions by peers and others

① Introduce

Bring in black and white photographs of different families. Pass them around and ask students to identify the medium. Explain that these are examples of still photography and that the photographers used sensory knowledge to help them communicate ideas. Point out areas where the photographer captured interesting values, shapes, and textures. Call on students to tell how they can use sensory knowledge to communicate ideas about family in a photograph.

Ask students what other kinds of photographs they have seen. Then discuss the different purposes of photography, such as documenting events and special occasions. Review neutral colors with students and remind them that values refer to shades of light and dark, with white being the lightest value and black being the darkest.

Photography

Photography is the process of capturing images on film, videotape, or another medium. You often see **still photography** when you read a newspaper or open a textbook. Have you seen a photograph of your family? Explain.

Annie Leibovitz. *Louise Bourgeois, Sculptor,* 1999. Black and white photograph. © Annie Leibovitz-Contact Press Images.

128

Art Background

Louise Bourgeois The subject of Leibovitz's portrait is French American sculptor Louise Bourgeois. Bourgeois is known for creating emotionally powerful sculptures of wood, marble, plaster, bronze, and other media.

About the Artist American photographer Imogen Cunningham (1883–1976) is best known for her portraits and botanical studies, including her sharply detailed images of magnolia blossoms and calla lilies.

ESL Notes

Have students work in groups to find examples of still photography in magazines. Have each group share its findings and tell the subject of the photographs.

ESL TEKS 4.5G Employ content area vocabulary words in context

Photographers may use their work to record history, tell a story, or help viewers think about a subject in a new way. Many photographers make black-and-white photographs. Look at the values in the photographs on these pages. The differences in light and dark areas add interest. The neutral colors of black, gray, white, and sometimes brown help guide your eye.

How are these two photographs alike? How are they different from color photographs you have seen?

Art in My World

Find a black-and-white photograph in a newspaper, magazine, or other source. How does the photograph express the photographer's point of view toward or feelings about the subject? Write about it.

Technology

Digital Photography Show students how to use a digital camera. Explain how to zoom in and out and how to frame photos. Guide students to photograph each other and create a digital gallery of the class. Then download the photographs onto the class computer and include student portraits alongside their artworks. Invite students to alter their portraits using computer software. First, model how to perform the program's basic functions.

Tech TEKS 4.1C Identify and describe digital input, processing, and output
Tech TEKS 4.2A Use a variety of input devices

② Teach

Have students read pages 128 and 129 and look at Leibovitz's photograph. Ask:

• **What details do you see in this photograph?** (wrinkles, earring, long hair, hand) DESCRIBE
• **Where do you see the details most sharply? Where is the image blurred?** (face is sharp; shirt is blurred) ANALYZE

Point out the emphasis placed on the subject's hand. Explain that students can identify the main idea of the artwork by interpreting this area of emphasis. Ask:

• **What main idea does Leibovitz express about Bourgeois?** (Possible response: Her hands have played an important role in her life's work.) INTERPRET
• **Would you want to meet this person? Why or why not?** (Accept all responses.) JUDGE

Ask similar questions about Cunningham's photograph.

Art in My World Have students point out what is being emphasized in the photographs they find.

③ Close

Demonstrate how to explore photographic imagery with art media and materials. Then have students alter their newspaper photographs by adding details with markers, paint, or torn paper. Tell them to call attention to areas of natural emphasis in the photograph.

Visual Culture Discuss how photographs in magazines and advertisements are manipulated so that images look different from the way they do in real life. Mention airbrushing and digital retouching, especially of celebrities.

NVAS (K–4) #2 Using knowledge of structures and functions
NVAS (K–4) #5 Reflecting upon and assessing the characteristics and merits of their work and the work of others
NVAS (K–4) #6 Making connections between visual arts and other disciplines

Studio 3

At a Glance

Objectives

- Express ideas through photography.
- Demonstrate the use of shadows and textures through black-and-white photography.
- Evaluate original artworks by self and peers.

Materials

- disposable cameras with black and white film
- drawing paper, crayons or charcoal, poster board
- acid-free tape or glue
- Rubric 4 from **Unit-by-Unit Resources**

FA TEKS 4.2A Integrate a variety of ideas about self, life events, family, and community in original artworks

FA TEKS 4.2B Design original artworks

FA TEKS 4.2C Invent ways to produce artworks and to explore photographic imagery, using a variety of art media and materials

FA TEKS 4.4A Describe intent and form conclusions about personal artworks

❶ Introduce

Review still photography, value, and neutral colors. Have students draw on their experiences to describe photographs they have taken or seen.

Have students brainstorm subjects for their photographs. Explain to students that they can integrate ideas about themselves by choosing subjects with personal meaning. Ask:

- **What areas of the classroom do you find interesting?**
- **Which person would you like to photograph?**
- **How will your subject convey ideas about you?**

Quick Studio

Have students use a disposable or instant camera to photograph their desk, seating area, or locker.

Studio 3

Make a Photograph

Use black-and-white photography to express a mood or idea or just to show interesting shadows and textures.

1 Choose an area or a detail to photograph with black-and-white film.

2 Using crayons or charcoal, draw a plan for your black-and-white photograph.

Technique Tip

To take a photograph, frame the scene through the viewfinder. Keep the camera steady by holding your elbows against your body.

130

Meeting Individual Needs

Extend Take students for an excursion around the school. Have them use 35-millimeter cameras to take black and white photographs of interesting scenes. Then have groups create photomontages by cutting and gluing selected images onto poster board.

3 Look through the camera lens. Focus on the subject. Take the photograph.

4 After your photograph is developed, mount it on poster board. Give it a title.

Think Like an Artist

In what way is your photograph different from the drawing you planned? Explain.

131

Fine Arts Connection

Dance Show students photographs of dancers performing different styles of dance. Discuss why still photography is an effective medium for capturing images of dancers. Also have students discuss what moods and ideas are expressed in the photographs.

FA TEKS 4.5C Compare and contrast the ways ideas and emotions are depicted

② Create

Have students look at the pictures and follow the steps on pages 130–131. Then distribute materials.

- Have students describe how their subject expresses ideas about themselves.
- Tell students to choose a center of interest for their composition. Ask them where they want the viewer's attention to be focused.
- Instruct students on how to use the flash button to provide enough light to take the photographs.
- Use acid-free tape or glue to mount photographs so they are not damaged.

Technique Tip Tell students to think about the areas of light and shadow before taking the picture.

③ Close

Have students form conclusions about their photographs by answering the *Think Like an Artist* question. (Possible response: The angle of the picture changed the way the objects appeared.)

Ongoing Assessment

If . . . students have difficulty choosing an angle to shoot from,

then . . . have them look through the camera's viewfinder from several angles before taking the photograph.

See page 72 from **Unit-by-Unit Resources** for a rubric to assess this studio.

NVAS (K–4) #1 Understanding and applying media, techniques, and processes

NVAS (K–4) #3 Choosing and evaluating a range of subject matter, symbols, and ideas

NVAS (K–4) #5 Reflecting upon and assessing the characteristics and merits of their work and the work of others

Look and Compare

Look and Compare

At a Glance

Objectives

- Compare and contrast two artworks that show outdoor scenes.
- Respond to and make judgments about artworks.

Materials

- **Art Prints 13, 14, 15**
- **Fine Art Transparency**
- **Sketchbook Journal**

FA TEKS 4.3B Compare and contrast selected artworks from a variety of cultural settings

Explore

Display **Art Print 13,** *Yellow Still Life.* Help students recall this artwork by Gabriele Münter from page 118. As students look at the two artworks on pages 132 and 133, ask them to predict which one was also painted by Münter, and give reasons for their answer. (Possible response: *Cliff Portion of Bornholm;* The flattened shapes and vibrant colors are similar.)

Discuss

After students read pages 132 and 133, have them discuss the colors and moods of each artwork. Point out the bright hues that create a lighthearted mood in Münter's painting. Explain that the use of yellow and blue throughout the painting creates unity.

Then contrast the way O'Keeffe used neutral and muted colors to create a more serious mood. Mention that by incorporating red into the painting, O'Keeffe adds variety.

Outdoor Scenes

Gabriele Münter. *Cliff Portion of Bornholm,* 1919. Oil on canvas, 14 by 21 inches. Gabriele Münter and Johannes Eichner-Stiftung, Munich, Germany.

One way to discover artists' styles is to compare their artworks. Both paintings here show outdoor scenes. The credit lines offer some information. What other clues tell you they were painted by different artists?

132

Art Background

Cliff Portion of Bornholm Münter painted *Cliff Portion of Bornholm* while living in Copenhagen, Denmark, between 1918 and 1920. She used vibrant colors to portray the island beach, emphasizing the intensity of the sunlight and the vitality of the scene.

Grey Hills American painter Georgia O'Keeffe (1887–1986) based this painting and many others on desert hills in New Mexico. She compared the gray hills to "a mile of elephants . . . all about the same size with almost white sand at their feet."

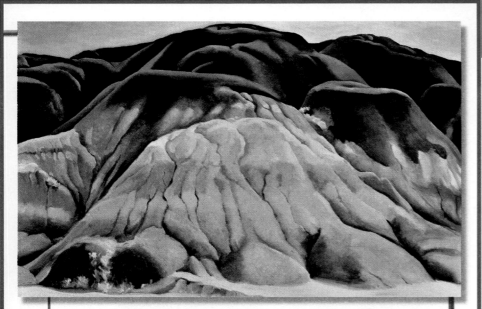

Georgia O'Keeffe. *Grey Hills,* 1941. Oil on canvas, 20 by 30 inches. Indianapolis Museum of Art, Gift of Mr. and Mrs. James W. Fesler.

Each artwork shows a mood. How would you describe the mood of the cliff scene on page 132? Now look at the desert hills shown above. They express a different mood. Notice the contrast of light and dark values on the hills. Does this contrast suggest a humorous or a serious mood? How does the painting make you feel?

Sketchbook Journal

Draw an outdoor scene. Use contrast to help show a mood. Your scene could include people, buildings, and natural objects. How will you express your own style?

133

Apply

Draw a chart like the one below on the chalkboard. Tell students that a chart is useful when comparing and contrasting two artworks.

Have students describe the colors in each painting. Fill in the chart as they point out how the colors create mood, unity, and variety. Possible responses are shown in blue.

Outdoor Scenes

	Cliff Portion of Bornholm	*Grey Hills*
Variety	bright and vibrant colors— violets, pinks, reds, greens	muted red
Unity	yellows and blues	neutral colors— black, white, gray, tan
Mood	lighthearted, playful	somber, serious

Close

Ask students what they have learned about painting outdoor scenes or landscapes. (Possible response: Colors can be used to create unity, variety, and mood.)

Sketchbook Journal Use a color wheel to help students choose color schemes that express different moods. Tell them to use one or two colors throughout the drawing to create unity.

 Reading Strategy

Relate to Personal Experience After students read the text and look at the paintings, have them discuss how the paintings relate to outdoor scenes they have seen. Ask if they have ever visited a beach like the one in *Cliff Portion of Bornholm.* Then ask if the colors and shapes in *Grey Hills* remind them of anything. (They may say elephants.)

TAKS Rdg. Obj. 1 Understand written texts
   ELA TEKS 4.14A Compare text events with readers' experiences

NVAS (K–4) #4 Understanding the visual arts in relation to history and cultures
NVAS (K–4) #5 Reflecting upon and assessing the characteristics and merits of their work and the work of others

Lesson 4

At a Glance

Objectives

• Identify and describe animation, motion pictures, and video art.

• Describe, analyze, interpret, and judge artworks.

Materials

• **Fine Art Transparency**
• animated cartoon clip

Vocabulary

animation, motion picture, video art

FA TEKS 4.3C Identify the roles of art in American society

FA TEKS 4.4B Interpret ideas and moods in original artworks, portfolios, and exhibitions by peers and others

① Introduce

Play a short cartoon, and have students discuss the types of movement shown. Explain that artists use this media to convey the perception of movement.

Explain that cartoons are a popular form of entertainment. Have students further discuss the role cartoons play in contemporary society. Invite students to talk about some of their favorite cartoons. Model examples by naming some of your own favorites. Discuss why artists might choose to use animation, motion pictures, or video art to express their ideas. Point out that moving pictures enable artists to show people, animals, and even inanimate objects in action.

Moving Pictures

Do you like to watch cartoons? They are a form of **animation,** a process of putting drawings or photographs together in a way that suggests motion. Each still picture appears in a frame. Each frame shows a picture that is slightly different from the one before it. Thousands of frames are joined to make a reel of film. A light shines through the moving film to display a **motion picture.**

Each motion picture frame is like a page in a flipbook.

134

🎨 Art Background

Art History Preceding the invention of moving film, animator Joseph Plateau invented the phenakistoscope, a spinning disk that created the illusion of movement when viewed in a mirror.

Art and Culture In 1965, Nam June Paik made a film using one of the first portable video recorders shipped to the United States. When it was shown at a club in New York City, the screening's announcement declared, "Someday artists will work with capacitors, resistors, and semi-conductors as they work today with brushes, violins, and junk." Paik proved this to be true as he eventually worked with all these materials.

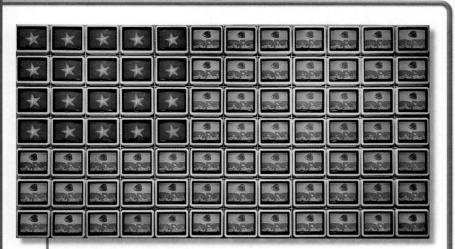

Nam June Paik. *Video Flag Z,* 1985. Television sets, videocassette players, videotapes, plexiglass modular cabinet, 74½ by 138¾ by 18 inches. Los Angeles County Museum of Art. Copyright © 1996 Museum Associates, Los Angeles County Museum of Art. Gift of the Art Museum Council.

Video art is another type of picture that moves. It uses television pictures as an art form. Artist Nam June Paik is a leader in this medium. He mixes video with other media, such as music and still photography.

What are some other ideas that you think would make interesting subjects for a work of video art?

Art Fact

The first television was demonstrated in London in 1926. People in the United States did not begin to buy television sets until almost twenty years later.

135

❷ Teach

Have students read pages 134 and 135 and look at the frames from the motion picture *Babe.* Ask:

- **What is the subject of these four frames?** (a pig) DESCRIBE
- **What has changed in each successive frame?** (The pig is gradually falling off the plank.) ANALYZE
- **What main idea does the artist express about Babe in this segment of film?** (Possible response: He is brave; He is clumsy.) INTERPRET
- **Would you like to be a part of a team that creates motion pictures, such as *Babe*? Why or why not?** (Responses will vary) JUDGE

Then have students discuss what they see in *Video Flag Z.*

Art Fact Have students work in small groups to research the history of television in the United States. Beginning with the 1940s, assign each group a decade to research.

❸ Close

Have each group present its findings to the class.

Assessment Have students take turns naming animated film, cartoon, or motion picture titles beginning with each letter of the alphabet, going around the class from A to Z.

NVAS (K–4) #2 Using knowledge of structures and functions
NVAS (K–4) #5 Reflecting upon and assessing the characteristics and merits of their work and the work of others
NVAS (K–4) #6 Making connections between visual arts and other disciplines

Studio 4

At a Glance

Objectives

- Express ideas by making moving pictures.
- Evaluate original artworks by self and peers.

Materials

- poster board and drawing paper
- rulers, safety scissors ⚠
- pencils with erasers, colored pencils or water-based markers
- tape, thumbtacks ⚠
- Rubric 4 from **Unit-by-Unit Resources**

FA TEKS 4.2B Design original artworks

FA TEKS 4.2C Invent ways to produce artworks and to explore photographic imagery, using a variety of art media and materials

FA TEKS 4.4A Describe intent and form conclusions about personal artworks

① Introduce

Remind students how to describe intentions about their artworks. Say: **Brainstorming ideas out loud can help you transform project ideas into a specific plan of action.**

Have students brainstorm subjects by asking:

- **What animal, person, or vehicle will you show in motion?**
- **What kind of activity will the subject be doing?**
- **What details will you include to show movement?**

Call on students to clearly define their intentions for the zoetrope.

Studio 4
Make a Zoetrope

Make your own moving pictures with this zoetrope.

1. Cut an 8-inch circle and a 24-by-3-inch strip from poster board.

2. Mark every 2 inches on the long edge of the strip. Cut a 1-inch slot on each mark.

Technique Tip

Show only slight changes from one picture to the next. Do not use too much detail in your drawings.

136

👥 Meeting Individual Needs

Reteach Have students work in small groups to make their zoetropes. Have each group brainstorm activities they can illustrate, such as doing sit-ups, climbing a ladder, or rolling down a hill. Have them think of a title for their animation.

Quick

Have students use index cards to draw a simple movement, with one drawing per card. Then have them flip cards to show movement.

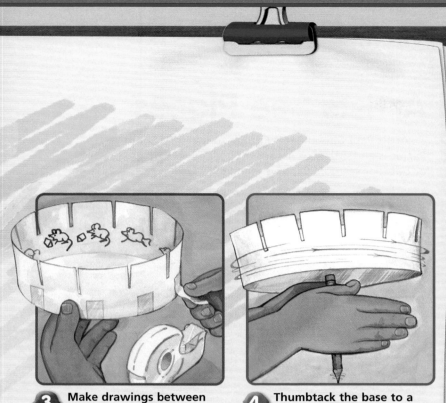

3 Make drawings between each slot. Attach the strip to the base.

4 Thumbtack the base to a pencil eraser. Spin the pencil between your hands.

Think Like an Artist

Does your zoetrope show the motion you hoped for? What changes would you make to improve it?

Fine Arts Connection

Music Show students a clip from the movie *Fantasia*. Explain that this film combines animation with classical music. Have students notice that the animation is seemingly intertwined with the rhythm of the music. Have students research the making of this movie and give a short report on their findings.

FA TEKS 4.5D Identify connections between music and the other fine arts

2 Create

Have students read pages 136–137. Then distribute materials.

- Provide students with safety compasses or precut cardboard circles to use to make their circles on the poster board.
- Have students draw a faint pencil line lengthwise across the strip of paper, one inch from the edge. Have them use this as a guide for cutting slots.
- Suggest that students work with a partner when taping their strip to the base.
- Suggest students stick the thumbtack through the base first, then into the eraser.

Technique Tip Have students make sketches of their animation sequences before drawing them on the strip.

3 Close

Have students answer the *Think Like an Artist* questions to form conclusions about their zoetropes. (Possible response: No; I need to redraw a few of the images to create less of a change.)

Ongoing Assessment

If . . . students have difficulty choosing a theme for their drawings,

then . . . suggest they feature a moving vehicle approaching the viewer.

See page 72 from **Unit-by-Unit Resources** for a rubric to assess this studio.

NVAS (K–4) #1 Understanding and applying media, techniques, and processes

NVAS (K–4) #3 Choosing and evaluating a range of subject matter, symbols, and ideas

NVAS (K–4) #5 Reflecting upon and assessing the characteristics and merits of their work and the work of others

Lesson 5

At a Glance

Objectives

- Identify and describe landscapes.
- Describe, analyze, interpret, and judge artworks.

Materials

- **Fine Art Transparency**
- examples of landscapes
- Sketchbook Journal
- travel advertisements

Vocabulary

landscapes, Expressionist, abstract

FA TEKS 4.4A Describe intent and form conclusions about personal artworks

FA TEKS 4.4B Interpret ideas and moods in original artworks, portfolios, and exhibitions by peers and others

① Introduce

Explain that landscapes are artworks that usually depict outdoor scenes of trees, lakes, mountains, and fields. Show the class some examples of landscapes from art books, magazines, or travel brochures.

Tell students that Expressionist artworks emphasize the artist's emotions, moods, and experiences with the subject. Say that abstract artworks are those that do not have easily recognizable subjects and accentuate a main feeling or idea.

Lesson 5

Artists See Places

Artist Paul Gauguin left Europe to live on a South Pacific island. Many of his artworks show **landscapes,** or outdoor scenes, from the island of Tahiti.

Paul Gauguin. *Tahitian Landscape,* 1891. Oil on canvas, 26¾ by 36½ inches. The Julius C. Eliel Memorial Fund. The Minneapolis Institute of Arts.

138

Art Background

About the Artist French painter, printmaker, and sculptor Paul Gauguin (1848–1903) worked in the merchant marines and as a stockbroker before devoting himself to painting. Disgusted by the corruption he saw in Parisian culture, he moved to Tahiti in the 1890s to pursue a romanticized "primitive" vision.

About the Artist Among other innovations, American Abstract Expressionist painter and printmaker Helen Frankenthaler (1928–) pioneered the stain technique of pouring very thin paint directly on unprimed canvas. The paint soaked the canvas and stained it with color.

Helen Frankenthaler.
Interior Landscape, 1964.
Acrylic on canvas, 104⅞
by 92⅞ inches. San
Francisco Museum of
Modern Art. Gift of the
Women's Board.

You can tell that Gauguin's colorful painting of Tahiti is a landscape even though it does not look just as it would in real life. The artwork is done in an **Expressionist** style. Painters of this movement do not try to paint realistically. Instead, they express their ideas or feelings through the use of bold colors and shapes. Frankenthaler's painting is also of the Expressionist style. Her artwork is abstract. The title of an abstract artwork may help you understand the artist's ideas.

What ideas or feelings do you think are expressed in these paintings? How do the

colors and styles of the paintings create or add to that message?

Sketchbook Journal

Have you ever dreamed about a place that didn't seem real? Draw an abstract landscape from memory.

139

Social Studies Have students work in small groups to research the geography of a region, including its climate, natural formations, and how people have modified the environment. Have them create a landscape based on their research. Ask them to give oral reports using visual materials they have created.

SS TEKS 4.9C Analyze consequences of human modification of the environment

 Notes

Have students draw a picture of a landscape that represents the country of their heritage. Then have them point to and name some features in their drawings, such as hills, mountains, or rivers.

ESL TEKS 4.5G Employ content area vocabulary words in context

➋ Teach

Have students read pages 138 and 139 and look at Gauguin's painting. Ask:

- **What colors do you see in the foreground and middle ground?** (Possible response: violet, yellow, orange, green, black) DESCRIBE
- **What kinds of colors did Gauguin mostly use?** (Possible response: warm colors, even the palm fronds show some orange) ANALYZE
- **What feelings or moods do these colors express?** (Possible response: happiness, warmth) INTERPRET
- **How would it feel to be in this landscape?** (Accept all responses.) JUDGE

Ask similar questions about Frankenthaler's painting.

Sketchbook Journal Help students form conclusions about their drawings. Say: **An abstract landscape will not have a recognizable subject, but will express a mood only.** Have students discuss the elements that make their drawing abstract and describe the mood their artwork conveys.

➌ Close

After students complete their drawings, have them give their artworks expressive titles.

Visual Culture Have students analyze how landscapes are portrayed in the travel industry to make places look inviting. Have them find travel advertisements in magazines or on the Internet and discuss the use of color schemes to express ideas and feelings.

NVAS (K–4) #2 Using knowledge of structures and functions

NVAS (K–4) #5 Reflecting upon and assessing the characteristics and merits of their work and the work of others

NVAS (K–4) #6 Making connections between visual arts and other disciplines

Studio 5

At a Glance

Objectives

- Express ideas by drawing a landscape.
- Evaluate original artworks by self and peers.

Materials

- 11" × 17" drawing paper
- colored pencils
- Sketchbook Journal
- Rubric 4 from **Unit-by-Unit Resources**

FA TEKS 4.2A Integrate a variety of ideas about self, life events, family, and community in original artworks

FA TEKS 4.2B Design original artworks

FA TEKS 4.2C Invent ways to produce artworks and to explore photographic imagery, using a variety of art media and materials

FA TEKS 4.4B Interpret ideas and moods in original artworks, portfolios, and exhibitions by peers and others

❶ Introduce

Have students draw on prior experience to describe landscapes of different places. Have them tell about the life events that brought them to the landscape and the effect it had on them. Model first with examples of your own. Have students brainstorm ideas. Ask:

- **Which outdoor scene has made an impact on you?**
- **What natural or human-made details did you see?**
- **Will you draw in a realistic or abstract manner?**

Quick Studio

Have students draw an imaginary landscape using crayons. Tell them to include one plant, an animal, and something blue.

Studio 5

Draw a Landscape

Recall a landscape that made an impression on you, or think of a real or imaginary scene you would like to visit.

1 Think of a realistic or abstract landscape. Draw it with a colored pencil.

2 Add details to show the season, time of day, and weather.

Technique Tip

Observe an outdoor scene to notice how sunlight affects colors and shadows at different times of the day.

🧍🧍🧍 Meeting Individual Needs

Inclusion Some students with special needs will benefit from encountering touchable sculpted landscapes in a variety of styles. Allow students to use textured materials, such as sandpaper, straw, and bubble wrap in their landscapes.

3 Think about the colors and details that will help you express your thoughts.

4 Color in your landscape, adding the effects of sunlight or moonlight.

Think Like an Artist

Ask a friend to try to identify the style and mood of your finished landscape.

141

 Fine Arts Connection

Theatre Invite a drama teacher or set designer to visit your class and ask him or her to explain how set designers create outdoor scenes for plays. Then have students work in small groups to design a set for an outdoor scene.

FA TEKS 4.3B Alter space to create suitable environments for play-making

❷ Create

Have students look at the pictures and read pages 140–141. Then distribute materials.

- Explain to students that choosing a landscape they have personally experienced will help them tell about a life event.
- Have students recall details, such as clouds, trees, rocks, plants, hills, rivers, animals, and snow, that they experienced.
- Review color schemes to help students determine which ones best express their mood.
- Tell students how to highlight areas using tints, and create shadows using shades.

Technique Tip Have students note differences in colors and values in their Sketchbook Journals. Then have them compare observations with other students.

❸ Close

Have students interpret mood in each other's drawings by completing the activity in the *Think Like an Artist* feature on page 141. (Responses will vary.)

Ongoing Assessment

If . . . students have difficulty adding the effects of sunlight and moonlight,

then . . . provide them with magazine images showing obvious day and night scenes.

See page 72 from **Unit-by-Unit Resources** for a rubric to assess this studio.

Lesson 6

At a Glance

Objectives

- Identify and describe technology in artworks.
- Describe, analyze, interpret, and judge artworks.

Materials

- **Fine Art Transparency**
- dictionary
- Sketchbook Journal

Vocabulary

technology, mixed-media, installation

FA TEKS 4.4B Interpret ideas and moods in original artworks, portfolios, and exhibitions by peers and others

➊ Introduce

Have a volunteer read the dictionary definition of *technology*. Then have students brainstorm ways they use technology. Ask which form of technology they would least like to give up and why.

Tell students that artists also use technology in artworks. Have them look at the two artworks featured in this lesson and read the credit lines. Then ask students to name other technological media that could be used in a mixed-media installation.

Lesson 6

Technology as Expression

Name some kinds of **technology,** or ways that you use tools and machines. Some artists rely on technology to help them express their thoughts and feelings. Thana Lauhakaikul, for example, used electronic media to create *Celebration*.

Thana Lauhakaikul. *Celebration*, 1983–1985. Mixed-media installation with projected light and sound, 3 by 16 by 25 feet. Photograph courtesy of Chronicle Books.

142

🎨 Art Background

About the Artist Thai American artist Thana Lauhakaikul (1941–) has created numerous installations in the United States and Thailand. A recipient of National Endownment for the Arts and Rockefeller Foundation awards, Lauhakaikul says, "I make art solely for love, balance, and to explore my true nature."

About the Artist Texas-based neon artist and light sculptor Ben Livingston (1958–) apprenticed under master neon glass benders in New Zealand and the United States. A recipient of National Endowment for the Arts and other awards, he has exhibited his sculptures widely throughout the United States.

Ben Livingston. *Neon Mural #1*, 1987. Neon, computer-animated story, 14 by 40 feet. © Ben Livingston. Photograph © Carrington Weems.

Celebration, a **mixed-media** installation, uses more than one medium, including sound and projected light. An **installation** is an artwork that is exhibited for a short time. Then the materials are taken apart and may be moved to another location for exhibition.

Ben Livingston uses technology as his paintbrush. He works with neon and other gases sealed in glass tubes that are bent to make different shapes. *Neon Mural #1* is fourteen feet wide. Where might it fit in your school?

Sketchbook Journal

Make some sketches of an installation you might like to assemble. Tell what media you will use. Indicate how large the installation will be. What senses will viewers use as they visit it?

143

② Teach

Have students read pages 142 and 143 and look at Lauhakaikul's artwork. Instruct them to read the credit line and ask:

- **How big is this installation?** ($3' \times 16' \times 25'$)
  DESCRIBE
- **What senses would you use to experience Lauhakaikul's artwork?** (sight and hearing)
  ANALYZE
- **Why do you think he gave the artwork the title** *Celebration*? (Possible response: It celebrates varieties of sound and sight.) **INTERPRET**
- **How do you think it would feel to move around this installation?** (Responses will vary.)
  JUDGE

Ask similar questions about Livingston's artwork.

Sketchbook Journal Tell students to also think about where they would like to install their installations and how that space would affect their plans.

③ Close

Have volunteers present their installation sketches.

Assessment Place students in small groups. Assign each group a different item of technology, such as a light bulb, blender, or radio. Have each group design an artwork using that medium.

NVAS (K–4) #2 Using knowledge of structures and functions

NVAS (K–4) #5 Reflecting upon and assessing the characteristics and merits of their work and the work of others

NVAS (K–4) #6 Making connections between visual arts and other disciplines

Curriculum Connection

Science Take students to a laboratory and have a science teacher demonstrate some of the technological tools scientists use to study the natural world. Tools used to collect and analyze information may include calculators, microscopes, hand lenses, thermometers, balances, and timing devices. Discuss how these devices can be used in artworks.

TAKS (Gr. 5) Sci. Obj. 1 Understand the nature of science
  Sci. TEKS 4.4A Collect and analyze information

 Notes

Have students point out examples of technology in the classroom. As they point to an object, name it and have students repeat after you.

ESL TEKS 4.5G Employ content area vocabulary words in context

Studio 6

Objectives

- Express ideas by creating an installation.
- Demonstrate the use of technology when creating an installation.
- Evaluate original artworks by self and peers.

Materials

- an assortment of found objects, such as sand, boxes, telephone wire, cellophane, maps, flashlights, strings of colored or white lights, cassette recorders, and other audio or video equipment
- Rubric 4 from **Unit-by-Unit Resources**

FA TEKS 4.2B Design original artworks

FA TEKS 4.2C Invent ways to produce artworks and to explore photographic imagery, using a variety of art media and materials

FA TEKS 4.4A Describe intent and form conclusions about personal artworks

① Introduce

Review technology and mixed-media installations. Remind students that an installation is intended to be taken apart when the exhibition is over. That is why unusual items can be incorporated.

Have students bring in items to include in the installation. Caution against bringing items with monetary or sentimental value.

Have students brainstorm ideas for their installation. Ask:

- **What senses do you want viewers to use when observing your artwork?**
- **Which found objects and art materials will you include?**
- **What forms of technology will you include?**

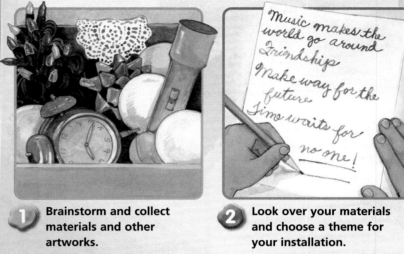

Studio 6

Create an Installation

Work with other artists—your classmates—to create an installation. Include technology as one of several media in your installation.

1 Brainstorm and collect materials and other artworks.

2 Look over your materials and choose a theme for your installation.

Technique Tip

Try to add some form of light or sound, such as popular music, that will draw in your viewers.

144

🏃 Meeting Individual Needs

Extend Have students create a permanent installation in the classroom. Designate an area of the room and use old bookshelves or other discarded furniture to set up the installation's framework.

If you can, include a computer as part of the installation to feature student artwork. Instruct students to choose a theme and, as the year progresses, have them add artworks and objects created by the class.

Quick Studio

Have students create a mixed-media installation using only discarded objects, such as recycled magazines, milk cartons, and old shoes.

③ Assemble the materials of your installation in an interesting way.

④ Present your installation. Encourage viewers to look closely and ask questions.

Think Like an Artist
What reaction did you hope your installation would produce? Were you successful? Explain.

 Fine Arts Connection

Music Have each group choose a song that goes with their theme and perform or record it as part of the installation. Students may sing the song or play instruments. If you have access to video recording equipment, have students make a music video as part of the installation.

FA TEKS 4.2A Sing or play an instrument

② Create

Have students look at the pictures and read pages 144–145. Place students in groups of three to five. Then distribute materials.

- Have students ask parents to donate items to use in the installation. Suggest that each student choose an item to include.
- Have students group like items together and look for a unifying idea.
- Use tape or string to assemble items, but remind students that the installation will need to be disassembled.
- Instruct students to stand by their artwork to answer questions.

Technique Tip Remind students that they can also create sounds by using their voices, by clapping, or by using musical instruments.

③ Close

Have students reflect on their installations by answering the *Think Like an Artist* questions. (Possible response: Surprise; Yes, people seemed surprised by our choice of materials.)

Ongoing Assessment

If . . . students have difficulty assembling their installation,

then . . . have them place heavier, larger objects near the bottom, and use lighter, smaller objects toward the top.

See page 72 from **Unit-by-Unit Resources** for a rubric to assess this studio.

NVAS (K–4) #1 Understanding and applying media, techniques, and processes

NVAS (K–4) #3 Choosing and evaluating a range of subject matter, symbols, and ideas

NVAS (K–4) #5 Reflecting upon and assessing the characteristics and merits of their work and the work of others

At a Glance

Objectives

- Read about a career in art.
- Identify the use of art in everyday life.
- Relate art to personal experiences.

Materials

- **Fine Art Transparency**
- Newspaper or magazine photograph (optional)

FA TEKS 4.3C Identify the roles of art in American society
FA TEKS 4.4B Interpret ideas and moods in original artworks, portfolios, and exhibitions by peers and others

Explore

Display a newspaper or magazine photograph showing a dramatic event. Explain that a photojournalist took the photograph to accompany an article about the event.

Have students guess the details of the event by looking at the photograph. Then read the article aloud.

Discuss

Guide students to set a purpose for reading. Then have them read pages 146–147. Ask:

- **What information does the photograph on page 147 convey?** (There is a strong storm.)
- **What mood or feeling does this photograph express?** (Possible response: danger, excitement)
- **What is the role of photojournalism in our country's society?** (Possible response: to convey visual information about a news event)
- **What kinds of technology does Barrera use?** (a laptop computer, a cellular telephone, camera gear)

Photojournalism

Photojournalist Ralph Barrera is always in search of an interesting subject to photograph.

Photojournalist Ralph Barrera might start his day in the newspaper office picking up his assignment. Then he heads out in search of a great shot for a news story. Later, he might work with a photo editor.

Barrera went to college to study engineering. Soon, though, he followed his heart and switched to journalism.

Technology is an important part of Barrera's job. Sometimes he travels with only a laptop computer, camera gear, and a cellular telephone. He uses the laptop and cellular telephone to transmit photographs back to the office. That way the pictures can appear in the newspaper the next day.

What makes a good photograph? Barrera believes it's all about the subject.

 Career Research

Have students work in small groups to research the skills necessary to become a photojournalist. Invite students to make a list of these skills and use them to write a job description. They may wish to read about other successful photojournalists to gain insight into the personal skills and strengths that are also necessary for the job.

"... Pictures that make you laugh or cry, or keep your interest, ... or remind you of someone" are the best. Barrera shows passion about being a photojournalist. "People have been taking pictures for over a hundred years," he says. "I'm just glad I get to take some tomorrow."

Ralph Barrera. *Central Texas Tornado,* 1997. Digital photograph.
© Austin American-Statesman, 1997.

147

Reading Strategy

Set a Purpose for Reading Before students read the text, have them set a purpose for reading. Discuss other *Artists at Work* features they have read and ask: **What do these features tell you?** (They tell about different careers in art.)

Tell them that they will be learning about photojournalism. Guide them to set a purpose, such as finding out what photojournalists do.

TAKS Rdg. Obj. 1 Understand written texts
ELA TEKS 4.10B Establish and adjust purposes for reading

Apply

Have students share their purpose for reading, such as understanding what photojournalists do. Tell them to make a list of observations based on the reading, such as the one below.

What Photojournalists Do

- take photographs for newspapers
- work with photo editors
- search for great shots for a news story
- use technology such as cellular phones and laptop computers
- transmit photographs using technology
- take photographs that hold people's interest

Close

Using photographs from newspapers and news magazines, have students create a classroom exhibition. Have students interpret the ideas and moods of the exhibition. First explain that they can interpret ideas by describing what the pictures make them think about. Have them tell whether the images offer new ideas about familiar subjects. They can interpret mood by describing facial expressions in subjects or how the photographs make them feel.

NVAS (K–4) #5 Reflecting upon and assessing the characteristics and merits of their work and the work of others

Portfolio Project

Portfolio Project

At a Glance

Objectives

- Develop and organize ideas from the environment.
- Demonstrate knowledge about still life, collage, abstract style, unity, and variety
- Evaluate original artworks by self and peers.

Materials

- drawing paper and colored pencils or crayons
- heavy paper stock and collage materials, such as colored construction paper, wallpaper, wrapping paper, tissue paper, old magazines, and fabric scraps
- safety scissors , glue
- Rubric 4 from **Unit-by-Unit Resources**

FA TEKS 4.2B Design original artworks

FA TEKS 4.2C Invent ways to produce artworks and to explore photographic imagery, using a variety of art media and materials

FA TEKS 4.4B Interpret ideas and moods in original artworks, portfolios, and exhibitions by peers and others

Make Abstract Art

Many artists rework themes and subjects to explore different styles. Now it is your turn to change a realistic still life into an abstract artwork.

1 Start by drawing a realistic still life of objects you collect.

2 On heavy paper, draw the still life in a new way. Use geometric forms in an abstract design.

3 Cut materials for your collage. Match the shapes in your abstract drawing.

4 Glue materials in place to finish your collage.

148

Plan

Direct students to read page 148. Ask:

- **What classroom or household objects will you use in your still life?**
- **What shapes, forms, and colors will you use to make an abstract design?**
- **What theme or message will you express?**

Quick Project

Set up a still life of one or two objects. Instruct students to draw the still life from three different perspectives.

Meeting Individual Needs

Reteach Have students cover their realistic drawing with tissue paper. Then ask them to draw over their image re-creating only the main shapes. Have students use the tissue paper drawing as a guide when they create their abstract artwork.

Extend Have students use a variety of found objects in their collage. Encourage them to use these objects to make patterns and create visual rhythm.

Brittany, Age 9. *Glass Fruit.* Collage.

Langley, Age 9. *Raccoon.* Collage.

How do these artworks by other fourth-graders show unity and variety?

Share Your Art

1. What were the subject and theme of your first drawing?

2. Describe the decisions you made as you turned the realistic still life into an abstract artwork. What elements did you use to show unity and variety?

149

Gallery Options

Restaurant Gallery Ask a local restaurant or café if they will display student artwork. Help students mount or mat their collages, sign them, and write a title card stating their first name, the artwork's title, their age, and the media they used.

Then model how to interpret ideas in the class exhibition. Say: **Many of these artworks include titles that hint at their subjects, but the subjects are shown in unfamiliar ways. The exhibition invites us to look at objects in our surroundings with a fresh perspective.** Call on students to interpret ideas in the exhibition and explain their responses.

Create

Gather the materials and guide students through the steps on page 148.

• You may want to set up a still life subject using three or four classroom objects.
• Have students add, take away, or change elements to make their designs more abstract.
• Encourage students to use a variety of textures and patterns.
• Tell students to cut out shapes from their drawing and glue them onto the paper to make an abstract collage.

Close

Point out the student portfolio art on page 149 and model how to interpret mood in artworks. Say: **The use of geometric shapes and warm colors in *Glass Fruit* give the collage an energetic mood.** Ask:

• **What feelings or moods are expressed in *Raccoon*? Explain.** (Possible response: *Raccoon* is serene because its curved lines create a sense of unity.)
• **How are these artworks similar to your own? How are they different?** (Responses will vary.)

Have students form conclusions about their own artwork by answering the *Share Your Art* questions on page 149. (Responses will vary.)

See page 72 from **Unit-by-Unit Resources** for a rubric to assess this project.

NVAS (K–4) #1 Understanding and applying media, techniques, and processes
NVAS (K–4) #3 Choosing and evaluating a range of subject matter, symbols, and ideas
NVAS (K–4) #5 Reflecting upon and assessing the characteristics and merits of their work and the work of others

At a Glance

Objectives

- Relate art terms to the environment.
- Identify theme, unity, variety, and value in artworks.
- Describe, analyze, interpret, and judge artworks.

Materials

- Art Print 16
- Fine Art Transparency

FA TEKS 4.1B Choose appropriate vocabulary to discuss the use of art elements such as color, texture, form, line, space, and value and art principles such as emphasis, pattern, rhythm, balance, proportion, and unity

FA TEKS 4.4A Describe intent and form conclusions about personal artworks

FA TEKS 4.4B Interpret ideas and moods in original artworks, portfolios, and exhibitions by peers and others

Think About Art

Possible responses:

still life (Point to fruit and vegetables.)
unity (Point to trees.)
photography (Point to both.)
variety (Point to fruit and vegetables.)
theme (Point to both.)
landscape (Point to trees.)

Write About Art

Before students write, ask:

- **How did the colors you used express unity or variety?** (Response will vary.)
- **What did you like or dislike about using this medium?** (Responses will vary.)

Unit Review

Think About Art

Read the art words. Then use the photographs to find an example for each word.

still life	photography	theme
unity	variety	landscape

Write About Art

You used a variety of media for the artworks in this unit. Name one artwork and write about the process you used to make something.

Talk About Art

- Look through your portfolio.
- Choose an artwork that is one of your best.
- Tell a friend what you tried to show in it.
- Describe unity and variety as they appear in your artwork.

150

 Assessment Options

Options for assessing student appear in the **Unit-by-Unit Resources.**

- Use the **Vocabulary Worksheets** on pages 65–68 for an informal assessment of Unit 4 vocabulary.

- Use the **Unit 4 Test** on pages 73–76 to assess students' mastery of unit vocabulary and concepts.

Put It All Together

1. Describe the subject and details of this photograph.

2. How do value and contrast help you see that this photograph was taken on a rainy day?

3. The photograph was taken during the Great Depression in a camp of migrant workers. What do you think the photographer was trying to say?

4. Where might you hang this artwork? Explain.

151

Art Background

About the Artist During the Great Depression, American photographer Dorothea Lange (1895–1965) photographed many portraits of people suffering from impoverishment.

In 1935, the Federal Resettlement Administration commissioned her to photograph migrant workers in order to draw public attention to their plight. Lange's most famous portrait, *Migrant Mother, Nipomo, California,* is considered an iconic image of the era and now hangs in the Library of Congress. Her detached but compassionate style has influenced generations of photographers.

Talk About Art

Prompt students to use words such as *unity, variety, theme,* and *value* to describe their artwork. Then have them interpret the moods and ideas in each other's portfolios. Explain that to interpret moods in a portfolio they must ask themselves how the total effect of the combined artworks make them feel. To interpret ideas, they must ask what the artworks make them think about and whether they offer a new perspective on a familiar subject.

Put It All Together

Use the questions on page 151 to evaluate the artwork. Possible responses follow.

1. A mother and three children. The mother looks worried and the two older children are hiding their faces. DESCRIBE
2. The lightest values in the photograph are on the mother's face and fingers. The rest of the photograph is much darker in value. ANALYZE
3. Lange's photograph expresses the desperate situation of the migrant family. The mood is somber, anxious, and sad. INTERPRET
4. Possible response: In a public place, so people could see it and respond. JUDGE

Display samples from Lange's portfolio from the Library of Congress (www.loc.gov/exhibits) or other source. Tell students to interpret both the moods and ideas in Lange's portfolio.

NVAS (K–4) #1 Understanding and applying media, techniques, and processes
NVAS (K–4) #2 Using knowledge of structures and functions
NVAS (K–4) #5 Reflecting upon and assessing the characteristics and merits of their work and the work of others

Unit 5 Overview

People have been creating art for centuries. Some methods for creating art are very old, such as weaving. Others, such as video art, are relatively new. In this unit, students will explore old and new art and its methods.

	Unit Opener, p. 152	Lesson 1, p. 154 Glass Studio 1, p. 156 Build a Model	Lesson 2, p. 158 Weaving Studio 2, p. 160 Make a Circle Weaving	Lesson 3, p. 162 Cartoons Studio 3, p. 164 Draw a Cartoon	Look and Compare, p. 166 Passengers
Artworks	**Red Grooms.** (Detail) *Ruckus Rodeo*, 1975–1976.	**Artist unknown,** Roman Empire (probably Italy). *Ribbon Glass Cup,* ca. first century A.D.	**Artist unknown,** Navajo culture. *Eye-dazzler Blanket,* 1975.	**PEANUTS,** June 24, 2003. PEANUTS reprinted by permission of United Feature Syndicate, Inc.	**Red Grooms.** *Subway (detail from Ruckus Manhattan),* 1976. **Frida Kahlo.** *The Bus,* 1929.
Vocabulary		glass art, tradition	eye-dazzler blanket, loom, warp, weft	cartoon	
Materials	• **Art Print 17** • **Fine Art Transparency** • Social Studies textbook	• **Fine Art Transparency** • objects made of glass, such as a light bulb or jar ⚠ • water-based markers • Sketchbook Journal • polystyrene foam balls, disposable drinking cups, plastic water bottles, cardboard tubes, and egg cartons • colored tissue paper, pipe cleaners ⚠, safety scissors ⚠, tape, glue, water-based markers	• **Fine Art Transparency** • woven item, such as a blanket or hat • Sketchbook Journal • 8" × 10" blue construction paper • scissors ⚠, glue, strips of colored construction paper, wallpaper, or wrapping paper, yarn, feathers, ribbons • tagboard circles, rulers and pencils (optional)	• **Fine Art Transparency** • newspaper comic strips • Sketchbook Journal • drawing paper, thin water-based markers • rulers (optional)	• **Art Prints 17, 18, 19** • **Fine Art Transparency** • Sketchbook Journal
Connections	**Home Connection** traditional artworks at home **Bookshelf** *Songs from the Loom: A Navajo Girl Learns to Weave* by Monty Roessel, Lerner Publications Company, 1995	**Curriculum Connection** Science: glass in nature **ESL Notes** **Fine Arts Connection** Music: glass harmonica **Meeting Individual Needs** Extend	**Curriculum Connection** Social Studies: Navajo weaving **ESL Notes** **Fine Arts Connection** Music: weaving a melody **Meeting Individual Needs** Reteach, Extend	**Technology** Search the web **ESL Notes** **Fine Arts Connection** Theatre: cartoons and plays **Meeting Individual Needs** Inclusion	**Reading Strategy** Identify details
Assessment Opportunities		Visual Culture Rubric 5 from **Unit-by-Unit Resources** Ongoing Assessment	Informal Assessment Rubric 5 from **Unit-by-Unit Resources** Ongoing Assessment	Informal Assessment Rubric 5 from **Unit-by-Unit Resources** Ongoing Assessment	

Lesson 4, p. 168 **Industrial Design** Studio 4, p. 170 **Design with Wire**	Lesson 5 p. 172 **Portraits and Proportion** Studio 5, p. 174 **Draw a Self-Portrait**	Lesson 6, p. 176 **The Human Form** Studio 6, p. 178 **Show Proportion**	Artist at Work, p. 180 **Stage Designs**	Portfolio Project, p. 182 **Design a Cartoon Car**	Unit Review, p. 184
 Chava Hernandez. *Lowrider Bike,* ca. 1994.	 **Andy Warhol.** *Marilyn,* 1964.	 **Thomas Gainsborough.** *Jonathan Buttall: The Blue Boy,* ca. 1770.	 Stage model by **José González.**		 **Red Grooms.** *Dali Salad,* 1980–1981.
industrial design	portraits, self-portrait, proportions	pose, model			
• **Fine Art Transparency** • item of industrial design, such as a watch or thermos • Sketchbook Journal • pencil and drawing paper • colored narrow gauge wire ⚠, wire snips ⚠ • safety scissors ⚠ • wooden blocks (optional)	• **Fine Art Transparency** • pencil and paper • Sketchbook Journal • pencils, drawing paper, small mirrors ⚠	• **Fine Art Transparency** • measuring tape • butcher paper • measuring tape, drawing paper, pencils, tempera paints, and paintbrushes • rulers (optional)	stage prop (optional)	• heavy drawing paper or construction paper • pencil, water-based markers, glue • decorating materials, such as pipe cleaners, nuts, bolts, and other mechanical parts ⚠	• **Art Print 20** • **Fine Art Transparency**
Curriculum Connection Social Studies: functional objects **ESL Notes** **Fine Arts Connection** Music: compare and contrast designs **Meeting Individual Needs** Reteach, Extend	**Curriculum Connection** Math: measure proportions **ESL Notes** **Fine Arts Connection** Theatre: character portraits **Meeting Individual Needs** Extend	**Curriculum Connection** Physical Education/Health: observe movement **ESL Notes** **Fine Arts Connection** Dance: portrait of a dancer **Meeting Individual Needs** Inclusion	**Career Research** Stage designers **Reading Strategy** Summarize and paraphrase information	**Gallery Options** Community display **Meeting Individual Needs** Extend	
Informal Assessment Rubric 5 from **Unit-by-Unit Resources** Ongoing Assessment	Visual Culture Rubric 5 from **Unit-by-Unit Resources** Ongoing Assessment	Informal Assessment Rubric 5 from **Unit-by-Unit Resources** Ongoing Assessment		Rubric 5 from **Unit-by-Unit Resources**	**Unit-by-Unit Resources** Vocabulary Worksheets, pp. 83–86 Unit 5 Test, pp. 91–94

Unit 5

At a Glance

Objectives

- Identify traditional and new ways of creating artworks.
- Relate art to personal experiences.
- Respond to and make judgments about artworks.

Materials

- **Art Print 17**
- **Fine Art Transparency**
- Social Studies textbook

FA TEKS 4.1A Communicate ideas about self, family, school, and community, using sensory knowledge and life experiences

FA TEKS 4.4B Interpret ideas and moods in original artworks, portfolios, and exhibitions by peers and others

Introduce the Unit

Ask students to look through their Social Studies books to find examples of artworks from the past. Have them describe the artworks and identify the media using appropriate language to discuss the elements or art and principles of design. Then discuss artistic traditions, such as weaving, glass art, and pottery.

Next ask a volunteer to read the title of this unit. Ask: **What qualities make an artwork seem old or new?** (Responses will vary.)

As you introduce the unit, have students look through it and say which artworks seem older and which seem more recent.

Red Grooms. (Detail) *Ruckus Rodeo*, 1975–1976. Sculpture wire, celastic, acrylic, and burlap, 174 by 606 by 294 inches. Collection of the Modern Art Museum of Fort Worth, Fort Worth, TX.

152

Art Background

Ruckus Rodeo This mammoth installation, which takes up 1,237 square feet and consists of painted surfaces and sculptured figures, captures the Fort Worth rodeo. The "sculpto-pictorama" includes a rodeo queen, a bucking bronco, rodeo clowns, and an enormous yellow bull named Butter.

Home Connection

Have students find an example of traditional artwork in their homes, such as a quilt, ceramics, or woodwork. Ask them to use their senses to examine the artwork. Then have them write about its history including what it looks and feels like, who made it, and why it is important to their family.

Art, Old and New

Clothing styles and car designs change from year to year. In fact, many parts of a culture change over time. Art styles, media, and techniques may change too, even as artists borrow from the past. How do you think this large artwork by Red Grooms draws on the past?

Meet the Artist

Artist Red Grooms is known for what he calls his "sculpto-pictoramas." He mixes media in different ways. His scenes are often cartoonlike.

Charles Rogers Grooms was born in Nashville, Tennessee. His nickname, Red, reflects the color of his hair. Look for another artwork by Grooms later in this unit.

Red Grooms. *Self-Portrait as a Bus Driver,* 1998.

153

Bookshelf

Songs from the Loom:
A Navajo Girl Learns to Weave
by Monty Roessel
Lerner Publications Company, 1995

In this photo-essay, Roessel describes how his mother taught his ten-year-old daughter the art of weaving, from shearing the sheep to working a loom. Students will enjoy the traditional stories about weaving, as well as the contemporary photographs, maps, and insights.

Discuss Unit Concepts

Have students read page 152 and look at the artwork. Invite them to interpret the ideas and mood portrayed in *Ruckus Rodeo.* Ask: **What mood do you think the artist was trying to convey?** (a playful, lively, humorous mood)

Discuss how these details recall the Texas tradition of the rodeo, a competition involving lassoing, wrangling, and roping cows. Engage students in a discussion about events that are important in your community. Model how to communicate ideas by sharing an experience you have had at a community event, such as an annual festival. Have students share their own experiences of a community event.

Art Prints 17–20 and **Transparencies** are available for fine art in the unit.

Meet the Artist

Red Grooms (1937–) Described as "a social historian with a hot glue gun," American artist Red Grooms uses a complex mix of media and techniques to produce his life-sized painted environments and portraits.

Drawing on the theatre, comic books, folk art, and traditional art styles, Grooms' highly idiosyncratic, humorous artworks include carnivalesque urban panoramas, three-dimensional depictions of cultural icons, such as Elvis Presley and Gertrude Stein, and small, intimate sketches of family and friends.

NVAS (K–4) #5 Reflecting upon and assessing the characteristics and merits of their work and the work of others

Lesson 1

Lesson 1

At a Glance

Objectives

- Identify and describe the art of glassmaking.
- Describe, analyze, interpret, and judge artworks.

Materials

- **Fine Art Transparency**
- objects made of glass, such as a light bulb or jar ⚠
- water-based markers
- Sketchbook Journal

Vocabulary

glass art, tradition

FA TEKS 4.1A Communicate ideas about self, family, school, and community, using sensory knowledge and life experiences

FA TEKS 4.3C Identify the roles of art in American society

FA TEKS 4.4B Interpret ideas and moods in original artworks, portfolios, and exhibitions by peers and others

① Introduce

Display objects made of glass, such as a light bulb, a paperweight, and a jelly jar. Ask students to identify the medium. Then have students identify other glass objects they use at home. Ask them to use their senses to describe a favorite glass object (such as what it looks like, what it may sound like, and how it feels), and tell how the family uses the object. Model first with an object of your own.

Have students describe the texture and other properties of glass. (Possible responses: hard, shiny, transparent, and reflective) Tell students that glass art has a tradition lasting thousands of years.

Glass

Some art forms are brand new. Glassmaking, however, has been around for thousands of years. You may think of glass as a material for useful objects, such as windows, light bulbs, or drinking glasses. Glass is also a medium for decorative objects.

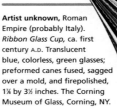

Artist unknown, Roman Empire (probably Italy). *Ribbon Glass Cup,* ca. first century A.D. Translucent blue, colorless, green glasses; preformed canes fused, sagged over a mold, and firepolished, 1⅞ by 3½ inches. The Corning Museum of Glass, Corning, NY.

What elements of art show rhythm in this cup?

154

🎨 Art Background

Art History Glass art dates back to about 2500 B.C. in the area of Mesopotamia and later Egypt, where glass was used in luxury items, such as beads and perfume bottles. From there, glassmaking traveled to Phoenicia, Cyprus, Greece, and the Italian peninsula. The Romans used glass to make many objects, including mosaics, lamps, and mirrors.

Fiesta Tower Rising to almost twenty-seven feet, *Fiesta Tower* weighs about forty-five hundred pounds and took four people four days to assemble. The artwork is permanently installed in the atrium of the San Antonio Public Library.

Glass art uses glass as a medium for decorative or functional artworks. Dale Chihuly is a glass artist whose studio is in Seattle, Washington. He studied glassblowing in Venice, Italy, where the art form has a long **tradition.** The artwork shown here contains nine hundred eighty separate parts of blown glass. The colors were inspired by confetti Chihuly saw in a spring fiesta, or party.

To make glass art, Chihuly first designs the artwork. Then he, or sometimes his team, blows the hot glass and assembles the parts. Compare Chihuly's glass art with the Roman cup. Notice the rhythm shown in each artwork. What mood does each one convey?

Dale Chihuly. *San Antonio Public Library Fiesta Tower,* 2003. Hand-blown glass over steel armature, approximately 21 by 10 feet. San Antonio, TX.

Sketchbook Journal

Use markers to make a sketch of a glass sculpture you might create. Show rhythm. Where would you display your sculpture?

155

Curriculum Connection

Science Tell students that sometimes glass is formed in nature. For example, some volcanoes produce the mineral obsidian, a black glass that Native Americans in the Southwest have used to make carvings and tools. Take the class to a science museum to see examples of natural glass and minerals, or show them examples from a book.

TAKS (Gr. 5) Sci Obj. 4 Understand earth science
Sci TEKS 4.8A Identify characteristics of nonliving objects

 **Notes**

Give students a variety of glass objects. Have them describe their tactile and visual texture using one-word descriptors, such as *shiny, smooth,* or *hard.*

ESL TEKS 4.5G Employ content area vocabulary words in context

---

② Teach

Have students read pages 154–155 and look at the *Ribbon Glass Cup.* Ask:

- **What colors and types of lines do you see?** (Possible responses: blue, yellow, red, black, green, white; curved, diagonal) DESCRIBE
- **How do the lines and colors create visual rhythm?** (repeated curved lines on the sides and repeated blue and white lines along the rim) ANALYZE
- **What mood do you think this artwork expresses?** (Possible response: festive) INTERPRET
- **How would you use this artwork?** (Possible response: to hold drinks) JUDGE

Then ask similar questions about Chihuly's artwork.

Sketchbook Journal Encourage students to use repeated colors, lines, and shapes to create pattern and rhythm.

③ Close

After students complete their sketches, have them give their drawing a title.

Visual Culture Have students identify functional objects made from glass, such as eyeglasses, windows, mirrors, display cases, and bottles. Invite them to discuss why glass is a useful medium in these examples.

NVAS (K–4) #4 Understanding the visual arts in relation to history and cultures

NVAS (K–4) #5 Reflecting upon and assessing the characteristics and merits of their work and the work of others

NVAS (K–4) #6 Making connections between visual arts and other disciplines

Studio 1

At a Glance

Objectives

- Express ideas by creating a model for a glass sculpture.
- Evaluate original artworks by self and peers.

Materials

- polystyrene foam balls, disposable drinking cups, plastic water bottles, cardboard tubes, and egg cartons
- colored tissue paper, pipe cleaners ⚠, safety scissors ⚠, tape, glue, water-based markers
- Rubric 5 from **Unit-by-Unit Resources**

FA TEKS 4.2B Design original artworks

FA TEKS 4.2C Invent ways to produce artworks and to explore photographic imagery, using a variety of art media and materials

FA TEKS 4.4A Describe intent and form conclusions about personal artworks

① Introduce

Explain to students that having a clear plan for an artwork can help glass artists convey their ideas. Model how to describe intentions. Say: **In my next artwork, I want to show geometric forms with radial balance. Designing a model will help me plan for a larger sculpture.** Have students describe their intentions. Ask:

- **What forms will you include in your model?**
- **What textures and colors will you use? Think about examples you may have seen in your home.**
- **How will you show variety?**

Studio 1
Build a Model

Sculptors often make models before building a sculpture. Make a model for a glass artwork you might want to build.

1 Build an armature of three-dimensional objects.

2 Cover the armature with torn strips of tissue paper.

Technique Tip

To create spiral forms, wrap pipe cleaners around a pen or pencil.

156

🚶🚶 Meeting Individual Needs

Extend Have students demonstrate rhythm by applying the tissue paper to their models in a regular color pattern. Suggest they also use repetition in their choice and placement of forms.

Quick Studio

Display a glass bottle or figurine and have students draw it from several points of view using crayons or markers.

3 Use colored markers to add designs.

4 Use pipe cleaners to add interesting lines and forms.

Think Like an Artist

Look at your model from different viewpoints. How does each view change your thinking about the model?

 Fine Arts Connection

Music Set up several glasses filled with varying amounts of water. Tap each glass lightly with a metal spoon and ask students to listen for a difference in the sounds generated. Explain that in this activity sound waves are produced, and the amount of water in the glass changes the pitch of the sound.

Tell students that Benjamin Franklin used this concept to create an instrument called the "Armonica" or the "Glass Harmonica." Have students research this strange instrument and share their findings with the class.

FA TEKS 4.1B Use standard terminology in explaining music

---

② Create

Have students look at the pictures and read the directions on pages 156–157. Then distribute materials.

- Help students find ways to cut and bend objects so that they can be glued or taped together.
- Remind students to use only a small amount of glue when adding paper to their models.
- Encourage students to create patterns and rhythm as they add to their design.
- In Step 4, review types of lines and forms if necessary.

Technique Tip Show students how to twist pipe cleaners together to create forms.

③ Close

Have students form conclusions about their artwork by answering the *Think Like an Artist* question on page 157. (Possible response: It makes you notice angles and shapes you would not normally see.)

Ongoing Assessment

If . . . students have difficulty gluing tissue paper to their model,

then . . . have them apply glue using a small paintbrush.

See page 90 from **Unit-by-Unit Resources** for a rubric to assess this studio.

NVAS (K–4) **#1** Understanding and applying media, techniques, and processes

NVAS (K–4) **#3** Choosing and evaluating a range of subject matter, symbols, and ideas

NVAS (K–4) **#5** Reflecting upon and assessing the characteristics and merits of their work and the work of others

Lesson 2

At a Glance

Objectives

- Identify and describe artworks made by weaving.
- Describe, analyze, interpret, and judge artworks.

Materials

- **Fine Art Transparency**
- woven item, such as a blanket or hat
- Sketchbook Journal

Vocabulary

eye-dazzler blanket, loom, warp, weft

FA TEKS 4.1B Choose appropriate vocabulary to discuss the use of art elements such as color, texture, form, line, space, and value and art principles such as emphasis, pattern, rhythm, balance, proportion, and unity.

FA TEKS 4.3C Identify the roles of art in American society

FA TEKS 4.4A Describe intent and form conclusions about personal artworks

①Introduce

Bring in a woven blanket, hat, or cloth and show it to students. Have them feel the object's texture and describe its patterns. Inform students that weaving plays an important role in our society. Ask students to identify items made by weaving that our society uses every day. (Some examples may be dishcloths, potholders, and clothing.) Then ask students to tell how each item is used.

Discuss how traditional weavers use a loom with a warp and weft to make cloth for items such as the eye-dazzler blanket. Mention that technology now allows some artists to use a computer to create designs for their weaving.

Lesson 2

Weaving

Weaving is an ancient art. Navajo women in the southwestern United States have woven beautiful, useful blankets for hundreds of years. This **eye-dazzler blanket** has a colorful design made with dyed wool. The earliest Navajo weavers used mostly undyed wool in natural tones.

Artist unknown, Navajo culture. *Eye-dazzler Blanket,* 1975. Cotton warp, 40¼ by 60¾ inches. School of American Research, Santa Fe, NM. Catalog no. SAR1989-7-352.

 **Art Background**

Art History The Navajo weaving tradition dates back to the 1600s. However, the introduction of aniline dyes in the 1800s dramatically increased the range of colors available for dying wool. These new colors led to the creation of eye-dazzler designs, which originated in the 1860s.

These designs typically featured a central pattern of concentric diamonds with serrated edges on a background of zigzag stripes.

ESL Notes

Have students work a partner to describe the shapes, colors, and textures in a weaving you display.

ESL TEKS 4.31F Describe how color, shape, and line influence the message

In what ways do Navajo artists design and create their weavings?

Traditional weavers use a **loom,** a tool or frame that holds fibers as a weaver works with them. The fibers that stretch vertically on the loom, above, are called the **warp.** The fibers woven from side to side, under and over the warp, are the **weft.**

Today, some weavers plan their designs on computer. They adjust line and color with the help of software. In this way, the artists create one artwork with two media.

Sketchbook Journal

Use colored pencils to draw a design for an eye-dazzler weaving. You may wish to draw a second design on a computer. How would your design show traditional patterns?

159

Curriculum Connection

Social Studies Tell students that Navajo weaving flourished during the Classic period from 1800–1863, which ended with the imprisonment of the Navajo people near Fort Sumner from 1863–1868. Have students work in groups to research Navajo history during this period and the internment's impact on weaving.

SS TEKS 4.4A Describe the impact of the Civil War and Reconstruction on Texas

② Teach

Have students read pages 158–159 and look at the artwork. Ask:

• **What shapes, lines, and colors do you see?** (Possible response: diamond shapes, zigzag lines, and red, black, white, and orange colors) **DESCRIBE**

• **How did the artist use pattern and rhythm?** (through the repetition of colors, lines, and shapes) **ANALYZE**

• **Why do you think this artwork is called an eye-dazzler blanket?** (Possible response: It dazzles the eye with its bright colors and energetic pattern.) **INTERPRET**

• **Would you want to use this blanket? Why or why not?** (Possible response: Yes; because it is beautiful.) **JUDGE**

Sketchbook Journal Find other examples of eye-dazzler blankets in books or on the Internet to show students.

③ Close

Model how to form conclusions about artworks, using a volunteer's sample. Say, for example: **The artist's use of diamond shapes and zigzag lines tells me she wished to show a traditional eye-dazzler pattern.** Have students share their own conclusions about their designs.

Assessment Have the class identify and list various functions of weavings.

NVAS (K–4) #4 Understanding the visual arts in relation to history and cultures

NVAS (K–4) #5 Reflecting upon and assessing the characteristics and merits of their work and the work of others

NVAS (K–4) #6 Making connections between visual arts and other disciplines

Studio 2

At a Glance

Objectives

- Express ideas about family in a weaving.
- Evaluate original artworks by self and peers.

Materials

- 8" x 10" blue construction paper
- scissors ⚠, glue, strips of colored construction paper, wallpaper, or wrapping paper, yarn, feathers, ribbons
- Rubric 5 from **Unit-by-Unit Resources**
- tagboard circles, rulers, and pencils (optional)

FA TEKS 4.1A Communicate ideas about self, family, school, and community, using sensory knowledge and life experiences

FA TEKS 4.2A Integrate a variety of ideas about self, life events, family, and community in original artworks

FA TEKS 4.2B Design original artworks

FA TEKS 4.2C Invent ways to produce artworks and to explore photographic imagery, using a variety of art media and materials

FA TEKS 4.4A Describe intent and form conclusions about personal artworks

1 Introduce

Review weaving, weft, and warp, as well as regular and irregular patterns.

Have students brainstorm ideas for their weavings. Invite them to integrate ideas from weavings they may have seen in their homes or communities. Ask:

- **Which materials will you use?**
- **Will you make a regular or an irregular pattern?**
- **What colors will you include?**

Quick Studio

Have students create a warp by cutting vertical slits into a square of construction paper. Use strips of paper to create the weft.

Studio 2

Make a Circle Weaving

Create a mixed-media weaving in a circular form. Use paper for the warp and a collection of objects with interesting textures and colors for the weft.

1. Draw and cut out a large circle. Fold it in half.

2. Cut lines from the fold to about an inch from the edge.

Technique Tip

Wrap a small piece of masking tape around the tip of the materials you weave.

160

Meeting Individual Needs

Reteach Provide students with precut paper warps. Have them use one color of paper strips for the weft to simplify the activity.

Extend Have students punch holes along the edge of the circle and string yarn through the holes to add decorative elements. Invite them to invent other ways to embellish their weaving using a variety of art media and materials.

3 Weave the strips over and under. On the next row, go under and over.

4 Trim, then glue the ends of the strips on the edges of the weaving.

Think Like an Artist
Did you use a regular or an irregular pattern in the materials you added for the weft? How would a different pattern change your design?

161

Fine Arts Connection

Music Ask students if they have ever heard of someone weaving a melody. Tell them that the melody is the part of music you recognize and that it consists of a series of notes with a distinctive rhythm. Discuss why the word *weaving* suits the making of music as well as cloth.

FA TEKS 4.5D Identify connections between music and other fine arts

② Create

Have students look at the pictures and read the directions on pages 160–161. Then distribute materials.

- Provide tagboard circles for students to use as templates.
- Provide students with rulers to help them make their lines as straight and parallel as possible.
- Have students look over the materials to think about the patterns they will create.
- Remind students to use as little glue as possible to secure the ends of the strips.

Technique Tip After students have woven three or four strips, have them gently push the strips close together so that the weaving will be even.

③ Close

Have students form conclusions about their artwork by answering the *Think Like an Artist* questions. (Possible responses: irregular pattern; A different pattern would be less interesting.)

Ongoing Assessment

If . . . students have difficulty making an even warp,

then . . . provide them with templates or rulers.

See page 90 from **Unit-by-Unit Resources** for a rubric to assess this studio.

NVAS (K–4) #1 Understanding and applying media, techniques, and processes

NVAS (K–4) #3 Choosing and evaluating a range of subject matter, symbols, and ideas

NVAS (K–4) #5 Reflecting upon and assessing the characteristics and merits of their work and the work of others

Lesson 3

At a Glance

Objectives

• Identify and describe cartoons.
• Describe, analyze, interpret, and judge artworks.

Materials

• **Fine Art Transparency**
• newspaper comic strips
• Sketchbook Journal

Vocabulary

cartoon

FA TEKS 4.3C Identify the roles of art in American society
FA TEKS 4.4B Interpret ideas and moods in original artworks, portfolios, and exhibitions by peers and others

❶ Introduce

Pass around the comics from your local newspaper. Have students discuss the cartoons and say what they have in common.

Point out that cartoons involve drawings and are often humorous. Have students identify ways cartoons are used in the United States, such as in newspapers, comic books, and on television. Invite them to name their favorite cartoons and say what they like about them.

Mention that cartoons have been a popular form of entertainment for more than two hundred years. Then have students discuss how cartoonists use the elements of art and principles of design.

Lesson 3

Cartoons

An artist in the 1400s would have said that a cartoon was a drawing made before creating a final painting or a tapestry, a large woven picture. Today, the word has a different meaning. A **cartoon** is a drawing or animation that pokes fun at or makes you think in a new way about a person or an idea.

PEANUTS, June 24, 2003. PEANUTS reprinted by permission of United Feature Syndicate, Inc.

162

🎨 Art Background

Peanuts American cartoonist Charles M. Schulz (1922–2000) created the *Peanuts* comic strip in 1950 under the original title *Li'l Folks*. With its cast of charming, neurotic 3- to 5-year-old characters, the strip revolutionized the form and has been read by hundreds of millions of readers around the world.

Garfield American cartoonist Jim Davis debuted *Garfield* in 1978. The most widely distributed comic in the world, it appears in more than 2,500 newspapers and has spurred sales of 130 million books.

162

GARFIELD © 2003 Paws, Inc. Reprinted with permission of UNIVERSAL PRESS SYNDICATE. All rights reserved.

In what ways does Garfield look like a real cat? Which of his features are *not* realistic?

Cartoons became popular in newspapers in the late 1800s. They were meant for adults and they usually poked fun at politicians.

Today, political cartoons appear on editorial pages of most newspapers. You can also find cartoons, or comic strips, in the funny pages of the newspaper. What are your favorite comic strips and characters? What do you like about them?

Art in My World

Look in a newspaper for a comic strip that appeals to you. Study it to see how the artist uses line and shading and shows motion. Keep checking the strip to watch for new techniques.

163

② Teach

Have students read pages 162–163 and look at the *Peanuts* cartoon. Ask if students are familiar with the boy, Charlie Brown, and his dog, Snoopy. Ask:

- **What happens in the cartoon?** (Charlie Brown gives Snoopy a menu to order food, and Snoopy questions why he bothers to look at it.) DESCRIBE
- **How does Schulz use the elements of art to express humor?** (lines show simple yet comical facial expressions, shapes show comical features such as ears) ANALYZE
- **What mood do you think is expressed?** (Possible response: resigned) INTERPRET
- **Would you want to read more cartoons like this one? Why or why not?** (Possible response: Yes; because it is funny.) JUDGE

Now ask similar questions about the comic strip on page 163.

Art in My World Provide a variety of newspapers from which students can choose their strip. Review line and shading if necessary.

③ Close

Gather from the library and display a variety of books featuring the artworks of famous cartoonists, such as Charles Schulz or Jim Davis. Explain that these books document the artists' portfolios because they show many examples of their works. Model how to interpret the ideas and moods of an artwork with a sample cartoon. Then ask students to interpret the ideas and moods of the portfolio.

Assessment Make a transparency of a comic strip. Point to different types of lines and invite students to name them.

 **Technology**

Search the Web Have students work in small groups to search the Internet for information about their favorite cartoon and cartoonist. Ask them to find out when the cartoon started and how the cartoonist developed the idea. Have them present their findings to the class.

Tech TEKS 4.2A Use a variety of input devices
Tech TEKS 4.4A Apply appropriate electronic search strategies
Tech TEKS 4.4B Select strategies to navigate and access information

ESL Notes

Have students use one-word descriptors, such as *wavy, zigzag,* or *straight,* to name the kinds of lines they see in the comic strips on these pages.
ESL TEKS 4.5G Employ content area vocabulary words in context

NVAS (K–4) #4 Understanding the visual arts in relation to history and cultures

NVAS (K–4) #5 Reflecting upon and assessing the characteristics and merits of their work and the work of others

Studio 3

At a Glance

Objectives

• Express ideas by drawing a cartoon.
• Evaluate original artworks by self and peers.

Materials

• drawing paper, thin water-based markers
• Rubric 5 from **Unit-by-Unit Resources**
• rulers (optional)

FA TEKS 4.2B Design original artworks

FA TEKS 4.2C Invent ways to produce artworks and to explore photographic imagery, using a variety of art media and materials

FA TEKS 4.4A Describe intent and form conclusions about personal artworks

① Introduce

Review cartoons and have students describe cartoons they may have seen and read.

Have them brainstorm ideas for a cartoon and describe their intentions. Ask:

• **What animal, person, or imaginary creature will you draw?**
• **What personality will your character have? Is this personality similar to your own or that of a family member?**
• **What kinds of lines will you use to show different expressions and actions?**

Quick Studio

Have students draw a one-panel cartoon showing one character helping another.

Studio 3

Draw a Cartoon

Does a career as a cartoonist seem like fun? Create your own cartoon!

1 Create a cartoon character. Give it unusual features.

2 Draw a plan for the action in three or four frames.

Technique Tip

Give your character a facial feature that will make the character recognizable as well as easy to redraw.

164

Meeting Individual Needs

Inclusion Substitute instant cameras for students who are unable to draw representational images. Have them investigate photographic imagery by creating a four-panel strip using the camera.

③ Turn your plan into drawings.

④ Write dialogue in speech balloons. Add details to the drawings.

MAYBE IF I BEG.

Think Like an Artist

Does your character's appearance match his or her personality? What changes would you make for a better match and more humor?

Fine Arts Connection

Theatre Tell students that cartoons, such as *Peanuts,* have been adapted as plays, films, and television shows. Show them one of these programs, such as *It's the Great Pumpkin, Charlie Brown.* Then have them work in groups to write and act out a play based on a cartoon.

FA TEKS 4.2D Dramatize literary selections
FA TEKS 4.3C Plan brief dramatizations
FA TEKS 4.3D Interact cooperatively with others
FA TEKS 4.4B Identify the role of live theatre in American society

② Create

Have students look at the pictures and read the directions on pages 164–165. Then distribute materials.

- Tell students to draw several sketches until they are satisfied with their character.
- Have students write their plan in words first. Then have them use the written plan to create their action sketches.
- Have students draw four panels using a ruler and black markers, or fold the drawing paper in half and then in half again to make the panels.
- Have students write the title of their comic strip and their name somewhere on the cartoon.

Technique Tip Tell students to add distinctive features to their characters, such as an unusual hair style or a funny hat.

③ Close

Ask students to form conclusions about their cartoons by answering the *Think Like an Artist* questions. (Possible response: Yes; but I could make the eyes bigger to make her look more surprised.)

Ongoing Assessment

If . . . students have difficulty thinking of a character,

then . . . have them draw their pet or the school mascot.

See page 90 from **Unit-by-Unit Resources** for a rubric to assess this studio.

NVAS (K–4) #1 Understanding and applying media, techniques, and processes
NVAS (K–4) #3 Choosing and evaluating a range of subject matter, symbols, and ideas
NVAS (K–4) #5 Reflecting upon and assessing the characteristics and merits of their work and the work of others

Look and Compare

Passengers

Red Grooms. *Subway (detail from Ruckus Manhattan)*, 1976. Mixed media, 108 by 223 by 446 inches. © 1997 Red Grooms/Artists Rights Society (ARS), NY. Photograph courtesy Marlborough Gallery, New York.

Artist Red Grooms observed the subway, or underground train, in New York City as a subject for this artwork. The three-dimensional scene shown here is part of a large multimedia installation.

166

At a Glance

Objectives

- Compare and contrast two artworks showing passengers.
- Respond to and make judgments about artworks.

Materials

- **Art Prints 17, 18, 19**
- **Fine Art Transparency**
- Sketchbook Journal

FA TEKS 4.3A Identify simple main ideas expressed in art

FA TEKS 4.3B Compare and contrast selected artworks from a variety of cultural settings

Explore

Display **Art Print 17,** *Ruckus Rodeo.* Help students recall this artwork by Red Grooms from page 152. Have them predict which one was also created by Grooms and give reasons for their answer. (Possible response: *Ruckus Manhattan;* The humorous, cartoonish imagery is similar.)

Discuss

After students read pages 166 and 167, have them discuss the subject, media, and styles each artist used. Point out that both artworks show passengers on public transportation, but Grooms' artwork is created in a cartoon-like style. Students can then contrast this with Kahlo's artwork, which is done in a more serious style.

Then discuss the cultural similarities and differences between the artworks. Point out that while both depict urban settings, Grooms' artwork portrays life in a United States city while Kahlo's portrays a Mexican setting. Ask students to point out clues that identify cultural settings. (clothing styles)

Art Background

Subway Grooms created this artwork and other parts of *Ruckus Manhattan* in collaboration with his wife, Mimi Grooms. A huge mixed-media installation, *Ruckus Manhattan* reflects their obsession with New York, inviting the viewer to experience the vitality of city life.

The Bus Unlike Kahlo's (1907–1954) dramatic and often anguished self-portraits, *The Bus* shows a rather serene scene from urban daily life. The subject, bright colors, and flattened shapes, reflect the influence of Mexican folk art.

Frida Kahlo. *The Bus,* 1929. Oil on canvas, 10¼ by 22 inches. Collection of Dolores Olmedo, Mexico City, Mexico.

Frida Kahlo lived and painted in Mexico and the United States. Some viewers think her work has a dreamlike quality, but Kahlo said, "I never painted dreams. I painted my own reality."

Compare the style of *The Bus* with that of *Subway.* How are the subjects and media of these artworks similar and different? How can you tell that the artworks show different places?

167

Sketchbook Journal

Would you find it more interesting to be a passenger in *Subway* or on *The Bus?* What kinds of sights and smells might you experience in each place? Write about it.

Apply

Draw a Venn diagram like the one below. Have students identify simple main ideas by first comparing the two artworks and saying how they are similar. Then guide students to contrast the artworks to find differences in media, style, and place.

Artworks Showing Passengers

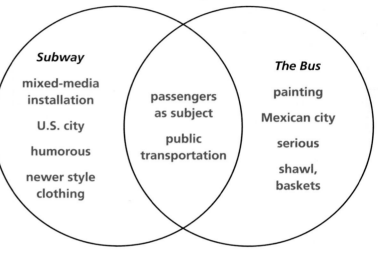

Subway
- mixed-media installation
- U.S. city
- humorous
- newer style clothing

passengers as subject
public transportation

The Bus
- painting
- Mexican city
- serious
- shawl, baskets

Close

Share an experience you have had taking public transportation in your community, such as riding a bus or a train, and invite students to tell stories of their own. Have them describe how they could communicate ideas about their community in an artwork based on these experiences.

Sketchbook Journal Have students compare the scenes in the artworks to their own experiences riding community transportation.

NVAS (K–4) #4 Understanding the visual arts in relation to history and cultures

NVAS (K–4) #5 Reflecting upon and assessing the characteristics and merits of their work and the work of others

Reading Strategy

Identify Details Tell students that identifying details while reading can help them understand what they read. Have them reread page 166 and identify details in the text that will help them answer the questions on page 167.

Point out the phrases: *subway, underground train,* and *large multimedia installation.* Tell students that these details provide answers about Grooms' subject and media.

TAKS Rdg. Obj. 1 Understand written texts
ELA TEKS 4.10F Determine how ideas are supported with details

Lesson 4

At a Glance

Objectives

- Identify and describe industrial design.
- Describe, analyze, interpret, and judge artworks.

Materials

- **Fine Art Transparency**
- item of industrial design, such as a watch or thermos
- Sketchbook Journal

Vocabulary

industrial design

FA TEKS 4.1A Communicate ideas about self, family, school, and community, using sensory knowledge and life experiences

FA TEKS 4.3C Identify the roles of art in American society

FA TEKS 4.4B Interpret ideas and moods in original artworks, portfolios, and exhibitions by peers and others

① Introduce

Display a watch, thermos, or other example of industrial design. Have students describe the object and its function in their lives.

Ask students to name other examples of industrial design in the classroom, such as computers, clocks, and pencil sharpeners. Invite them to share experiences they have had at school using these objects. Model first by relating a story of your own. For example, you might share a story about a time you used a school computer. Ask students to tell whether they would change the design of these objects based on their experiences.

Then discuss the role industrial design plays in our society. Point out how industrial designers use the elements of art and principles of design to make their objects both functional and decorative.

168

Lesson 4

Industrial Design

Have you ever noticed that many functional objects are beautiful and interesting? Cars, bicycles, appliances, and other machines are examples of **industrial design.** They have a purpose but may also be pleasing to see and use.

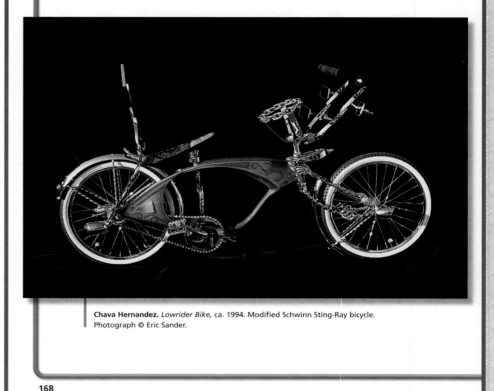

Chava Hernandez. *Lowrider Bike,* ca. 1994. Modified Schwinn Sting-Ray bicycle. Photograph © Eric Sander.

168

Art Background

Lowrider Bike Chava Hernandez built his lowrider bicycle from a Schwinn Sting-Ray. He added special touches, such as gold-plated pedals and chain, and applied an elaborate paint job. Hernandez also included an ornately decorated banana-style seat, the kind popular on many bicycles in the 1970s.

Pirovano Watch Designed by Italian artist Stefano Pirovano (1961–), the 1000 series watch features bright colors and concave crystals. The polyurethane case and strap are created in a single mould.

Stefano Pirovano.
Pirovano Watch (Calumet 1000 Series),
2000. Urethane, diameter 1½ inches. Museum of Modern Art Design Store, New York. Distributed and marketed by Seiko Instruments (SII), Austin, USA, and Alessi s.p.a., Crusinallo, Italy.

Industrial designers ask themselves many questions as they plan a new design. They must consider an object's purpose as well as how to make it attractive, affordable, and easy to use.

Take a close look at the bicycle and the watch. How do you think the designers answered the following questions: Who will use this object? What kind of design would this person like? What features are important to this user?

> **Sketchbook Journal**
>
> Draw a picture of a brand new design for a bicycle that you would like to ride. Include features that make it attractive or comfortable to use. How would you feel riding this bicycle?

169

② Teach

Have students read pages 168–169 and look at the *Pirovano Watch.* Ask:

- **What colors, shapes, and forms do you see?** (green, orange, and silver; circles, teardrops; organic) DESCRIBE
- **How does the watch show balance?** (It shows radial balance in the watch face and symmetrical balance side to side.) ANALYZE
- **What kind of person do you think the designer had in mind when he created this watch?** (Possible responses: sporty, busy) INTERPRET
- **Would you wear this watch? Why or why not?** (Yes; I think it would be fun to wear.) JUDGE

Discuss how the lack of detail, colors, and simplified shapes and forms appeal to someone who is sporty and on the go. Then ask similar questions about the bicycle.

Sketchbook Journal Tell students to think about radial and symmetrical balance when designing their bicycles.

③ Close

Have an exhibition of the students' bicycle designs in the classroom. Model how to interpret moods and ideas in an artwork, using a volunteer's sample. Then ask students to interpret the moods and ideas in the exhibition. Discuss how these moods and ideas contribute to the decoration and functionality of the bicycle.

Assessment Take students to the library or cafeteria and have them point out examples of industrial design.

NVAS (K–4) #2 Using knowledge of structures and functions
NVAS (K–4) #4 Understanding the visual arts in relation to history and cultures
NVAS (K–4) #5 Reflecting upon and assessing the characteristics and merits of their work and the work of others
NVAS (K–4) #6 Making connections between visual arts and other disciplines

Curriculum Connection

Social Studies Have students work in small groups to research the history of a functional object they use, such as a bicycle, watch, or telephone. Have them find out who first designed or invented the object, what was the source of their inspiration, and the role this object plays in our society.
SS TEKS 4.21A Identify famous inventors and their contributions

ESL Notes

Have students work with a partner to find an example of industrial design in the classroom and then say its name. You may wish to have students work with an English-speaking partner to describe the object's function.
ESL TEKS 4.5G Employ content area vocabulary words in context

Studio 4

Studio 4

Design with Wire

Industrial design reflects the time in which objects are created. Design a bicycle from the past, present, or future and build it from colored wire.

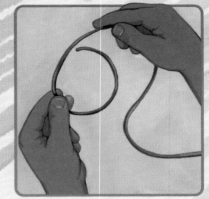

1 Draw a design for your bicycle.

2 Bend and twist the wire for each part of the bicycle.

Technique Tip

When you snip off pieces of wire, hold the wire away from your own and other people's eyes.

170

At a Glance

Objectives

- Express ideas by designing a bicycle from colored wire.
- Evaluate original artworks by self and peers.

Materials

- pencil and drawing paper
- colored narrow gauge wire ⚠, wire snips ⚠
- safety scissors ⚠
- Rubric 5 from **Unit-by-Unit Resources**
- wooden blocks (optional)

FA TEKS 4.1A Communicate ideas about self, family, school, and community, using sensory knowledge and life experiences

FA TEKS 4.2B Design original artworks

FA TEKS 4.2C Invent ways to produce artworks and to explore photographic imagery, using a variety of art media and materials

FA TEKS 4.4A Describe intent and form conclusions about personal artworks

❶ Introduce

Review industrial design. Have students describe examples of industrial design, including bicycles.

Then engage students in a discussion about bicycles they have owned or ridden. Discuss experiences they have had with bicycles and what features made the bicycle functional.

Have students brainstorm ideas for a bicycle and describe their design intentions. Ask:

- **What time period will you use as inspiration for your bicycle?**
- **What colors and special features will the bicycle include?**
- **How will you show unity and variety?**

Quick Studio

Have students use pipe cleaners to build a model of the bicycle they have designed.

👥 Meeting Individual Needs

Reteach Have students focus on creating parts of the bicycle, such as the wheels, the handlebars, or the seat.

Extend Have students design a bicycle from the 1800s. Invite them to first research the style of bicycles popular during the time period and gather several pictures to use as a guide. After completing their model, have students write a paragraph comparing the bicycle they built to ones from today.

③ Connect separate bicycle parts with more wire.

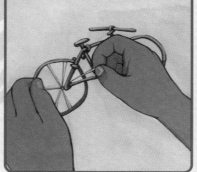

④ Wind and weave more wire to add details to your design.

Think Like an Artist

Describe the kind of person who would enjoy owning the bicycle you designed.

171

Fine Arts Connection

Music Have students find examples of radios, compact disc players, or stereos in advertisements, or provide different examples for students to view. Have them compare and contrast the different designs, and discuss how the designs serve their functions.

FA TEKS 4.5D Identify connections between music and other fine arts

② Create

Have students look at the pictures and read the directions on pages 170–171. Then distribute materials.

- If students completed the *Sketchbook Journal* activity in Lesson 4, have them consult their designs.
- Have students cut twenty 30-inch lengths of wire, or precut the wire for student use.
- To create strength, tell students to twist several wires together and then bend them into forms.
- If you wish, have students attach their finished bicycles to a wood base, or encourage them to invent their own method for mounting their artwork.

Technique Tip Demonstrate how to use the wire snips safely to bend the wires.

③ Close

Tell students to form conclusions by answering the *Think Like an Artist* question. (Possible response: someone sporty who likes to ride up and down hills)

Ongoing Assessment

If . . . students have difficulty bending the wires,

then . . . provide youth-sized garden gloves to protect their fingers and to help them grip the wire.

See page 90 from **Unit-by-Unit Resources** for a rubric to assess this studio.

NVAS (K–4) #1 Understanding and applying media, techniques, and processes

NVAS (K–4) #3 Choosing and evaluating a range of subject matter, symbols, and ideas

NVAS (K–4) #5 Reflecting upon and assessing the characteristics and merits of their work and the work of others

Lesson 5

At a Glance

Objectives

- Identify and describe portraits, self-portraits, and proportions in artworks.
- Describe, analyze, interpret, and judge artworks.

Materials

- **Fine Art Transparency**
- pencil and paper
- Sketchbook Journal

Vocabulary

portraits, self-portrait, proportions

FA TEKS 4.1B Choose appropriate vocabulary to discuss the use of art elements such as color, texture, form, line, space, and value and art principles such as emphasis, pattern, rhythm, balance, proportion, and unity

FA TEKS 4.3B Compare and contrast selected artworks from a variety of cultural settings

FA TEKS 4.4B Interpret ideas and moods in original artworks, portfolios, and exhibitions by peers and others

① Introduce

Place students in pairs and have them take turns making a quick drawing of their partner's face. Tell students they have made a portrait.

Have students look at the portraits in this lesson. Ask them to tell what we can learn about people from their portraits. Point out that we can learn how people dressed, how they worked or played, how they felt about themselves, or even what culture they are from.

Point out that this type of information is especially helpful when we look at portraits from long ago. Then have students notice the facial features in each portrait. Invite them to use their fingers to measure the proportions of the features in relation to the rest of the face, and use appropriate vocabulary to discuss their findings. Ask them to compare and contrast the artworks for cultural differences.

172

Portraits and Proportion

Long before cameras were invented, artists created portraits. **Portraits** show people or animals as their subjects.

Andy Warhol. *Marilyn*, 1964. Synthetic polymer paint and silkscreen ink on canvas, 40 by 40 inches.

172

🎨 Art Background

About the Artist American artist and filmmaker Andy Warhol (1928–1987) began mass-producing images of consumer goods, such as soup cans, and celebrity portraits by silk-screening them. His technique and use of flat, garish colors emphasized the disposability of cultural products.

About the Artist Rembrandt van Rijn (1606–1669) is considered by some to be the greatest artist of the Netherlands. A master of light and shadow, he is known for his etchings, religious paintings, landscapes, and portraits. He created over fifty self-portraits.

The portraits on these two pages are from different centuries. How can you tell which one is old and which one is new?

Some artists use themselves as the subjects of their artworks. A **self-portrait** shows an image of the artist.

The **proportions** of a face show how facial features relate to each other in terms of size and placement. For example, notice how the eyes in many portraits fall midway between the top of the head and the chin.

Research

Find a portrait by one of these painters: Diego Velázquez, Mary Cassatt, or Alice Neel. Who is the subject? What can you tell about that person?

173

② Teach

Have students read pages 172–173 and look at *Marilyn.* Tell students that the subject, Marilyn Monroe, was a famous movie star. Ask:

- **What colors do you see?** (mint green, pink, red, bright yellow, brown) DESCRIBE
- **How does the use of color contribute to the main idea?** (Possible response: It shows the subject in an unrealistic way.) ANALYZE
- **What ideas do you think Warhol expresses in this portrait?** (Possible response: Celebrities do not seem like real people.) INTERPRET
- **Would you want to meet this person? Why or why not?** (Accept all responses.) JUDGE

Ask similar questions about Rembrandt's self-portrait and have students tell which artwork is new and which is old. Students may say that they know Warhol's portrait is more recent because Monroe is a twentieth century personage and the colors seem modern.

Research Ask a librarian to instruct students on how to find portraits in art books or journals.

③ Close

Have students display an exhibition of the portraits they found and interpret the ideas and moods that the artists conveyed about the subjects. Model first with a sample artwork.

Visual Culture Discuss how portraits are used to sell products, such as cereal, perfume, and jeans. Talk about what ideas these images express.

NVAS (K–4) #2 Using knowledge of structures and functions

NVAS (K–4) #4 Understanding the visual arts in relation to history and cultures

NVAS (K–4) #5 Reflecting upon and assessing the characteristics and merits of their work and the work of others

Curriculum Connection

Math Place students in pairs and have them measure the length and width of each other's face. Then have them measure the distance between the eyes and the top of the forehead, the nose and top of the forehead, and mouth and chin.

Have them use these measurements to make life-sized portraits. Once students have drawn the facial features, tell them to add hair and other details.

TAKS Math Obj. 4 Understand measurement
Math TEKS 4.12 Apply measurement concepts

 **Notes**

Have students draw quick self-portraits and then name each part of the face.

ESL TEKS 4.1C Understand major ideas in spoken messages

Studio 5

At a Glance

Objectives

• Express ideas by drawing a self-portrait.
• Evaluate original artworks by self and peers.

Materials

• pencils, drawing paper, small mirrors ⚠
• Rubric 5 from **Unit-by-Unit Resources**

FA TEKS 4.1A Communicate ideas about self, family, school, and community, using sensory knowledge and life experiences.

FA TEKS 4.2A Integrate a variety of ideas about self, life events, family, and community in original artworks

FA TEKS 4.2B Design original artworks

FA TEKS 4.4A Describe intent and form conclusions about personal artworks

❶ Introduce

Review *portrait* and *self-portrait*. Have students point out portraits or self-portraits in their Social Studies textbook.

Remind students that artists use their senses to communicate ideas about themselves. Demonstrate how to use your sense of touch and sight to communicate ideas about your facial features. Then have students look in a mirror or feel their features with their fingertips and share their ideas. Have them tell how they will use this sensory knowledge to tell about themselves in an artwork. Ask:

• **What kinds of lines and shapes will you use?**
• **How will you use shading to create values?**
• **What details about yourself will you integrate into your portrait?**

Quick Studio

Have students draw a portrait of a friend using the folded paper grid to guide them.

Studio 5

Draw a Self-Portrait

Have you ever looked closely at the proportions of your face in a mirror? Studying facial features helps artists draw self-portraits.

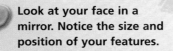

❶ **Look at your face in a mirror. Notice the size and position of your features.**

❷ **Fold a piece of paper into eight sections.**

Technique Tip

Use the side of your pencil point for shading. You can also blend the shadows with a tissue.

174

👥 Meeting Individual Needs

Extend Have students create more complete self-portraits on larger sheets of paper. Have them use crayons, oil pastels, or tempera paints to add the details and color. Then encourage them to invent ways to include other art media into their self-portraits, such as foil, raffia, beads, and fabric.

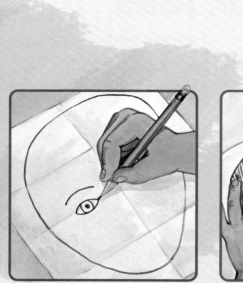

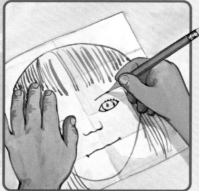

③ Draw your face using the grid as a guide. Look in the mirror as necessary.

④ Place your other features, using the grid to help.

Think Like an Artist

How is your self-portrait likely to be different from a portrait of you painted by someone else?

 Fine Arts Connection

Theatre Read aloud a play to students or take the class to see a play. Then have students choose their favorite character and create a portrait of him or her. When they have finished, display the portraits. Ask the students to try to identify who the characters are in the portraits. If the students are correct, ask them to tell what features or details helped them to identify the character.

FA TEKS 4.5A Identify and apply appropriate audience behavior

② Create

Have students look at the pictures and read the directions on pages 174–175. Then distribute materials.

- Tell students to study proportion by noting the amount of space between features, such as between the mouth and chin.
- Tell students to fold the paper once vertically, then twice horizontally.
- Have students draw the shape of the head first, and then draw the neck, hair, and ears.
- Show students that the eyes are about halfway down the face. The nose is above the bottom guideline and the mouth is below.

Technique Tip Tell students to work from left to right if they are right-handed or from right to left if they are left-handed so that the drawing will not smear.

③ Close

Have students form conclusions about their portraits by answering the *Think Like an Artist* question. (Possible response: I may see myself differently than how other people see me.)

Ongoing Assessment

If . . . students have difficulty using the grid,

then . . . go over the instructions for Steps 3 and 4 with them individually.

See page 90 from **Unit-by-Unit Resources** for a rubric to assess this studio.

NVAS (K–4) #1 Understanding and applying media, techniques, and processes

NVAS (K–4) #3 Choosing and evaluating a range of subject matter, symbols, and ideas

NVAS (K–4) #5 Reflecting upon and assessing the characteristics and merits of their work and the work of others

175

Lesson 6

At a Glance

Objectives

• Identify and describe the human form in artworks.

• Describe, analyze, interpret, and judge artworks.

Materials

• **Fine Art Transparency**
• measuring tape
• butcher paper

Vocabulary

pose, model

FA TEKS 4.1B Choose appropriate vocabulary to discuss the use of art elements such as color, texture, form, line, space, and value and art principles such as emphasis, pattern, rhythm, balance, proportion, and unity

FA TEKS 4.4B Interpret ideas and moods in original artworks, portfolios, and exhibitions by peers and others

1 Introduce

Have a volunteer come to the front of the class. Use a measuring tape to measure the student's height and the vertical length of his or her head.

Using a large piece of butcher paper, show how many times the head length is repeated in order to equal the length of the body. Write this ratio on the board. Explain that this proportion will be roughly the same in most full-length portraits of children. Point out that since adults are taller, their proportion is 8 head lengths to body length.

Next, discuss how artists have models strike poses to express different ideas. Invite students to practice making different poses.

The Human Form

Throughout history, artists have created artworks showing the entire human form. Portrait painters often show subjects in a realistic **pose,** or position, to make the people look as lifelike as possible. A person who poses for a portrait is called a **model.**

Thomas Gainsborough. *Jonathan Buttall: The Blue Boy,* ca. 1770. Oil on canvas, 70⅝ by 48¾ inches. The Huntington Gallery, San Marino, CA.

176

 Art Background

About the Artist English portrait and landscape painter Thomas Gainsborough (1727–1788) is considered one of the most versatile English artists of the 1700s. Influenced by many other painters, he drew his images from contemporary life and often painted portraits of the fashionably rich.

ESL Notes

Show students a full-length portrait and have students name different parts of the human form.

ESL TEKS 4.4A Connect experiences with those of others

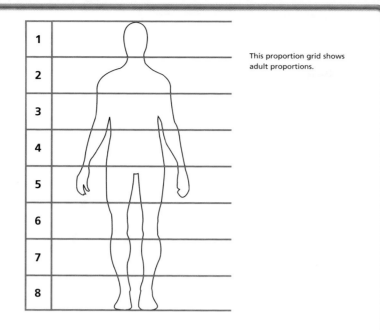

This proportion grid shows adult proportions.

1
2
3
4
5
6
7
8

Just as artists look at proportions when drawing faces, they also pay attention to proportions when drawing an entire figure. A grid for an adult figure shows that the body is approximately eight "heads" tall. A grid for a child's figure should show only about six head lengths.

Art Fact

The ancient Roman architect Vitruvius created a model of the human body with what he thought were ideal proportions. Leonardo da Vinci used those measurements too.

177

Curriculum Connection

Physical Education/Health Tell students that artists study movement in the human form to make their portraits appear lifelike. Take students to a large open space. Divide the class into two groups. Have one group sit while the other group performs.

Call out physical activities, such as running, walking, jumping, or crawling. Have the acting group perform the suggested activity while the other group observes the movement. Have students pay particular attention to how the arms, and legs change position during the activities. Then have the groups switch roles.

PE TEKS 4.1E Perform sequences showing good body control

② Teach

Have students read pages 176–177 and look at the painting. Ask:

- **What is the subject of the painting? What details do you see?** (a boy; fancy clothes, a feathered hat, ribbons on shoes, a wild, windy landscape) DESCRIBE
- **How would you describe the mood of this portrait based on the boy's expression?** (Possible response: serious) ANALYZE
- **What does the portrait tell you about the person that you might not know if you only saw the face?** (Possible response: The boy is probably rich.) INTERPRET
- **Would you introduce this person to your friends? Why or why not?** (Accept all responses.) JUDGE

Art Fact Have students research how ideas about ideal human proportions have changed over time.

③ Close

After students finish researching, have them discuss whether they think there is such a thing as ideal human proportion. (Accept all responses.)

Assessment Have students find examples of the human form in other artworks in their school or home environments. Then have them describe these examples using their life experiences as the basis for discussion.

NVAS (K–4) #2 Using knowledge of structures and functions

NVAS (K–4) #4 Understanding the visual arts in relation to history and cultures

NVAS (K–4) #5 Reflecting upon and assessing the characteristics and merits of their work and the work of others

NVAS (K–4) #6 Making connections between visual arts and other disciplines

Studio 6

At a Glance

Objectives

- Express ideas by creating a full-length portrait.
- Evaluate original artworks by self and peers.

Materials

- measuring tape, drawing paper, pencils, tempera paints, and paintbrushes
- Rubric 5 from **Unit-by-Unit Resources**
- rulers (optional)

FA TEKS 4.2A Integrate a variety of ideas about self, life events, family, and community in original artworks

FA TEKS 4.2B Design original artworks

FA TEKS 4.2C Invent ways to produce artworks and to explore photographic imagery, using a variety of art media and materials

FA TEKS 4.4A Describe intent and form conclusions about personal artworks

① Introduce

Review drawing the human form. Provide students with examples of full-length portraits from art books and journals.

Have students brainstorm ideas and describe intent for their portraits. Ask:

- **What kinds of lines will you use to show the model's hair?**
- **What details will you add for the clothing?**
- **What details from your school will you add to the background?**

Have students communicate ideas about school based on their experiences. Ask them to describe how they will incorporate these details into their portrait background. Model first with stories of your own school experiences.

Quick Studio

Have students draw a full-length portrait of a classmate. Remind them to use realistic proportions.

Studio 6
Show Proportion

Draw a portrait of a classmate. Measure how many head lengths you will need for the height.

1 Draw the form of your model's body. Use a grid to show realistic proportions.

2 Paint the figure in your drawing.

Technique Tip

Look at the illustration on page 177. Then use the size of your subject's head to figure out proportions of other body parts.

Meeting Individual Needs

Inclusion Some students with severe disabilities may not have the skills to create a representative portrait with drawing materials. Consider having students invent ways to use an instant camera for this purpose.

They can also explore photographic images in magazines to identify and collect full-length portraits, which can be embellished using a variety of art media and materials.

3 Add details to show the clothing, face, and hair.

4 Add a familiar indoor or outdoor setting around the figure.

Think Like an Artist

Does your portrait capture the posture and proportions of your model? What would you do differently in your next portrait painting?

179

Fine Arts Connection

Dance Have students make a full-length portrait of someone dancing. Have them consider the costume or clothing the dancer is wearing and how to show movement. Provide images for students to use as a guide, or show a short video of a dance performance and have students study the dancers' movements.

PE TEKS 4.2B Identify ways movement concepts can be used to refine movement skills

② Create

Have students read the directions and look at the pictures on pages 178–179. Then distribute materials.

- Provide students with tape measures. Assist them as they determine their partner's head length to height ratio.
- Remind students to use the tip of the brush to make thin lines and push down for thick lines.
- Tell students to hold the brush at different angles to create different effects.
- Have them integrate a variety of ideas about the subject based on his or her experiences at school.

Technique Tip Point out that children's bodies are smaller proportionally so their grids will be different than the one of page 177.

③ Close

Ask students to reflect on their portraits and form conclusions by answering the *Think Like an Artist* questions. (Possible response: No; I would make the feet bigger.)

Ongoing Assessment

If . . . students have difficulty making a grid,

then . . . have them use a ruler to mark off measurements.

See page 90 from **Unit-by-Unit Resources** for a rubric to assess this studio.

Stage Designs

José González says it takes a team to put on a play. He is a stage designer, or a person who plans a play's set—the painted backgrounds, the furniture, and other scenery.

González starts planning a stage design by reading the playscript. He meets with the director and the lighting and costume designers. They share ideas and agree on a general "look" for the play. Then

González makes sketches of his stage design ideas.

González often builds three-dimensional models of his designs. He starts with a simple white model. Later he adds details and color so everyone can see how the set will look during the play. González believes that a successful stage design helps move along the action of the play.

González had to learn many skills to get his job. He had no experience designing stages when he first worked on a stage set years ago. He apprenticed, or learned on the job, for weeks without pay. Now, González is Executive Director of a theater group in Oregon. What he likes best about his job is seeing an idea come to life.

José González designs sets for the Miracle Theatre Group in Portland, Oregon.

180

At a Glance

Objectives

- Read about a career in art.
- Identify the use of art in everyday life.
- Relate art to personal experiences.

Materials

- stage prop (optional)

FA TEKS 4.1A Communicate ideas about self, family, school, and community, using sensory knowledge and life experiences.

Explore

Display a stage prop, such as a fake rock. Allow students the opportunity to touch and lift it. Tell students that stage designers use a variety of media to create the setting for a play.

Then ask students if they have ever seen a play. If so, have them describe elements of the scenery that they remember and identify the role that the set design played in the performance they saw.

Discuss

Have students read pages 180–181. Ask:

- **How is Gonzalez's model similar to the actual set design? How is it different?** (The colors are the same as are the large structures; The actual set has more details and includes additional props.)
- **Do you think the actors seem to fit with the stage design? Why or why not?** (Yes; Their costume colors match the background.)
- **What skills does Gonzalez need to do his job well?** (Possible responses: imagination, ability to see pictures from words, building skills)
- **Do you think stage design is an interesting career? Why or why not?** (Possible response: Yes; Each play gives you a new challenge.)

 Career Research

Take students to visit a community theatre or the theatre of a local high school or college. Ask if students can tour the prop area or possibly walk through the set of a currently running play.

Have the theatre manager or set designer explain the reasoning behind the design and possibly show how actors use different elements of the space in the play. Encourage students to pay attention to ways stage designers use the elements of art and principles of design to create functional and visually pleasing scenery.

Gonzáles used the model shown above to plan this stage design.

181

Reading Strategy

Summarize and Paraphrase Information Place students in groups of four. Have them read the passage and look at the images. Then, have them take turns summarizing aloud each of the four paragraphs. You may want to have them think about what the main idea of each paragraph is.

TAKS Rdg. Obj. 3 Uses strategies to analyze texts
ELA TEKS 4.10G Summarize text to organize ideas

Apply

Have students summarize each of the paragraphs about stage design. Display a web such as the one below. Fill it in together as students name the main idea and supporting details for each paragraph.

Main Idea, Paragraph 1

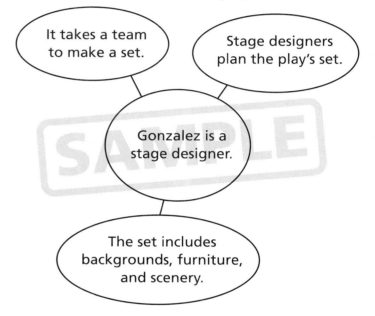

Close

Review the completed web and ask: **What does a stage designer do?** (A stage designer plans the play's set.)

Have students share their experiences about plays they have seen or performed in at school. Ask them to describe the set and tell whether it enhanced the school play. Model first by sharing an experience of your own.

NVAS (K–4) #5 Reflecting upon and assessing the characteristics and merits of their work and the work of others

Portfolio Project

Portfolio Project

At a Glance

Objectives

- Develop and organize ideas.
- Demonstrate knowledge about cartoons and industrial design.
- Evaluate original artworks by self and peers.

Materials

- heavy drawing paper or construction paper
- pencil, water-based markers, glue
- decorating materials, such as pipe cleaners, nuts, bolts, and other mechanical parts ⚠Ⓢ
- Rubric 5 from **Unit-by-Unit Resources**

FA TEKS 4.2B Design original artworks

FA TEKS 4.2C Invent ways to produce artworks and to explore photographic imagery, using a variety of art media and materials

FA TEKS 4.4B Interpret ideas and moods in original artworks, portfolios, and exhibitions by peers and others

Design a Cartoon Car

Combine your new skills as a cartoonist and industrial designer. Design a car for your favorite cartoon character.

1 Design a car for a cartoon character.

2 Add details to your car.

3 Draw your favorite cartoon character in or near the car.

4 Complete your car by gluing on pipe cleaners, nuts, bolts, and other mechanical parts.

182

Plan

Direct students to read page 182. As they brainstorm ideas for their original design, ask:

- **What kinds of cars have you been in, seen, or imagined?**
- **What features will you include to make the car comfortable?**
- **What features will you include to make the car fast or beautiful?**

Review industrial design and cartoons. Tell students that they can use exaggeration and symbols to make their car "cartoonish."

Quick Project

Have students use markers or crayons to draw a cartoon train, subway car, or bus.

👥 Meeting Individual Needs

Extend Have the students design cars that incorporate the features of their favorite cartoon characters, making the car resemble the character. Before they begin, suggest that students make a list of the exaggerated features of their favorite character to use as a guide when creating their car.

Paige, Age 9. *Rabbit Mobile.* Markers, pipe cleaners, bottlecaps, and mechanical parts on paper.

How are these students' car designs attractive and useful?

Sophie, Age 9. *Star Car.* Markers, pipe cleaners, bottlecaps, and mechanical parts on paper.

Share Your Art

1. Would you describe your car as modern or old-fashioned? Explain.
2. What makes the car design well-suited to your cartoon character?

183

Gallery Options

Community Display Ask a local business for permission to display student artwork. Have students write brief descriptions of their cartoon cars and hang the descriptions beneath each cartoon. Have students write invitations for their parents to visit the business for a gallery opening of the artwork.

Then, as a class, visit the exhibition of student art. Invite students to analyze each other's work in a nonjudgmental way. Then ask them to interpret the ideas and moods of each other's artworks. Explain that to interpret moods in an exhibition they must ask themselves how the total effect of the artwork makes them feel. To interpret ideas, they must ask whether the images offer a new perspective on familiar topics.

Create

Have students look at the pictures and read the directions on page 182. Gather together the nuts, bolts, and other mechanical objects.

- Have students make several drawings with a pencil before using markers.
- Encourage students to focus on one particular feature, such as speed or elasticity. Remind them that details should serve a purpose.
- Remind them to add a distinctive feature to their characters as well.
- Suggest that students arrange objects in different ways before gluing them down.

Close

Point out the student art on page 183. Explain that these artworks are from the portfolios of other fourth grade students. Have students interpret the ideas in these artworks by asking:

- **How did the students design their cars to fit with their characters?** (The rabbit car carries the character's food; The star car is shaped to fit the star cartoon.)
- **How are these cartoon cars similar to your own? How are they different?** (Responses will vary.)

Then use the *Share Your Art* questions on page 183 to help students evaluate and form conclusions about their own artwork. (Possible responses: modern; The car is full of gadgets and my character likes to fix things.)

See page 90 from **Unit-by-Unit Resources** for a rubric to assess this project.

NVAS (K–4) #1 Understanding and applying media, techniques, and processes

NVAS (K–4) #3 Choosing and evaluating a range of subject matter, symbols, and ideas

NVAS (K–4) #5 Reflecting upon and assessing the characteristics and merits of their work and the work of others

Unit 5 Review

At a Glance

Objectives

- Relate art terms to the environment.
- Identify proportion, cartoon, industrial design, weft, tradition, and portrait in artworks.
- Describe, analyze, interpret, and judge an artwork.

Materials

- **Art Print 20**
- **Fine Art Transparency**

FA TEKS 4.1B Choose appropriate vocabulary to discuss the use of art elements such as color, texture, form, line, space, and value and art principles such as emphasis, pattern, rhythm, balance, proportion, and unity

FA TEKS 4.4A Describe intent and form conclusions about personal artworks

FA TEKS 4.4B Interpret ideas and moods in original artworks, portfolios, and exhibitions by peers and others

Think About Art

Possible responses:

tradition (Point to weaving.)
proportion (Point to cartoon and alarm clock.)
cartoon (Point to cartoon.)
weft (Point to weaving.)
industrial design (Point to alarm clock.)
portrait (Point to cartoon.)

Write About Art

Before students write, ask:

- **What artistic skills or traditions from the past can you name?**
- **How might these skills and traditions be useful today?**

 Think About Art

Read the art words. Then explain how one of the pictures relates to that term.

tradition	cartoon	weft
proportion	industrial design	portrait

 Write About Art

What can artists today learn from the past? Write your ideas.

 Talk About Art

- Choose an artwork from your portfolio that shows a contrast with traditional art forms.
- Tell why you think the artwork is successful.
- Explain what you tried to show in this artwork. Use words you learned in this unit.

 Assessment Options

Options for assessing students appear in the **Unit-by-Unit Resources.**

- Use the **Vocabulary Worksheets** on pages 83–86 for an informal assessment of Unit 5 vocabulary.
- Use the **Unit 5 Test** on pages 91–94 to assess students' mastery of unit vocabulary and concepts.

Red Grooms. *Dali Salad*, 1980–1981. Color lithograph and silkscreen, cut out, glued, and mounted on rag paper (edition of 55), 26½ by 27½ by 12 inches. Courtesy Brooke Alexander Gallery, Inc., New York. Photograph © D. James Dee, New York. © 1998 Red Grooms/Artists Rights Society (ARS), New York.

Put It All Together

1. Describe the subject of the artwork.

2. What makes this three-dimensional portrait unusual?

3. Do you think this artwork is serious or humorous? Explain.

4. Would you like to own this artwork? Explain.

185

Art Background

Dali Salad This artwork refers to Spanish painter, sculptor, graphic artist, and designer Salvador Dalí (1904–1989), who was a key exponent of Surrealism. His paintings are characterized by a blend of precise academic technique and fantastical, hallucinatory images.

Share samples from Dalí's portfolio by displaying his works from art books or from the Internet. (www.dali-gallery.com) Have students interpret the moods and ideas in Dalí's portfolio and relate them to the Hockney portrait. Model first by analyzing sample artworks.

Talk About Art

Prompt students to use words such as *proportion, tradition, portrait, cartoon, balance, unity,* and *variety* to describe their artworks. Then have partners interpret moods and ideas in each other's portfolios. Remind them that to interpret moods in a portfolio they must ask themselves how the combined artworks make them feel. To interpret ideas they can see whether the artworks offer a fresh perspective on familiar topics.

Put It All Together

Tell students that the title of the artwork refers to the artist Salvador Dalí. Use the questions on page 185 to have students form conclusions about and evaluate the artwork. Possible responses:

1. The subject is a portrait of Dalí amidst salad greens and butterflies. **DESCRIBE**
2. Most portraits do not show people as a salad ingredient. **ANALYZE**
3. Humorous. Dalí is shown with a silly expression on his face. **INTERPRET**
4. Yes; the odd details, such as the ribbons, make this a humorous portrait. **JUDGE**

Set up a classroom exhibition of famous portraits. Display *Dalí Salad, Marilyn, Self-Portrait* (Rembrandt), and *The Blue Boy* from this unit along with other portraits from art books or other textbooks. Ask students to interpret the ideas and moods of the artworks in this exhibition of famous portraits.

NVAS (K–4) #1 Understanding and applying media, techniques, and processes

NVAS (K–4) #2 Using knowledge of structures and functions

NVAS (K–4) #5 Reflecting upon and assessing the characteristics and merits of their work and the work of others

Unit 6 Overview

An artist chooses from a wide variety of subjects, media, and styles when creating art. The result can be an interesting or unusual combination of elements. In this unit, students will explore some more interesting art styles and materials. They will also use different media to create their own unique artworks.

	Unit Opener, p. 186	Lesson 1, p. 188 Mixed-Media Artworks Studio 1, p. 190 Design a Story Quilt	Lesson 2, p. 192 Relief Sculpture Studio 2, p. 194 Make a Relief Sculpture	Lesson 3, p. 196 Many Kinds of Folk Art Studio 3, p. 198 Create Papier-Mâché	Look and Compare, p. 200 Cultural Scenes
Artworks	Carmen Lomas Garza. *Haciendo Papel Picado/Making Paper Cutouts*, 1998.	Faith Ringgold. *Harlem Renaissance Party: Bitter Nest Part II*, 1988.	Artist unknown. *The Goddess Hathor and King Sethi*, ca. 1294–1279 B.C.	David Moctezuma. *Alebreje*, 2003.	Carmen Lomas Garza. *Barbacoa para Cumpleaños*, 1993. Grandma Moses. *Joy Ride*, 1953.
Vocabulary	cut-paper art, *papel picado*	mixed media, theme, story quilt, femmage	relief sculpture, profile	folk artist, folk art, papier-mâché, armature	
Materials	• **Art Print 21** • **Fine Art Transparency** • various art materials (optional)	• **Fine Art Transparency** • artworks using different media • Sketchbook Journal • 12" × 18" drawing paper • various media, such as colored pencils, paint, fabric, and chalk pastels • safety scissors ⚠ and glue • ruler (optional)	• **Fine Art Transparency** • Sketchbook Journal • cardboard, pencils, glue, tape, safety scissors ⚠ • assorted found objects, such as small wooden beads, yarn, buttons, and fabric strips • paintbrushes, aluminum foil • Social Studies textbook (optional)	• **Fine Art Transparency** • examples of folk art • Sketchbook Journal • heavy wire ⚠, scrap paper, newspaper, balloons, cardboard tubes, masking tape • newspaper strips, papier-mâché paste or other liquid adherent, plastic tubs • tempera paints, paintbrushes, glue • decorative objects, such as shells, yarn, buttons, and pipe cleaners	• **Art Prints 21, 22, 23** • **Fine Art Transparency**
Connections	**Home Connection** Traditional art forms **Bookshelf** *Magic Windows/Ventanas Magicas* by Carmen Lomas Garza, Children's Book Press, 1999	**Curriculum Connection** Social Studies: contributions of women in community **ESL Notes** **Fine Arts Connection** Theatre: story quilts based on play **Meeting Individual Needs** Inclusion	**Curriculum Connection** Physical Education/Health: benefits of good posture **ESL Notes** **Fine Arts Connection** Music: relief sculpture of musician **Meeting Individual Needs** Reteach, Extend	**Technology** Visit a museum website **ESL Notes** **Fine Arts Connection** Dance: traditional folk dance **Meeting Individual Needs** Reteach	**Reading Strategy** Ask questions
Assessment Opportunities		Visual Culture Rubric 6 from **Unit-by-Unit Resources** Ongoing Assessment	Informal Assessment Rubric 6 from **Unit-by-Unit Resources** Ongoing Assessment	Visual Culture Rubric 6 from **Unit-by-Unit Resources** Ongoing Assessment	

Lesson 4, p. 202 **Fiber Art** Studio 4, p. 204 **Weave Natural Objects**	Lesson 5 p. 206 **Murals** Studio 5, p. 208 **Make a Mural**	Lesson 6, p. 210 **Mosaics** Studio 6, p. 212 **Make a Paper Mosaic**	Artist at Work, p. 214 **Comic Illustrations**	Portfolio Project, p. 216 **Stitch Your Own Design**	Unit Review, p. 218
Billie Ruth Sudduth. *Fibonacci 5,* 1996.	**Yreina D. Cervantez.** *La Ofrenda (The Offering),* 1990.	**Artist unknown.** *Byzantine Emperor.*	**Stan Webb.** *Buffalo Soldier.*		**Artist unknown.** *Blanket: Map of the Four Corners Area,* ca. 1960.
fiber art, raffia cloth	mural, muralists	mosaics, tesserae			
• **Fine Art Transparency** • basket • raffia (optional) • small Y-shaped branches, colored yarn • natural fibers, such as raffia, straw, and grasses • other natural objects, such as feathers and craft sticks (optional)	• **Fine Art Transparency** • colored chalk • Sketchbook Journal • drawing paper, craft paper, pencils, rulers • tempera paint and paintbrushes	• **Fine Art Transparency** • pattern blocks • colored construction paper, cut or torn into an assortment of small pieces for tesserae • tagboard, cardboard, or construction paper for bases, glue or glue sticks • high-gloss varnish (optional)	comic book (optional)	• pencils, 8" squares of drawing paper • water-based markers, 8" burlap squares • colored yarn, large needles ⚠, fabric scraps	• **Art Print 24** • **Fine Art Transparency**
Curriculum Connection Science: prepare and use fiber **ESL Notes** **Fine Arts Connection** Theatre: costumes in plays **Meeting Individual Needs** Extend	**Curriculum Connection** Social Studies: create mural from historical event **ESL Notes** **Fine Arts Connection** Theatre: write play from mural **Meeting Individual Needs** Inclusion	**Curriculum Connection** Math: geometric shapes **ESL Notes** **Fine Arts Connection** Music: musical instrument **Meeting Individual Needs** Extend	**Career Research** Illustrator **Reading Strategy** Build background	**Gallery Options** Traveling exhibit **Meeting Individual Needs** Reteach	
Informal Assessment Rubric 6 from **Unit-by-Unit Resources** Ongoing Assessment	Informal Assessment Rubric 6 from **Unit-by-Unit Resources** Ongoing Assessment	Visual Culture Rubric 6 from **Unit-by-Unit Resources** Ongoing Assessment		Rubric 6 from **Unit-by-Unit Resources**	**Unit-by-Unit Resources** Vocabulary Worksheets, pp. 101–104 Unit 6 Test, pp. 108–112

Unit 6

Objectives

- Identify a variety of media and styles.
- Relate art to personal experiences.
- Respond to and make judgments about artworks.

Materials

- **Art Print 21**
- **Fine Art Transparency**
- various art materials (optional)

Vocabulary

cut-paper art, *papel picado*

FA TEKS 4.1A Communicate ideas about self, family, school, and community, using sensory knowledge and life experiences

FA TEKS 4.2A Integrate a variety of ideas about self, life events, family, and community in original artworks

Introduce the Unit

Have students recall the different media they have learned about in previous units. Ask them which of these they find most interesting and why.

Next, invite students to review the various artworks they have studied. Have them use appropriate vocabulary to discuss both the media and the style of these artworks. Ask: **What are some different purposes for creating artworks?** (Possible responses: to express ideas, to create something functional, to share cultural beliefs)

Then ask a volunteer to read the title of Unit 6. Explain that in this unit they will explore more interesting art styles and materials.

Carmen Lomas Garza. *Haciendo Papel Picado/Making Paper Cutouts,* 1998. Black paper cutout, 22 by 30 inches. Collection of Carmen Lomas Garza, San Francisco, CA. © 1998 Carmen Lomas Garza.

186

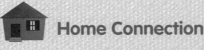 **Art Background**

Making Paper Cutouts In this artwork, Garza depicts people making *papel picado* banners called *banderitas,* which are hung in the plazas of Mexican towns.

Artists use hammers and chisels with special points to cut through many layers of tissue paper when mass-producing *papel picado.* Nonprofessional artists use scissors and folded tissue paper to make *banderitas* for special occasions.

Home Connection

Have students investigate and discuss traditional art forms and crafts practiced by family members and friends, such as weaving, woodwork, or quilting.

An Assortment of Art

You have read about various art forms and media, both old and new. In this unit, you will see a few more interesting art styles and materials.

Some artworks express the artist's cultural background. This artwork shows people making cut-paper art, a traditional Mexican art form called *papel picado*.

Meet the Artist

Much of the work of artist Carmen Lomas Garza shows special and everyday events in the lives of some Mexican Americans. Garza's artworks also appear as illustrations in books she has written. These children's books are based mostly on Garza's childhood in Texas. Find more *papel picado* by Garza later in this unit.

187

 Bookshelf

Magic Windows/Ventanas Mágicas
by Carmen Lomas Garza
Children's Book Press/Libros Para Niños, 1999

Students will enjoy seeing more cut-paper art by Garza on subjects ranging from a grandfather's garden to *Día de los Muertos* (Day of the Dead) celebrations described in English and Spanish. Read the book aloud to students as you display the cut-paper artworks.

You may also want to teach students how to make cut-paper art using Garza's companion book, *Making Magic Windows: Creating Papel Picado/Cut-Paper Art* (Children's Book Press/Libros Para Niños, 1999).

Discuss Unit Concepts

Have students read page 187 and look at the artwork. Ask students to tell the subject of the artwork and describe the details they see.

Discuss the medium Garza used. Ask: **How does the subject match with the medium in this artwork?** (The medium is cut paper; The subject is people making cut-paper art.)

Explain that, just as Garza shares ideas about family and culture, students can integrate their own ideas about family in artworks. Call on students to share ideas about family traditions. Have them use sensory language to describe a family event or celebration. Model first by sharing a family tradition of your own, such as an annual reunion. Describe specific sights, sounds, and smells involved in the event.

Have students tell what media they would use to share their ideas. Gather various art materials and invite students to create artworks that integrate ideas about family. Demonstrate how to use certain media, if necessary.

Art Prints 21–24 and **Transparencies** are available for fine art in the unit.

Meet the Artist

Carmen Lomas Garza (1948–) grew up in Texas during the 1950s. During her career she has worked for civil rights and the preservation of cultural identity for Mexican Americans.

In 1995, she became the first Mexican American artist to have a solo exhibition at the Hirshhorn Museum and Sculpture Garden in Washington, D.C. Her work is also featured in the National Museum of American Art's permanent collection.

NVAS (K–4) #4 Understanding the visual arts in relation to history and cultures

NVAS (K–4) #5 Reflecting upon and assessing the characteristics and merits of their work and the work of others

Lesson 1

At a Glance

Objectives

- Identify and describe mixed-media artworks, story quilts, and femmage.
- Identify and describe theme in artworks.
- Describe, analyze, interpret, and judge artworks.

Materials

- **Fine Art Transparency**
- artworks using different media
- Sketchbook Journal

Vocabulary

mixed media, theme, story quilt, femmage

FA TEKS 4.4B Interpret ideas and moods in original artworks, portfolios, and exhibitions by peers and others

❶ Introduce

Display several artworks and ask students to identify the media used in each. Have them brainstorm a list of other media that could be used for making art.

Tell students that mixed-media artworks are created by using two or more materials. For example, paint and fabric may be used to create a quilt. Have students discuss how other media might be used in combination to create artworks.

Point out that artists use different media to express themselves and share the message, or theme of their artwork. Often this message involves some aspect of their cultural heritage.

Mixed-Media Artworks

Sometimes artists use **mixed media** to express themselves. In mixed-media artworks, artists create with more than one medium. These artists may use their cultural heritage as the **theme,** or main message, of their artwork.

Faith Ringgold. *Harlem Renaissance Party: Bitter Nest, Part II,* 1988. Acrylic on canvas, printed, tie-dyed, and pieced fabric, 94 by 82 inches. © 1988 Faith Ringgold, Inc.

188

🎨 Art Background

About the Artist American artist Faith Ringgold (1930–) has used a diverse range of media including paint, fabric, and paper to create her original artworks, which focus on African American cultural life, slavery, and civil rights.

About the Artist In the 1970s, Canadian American artist Miriam Schapiro (1923–) developed a technique called *femmage,* which uses the media and methods traditionally employed by women, such as embroidery and appliqué, to create mixed-media artworks.

Miriam Schapiro. *Mechano/Flower Fan*, 1979. Acrylic and fabric collage on paper, 30 by 44 inches. The National Museum of Women in the Arts, Washington, D.C. Gift of Mary Ross Taylor, in honor of her mother, W. B. Abbott.

Faith Ringgold's **story quilt** combines fabric and paint to tell a story. It shows famous people who created a community of artists during a time known as the Harlem Renaissance. The words along the border tell their story.

Miriam Schapiro describes her art as **femmage,** a collage of fabrics traditionally made by women. What would you use in a collage to call attention to your interests? Why?

Sketchbook Journal

Think about a story you want to tell in a mixed-media artwork. Make a list of materials you could use, and illustrate your list. Draw a sketch of your theme.

189

---

② Teach

Have students read pages 188–189 and look at Ringgold's story quilt. Ask:

- **What do you see in the center of the artwork? What do you see on the borders?** (people sitting around a table and one woman dancing; colored fabrics and words) DESCRIBE
- **How did Ringgold create variety in her story quilt?** (Possible response: She used various media with different textures, such as paint and fabric.) ANALYZE
- **What is the theme of this artwork?** (Possible response: African American artists have made important contributions to society.) INTERPRET
- **What is your favorite part of the artwork? Why?** (Possible response: The woman dancing; she seems to be celebrating.) JUDGE

Now ask similar questions about Schapiro's artwork.

Sketchbook Journal Encourage students to use their cultural heritage as a basis for story ideas.

③ Close

After students complete their illustrated lists, have them discuss the theme of their proposed artworks.

Visual Culture Have a graphic designer visit the class to discuss how he or she uses a variety of technological media, such as video, print, and photography.

NVAS (K–4) #4 Understanding the visual arts in relation to history and cultures

NVAS (K–4) #5 Reflecting upon and assessing the characteristics and merits of their work and the work of others

---

 **Curriculum Connection**

Social Studies Have students work in small groups to research the contributions of women to their community or state. Provide a variety of materials for them to use in creating a mixed-media artwork based on their research.

SS TEKS 4.5B Identify accomplishments of notable individuals
SS TEKS 4.18C Identify the importance of historical figures

ESL Notes

Display a variety of media and write the name of each on an index card. Have students match each type of media with its label and say the name aloud.

ESL TEKS 4.5G Employ content area vocabulary words in context

Studio 1

At a Glance

Objectives

- Express ideas by creating story quilts.
- Demonstrate use of mixed media.
- Evaluate original artworks by self and peers.

Materials

- 12" × 18" drawing paper
- various media, such as colored pencils, paint, fabric, and chalk pastels
- safety scissors ⚠, glue
- ruler (optional)
- Rubric 6 from **Unit-by-Unit Resources**

FA TEKS 4.1B Choose appropriate vocabulary to discuss the use of art elements such as color, texture, form, line, space, and value and art principles such as emphasis, pattern, rhythm, balance, proportion, and unity

FA TEKS 4.2B Design original artworks

FA TEKS 4.2C Invent ways to produce artworks and to explore photographic imagery, using a variety of art media and materials

1 Introduce

Review mixed-media artworks and story quilts. Have students describe examples they may have seen.

Tell students that although most quilts use stitching, they will be making story quilts without sewing. Have students brainstorm ideas. Ask:

- **Will you choose a story from your life or from a book?**
- **Who are the main characters in the story?**
- **What details will you include to express your theme?**

Quick Studio

Have students use crayons to draw a scene from a familiar fairy tale. Then have them make a border using construction paper.

Studio 1

Design a Story Quilt

What story could you use as the subject of a story quilt? Think about design elements to include.

1 Choose a story that would make a good subject for a story quilt.

2 Begin writing a story along the borders of a sheet of paper.

Technique Tip

Cover the border with paper as you illustrate the center to avoid smearing your writing.

190

🚶🚶🚶🚶 Meeting Individual Needs

Inclusion Students who have difficulties with fine motor skills will benefit from having some materials pre-cut, such as paper shapes, fabric pieces, tissue paper, or foil. You may also wish to provide templates of various shapes for students to draw around as they create their center illustrations.

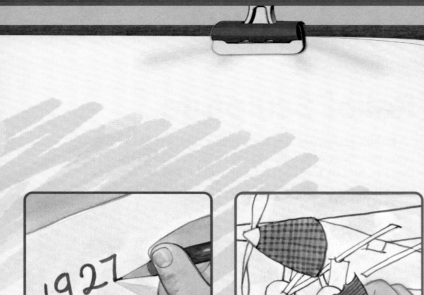

3 Decorate the border with colorful details as you write.

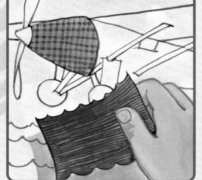

4 Choose a new medium to illustrate the story in the center of the quilt.

Think Like an Artist

Describe how the illustrations in the center complement the words around the border.

191

Fine Arts Connection

Theatre Read a play aloud to students or take them to a performance. Have them work in small groups to create story quilts based on the play.

Theatre 4.1F Represent environment, characterization, and actions

② Create

Have students look at the pictures and read the directions on pages 190–191. Then distribute materials.

- Have students discuss how they can arrange color values and positive and negative space to achieve a sense of unity in their design.
- Encourage students to write a draft of their story first. Suggest they use a ruler to mark the border before transferring the story.
- In Step 3, encourage students to use both words and symbols to express their themes.
- Suggest that students make a light drawing of their illustration on the quilt before applying the new medium.

Technique Tip Students can use scrap paper to cover the borders as they illustrate the center.

③ Close

Have students reflect on their story quilts by answering the *Think Like an Artist* question. (Possible response: Both the illustrations and the border show my theme of people working together.)

Ongoing Assessment

If . . . students have difficulty choosing a story,

then . . . assign one they have recently read.

See page 108 from **Unit-by-Unit Resources** for a rubric to assess this studio.

NVAS (K–4) #1 Understanding and applying media, techniques, and processes

NVAS (K–4) #3 Choosing and evaluating a range of subject matter, symbols, and ideas

NVAS (K–4) #5 Reflecting upon and assessing the characteristics and merits of their work and the work of others

Lesson 2

At a Glance

Objectives

- Identify and describe relief sculpture.
- Identify and describe profiles in artworks.
- Describe, analyze, interpret, and judge artworks.

Materials

- **Fine Art Transparency**
- Sketchbook Journal

Vocabulary

relief sculpture, profile

FA TEKS 4.3B Compare and contrast selected artworks from a variety of cultural settings

FA TEKS 4.4B Interpret ideas and moods in original artworks, portfolios, and exhibitions by peers and others

❶ Introduce

Have students look at the artwork on page 192. Then have them try to stand like the king in the relief sculpture. Ask if they are comfortable in this position.

Tell students that Egyptian artists often cast their subjects in this pose, which shows all parts of a figure's body. Next invite students to compare and contrast this artwork with the one on page 193.

Explain that both artworks show the heads and bodies of their subjects, but the sculpture from Mesopotamia shows a complete side view of the harpist. It also shows the image without added color, unlike the Egyptian artwork, which includes reds, blacks, whites, and brown tones.

Lesson 2

Relief Sculpture

Relief sculpture is a form of art that is thousands of years old. Parts of a relief sculpture are raised to make them stand out from a flat background. The relief in this sculpture was created by carving away the background areas.

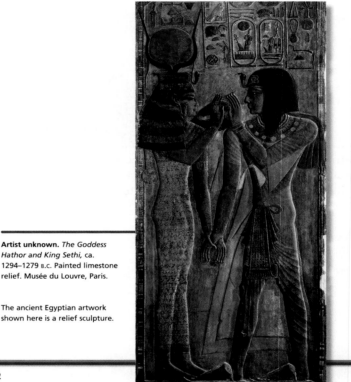

Artist unknown. *The Goddess Hathor and King Sethi,* ca. 1294–1279 B.C. Painted limestone relief. Musée du Louvre, Paris.

The ancient Egyptian artwork shown here is a relief sculpture.

192

🎨 Art Background

Art and Culture In ancient Egyptian religion, Hathor was the goddess of women and love. Associated with the sky and the cow, she was sometimes represented as a star-studded cow or a woman with the head of a cow.

Harpist This relief sculpture is made from terra cotta, or clay baked to be hard and compact. The fringed robe and skull cap of the harpist are characteristic of Mesopotamian sculptures from the second millennium B.C. Plaques from this period often show musicians playing a variety of instruments.

Artist unknown. *Harpist,* ca. 1800 B.C. Terra-cotta plaque, 3 by 4⅜ inches. Musée du Louvre, Paris.

Notice how the head in the Egyptian relief sculpture is shown in **profile,** or from a side view. However, the body faces forward. This style was used in Egyptian art for thousands of years.

Compare the terra-cotta relief sculpture above with the Egyptian sculpture. Talk about similarities and differences in how the figures are portrayed.

Sketchbook Journal

How would an Egyptian artist have portrayed you? Draw a picture of yourself as a figure in an Egyptian relief sculpture. Describe and explain the point of view.

193

Curriculum Connection

Physical Education/Health Have a nurse or other health professional visit the class and discuss the benefits of good posture both when standing and sitting. Have students take notes and then write a short report on why they should practice good posture. Ask students to practice this posture as they move through their school day.
Health TEKS 4.2A Describe how health behaviors affect body systems

 **Notes**

Provide magazine images of people in obvious profile or frontal positions. Have students sort them accordingly and name each position.
ESL TEKS 4.5G Employ content area vocabulary words in context

② Teach

Ask students to read pages 192–193 and look at *The Goddess Hathor and King Sethi.* Ask:

- **What is the subject of this relief sculpture?** (a goddess and a king facing each other) DESCRIBE
- **What mood does the artist convey? How?** (Possible response: The artist shows an affectionate mood. The position of the subjects' hands shows that they care for one another.) ANALYZE
- **How can you tell that the two figures are important?** (Possible response: They are wearing fancy clothes and they stand out against the background.) INTERPRET
- **Which of the two figures would you rather meet? Why?** (Possible response: The goddess Hathor; her headgear is more interesting.) JUDGE

Ask similar questions about the *Harpist.*

Sketchbook Journal You may want to show students more examples of ancient Egyptian relief sculptures to guide them. Remind them to show their head in profile and their body facing forward.

③ Close

After students complete their drawings, have them trade with a partner and describe the points of view in each other's work.

Assessment Have students identify figures in profile in posters around the school.

NVAS (K–4) #2 Using knowledge of structures and functions
NVAS (K–4) #4 Understanding the visual arts in relation to history and cultures
NVAS (K–4) #5 Reflecting upon and assessing the characteristics and merits of their work and the work of others
NVAS (K–4) #6 Making connections between visual arts and other disciplines

Studio 2

At a Glance

Objectives

- Express ideas by creating a relief sculpture.
- Evaluate original artworks by self and peers.

Materials

- cardboard, pencils, glue, tape, safety scissors ⚠
- assorted found objects, such as small wooden beads, yarn, buttons, and fabric strips
- paintbrushes, aluminum foil
- Social Studies textbook (optional)
- Rubric 6 from **Unit-by-Unit Resources**

FA TEKS 4.2B Design original artworks

FA TEKS 4.2C Invent ways to produce artworks and to explore photographic imagery, using a variety of art media and materials

1 Introduce

Review relief sculpture. Remind students that parts of a relief sculpture are raised to stand out from a flat background.

Have students brainstorm ideas for their sculptures. Ask:

- **What person from history will you portray?**
- **What features of this person will you include?**
- **What found objects will you use to create a three-dimensional effect?**

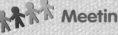

Quick Studio
Have students use colored yarn and glue on cardboard to create a portrait of a person they admire.

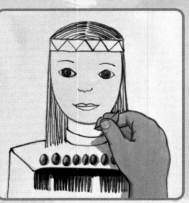

Studio 2
Make a Relief Sculpture

Follow these steps to turn a three-dimensional collage of a historical person into a relief sculpture.

1. **Make a sketch of a person from history. Draw from memory or imagination.**

2. **Glue cut cardboard and found objects to create a relief sculpture.**

Technique Tip

Build the relief material up to one inch deep. Press the foil gently with a pencil eraser to form the relief.

194

🚶🚶🚶 Meeting Individual Needs

Reteach Have students create a portrait of a friend by gluing pieces of cardboard to an oval cardboard shape. Then have them cover the oval with aluminum foil and use markers to add details.

Extend Provide students with self-hardening clay. Have them use the clay to form some of the features of their historical person. Then encourage them to continue by adding found objects for additional details and texture.

3 After the portrait dries, brush thinned white glue over the entire surface.

4 Starting from the center, gently press a sheet of foil over the entire portrait.

Think Like an Artist

Explain how successful you were in creating the flat and raised forms that you planned. Does your relief sculpture have light and dark areas?

195

Fine Arts Connection

Music Have students research famous musicians and composers, such as Mozart, Beethoven, and Anna Bon. Invite them to find out three interesting facts about the musician, and a picture of him or her. Then have them make a relief sculpture of the musician. The relief sculptures can be displayed in the music room.

FA TEKS 4.5D Identify connections between music and other fine arts

2 Create

Ask students to look at the pictures and follow the directions on pages 194–195. Cut cardboard squares and foil pieces beforehand. Be sure the foil is slightly larger than the cardboard.

- Suggest students look through their Social Studies books to find a subject for their relief sculpture.
- Remind students to think about how the shapes will look when covered with foil.
- Be sure students spread the glue in a thin, even layer to avoid puddles of glue in the crevices.
- Tell students to tuck the foil edges under the cardboard and secure with tape.

Technique Tip Demonstrate how to use the pencil eraser to gently press the foil. Tell students to avoid poking at the foil or using their fingernails as this may cause tears.

3 Close

Have students reflect on their artworks by answering the *Think Like an Artist* question. (Possible responses: I made the nose a little too flat, but otherwise my forms look good; There are light areas on the raised forms.)

Ongoing Assessment

If . . . students have difficulty envisioning how their sculptures will look,

then . . . provide an extra sheet of foil for them to lay over their collage to determine if they have created sufficient relief.

See page 108 from **Unit-by-Unit Resources** for a rubric to assess this studio.

NVAS (K–4) #1 Understanding and applying media, techniques, and processes

NVAS (K–4) #3 Choosing and evaluating a range of subject matter, symbols, and ideas

NVAS (K–4) #5 Reflecting upon and assessing the characteristics and merits of their work and the work of others

Lesson 3

At a Glance

Objectives

- Identify and describe folk art.
- Identify and describe papier-mâché artworks.
- Describe, analyze, interpret, and judge artworks.

Materials

- **Fine Art Transparency**
- examples of folk art
- Sketchbook Journal

Vocabulary

folk artist, folk art, papier-mâché, armature

FA TEKS 4.1B Choose appropriate vocabulary to discuss the use of art elements such as color, texture, form, line, space, and value and art principles such as emphasis, pattern, rhythm, balance, proportion, and unity

FA TEKS 4.3C Identify the roles of art in American society

FA TEKS 4.4B Interpret ideas and moods in original artworks, portfolios, and exhibitions by peers and others

①Introduce

Bring examples of folk art for students to observe, such as a quilt, a wooden toy, or pottery. Have students describe the colors, forms, and lines they see.

Explain the role folk art plays in our society by describing the use and/or function of each object. Further explain that folk art is usually not created by professional artists. Folk artists often have another career and create their art for pleasure or for the enjoyment of others. They sometimes carry on artistic traditions that are passed down from generation to generation.

Ask students to describe other folk art objects they have seen in their homes or communities, including those made of papier-mâché, such as piñatas, masks, or decorative figures.

Lesson 3

Many Kinds of Folk Art

Do you know someone who whittles wooden toys, makes decorative quilts, or carves birds? If so, you probably know a **folk artist,** a self-taught artist. Folk artists create artworks, called **folk art,** that often reflect the artists' cultural symbols and beliefs.

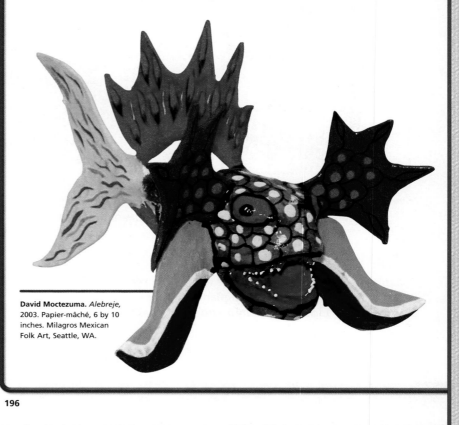

David Moctezuma. *Alebreje,* 2003. Papier-mâché, 6 by 10 inches. Milagros Mexican Folk Art, Seattle, WA.

Art Background

About the Artist Pedro Linares (1906–1992) began making papier-mâché animals and figures in 1957. Today, six of Linares' sons and grandsons, including featured artist David Moctezuma, continue the folk art tradition of *cartonería,* or making papier-mâché objects for fiestas.

About the Artist Clark Coe (1847–1919), a farmer and basketmaker by trade, is most noted for his creation of life-size, movable figures that he constructed on his land. The figures, known as the *Killingworth Images,* were created from barrel staves, slats, driftwood, and tree stumps. They move by water power.

Clark Coe. *Killingworth Image, Man on a Hog*, ca. 1890. Carved, assembled, and painted wood, tinned iron, and textile remnants, 37 by 38 by 21¾ inches. Smithsonian American Art Museum, Washington, D.C.

This mixed-media sculpture is another example of folk art.

The Linares family of Mexico is known for its folk art **papier-mâché** sculptures. Paper strips are dipped in a watery paste and added in layers to an **armature,** or frame. It provides strength and shape. The grandfather, Pedro Linares, first made the sculptures. Now other family members, such as David Moctezuma, create these imaginative works as well.

Sketchbook Journal

Draw a picture of an unusually colorful fish or animal from memory, observation, or your imagination. Write a plan to create the sculpture based on your drawing.

197

2 Teach

Have students read pages 196–197 and look at *Alebreje.* Ask:

- **What medium is used in this artwork?** (papier-mâché) DESCRIBE
- **How does the artist use colors to show balance?** (Possible response: He shows purple and different values of blue on opposite sides of the form.) ANALYZE
- **What mood do you think the artist conveys?** (Possible response: playful, humorous) INTERPRET
- **Would you want this fish as a pet? Why or why not?** (Possible response: No; it seems monstrous.) JUDGE

Now ask similar questions about Clark Coe's artwork.

Sketchbook Journal Have students include a variety of colors, patterns, shapes, and lines in their drawings.

3 Close

After students complete their drawings, have them name their fish creations.

Visual Culture Have students look for examples of folk art in their homes. Invite them to interview family members to find out the history of each artwork.

NVAS (K–4) #2 Using knowledge of structures and functions
NVAS (K–4) #4 Understanding the visual arts in relation to history and cultures
NVAS (K–4) #5 Reflecting upon and assessing the characteristics and merits of their work and the work of others
NVAS (K–4) #6 Making connections between visual arts and other disciplines

Technology

Visit a Museum Website Have students work in small groups to find more images of folk art on museum Web sites, such as the Smithsonian **(www.si.edu),** American Folk Art Museum **(www.folkartmuseum.org),** or Museum of Craft & Folk Art **(www.sfcraftandfolk.org).** Invite students to make sketches of their favorite artworks and note the materials used in each.

Tech TEKS 4.2A Use variety of input devices
Tech TEKS 4.4A Apply appropriate electronic search strategies

ESL Notes

Have students find or bring in an example of folk art from their heritage countries. Ask them to point to and name colors and subjects in the artwork.

ESL TEKS 4.4A Connect experiences with those of others

Studio 3

Studio 3
Create Papier-Mâché

Design your own papier-mâché sculpture of an animal, a person, a plant, or an imaginary figure.

1 Form an armature using wire, an inflated balloon, or wadded-up newspaper.

2 Dip newspaper strips into paste and remove excess. Lay strips on armature.

Technique Tip

Use wide newspaper strips to cover wide forms. Thin strips will lie flat on small areas. Let each layer dry before you add another.

198

At a Glance

Objectives

• Express ideas by creating a papier-mâché sculpture.
• Demonstrate how to build an armature.
• Evaluate original artworks by self and peers.

Materials

• heavy wire ⚠, scrap paper, newspaper, balloons, cardboard tubes, masking tape
• newspaper strips, papier-mâché paste or other liquid adherent, plastic tubs
• tempera paints, paintbrushes, glue
• decorative objects, such as shells, yarn, buttons, and pipe cleaners ⚠
• Rubric 6 from **Unit-by-Unit Resources**

FA TEKS 4.2B Design original artworks

FA TEKS 4.2C Invent ways to produce artworks and to explore photographic imagery, using a variety of art media and materials

FA TEKS 4.4A Describe intent and form conclusions about personal artworks

❶ Introduce

Review papier-mâché. Ask students to describe papier-mâché artworks they have made or seen.

Have students brainstorm ideas for their sculptures and describe their intentions. Ask:

• **What subject will you portray?**
• **What forms will you use to create the armature?**
• **How will you arrange found objects to show variety?**

Quick Studio

Have students dip strips of colored tissue paper into paste and apply them to an inflated balloon. After it dries, add details with markers.

🏃 Meeting Individual Needs

Reteach Have students create papier-mâché cups and bowls using recycled plastic containers as molds. Instruct them to turn the tubs upside down and then apply strips to the inverted tubs.

When the strips are dry, have them separate the bowls or cups from the plastic forms. Have them trim the edges and paint the sculptures with tempera paints.

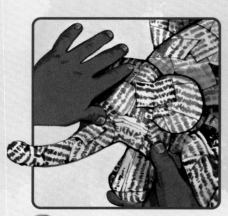

3 Continue adding strips until the main form is finished. Shape details.

4 After the paper dries, paint the sculpture. Add found objects for decoration.

Think Like an Artist

Would you describe your papier-mâché sculpture as folk art? Explain.

 Fine Arts Connection

Dance Have students research a traditional folk dance, such as the Mexican hat dance. Explain that dancers perform a sequence of hopping steps and heel-to-toe tapping around a large Mexican *sombrero,* or hat.

If possible, show a video of a hat dance being performed and practice the simple steps with students. Explain that this dance is often performed at festivals and celebrations. Then have students make a papier-mâché hat, which they can use as they perform the dance.

FA TEKS 4.1I Perform basic folk dance steps

2 Create

Ask students to read the directions on pages 198–199 and look at the pictures. Collect materials and prepare newspaper strips ahead of time. This studio will take several classes.

- Instruct students to be careful using wire. Show them how to tape parts of the armature together, using tape to make areas stronger.
- Show students how to crisscross the newspaper strips as they cover the armature.
- Tell students to let the first layer dry. Then have them add one or two more layers.
- Allow sufficient time for the sculpture to dry. Have students paint the dried form with tempera paint and add details with glue.

Technique Tip Demonstrate how to run strips through fingers to squeeze away most of the paste.

3 Close

Have students reflect on their sculptures by answering the *Think Like an Artist* question. (Possible response: Yes; because I am not a professional artist.)

Ongoing Assessment

If . . . students have difficulty applying the strips,

then . . . show them how to place strips one at a time until the armature is covered.

See page 108 from **Unit-by-Unit Resources** for a rubric to assess this studio.

NVAS (K–4) #1 Understanding and applying media, techniques, and processes

NVAS (K–4) #3 Choosing and evaluating a range of subject matter, symbols, and ideas

NVAS (K–4) #5 Reflecting upon and assessing the characteristics and merits of their work and the work of others

Look and Compare

Look and Compare

At a Glance

Objectives

- Compare and contrast two artworks showing cultural scenes.
- Analyze the influences of history and culture in artworks.
- Respond to and make judgments about artworks.

Materials

- **Art Prints 21, 22, 23**
- **Fine Art Transparency**

FA TEKS 4.3A Identify simple main ideas expressed in art

FA TEKS 4.3B Compare and contrast selected artworks from a variety of cultural settings

Explore

Display **Art Print 21.** Help students recall this artwork by Carmen Lomas Garza from page 186.

As students look at the two artworks on pages 200 and 201, ask them to predict which one was also created by Garza, and give reasons for their answer. (*Birthday Barbecue*; it also shows *papel picado* and the cultural setting is Mexican American.)

Discuss

After students read pages 200 and 201, have them discuss the colors, weather, and cultural differences in each painting. Have students notice the traditional Mexican cultural items in Garza's artwork, such as the piñata and the *papel picado.* Point out that Garza uses bright colors to show the warm weather of the region. Students can contrast this scene with the winter setting in Moses' painting. Point out the use of white to create a snowy, cold scene along with the sleigh rides and cultural dress.

Cultural Scenes

Grandma Moses created scenes of New England traditions long before Carmen Lomas Garza began to paint scenes of her own Mexican American culture. Unlike Garza, however, Grandma Moses did not begin to paint until she was in her seventies.

Carmen Lomas Garza. *Barbacoa para Cumpleaños (Birthday Barbecue),* 1993. Alkyds on canvas, 36 by 48 inches. Collection of Federal Reserve Bank of Dallas, Dallas, TX. © 1993 Carmen Lomas Garza (reg. 1994).

200

Art Background

Birthday Barbecue In this painting, Garza depicts a childhood memory of her sister Mary Jane's birthday party. The painting's central focus is of the birthday girl breaking her piñata while a multi-generational group of family and friends watch and encourage her. The precise details, unusual perspective, and flat, bright colors are typical of Garza's paintings.

Joy Ride Like most of Anna Mary Robertson Moses' (1860–1961) paintings, *Joy Ride* draws on rural scenes from the painter's life. This image has been widely reproduced in greeting cards and other media.

200

Grandma Moses. *Joy Ride*, 1953. Oil on pressed wood, 18 by 24 inches. © 1992, Grandma Moses Properties Co., New York.

Compare the subjects, styles, and cultures shown in these two paintings. Point out how each artist showed pattern and rhythm. What part of each painting does your eye go to first?

Which painting shows warm weather? Which one shows cold weather? How can you tell?

Research

Find a picture of either *Children's Games* or *Winter Scene* by Pieter Brueghel. Compare the Brueghel painting with either *Birthday Barbecue* or *Joy Ride*.

201

Ask Questions Tell students that asking questions while they read a passage or look at an artwork is an effective way to understand what they are reading or viewing. As students read pages 200–201 and look at the artworks, have them list questions they have, such as "What are the banners hanging in *Birthday Barbecue?*" (banderitas) and "What culture is shown in *Joy Ride?*" (a rural New England culture) Discuss their questions as a class after reading the text.

TAKS Rdg. Obj. 1 Understand written texts
ELA TEKS 4.13H Use compiled information to raise questions

Apply

Draw a Venn diagram like the one below on the board. Fill in the center of the diagram as students say how the artworks are alike.

Then guide students to look for differences as they focus on the colors, cultural setting, weather, and center of interest in each artwork. Possible responses are shown in blue.

Two Cultural Scenes

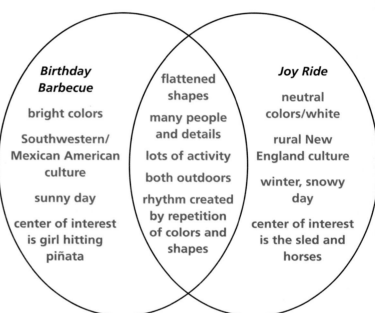

Birthday Barbecue

bright colors

Southwestern/ Mexican American culture

sunny day

center of interest is girl hitting piñata

flattened shapes

many people and details

lots of activity

both outdoors

rhythm created by repetition of colors and shapes

Joy Ride

neutral colors/white

rural New England culture

winter, snowy day

center of interest is the sled and horses

Close

Ask students what they learned about painting cultural scenes. (Possible response: There are many ways to show people celebrating.)

Research Students may find images of the Breughel paintings in books or at **www.artcyclopedia.com.** Have them compare the weather, cultural setting, and colors. Then have them identify simple main ideas in the artworks.

NVAS (K–4) #4 Understanding the visual arts in relation to history and cultures

NVAS (K–4) #5 Reflecting upon and assessing the characteristics and merits of their work and the work of others

At a Glance

Objectives

• Identify and describe fiber art.

• Describe, analyze, interpret, and judge artworks.

Materials

• **Fine Art Transparency**

• basket

• raffia (optional)

Vocabulary

fiber art, raffia cloth

FA TEKS 4.1B Choose appropriate vocabulary to discuss the use of art elements such as color, texture, form, line, space, and value and art principles such as emphasis, pattern, rhythm, balance, proportion, and unity

FA TEKS 4.3C Identify the roles of art in American society

❶ Introduce

Display a basket. Have students discuss some of the functional uses for baskets in our society. They may say baskets are used to carry items, such as laundry and fruit.

Tell students that baskets and cloth can be woven from fibers, such as raffia, which comes from a type of palm tree. If possible, bring in a piece of raffia for students to touch.

Then have them describe the texture of the raffia, as well as the texture of the basket. Ask them to identify examples of fiber art they may have seen at home or in their community.

Fiber Art

Many artists create useful objects, such as blankets, rugs, or baskets, by hand. They make **fiber art,** art created with thread or thread-like materials.

Billie Ruth Sudduth. *Fibonacci 5,* 1996. Hand-shaped and hand-dyed reed splints, with twill weave construction, 13 by 16½ inches. Smithsonian American Art Museum, Washington, D.C.

🎨 Art Background

About the Artist A former school psychologist, Billie Ruth Sudduth became interested in basketry after learning the skill in a summer course. Eventually her hobby became her life's work and her passion. Known for incorporating a mathematical sequence called the Fibonacci series into her pattern development, Sudduth's baskets have become world-renowned.

Art and Culture Raffia is a natural fiber derived from the cut leaves and bark of raffia palm trees. During the 1600s, textiles made from raffia, which provide a rich range of color and velvety texture, became the basis of wealth and currency in Central Africa.

The basket artist used natural fibers to weave an object that is both beautiful and useful. Sometimes baskets are woven so tightly that they can hold water.

The cloth weaving above is a **raffia cloth.** It is woven from raffia, a fiber that is also used to make baskets.

How are the texture and designs on these two objects similar?

Art in My World

Look around your home, classroom, or community. See how many ways people use baskets, a traditional fiber craft object seen in many parts of the world. Describe the design of a basket.

203

② Teach

Have students look at the basket and read pages 202–203. Ask:

- **What material was used to make the basket?** (hand-shaped and hand-dyed reed splints) DESCRIBE
- **How is the design created in this basket?** (by weaving different colored reeds in a pattern) ANALYZE

Review functional and decorative artwork. Then ask:

- **Would you describe this artwork as functional or decorative? Why?** (Possible response: Both; because it is useful and interesting to look at.) INTERPRET
- **How would you use this basket?** (Possible response: to hold flowers) JUDGE

Ask similar questions about the raffia cloth. Discuss how the texture of both artworks is rough or prickly and how both use lines that cross over and under each other.

Art in My World Have students draw a basket they find in their home or community and write about how it is used.

③ Close

Have students identify the material used to make the basket they found.

Assessment Have students list items that are made with fibers. If possible, have them find examples of fiber art in the classroom.

Curriculum Connection

Science Have students work in small groups to research natural fibers, such as cotton and wool. Have them investigate the process used to prepare these fibers for weaving, and make a list of ways the fibers are used in U.S. society. Then invite groups to present their findings to the class.

TAKS (Gr. 5) Sci Obj. 1 Understand the nature of science
  Sci TEKS 4.3E Connect Grade 4 science concepts with the history of science

 **Notes**

Have students describe the tactile texture of a basket or cloth using words such as *soft, rough,* or *scratchy.*
ESL TEKS 4.5G Employ content area vocabulary words in context

NVAS (K–4) #2 Using knowledge of structures and functions
NVAS (K–4) #4 Understanding the visual arts in relation to history and cultures
NVAS (K–4) #5 Reflecting upon and assessing the characteristics and merits of their work and the work of others
NVAS (K–4) #6 Making connections between visual arts and other disciplines

Studio 4

At a Glance

Objectives

- Express ideas by making fiber art.
- Demonstrate weaving using natural fibers.
- Evaluate original artworks by self and peers.

Materials

- small Y-shaped branches, colored yarn
- natural fibers, such as raffia, straw, and grasses
- other natural objects, such as feathers and craft sticks (optional) ⚠
- Rubric 6 from **Unit-by-Unit Resources**

FA TEKS 4.2B Design original artworks

FA TEKS 4.2C Invent ways to produce artworks and to explore photographic imagery, using a variety of art media and materials

FA TEKS 4.4A Describe intent and form conclusions about personal artworks

❶ Introduce

Review fiber art, weaving, warp, and weft. Ask students to name natural fibers they can use in a weaving.

Remind students that having a clear plan for an artwork can help make the project run smoothly. Have students describe their intentions for the weaving. Ask:

- **What color yarn will you use?**
- **What patterns will you create?**
- **How will you show texture with natural fibers?**

Quick Studio

Have students make bookmarks using strips of burlap. Have them pull threads out and tie other ones together to create patterns.

Studio 4

Weave Natural Objects

Weavers use looms of many shapes and sizes. Try this fiber art project using a branch for a loom.

1 Find a small tree branch that is shaped like the letter Y.

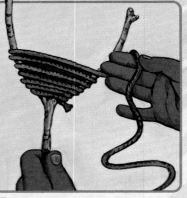

2 Wrap yarn around the outer parts of the Y for the warp.

Technique Tip

Wrap the warp tightly around each side of the Y so it will not slip. Knot the beginning and end of the warp.

204

👫👫 Meeting Individual Needs

Extend Have students make a mixed-media wall hanging using clay, yarn, and natural fibers. Tell them to make a rectangular frame with slabs of self-hardening clay. Then have them use a plastic soda straw to make holes through the top and bottom edges.

When the clay is hard have them make a warp by pulling yarn through the holes. Then have them weave the weft using natural fibers.

204

3 Next, weave in various fibers to make the weft. Do not pull the weft too tight.

4 Use your fingertips to adjust the spacing of the warp and weft.

Think Like an Artist

Explain why an artist might make a weaving like yours instead of one on a traditional loom. How did you consider unity and color in your weaving?

205

Fine Arts Connection

Theatre Have students write or choose a short play to perform. Then invite them to design and create costumes and props made with fiber art to use in their performance. You may want to suggest that they design belts, hats, capes, baskets, or other objects made by weaving.

FA TEKS 4.2C Develop characters and assume roles in short improvised scenes
FA TEKS 4.3A Demonstrate safe use of props

2 Create

Have students look at the pictures and read the directions on pages 204–205. Then distribute materials.

- Have students collect branches that have already fallen off trees. You may want to gather them ahead of time.
- Assist students in knotting the yarn around the base of one side of the *Y* to begin. Then demonstrate how to wrap the remaining yarn.
- Encourage students to invent interesting patterns and textures using the fibers.
- Invite students to add other natural objects, such as feathers, to add variety and texture.

Technique Tip Show students how to use a craft stick to push the fibers under and over the warp.

3 Close

Tell students to reflect on their weavings by answering the *Think Like an Artist* questions. (Possible responses: Because non-traditional looms are more interesting; The natural colors of the materials worked to create unity.)

Ongoing Assessment

If . . . the branch is smooth,

then . . . have students loop each thread in the warp around the branch to keep it from slipping.

See page 108 from **Unit-by-Unit Resources** for a rubric to assess this studio.

NVAS (K–4) #1 Understanding and applying media, techniques, and processes

NVAS (K–4) #3 Choosing and evaluating a range of subject matter, symbols, and ideas

NVAS (K–4) #5 Reflecting upon and assessing the characteristics and merits of their work and the work of others

Lesson 5

At a Glance

Objectives

- Identify and describe murals.
- Describe, analyze, interpret, and judge artworks.

Materials

- **Fine Art Transparency**
- colored chalk
- Sketchbook Journal

Vocabulary

mural, muralists

FA TEKS 4.3C Identify the roles of art in American society

FA TEKS 4.4B Interpret ideas and moods in original artworks, portfolios, and exhibitions by peers and others

① Introduce

Take students to the playground or school sidewalk. Using colored chalk, have each student draw something he or she likes about the school. Then invite the class to stand back and view the drawings as one.

Tell students that they have just created a mural, or a large artwork that decorates a public place. Explain that muralists make murals as a form of public art, often seen on walls both inside and outside of buildings. Go on to explain the roles murals play in our society by explaining that often murals depict a social or political statement. Or, they may document the history and traditions of a particular time and place.

Ask students if they have seen a mural, and if so, what was its subject and location. Have students describe the message of the mural and its role in the community.

Lesson 5

Murals

You might see a **mural** in almost any big city in the United States. These large artworks are usually painted directly on a ceiling or a wall in a public place. Some murals are indoors. Others decorate outdoor spaces.

Yreina D. Cervantez. *La Ofrenda (The Offering),* 1990. Mural. Los Angeles, CA. Commissioned by SPARC, through its Great Walls Unlimited: Neighborhood Pride Program. Photo courtesy of SPARC (www.sparcmurals.org).

Describe some details you see in this mural. What elements of art did the artist use to create unity and variety?

🎨 Art Background

The Offering Located in downtown Los Angeles, this mural celebrates everyday life, hard work, and the central role played by women in the community. Specifically, this mural honors the struggle and strength of farmworkers, such as Dolores Huerta, a longtime leader of the United Farmworkers Union.

About the Artist American painter John Steuart Curry (1897–1946) was a Regionalist artist known for his depictions of rural Kansas. From 1936–1938, he created murals commissioned under the New Deal.

John Steuart Curry. (Detail) *Kansas Pastoral*. Mural at the Kansas State House, Topeka, KS.

What can you learn about Kansas from Curry's mural? What values do you think Curry wanted to reflect?

Muralists often use their artwork to tell a story about something important to them. What story do you think these **muralists** wanted to show?

Sometimes murals are painted by one person. At other times a group of muralists works together to design and create a mural. The mural above was designed by one artist. How does the credit line reflect this information?

Sketchbook Journal

Draw a place in your community where you think a mural would look just right. What story would the mural tell? Write a list of words for your story.

207

Curriculum Connection

Social Studies Have students work in groups to research a historical event that has shaped their community. After researching the occurrence, have them plan and create a mural illustrating the event.

SS TEKS 4.23C Express ideas orally based on research and experience

 **Notes**

Point to details from each of the murals on pages 206 and 207, such as a candle in *The Offering* or the pig in *Kansas Pastoral*. Name the detail and have students repeat.

ESL TEKS 4.1C Understand major ideas in spoken messages

---

② Teach

Have students read pages 206–207 and look at the Cervantez mural. Ask:

- **Where is this mural located?** (in Los Angeles)
  DESCRIBE
- **How does the artist show the center of interest?** (in the details of the woman's face)
  ANALYZE
- **What culture do you think this mural honors? How do you know?** (Possible response: Mexican American; Some words are written in Spanish.)
  INTERPRET
- **Do you think this mural conveys a powerful message? Why or why not?** (Accept all responses.) JUDGE

Then ask similar questions about the Curry mural. Discuss how the credit line shows that Curry is the only artist who created this mural.

Sketchbook Journal You may want to take students for a walk around the neighborhood to inspire ideas about the location for their mural. Invite volunteers to share experiences they have had in the community to brainstorm ideas for a mural theme.

③ Close

Have students discuss how their story fits with the location they chose.

Assessment Ask students to discuss the steps they would take to make a mural.

NVAS (K–4) #4 Understanding the visual arts in relation to history and cultures

NVAS (K–4) #5 Reflecting upon and assessing the characteristics and merits of their work and the work of others

Studio 5

At a Glance

Objectives

- Express ideas by creating a mural.
- Evaluate original artworks by self and peers.

Materials

- drawing paper, craft paper, pencils, rulers
- tempera paint and paintbrushes
- Rubric 6 from **Unit-by-Unit Resources**

FA TEKS 4.2A Integrate a variety of ideas about self, life events, family, and community in original artworks

FA TEKS 4.2B Design original artworks

FA TEKS 4.2C Invent ways to produce artworks and to explore photographic imagery, using a variety of art media and materials

FA TEKS 4.4A Describe intent and form conclusions about personal artworks

1 Introduce

Review murals. Have students describe any murals they have seen in the community.

Place students in groups of three to five and have them brainstorm ideas for a mural scene. Ask:

- **What scene from your community would you like to portray?**
- **What events will you depict?**
- **What colors, shapes, and lines will you use to create unity?**

Quick Studio

Have students draw a mural showing a school activity. Then have them transfer their idea to butcher paper using water-based markers.

Studio 5
Make a Mural

Take your place in history. Help create a mural for a wall in your school.

1 Work with your group to brainstorm and draw ideas for a mural.

2 Combine the sketches and make a grid of one-inch squares over the sketch.

Technique Tip

Fill in one square at a time when transferring the sketch. Match each square on the mural with the same square in the original sketch.

208

Meeting Individual Needs

Inclusion To accommodate students in wheelchairs, tape the craft paper to a wall before the image is transferred. Then assign those students the job of drawing or painting the lower sections that are at a comfortable and accessible height for them.

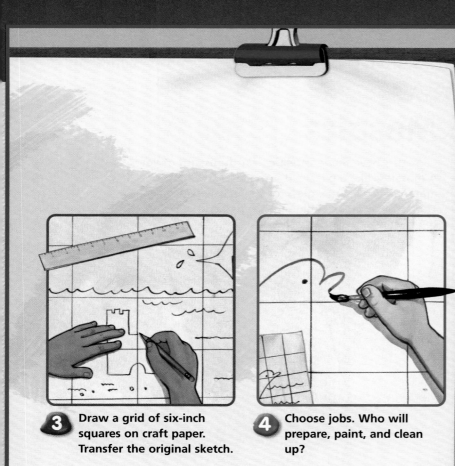

3 Draw a grid of six-inch squares on craft paper. Transfer the original sketch.

4 Choose jobs. Who will prepare, paint, and clean up?

Think Like an Artist

How did you create unity among the different parts of your mural?

209

Fine Arts Connection

Theatre After groups complete their murals, have them write and act out short plays dramatizing the scenes they depicted. Have them perform the plays during a gallery night or parents' night.

FA TEKS 4.1E Imitate and synthesize life experiences in dramatic play
FA TEKS 4.2C Develop characters and assume roles in short improvised scenes
FA TEKS 4.3C Plan brief dramatizations
FA TEKS 4.3D Interact with others in brief dramatizations

❷ Create

Tell students to look at the pictures and read the directions on pages 208–209. Then distribute materials.

- Have students draw their ideas individually.
- Then have them work together to incorporate ideas into a master drawing on a sheet of drawing paper.
- Distribute craft paper to groups. Provide at least two feet of paper for each student. Help groups draw grids using a long ruler.
- Have students use tempera paints to complete the murals. Suggest that they take turns performing each job.

Technique Tip When students make their larger grid, make sure that it has the same number of squares as the smaller grid.

❸ Close

Have students form conclusions about their murals by answering the *Think Like an Artist* question. (Possible response: We created unity by using the color blue throughout.)

Ongoing Assessment

If . . . students have difficulty creating shadows and light areas,

then . . . review how to mix shades and tints to create values.

See page 108 from **Unit-by-Unit Resources** for a rubric to assess this studio.

NVAS (K–4) #1 Understanding and applying media, techniques, and processes

NVAS (K–4) #3 Choosing and evaluating a range of subject matter, symbols, and ideas

NVAS (K–4) #5 Reflecting upon and assessing the characteristics and merits of their work and the work of others

Lesson 6

At a Glance

Objectives

- Identify and describe mosaics.
- Describe, analyze, interpret, and judge artworks.

Materials

- **Fine Art Transparency**
- pattern blocks

Vocabulary

mosaics, tesserae

FA TEKS 4.4B Interpret ideas and moods in original artworks, portfolios, and exhibitions by peers and others

① Introduce

Provide students with pattern blocks. Invite them to manipulate the blocks to create designs. Challenge them to show a recognizable image with the blocks. Point out to students that working with pattern blocks is similar to putting together a puzzle since both involve assembling small pieces.

Explain that mosaics are made of tesserae or small bits of materials, such as stone, glass, and shells. The pieces are then glued or cemented to a surface, leaving a small space between them.

Ask if students have seen a mosaic, and invite them to tell where. They may mention tile floors, trivets, walls, or counters in bathrooms or the kitchen.

Mosaics

Artists have made **mosaics** for thousands of years. A mosaic is like a puzzle. It is made of small bits of material, usually tile, glass, or stone, called **tesserae.** The artist creates a design by arranging and gluing the tesserae.

Artist unknown.
Byzantine Emperor.
Mosaic.

210

🎨 Art Background

Art History Mosaics have been used as a decorative medium for more than five thousand years. The Romans made mosaic floors, walls, and vaults, using tesserae made of marble, limestone, shells, glass, and pumice. Floor mosaics were usually black and white, while wall and vault mosaics were more colorful and pictorial.

Güell Park Antonio Gaudí (1852–1926) designed Güell Park to stand "like a tree" without internal or external bracing. The garden park is comprised of a market hall with columns, multi-colored entrance lodges, fountains, curving benches, and other elements covered with mosaics in abstract designs.

Antonio Gaudí. *Güell Park*, Barcelona, Spain.

Gaudí spent fourteen years constructing Güell Park in Barcelona, Spain.

In ancient Rome, mosaics, such as the one shown on page 210, decorated a wall or floor. Notice how the artist used heavy dark lines to emphasize facial features.

Gaudí used mosaics to cover sculptures, benches, and other three-dimensional structures in this park. Why do you think the mosaics glitter in the light?

Art Fact

Many mosaics were found in good shape when ash from a volcanic eruption was cleared away from the ancient city of Pompeii in Italy. The volcano erupted in A.D. 79.

211

② Teach

Have students read pages 210–211 and look at *Byzantine Emperor*. Ask:

- **What shapes and lines do you see?** (Possible response: shapes: squares, circles, ovals, teardrops; lines: curved, thick) DESCRIBE
- **What visual texture do you see?** (shiny) ANALYZE
- **What ideas about the subject does the artist express?** (Possible response: The subject is serious and wealthy.) INTERPRET
- **Do you think mosaic is a good medium for this portrait? Why or why not?** (Possible response: Yes; because it lasts a long time.) JUDGE

Ask similar questions about Gaudí's mosaic sculpture. Tell students that mosaics often glitter because many are made of reflective substances such as glass or ceramic.

Art Fact Have students discuss why mosaics might last a long time. (They are usually made of hard materials that can withstand force; They are made of many small pieces instead of one large piece so they do not shatter.)

③ Close

Ask students what subjects they would want to depict using mosaics.

Visual Culture Have students discuss why mosaics are used in countertops, tubs, and floors.

NVAS (K–4) #4 Understanding the visual arts in relation to history and cultures

NVAS (K–4) #6 Making connections between visual arts and other disciplines

 Curriculum Connection

Math Tell students that many tesserae are geometrically shaped. Have them identify the geometric shapes in the mosaics on pages 210–211. (circles, squares, rectangles) Then ask them to draw a design for a mosaic using geometric shapes that fit together.

TAKS Math Obj. 3 Understand geometry
    Math TEKS 4.8C Describe shapes and solids

 **Notes**

Have students point to and name shapes and colors they see in the *Byzantine Emperor.*

ESL TEKS 4.31F Describe how color, shape, and line influence the message

Studio 6

At a Glance

Objectives

- Express ideas by creating a mosaic.
- Evaluate original artworks by self and peers.

Materials

- colored construction paper, cut or torn into an assortment of small pieces for tesserae
- tagboard, cardboard, or construction paper for bases, glue or glue sticks
- high-gloss varnish (optional)
- Rubric 6 from **Unit-by-Unit Resources**

FA TEKS 4.2B Design original artworks

FA TEKS 4.2C Invent ways to produce artworks and to explore photographic imagery, using a variety of art media and materials

FA TEKS 4.4A Describe intent and form conclusions about personal artworks

① Introduce

Review mosaic. Remind students that the small bits of material used in a mosaic are called tesserae.

Have students brainstorm ideas for their mosaics. Ask:

- **What person, plant, or animal will you depict?**
- **How will you use tesserae to show your subject?**
- **What colors, shapes, and patterns will you use?**

Quick Studio

Provide students with 1-by-6-inch pieces of tagboard. Have them design an abstract mosaic bookmark using scrap construction paper.

Studio 6

Make a Paper Mosaic

Try this version of the ancient art of mosaic.

1 Sort your paper bits, or tesserae, by color, size, and shape.

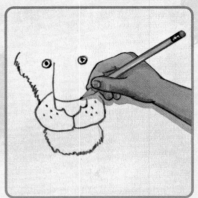

2 Draw the outline of a design that you like.

Technique Tip

Glue tesserae from the center of the design outward. Leave a little space between the tesserae.

👥 Meeting Individual Needs

Extend Have students make a mosaic showing a landscape, still life, or human figure. Provide them with shells, stones, tile, marbles, or other three-dimensional media for the tesserae.

3 Put glue on the paper and place the tesserae one at a time.

4 Continue gluing down the tesserae until your design is complete.

Think Like an Artist

How could you add more relief to the surface of your mosaic? Name some objects you could use in place of a few tesserae.

213

 Fine Arts Connection

Music Have students work in groups to research a musical instrument. Ask the group to prepare a short presentation on the history of the instrument.

Have each group create a mosaic of their instrument to display during their presentation. Provide a variety of media for the tesserae. After the presentations are complete, display the mosaics in the music room.

FA TEKS 4.5D Identify connections between music and other fine arts

2 Create

Have students look at the pictures and follow the steps on pages 212–213 to create mosaics. Then distribute materials.

- Have students tear paper bits to create texture. Tell them to select a background color that contrasts with the tesserae.
- Encourage them to make many sketches before creating their final design.
- Instruct students to leave a small amount of space around each tesserae.
- You may want to apply a high-gloss varnish to the finished artworks. Be sure to do this away from students and in a well-ventilated area.

Technique Tip Check to make sure that students are not leaving too much space between the tesserae.

3 Close

Students can reflect on their mosaics by answering the *Think Like an Artist* questions. (Possible response: You could use three-dimensional objects; shells, marbles, stones, old jewelry, tiles)

Ongoing Assessment

If . . . students have difficulty applying tesserae,

then . . . tell them to spread a thin layer of glue over a small area, then press a few tesserae to the surface.

See page 108 from **Unit-by-Unit Resources** for a rubric to assess this studio.

NVAS (K–4) #1 Understanding and applying media, techniques, and processes

NVAS (K–4) #3 Choosing and evaluating a range of subject matter, symbols, and ideas

NVAS (K–4) #5 Reflecting upon and assessing the characteristics and merits of their work and the work of others

Artist at Work

Artist at Work

Comic Illustrations

How do artists make comic books? Illustrator Stan Webb follows many steps. First, he conducts research. Webb works with a writer to study the subject. Then, he and the writer do much thinking and planning to develop the characters.

Finally, the writer writes the story. Webb draws the illustrations, then scans them into a computer and adds color. It takes about thirty days for Webb to illustrate one comic book.

Webb's favorite part of the process is drawing the characters. He enjoys making them seem like real people. According to Webb, the best comic books combine two traits. He values great story-telling and great illustrations with a lot of action and details. What characteristics do *you* value in a comic book?

Stan Webb, comic book illustrator

At a Glance

Objectives

- Read about a career in art.
- Identify the use of art in everyday life.
- Relate art to personal experiences.

Materials

- comic book (optional)

FA TEKS 4.3C Identify the roles of art in American society

Explore

Display examples of various age-appropriate comic books. Ask students what comic books they have read, if any. Then ask them why they find those comic books appealing. Explain that an illustrator draws the pictures for a comic book, while a writer writes the words.

Discuss

Have students read page 214 and look at the artwork on page 215. Ask:

- **What story do you think is being told in the illustration?** (Possible response: Two people are riding very fast, perhaps to catch someone, or escape.)
- **How does Webb focus attention on the riders?** (Possible response: It appears that the soldiers are riding directly at the viewer.)
- **According to Webb, what traits are essential to the best comic books?** (great storytelling and great illustrations)
- **What skills does Webb need to illustrate comic books?** (Possible responses: computer skills; the ability to draw characters and action; design skills)

 Career Research

Have students work in small groups to research other projects that an illustrator might do, such as greeting cards, children's books, or diagrams for instructional material. If possible, invite someone from the community, such as a graphic artist, to speak to the class.

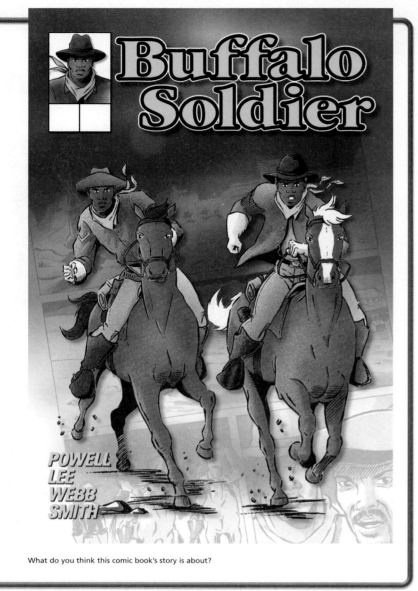

Buffalo Soldier

POWELL
LEE
WEBB
SMITH

What do you think this comic book's story is about?

215

Reading Strategy

Build Background Before students read the lesson, have them look at several comic books that you provide. Then have the class discuss how artists often work with writers to create a variety of materials, such as comic books, children's books, instruction manuals, and medical texts. Have students think of other jobs in which drawing is an essential skill. Then have them read the lesson.

TAKS Rdg. Obj. 4 Apply critical thinking
ELA TEKS 4.13G Draw conclusions from information gathered from multiple sources

Apply

Build Background Have students work in small groups to name other careers in which artists work with writers. Draw a chart such as the one below on the board. Fill in the chart as students identify other careers. Possible responses are shown below.

Artists Working with Writers

Careers	What They Create
children's book illustrator	children's books
medical or science illustrator	medical or scientific books, posters, and diagrams
graphic designer	magazines, newspapers, Web sites

Close

Review the completed table and ask:

- **What would you create if you were making artworks with a writer?** (Possible response: a sports magazine for kids)
- **What role do illustrators play in our society?** (Possible response: They create the images we see in comic books, textbooks, and magazines.)

NVAS (K–4) #5 Reflecting upon and assessing the characteristics and merits of their work and the work of others

Portfolio Project

Portfolio Project

At a Glance

Objectives

- Develop and organize ideas from the environment.
- Demonstrate knowledge about story quilts, theme, and fiber art.
- Evaluate original artworks by self and peers.

Materials

- pencils, 8" squares of drawing paper
- water-based markers, 8" burlap squares
- colored yarn, large needles ⚠, fabric scraps
- Rubric 6 from **Unit-by-Unit Resources**

FA TEKS 4.2A Integrate a variety of ideas about self, life events, family, and community in original artworks

FA TEKS 4.2B Design original artworks

FA TEKS 4.2C Invent ways to produce artworks and to explore photographic imagery, using a variety of art media and materials

FA TEKS 4.4B Interpret ideas and moods in original artworks, portfolios, and exhibitions by peers and others

Stitch Your Own Design

Needlework is one of the ways artists around the world express their creativity. Add your creative square to a class quilt.

1 Draw a design that has your initials and a symbol of a way you express yourself.

2 Cut out your design and transfer it onto a square of burlap.

3 Use a large needle and yarn to stitch over the initials and symbol you drew.

4 Add your square to those of your classmates to form a quilt.

216

Plan

Have students read page 216. Explain that they will create a square that expresses ideas about themselves to add to a class quilt. Then ask:

- **What is an art form, such as dance, music, or poetry, that you enjoy?**
- **What symbols will you use to show your form of expression?**

Have students think about the themes or stories they want to express. Tell them to look through their Sketchbook Journals for ideas or find books about a favorite activity at the library.

Quick Project

Assign each student a different letter of the alphabet. Have them use yarn to stitch their letters. Display the completed alphabet together.

👥 Meeting Individual Needs

Reteach For students who may have difficulty transferring their designs to the burlap, have them draw their original design onto tissue paper. Then pin the tissue paper to the burlap. Have students stitch directly over their design, then tear away the paper.

Timothy, Age 10, and Joseph, Age 9. *Baseball Is the Best!* and *Reading is Fun.* Burlap and yarn.

Henry, Age 9, and Jennifer, Age 10. *Drums* and *Plants.* Burlap and yarn.

What symbols did these students stitch to express their creativity?

Share Your Art

1. What is the theme of your stitchery?

2. Could your class quilt be described as both a story quilt and a work of fiber art? Explain.

217

Gallery Options

Traveling Exhibit Stitch the burlap squares to a large piece of fabric to make a quilt and have different stores, restaurants, and community centers display the quilt at different times. Have students write artist biographies for themselves to travel with the exhibit.

Create

Guide students through the steps on page 216 to complete the project.

- Have students draw their designs on scrap paper or in their Sketchbook Journals.
- Suggest students use the same color marker to transfer their design as the color of yarn they will use to stitch.
- Before students begin this step, have them practice making stitches on fabric scraps. Demonstrate how to use needles safely.
- Help students pin their squares to a bulletin board.

Be sure the needles are safely returned to a central location so they will not be dropped or lost.

Close

Point out the student art on page 217. Explain that these artworks are from the portfolios of other fourth-grade students. Have students interpret the ideas in these artworks by asking:

- **What symbols do you see?** (Possible responses: a baseball and a book; a drum and a plant)
- **How are these artworks similar to your own? How are they different?** (Responses will vary.)

Then use the *Share Your Art* questions on page 217 to help students make judgments about their artwork. (Possible responses: dance; Yes, because it tells stories about us and uses fibers as a medium.)

See page 108 from **Unit-by-Unit Resources** for a rubric to assess this project.

NVAS (K–4) #1 Understanding and applying media, techniques, and processes

NVAS (K–4) #3 Choosing and evaluating a range of subject matter, symbols, and ideas

NVAS (K–4) #5 Reflecting upon and assessing the characteristics and merits of their work and the work of others

Unit 6 Review

At a Glance

Objectives

- Relate art terms to the environment.
- Identify fiber art, story quilt, mural, mosaic, relief sculpture, and folk art.
- Describe, analyze, interpret, and judge an artwork.

Materials

- **Art Print 24**
- **Fine Art Transparency**

FA TEKS 4.1B Choose appropriate vocabulary to discuss the use of art elements such as color, texture, form, line, space, and value and art principles such as emphasis, pattern, rhythm, balance, proportion, and unity

FA TEKS 4.4A Describe intent and form conclusions about personal artworks

FA TEKS 4.4B Interpret ideas and moods in original artworks, portfolios, and exhibitions by peers and others

Think About Art

Possible responses:

fiber art (Point to *Tomb Guardian*.)
mosaic (Point to the mosaic mask.)
theme (Point to the mural on building.)
relief sculpture (Point to the relief sculpture.)
folk art (Point to the mosaic mask.)
mural (Point to the mural on building.)

Write About Art

Before students write, ask:

- **What media was used to create the art form you chose? How would you describe the style?** (Responses will vary.)

Unit Review

Think About Art

Point to a picture that matches each word. Explain how the picture illustrates what the word means.

fiber art   theme   folk art
mosaic   relief sculpture   mural

Comic Mosaic Mask,
A.D. 1st century.

Tomb Guardian,
A.D. 1000–1470.

Write About Art

Which of the new art forms that you explored in this unit was the most interesting and unusual? Describe it, and explain your choice.

Talk About Art

- Look through your portfolio.
- Choose an artwork that surprised you in some way.
- Tell a friend what you discovered by making it.
- Explain what you learned in this unit that you tried to show in this artwork.

218

 Assessment Options

Options for assessing the students appear in the **Unit-by-Unit Resources.**

- Use the **Vocabulary Worksheets** on pages 101–104 for an informal assessment of Unit 6 vocabulary.
- Use the **Unit 6 Test** on pages 108–112 to asses students' mastery of unit vocabulary and concepts.

Artist unknown, Navajo culture, Arizona. *Blanket: Map of the Four Corners Area,* ca. 1960. Tapestry-woven wool, 38 by 29¼ inches. From the Girard Foundation Collection, in the Museum of International Folk Art, a unit of the Museum of New Mexico, Santa Fe, NM.

Put It All Together

1. What is this weaving about?

2. How did the artist show both unity and variety?

3. What theme do you think the weaver had in mind?

4. Do you think this weaving should be considered folk art? Explain.

219

Art Background

Art and Culture Four Corners is the point in the southwestern United States where the states of Colorado, Arizona, New Mexico, and Utah meet. These states encompass the Colorado Plateau of the Rocky Mountains. The region is home to hundreds of thousands of Native Americans, including the Navajo Indian Reservation and the Hopi Indian Reservation.

Talk About Art

Prompt students to use words such as *theme, profile, relief sculpture, fiber art, mural,* or *mosaic* as well as the elements of art and principles of design to describe their artwork.

Remind students how to form conclusions about their artwork. Use a volunteer's sample to model forming conclusions. Say, for example: **The artist's use of three-dimensional tesserae adds texture to the overall design. Her inclusion of other media adds variety.**

Have students form conclusions about their own artworks and share their ideas with a partner.

Put It All Together

Use the questions on page 219 to evaluate the artwork. Possible responses:

1. The states that make up Four Corners. **DESCRIBE**
2. The artist shows unity through the repetition of diagonal and horizontal lines and the colors blue, white, orange, brown, and black. The artist shows variety with the use of red and variations in the lettering. **ANALYZE**
3. The theme may be that the Four Corners area is a special place worth commemorating as the home of many Navajo people. **INTERPRET**
4. Yes; weaving is a tradition in Navajo culture, so the skills used to make the artwork were probably passed down through many generations. **JUDGE**

NVAS (K–4) #1 Understanding and applying media, techniques, and processes

NVAS (K–4) #2 Using knowledge of structures and functions

NVAS (K–4) #5 Reflecting upon and assessing the characteristics and merits of their work and the work of others

Elements of Art

Line

straight

curved

zigzag

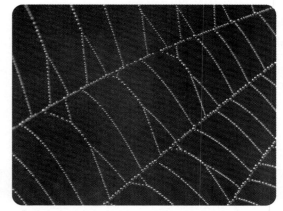
thin

thick

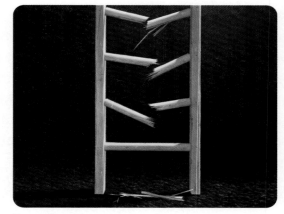
broken

220

Color

cool

warm

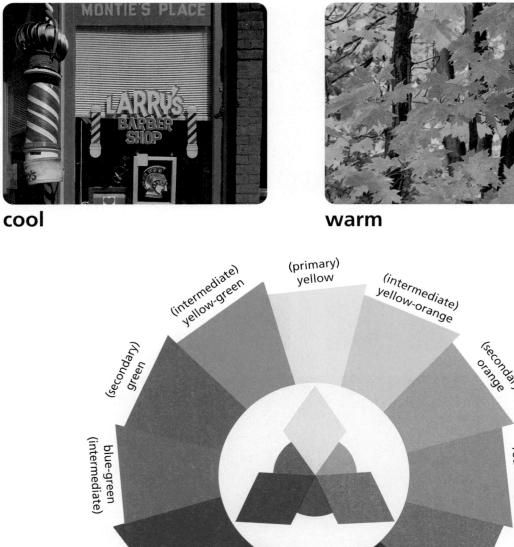

(primary)
yellow

(intermediate)
yellow-green

(intermediate)
yellow-orange

(secondary)
green

(secondary)
orange

blue-green
(intermediate)

(intermediate)
red-orange

blue
(primary)

red
(primary)

blue-violet
(intermediate)

red-violet
(intermediate)

violet
(secondary)

color wheel

221

Value

Shape

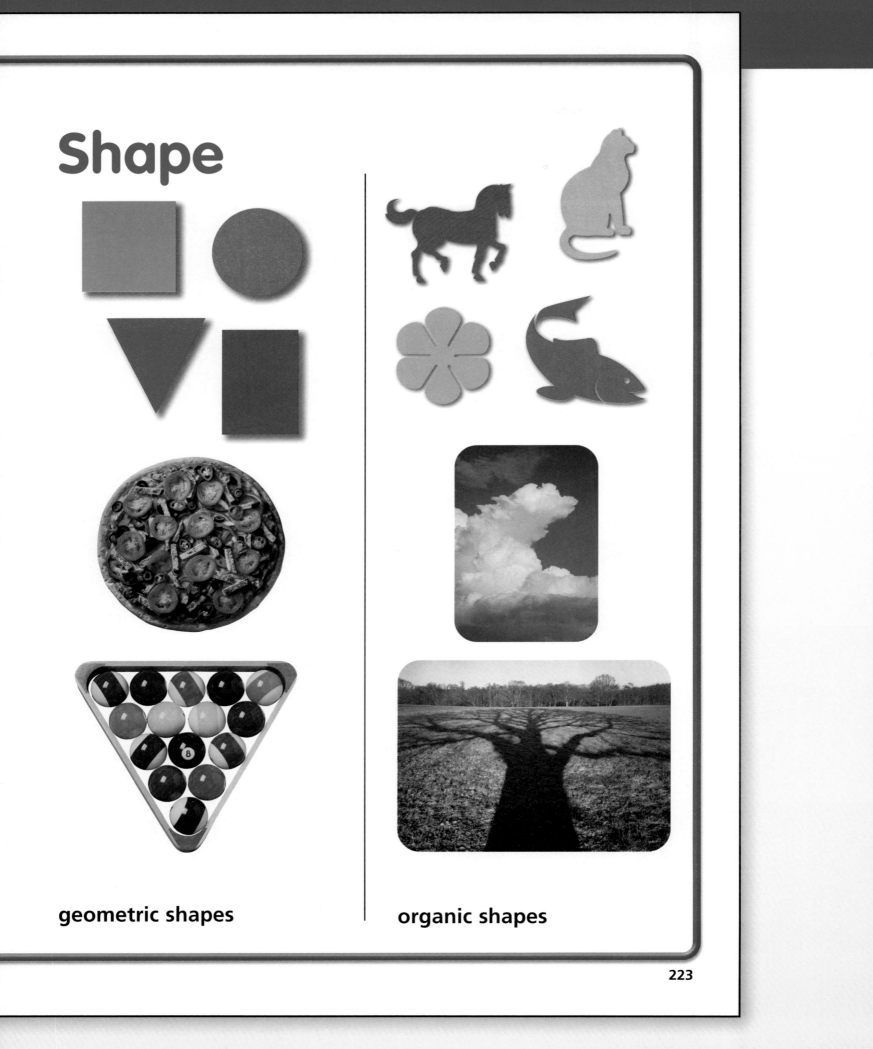

geometric shapes

organic shapes

223

Texture

bumpy

soft

shiny

prickly

sticky

fluffy

224

Form

geometric forms

organic forms

225

Space

positive space

negative space

Principles of Design

Unity

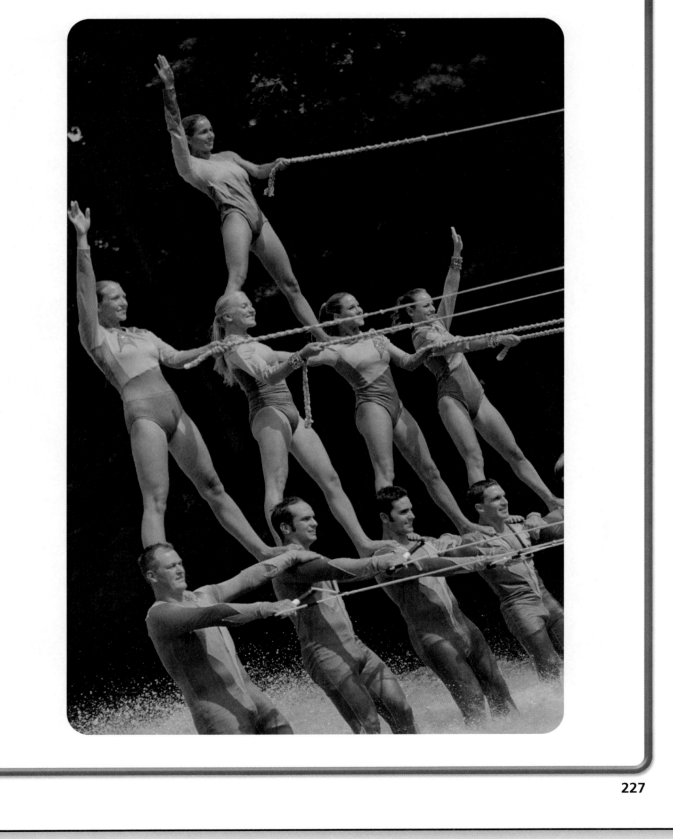

Principles of Design

Variety

228

Emphasis

Balance

230

Proportion

Pattern

Rhythm

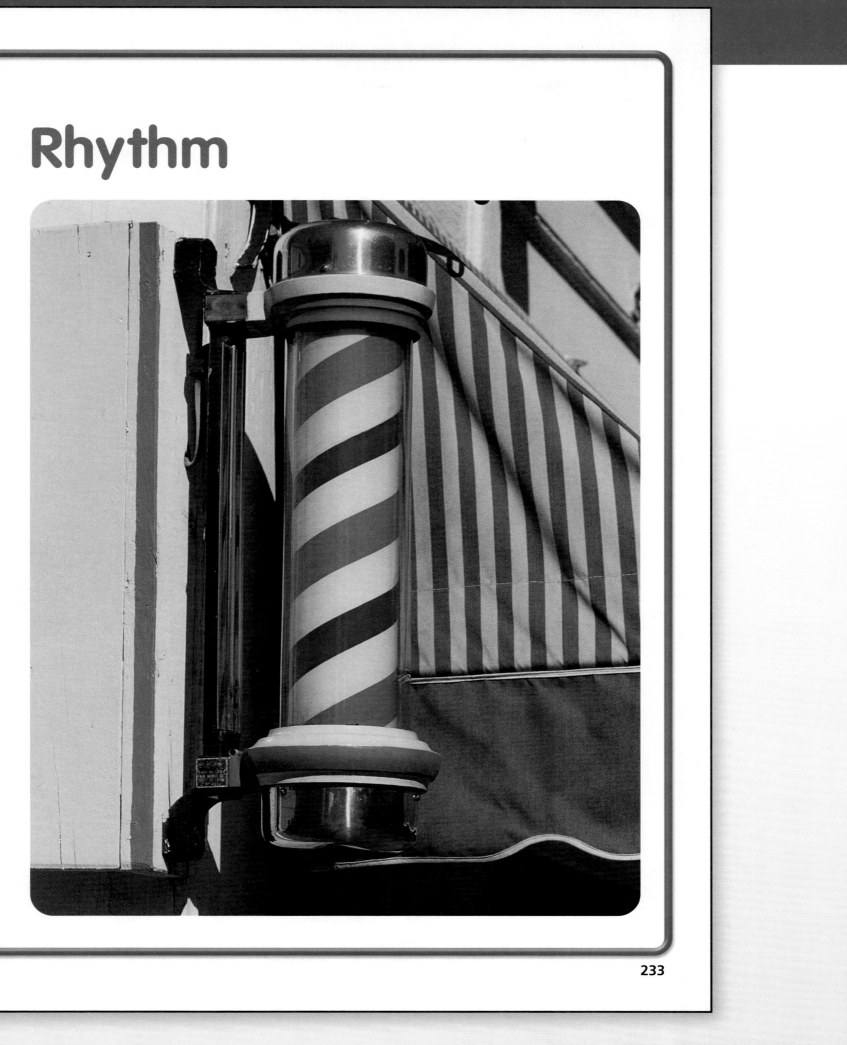

Think Safety

Read these safety rules. Be sure to follow these rules when you create artworks.

1. Keep art materials away from your face, especially your mouth and eyes.

2. Be careful when you work with scissors. If you use a sharp object, point it away from your body.

3. Read the labels on art materials. Look for the word *nontoxic*. This label tells you the materials are safe to use.

4. Do not breathe chalk dust or art sprays.

5. If you have a problem with any art materials, ask your teacher for help.

6. If an art material makes you feel sick, tell your teacher right away.

7. If you spill water or paint on the floor, be sure to clean it up quickly. A wet floor is unsafe to walk on.

8. Clean up after you finish an artwork. First, wash your hands with soap and water. Then, wash the tools you want to save, such as paintbrushes. Return art materials to their proper places.

Can you think of more ways to be safe?

234

List of Artists

Unknown Artists

List of Artists

Glossary

A

abstract [ab strakt´] A style of art in which the subject of an artwork has been simplified or rearranged. Abstract art emphasizes moods and impressions and is characterized by the use of bold colors, lines, and flat shapes.

actual line A line that is real. It is a line you can actually see.

analogous [ə na´ lə gəs] The name given to colors that are next to each other on the color wheel (for example, yellow, yellow-orange, and orange). They are also called *related colors*.

animation The process of showing in rapid succession a series of drawings or photographs, each image having a small change in the position of the subject(s). This process creates the illusion of motion.

architect [är´ ka tekt] A professional who designs buildings.

architecture [är´ kə tek chər] The art and science of designing buildings and other large-scale, functional structures.

armature [är´ mə chùr] In sculpture, a framework used to support material, such as clay or papier-mâché, that is being formed.

assemblage [ə sem´ blij] A type of three-dimensional art created by combining and connecting a variety of objects to create a pleasing whole.

asymmetrical [ā sə me´ tri kəl] **balance** A type of balance in which two sides of an artwork are not alike but carry equal or nearly equal visual weight. It is also known as *informal balance*.

asymmetry [ā si´ mə trē] A type of balance that lacks symmetry.

B

background The part of an artwork that appears to be farthest from the viewer, often in the distance of a scene.

balance The arrangement of the parts of an artwork to give an overall sense of equality in visual weight. Balance can be symmetrical, asymmetrical, or radial. Balance is a principle of design.

basket A hollow vessel created by weaving together stiff fibers such as twigs or reeds.

blueprint A large print of an architectural plan shown with white lines on a blue background.

brayer [brā´ ər] In printing, a rubber roller used to spread ink over a surface.

cartoon A drawing, as in a newspaper or magazine, intended to amuse the reader. A cartoon often has a caption.

cartoon character A person, animal, or thing shown in an artwork that is humorous. Words often go with the drawings.

cartoon strip A series of cartoon drawings that tell a story.

center of interest The part of an artwork the viewer notices first. It is the most important part of an artwork.

ceramic [sə ra´ mik] A hard material made by baking, or firing, clay. It is also the artwork made of the ceramic.

clay A powdery substance found in the earth that becomes pliable, or flexible, when moistened and hardens when baked. Clay is used to create artworks such as sculpture and pottery.

collage [kə läzh´] An artwork created by arranging and gluing small pictures or photographs, pieces of paper, fabric, or other materials, onto a larger, flat surface.

Jane Sterrett. *Diversity Collage.*

color The visual quality of objects, as they reflect hues on the color wheel, caused by the amount of light reflected by them. Color is an element of art.

color scheme A plan for combining color in an artwork.

239

complementary colors Colors that contrast strongly with one another and are directly across from one another on the color wheel.

composition [käm pə zi´ shən] The arrangement of the various parts of an artwork into a pleasing whole. Composition also refers to a work of art.

contrast To show a large difference between two elements of art.

cool colors Related colors that range from green through blue and violet. Cool colors often bring to mind cool objects, places, and feelings.

cut-paper art (papel picado) Traditional Mexican art of cutting decorative and patterned designs into sheets of tissue paper.

D

decorative art A handicraft that results in beautiful, useful objects. Rug and fabric design, furniture-making, and glassblowing are all decorative arts.

detail A small part of an artwork that has been pulled out and usually enlarged for close inspection. A detail is also a tiny or particularly interesting part of an artwork.

diagonal line A line that slants in one direction. A diagonal line is neither vertical nor horizontal.

E

elements of art The basic parts of an artwork, including line, color, value, shape, texture, form, and space.

emphasis [em´ fə səs] The visual accent, stress, or sense of importance created in an artwork by the color, size, shape, or placement of an object or area. Emphasis is a principle of design.

Expressionistic [ik spre shə nis´ tik] A style of art in which the artist boldly expresses personal experiences and emotions about a subject using simple designs and brillant colors. Expressionism began in Germany during the early 1900s. It became popular in the United States during the 1940s and 1950s.

Eye-Dazzler Blanket A blanket woven in a specific and traditional Navajo style, with intricate patterns of bright colors.

240

F

fantasy Refers to art made from the creative imagination.

femmage [fem´ äzh] A type of collage made by women that usually includes vintage fabric items sewn and used by women.

fiber art Artwork created from yarn, thread, or cloth. Stitchery and weaving are examples of fiber art.

Artist unknown. *Otal avo Indian Weaving* (Detail).

firing Baking clay in a kiln. Firing causes the clay to retain its hardness.

floor plan A drawing that shows the arrangement of rooms in a building, as seen from a bird's-eye view.

folk art Artwork that often reflects traditions of a particular culture, especially images made by artists who do not have formal training. Instead, they are usually self-taught or learn from their friends and relatives.

foreground The part of an artwork that appears to be nearest the viewer.

form A three-dimensional object, such as a cube or a sphere, that is shown in three-dimensional artworks. Form is defined by height, depth, and width and is an element of art.

functional art Art created and used for a specific purpose.

G

geometric shape A shape that is mathematically defined or regular in appearance, such as a triangle, circle, square, or rectangle.

glaze A glassy substance that is applied to clay before firing in a kiln. It forms a hard surface that can protect the clay and serve as decoration.

Artist unknown. *Horse*, 8th Century.

H

horizontal line A line that is straight and flat, parallel to the horizon.

hue [hyü´] Another word for color.

implied line A line that is not shown but is implied, or suggested, by the placement of other lines, shapes, and colors.

industrial design The design of objects, such as automobiles, appliances, and telephones, manufactured and sold by industry.

installation An artwork asembled for an exhibition and dissambled when the exhibition is over.

intermediate color A color created when a primary color (yellow, red, or blue) is mixed with a secondary color (orange, violet, or green). Some examples are red-violet and blue-green.

jewelry [jü´ əl rē] Ornaments or decorative objects that people wear, such as rings, bracelets, and necklaces. Artists design and make jewelry.

kiln A hot oven used to bake and harden artworks made of clay, such as pottery or ceramics.

landscape An artwork showing an outdoor scene or scenery.

line The thin path of a point, usually created by a pen, pencil, or paintbrush. Lines can be actual or implied. A line can be thick or thin and can be curved, straight, zigzag, wavy, spiral, or broken. Line is an element of art.

loom [lüm´] A frame-like tool used to hold fibers for weaving fabric.

mask An artwork made to be placed over a person's face for disguise and decoration.

Artist unknown. Native American. *Northern Kwakiutl Mask of a Man.*

media [mē´dē ə] The materials used to create artworks, such as charcoal, pastels, oil paints, or clay. Media also refers to the techniques used to make an artwork, such as painting, sculpting, or drawing. The singular of *media* is *medium*.

middle ground The part of an artwork that appears to lie between the foreground and the background.

mixed media Artworks created by using more than one medium. For example, collage can be a mixed-media artwork in which drawing, painting, and photography are combined.

model Someone or something the artist uses as an example when creating an artwork. Also, in architecture, a model is a small version that represents a larger building or structure.

monument A three-dimensional artwork created to honor a person or an event.

mosaic [mō zā´ik] An artwork created by setting tesserae into mortar or onto another adhesive background to create a unified pattern or image. See *tesserae*.

motion picture A series of slightly changing images recorded on a filmstrip. When viewed in rapid succession, the rapidly changing images create the illusion of continuous motion.

movement In an artwork, a quality that evokes a sense of action, often created using lines or patterns.

mural [myûr´əl] A large artwork, usually a painting, applied to a wall or ceiling. Murals often appear on or in public buildings.

negative space The empty space that surrounds a form or shape in an artwork.

neutrals [nü´trəls] A term used for black, white, and tints and shades of gray. Some artists also consider browns to be neutral.

nonobjective [nän əb jek´tiv] **style** A term used to describe artworks that have no recognizable subject matter. This style does not represent real objects.

object Something in an artwork that usually can be named by the viewer.

organic shape Shapes and forms that are irregular, particularly those resembling objects in nature, such as the shape of a leaf or the form of an animal.

overlap To partly or completely cover one shape or form with another.

P

papier-mâché [pā pər mə shā´] A material made from paper pulp that can be molded when wet and painted when dry. It is also the technique for making sculptures from this material.

pattern Repetition of color, line, shape, or form in an artwork. Pattern is a principle of design. Also, a pattern is a plan or model to be followed when making something.

photography The art of creating photographs.

plate See *printing block*.

Pop Art A style of art developed during the 1950s. Pop Artists show people, objects, or scenes from popular culture and use graphics similar to those found in advertisements or comic strips.

portrait [pōr´ trət] An artwork that features a person, an animal, or a group of people, often placing emphasis on the face.

Christian Pierre. *Troy.* 1962.

pose The way people or animals sit or stand while an artist creates a portrait of them.

positive space Shapes, forms, or lines that stand out from the background or negative space in an artwork.

primary color One of the three colors (yellow, red, and blue) from which other colors are made

principles of design Guidelines artists use to arrange elements of art. The principles of design are unity, variety, emphasis, balance, proportion, pattern, and rhythm.

print An artwork created by coating a surface, such as a carved wood block, with wet color and then pressing paper onto it. The paper is "pulled" as a print.

244

printing block A surface, such as wood or linoleum, into which an artist carves a design. Ink or paint is spread across the surface and paper is pressed onto it to make a print, an impression of the design.

printmaker A person who creates prints, or multiple images, by using the same printing block.

profile Something that is seen or shown from the side, such as a side view of a face.

proportion [prə pōr´ shən] The size relationship of one part of an artwork to another part or to the whole. For example, the size relationship of the nose to the face shows proportion. Proportion is a principle of design.

 Q

quilt A padded bedcover made from two layers of cloth that are sewn together. Usually, one layer is made from  scraps of fabric that have been arranged and stitched together in a colorful design. Also, the term is used to mean creating a quilt.

quilt block A section of a quilt top, usually square or rectangular.

 R

radial [rā´ dē əl] **balance** A type of balance in which lines or shapes spread out from a center point.

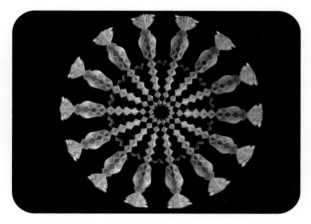

raffia [ra´ fē ə] **cloth** Cloth woven from the leaf fibers of the raffia, an African palm tree.

realistic A style of art that describes artworks showing objects and scenes as they actually look to most viewers.

relief [ri lēf´] **print** An artwork made by rolling ink onto a carved surface showing a raised design and then pressing paper onto it.

relief sculpture [ri lēf´ skəlp´ chər] A kind of sculpture that stands out from a flat background.

245

rhythm [ri´ thəm] A sense of visual movement or motion caused by the repetition of one or more elements of art, such as color, line, shape, or form, in an artwork. Rhythm is a principle of design.

S

sculpture [skəlp´ chər] An artwork made by modeling, carving, or joining materials into a three-dimensional whole. Clay, wood, stone, and metal are some common materials used for sculpture. Sculpture is also the process of making such an artwork.

secondary color A color created by mixing two primary colors. The secondary colors are orange (made from yellow and red), violet (made from red and blue), and green (made from blue and yellow).

self-portrait [self´ pōr´ trət] An artwork showing a likeness of the artist who created it.

shade A darker value created by adding black to a color or by adding black to white.

shading A way of showing gradual changes of darker values in an artwork. Shading helps make a flat artwork appear three-dimensional.

shape A two-dimensional flat area made by lines that enclose it. A shape can be geometric, such as a circle or square, or organic, having an irregular outline. Shape is an element of art.

space The open or empty area around, above, between, within, or below objects. Shapes and forms are defined by the empty space surrounding them (negative space) and by the space they occupy (positive space). Space is an element of art.

still life An artwork showing an arrangement of objects that do not move on their own.

still photograph A photograph that does not move, as compared to a motion picture.

story quilt A quilt showing pictures and words that tell a story.

style An artist's own special way of creating art through the use of specific media, methods, materials, or subjects. Artistic style can also represent certain techniques of a group of artists in a specific culture or time.

subject What an artwork is about. It can be a person, object, or scene. A subject is the recognizable topic of an artwork.

246

symbol [sim´bəl] A letter, color, sign, or picture used to represent a word, message, or idea.

symmetrical [sə me´tri kəl] **balance** A type of balance in which both sides of a center line are the same or about the same. A cat's face, for example, is symmetrically balanced along a vertical line through the middle of the nose. Symmetrical balance is also known as *formal balance*.

symmetry [si´mə trē] Balance created by making both sides of an artwork the same or about the same.

T

tactile texture [tak´təl teks´chər] Texture that can be understood by the sense of touch. It is also called *actual texture*. Tactile textures, which artists show in their compositions, include rough, smooth, silky, pebbly, soft, hard, bumpy, and scratchy. See *texture*.

technology The way human beings use machines and other tools to make or do something. Technology in art helps artists solve problems in making and doing art.

tesserae [te´sə rə] In a mosaic, the small pieces of glass, tile, stones, paper, or similar material set into mortar or onto another adhesive surface to create a unified pattern. See *mosaic*.

Artist unknown. Roman. *Mosaic-Two Roman Figures.*

texture [teks´chər] The way a surface feels (actual or tactile texture) or looks (visual texture). Words such as shiny, dull, rough, and smooth are used to describe texture. Texture is an element of art.

theme The artist's particular interpretation of a broad or abstract topic, such as nature, love, or beauty.

three-dimensional Having height, width, and depth or thickness. Something that is three-dimensional is not a flat shape. It is a form.

tint A light value of a color created by mixing the color with white.

247

traditional style A style that conforms to knowledge, beliefs, and customs passed down from one generation to the next. See *style*.

two-dimensional Having height and width but not depth. Something that is two-dimensional is flat.

unity [yü´ nə tē] A quality that occurs when all parts of an artwork combine to create a sense of wholeness and completion. Unity is a principle of design.

value [val´ yü] The lightness or darkness of a color. Tints have a light value. Shades have a dark value. For example, pink is a light value of red, while navy is a dark value of blue. Value is an element of art.

variety [vē rī´ ə tē] The combination of elements of art, such as line, shape, or color, that adds interest to an artwork. Variety is a principle of design.

vertical line A line that goes straight up and down.

visual texture [vi´ zhə wəl teks´ chər] The way a surface appears through the sense of vision. For example, the surface of a sculpture may be shiny or dull. See *texture*.

warm colors The family of related colors that range from yellow through orange and red. Warm colors usually remind people of warm objects, places, and feelings.

warp [wȯrp´] In weaving, fibers stretched vertically, top to bottom, on a loom and through which the weft is woven.

weave [wēv´] To make cloth-like artworks by interlacing, or weaving, warp and weft threads, or other fiber, often on a loom.

weft In weaving, fibers woven over and under, from side to side, through the warp on a loom.

Index

Index

Acknowledgments

ILLUSTRATIONS
20, 21, 24, 25, 28, 29, 34, 35, 38, 39, 42, 43, 54, 55, 58, 59, 62, 63, 68, 69, 72, 73, 76, 77, 88. 89, 92, 93, 96, 97, 102, 103, 105, 106, 107, 110, 111, 122, 123, 126, 127, 130, 131, 136, 137, 140, 141, 144, 145, 156, 157, 160, 161, 164, 165, 170, 171, 174, 175, 178, 179, 182, 190, 191, 194, 195, 198, 199, 204, 205, 208, 209, 212, 213, 216 Carol Newsom

46, 80, 114, 148 Connie McLennan

PHOTOGRAPHS
Every effort has been made to secure permission and provide appropriate credit for photographic material. The publisher deeply regrets any omission and pledges to correct errors called to its attention in subsequent editions.

Unless otherwise acknowledged, all photographs are the property of Scott Foresman, a division of Pearson Education.

Photo locators denoted as follows: Top (t), Center (c), Bottom (b), Left (l), Right (r), Background (Bkgd)

Front Matter
Page 7, © SuperStock; 7, Sisse Brimberg, © National Geographic; 10, © Smithsonian American Art Museum, Washington, D.C./Art Resource, NY; 14, © Erich Lessing/Art Resource, NY. © 2004 Estate of Pablo Picasso/Artists Rights Society (ARS), New York.

Units 1–6
Page 16, © Réunion des Musées Nationaux/Art Resource, NY; 17, Claude Monet. *Self-Portrait,* 1917. Oil on canvas, 27 1/3 by 21 1/2 inches. Musée d'Orsay, Paris, France. © Erich Lessing/Art Resource, NY; 30, © Francis G. Mayer/Corbis; 32, Photo by Doug Parker Studios, courtesy of Frank Romero; 37, © Corbis; 40, Fine Arts Museums of San Francisco, Achenbach Foundation for Graphic Arts, Gift of Mr. and Mrs. Robert Marcus,1990.1.116; 44 (tr), © Toba Garrett; 44 (bc), 45, Photography by Steven Mark Needham, cake photo courtesy of The Well Decorated Cake, © 2003/Courtesy of Sterling Publishing; 48, © Getty Images, 48, © Frans Lemmens/Getty Images; 48, © Corbis; 49, © 2004 Artists Rights Society (ARS), New York/VG Bild Kunst, Bonn.; 50, © 2004 Jacob Lawrence Foundation/Artists Rights Society (ARS), New York; 51, Collection of the National Academy of Design, New York, NY. © 2004 Jacob Lawrence Foundation/Artists Rights Society (ARS), New York; 56, © Fiduciario en el Fideicomiso relativo a los Museos Diego Rivera y Frida Kahlo. Reproduction authorized by the Bank of Mexico, Mexico City; 60, The Baltimore Museum of Art, The Cone Collection, formed by Dr. Claribel Cone and Miss Etta Cone of Baltimore, Maryland BMA 1950.196; 61(tr), © Corbis; 64, © Smithsonian American Art Museum, Washington, D.C./Art Resource, NY. © 2004 Jacob Lawrence Foundation/Artists Rights Society (ARS), New York; 65, Toledo Museum of Art, purchased with funds from the Libbey Endowment, gift of Edward Drummond Libbey, 1976.34. © Richard Estes/Toledo Museum of Art; 67, © Adam Woolfitt/Corbis; 67, © Bob London/Corbis; 70, Collection of the American Folk Art Museum, New York; 71, © Peter Harholdt/SuperStock; 78, 79, © Annamaree Rea; 82, © Peter Harholdt/SuperStock; 82, © Burstein Collection/Corbis; 83, © SuperStock; 84, © 2004 Estate of Louise Nevelson/Artists Rights Society (ARS), New York; 85, Hans Namuth. *Louise Nevelson,* 1977. Cibachrome, 16 7/8 by 15 1/3 inches. National Portrait Gallery, Smithsonian Institution/Art Resource, NY; 86, © North Carolina Museum of Art/Corbis; 91, © Estate of Fernand Léger/Artists Rights Society (ARS), NY; 94, Photo by Teresa N. Rishel, courtesy of Chihuly Studio; 95, © Museum of Fine Arts, Houston/Bridgeman Art Library; 98, © 2004 Estate of Louise Nevelson/Artists Rights Society (ARS), New York; 100, Digital image © The Museum of Modern Art/Licensed by SCALA/Art Resource, NY; 101, © David Gilhooly; 104, © Scala/Art Resource, NY; 105, © Bill Ross/Corbis; 109, Photograph © 1982 Medford Taylor/Black Star; 112(bl), © Les Orenstein; 113, Peter Yang/© Les Orenstein; 116, © Richard Cummins/Corbis; 116, © William Manning/Corbis; 116, © SuperStock; 117, © Danny Lehman/Corbis; 118, © 2004 Artists Rights

251

Society (ARS), New York/VG Bild Kunst, Bonn.; 119, Wassily Kandinsky. *Lady (Portrait of Gabriele Münter),* ca. 1910. Oil on canvas, 44 by 43 1/2 inches. Munich, Lenbachhaus. Photograph © AKG London. © 2004 Wassily Kandinsky/Artists Rights Society (ARS), New York; 120, © The Tate Gallery, London/Art Resource, New York. © 2004 Succession H. Matisse, Paris/Artists Rights Society (ARS), New York; 121, © Musée Picasso, Paris/Peter Willi/SuperStock. © 2004 Estate of Pablo Picasso/Artists Rights Society (ARS), New York; 124, Digital Image © The Museum of Modern Art/Licensed by SCALA/Art Resource, NY; 125(t), Chris Gomien/Carl Solway Gallery, Cincinnati, Ohio; 128, Contact Press Images; 129, Portland Museum of Art, Portland, OR. Gift of David and Nissa Shaw. © 1970 Imogen Cunningham Trust; 132, © 2004 Artists Rights Society (ARS), New York/VG Bild Kunst, Bonn.; 133, © 2004 The Georgia O'Keeffe Foundation/Artists Rights Society (ARS), New York; 134, Photographs courtesy of the Everett Collection, Inc., New York; 139, © Helen Frankenthaler; 142, From *50 Texas Artists,* by Annette Carlozzi, © 1986, published by Chronicle Books, San Francisco. Courtesy of Chronicle Books; 146(tl), Photo by Peter Yang; 146(br), Corbis; 147, © Ralph Barrera; 150, © GoodShoot/SuperStock; 150, © Corbis; 152, Museum purchase and commission with funds from the National Endowment for the Arts, and The Benjamin J. Tillar Memorial Trust. © 2004 Red Grooms/Artists Rights Society (ARS), New York; 153, Red Grooms. *Self-Portrait as a Bus Driver,* 1998. Acrylic on paper. Palmer Museum, Pennsylvania State University, University Park, PA. © 2004 Red Grooms/Artists Rights Society (ARS), New York; 155, Photo by Parks Anderson, courtesy of Chihuly Studio; 158, Catalog Number SAR.1989-7-352, School of American Research; 159, © Kevin Fleming/Corbis; 167, © Schalkwijk/Art Resource, NY. © Fiduciario en el Fideicomiso relativo a los Museos Diego Rivera y Frida Kahlo. Reproduction authorized by the Bank of Mexico, Mexico City; 172, The Andy Warhol Foundation, Inc./Art Resource, NY. © 2004 Andy Warhol Foundation for the Visual Arts/ARS, New York; 176, © The Huntington Library, Art Collections, and Botanical Gardens, San Marino, California/SuperStock; 180(bl), © Jose Gonzalez; 181(t), 181(b), © Jose Gonzalez; 184(tc),© Paul Gilligan/Getty Images; 184, © Lynn Radeka/SuperStock; 184, © Spike Mafford/Getty Images; 186, Photo by Northern Lights, courtesy of Carmen Lomas Garza; 187, Photo © 1990 Hulleah Tsinhnahjannie, courtesy Bernice Steinbaum Gallery, Miami; 189, © Miriam Schapiro; 192, © Erich Lessing/Art Resource, NY; 193, Réunion des Musées Nationaux/Art Resource, NY; 197, © Smithsonian American Art Museum, Washington, D.C./ Art Resource, NY; 200, Photo by M. Lee Fatherree, courtesy of Carmen Lomas Garza; 202, © Smithsonian American Art Museum, Washington, D.C./Art Resource, NY; 206, Commissioned by SPARC through it's Great Walls Unlimited: Neighborhood Pride Program/Courtesy of Social and Public Art Resource Center. www.sparcmurals.org; 207, Photographed by Larry Colcher/Kansas State Historical Society; 210, © SuperStock; 211, © Steve Vidler/SuperStock; 214(b), 215 © Stan Webb; 218(tl), © Rudi Von Briel/Photoedit; 218 (tc), © Cummer Museum of Art and Gardens, Jacksonville, FL/Superstock; 218(tc), © Michael Freeman/Corbis; 218 (tr), © The Lowe Museum, The University of Miami/SuperStock.

Back Matter
Page 220, © Getty Images; 220, © Getty Images; 220, © Corbis; 220, Getty Images; 221, Getty Images; 221, digitalvisiononline.com; 222, © Darrell Gulin/Corbis; 222, © Eric Crichton/Corbis; 223, © Paul Chauncey/Corbis; 223, © Corbis; 223, © Pat Doyle/Corbis; 223, © Robert Yin/Corbis; 224, © David Frazier/Corbis; 224, © Peter Dazeley/Corbis; 224, © Richard Hamilton Smith/Corbis; 224, © Charles Gold/Corbis; 224, © Lance Nelson/Corbis; 225, © The Purcell Team/Corbis; 225, © Lindsey P. Martin/Corbis; 225, © Nik Wheeler/Corbis; 227, © Randy Faris/Corbis; 228, © Bob Krist/Corbis; 229, © Charles & Josette Lenars/Corbis; 230, © Mark Gibson/Corbis; 231, © Tom Bean/Corbis; 232, © Corbis; 233, © Getty Images; 238, © Corbis; 238, © Corbis; 239, (tl) © Corbis; 239, © Images.com/Corbis; 240, © Peter Harholdt/SuperStock; 241, © Holton Collection/SuperStock; 241, © The Lowe Art Museum, The University of Miami/SuperStock; 242, © Kim Sayer/Corbis; 243, © British Museum, London/Bridgeman Art Library, London/SuperStock; 244, © Christian Pierre/SuperStock; 245, © Roman Soumar/Corbis; 245, © Roger Allyn/SuperStock; 246, © Erik Slutsky/SuperStock; 247, © SuperStock; 248, © Corbis.

Teacher Resources

Art Connections

	Strands/Themes/Concepts	Fine Art Images	Studios/Projects
Social Studies	**History**	Moonwalk, U2 p. 75 Vietnam Veterans Memorial, U3 p. 109 Migrant Mother, Nipomo, California, U4 p. 151 Self-Portrait, U5 p. 173 Jonathan Buttall: The Blue Boy, U5 p. 176 The Goddess Hathor and King Sethi, U6 p. 192 (Detail) Kansas Pastoral, U6 p. 207 Byzantine Emperor, U6 p. 210	U3 Studio 6 p. 110 U6 Studio 5 p. 208
	Geography	Ranchos Church—Taos, U1 p. 31 The Old Chisholm Trail, U1 p. 36 Geraniums Before Blue Mountain, U2 p. 52 Mont Sainte-Victoire Seen from the Bibermus Quarry, U2 p. 60 Map, U4 p. 124 Cliff Portion of Bornholm, U4 p. 132 Tahitian Landscape, U4 p. 138 Central Texas Tornado, U4 p. 147 Güell Park, U6 p. 211 Blanket: Map of the Four Corners Area, U6 p. 219	
	Economics	The Washerwomen, U1 p. 26	
	Government	"In a Free Government, the security of civil rights...." (the words of James Madison), U2 p. 50 Video Flag Z, U4 p. 135	
	Citizenship	Vietnam Veterans Memorial, U3 p. 109	
	Culture	The Washerwomen, U1 p. 26 Ranchos Church—Taos, U1 p. 31 Rabbi Reading, U2 p. 74 Antelope Headdress, U3 p. 86 Kifwebe Mask, U3 p. 87 Cadillac Ranch, U3 p. 117 Space Kid, U4 p. 125 Ruckus Rodeo, U5 p. 152 Eye-dazzler Blanket, U5 p. 158 Haciendo Papel Picado/Making Paper Cutouts, U6 p. 186 Mechano/Flower Fan, U6 p. 189 Alebreje, U6 p. 196 African Raffia Cloth, U6 p. 203 Blanket: Map of the Four Corners Area, U6 p. 219	U2 Studio 3 p. 62 U2 Studio 6 p. 76 U3 Studio 6 p. 110 U3 Portfolio Project p. 114 U6 Studio 1 p. 190 U6 Studio 4 p. 204
	Science, Technology, and Society	Moonwalk, U2 p. 75 Lowrider Bike, U5 p. 168	
Science	**Life Science**	(Detail) Waterlilies: Green Reflections, U1 p. 16 Scamp in the Snow, U1 p. 32 No Added Hormones, U2 p. 79 Run, U2 p. 79 Hide, U2 p. 79 Tropical Storm with a Tiger (Surprise), U2 p. 83 Red Ikebana Flower, U3 p. 94 Frog Sandwich, U3 p. 101 Killingworth Image, Man on a Hog, U6 p. 197	U1 Studio 4 p. 34 U1 Studio 5 p. 38

	Strands/Themes/Concepts	Fine Art Images	Studios/Projects
	Earth Science	*Geraniums Before Blue Mountain,* U2 p. 52 *Mont Sainte-Victoire Seen from the Bibermus Quarry,* U2 p. 60 *Sand Brought to an Edge to Catch the Light,* U3 p. 108 *Grey Hills,* U4 p. 133 *Central Texas Tornado,* U4 p. 147	
	Physical Science	*Moonwalk,* U2 p. 75	
	Space and Technology	*Space Kid,* U4 p. 125 *Video Flag Z,* U4 p. 135 *Celebration,* U4 p. 142 *Neon Mural #1,* U4 p. 143	U4 Studio 6 p. 144
Reading	**Myself and Others**	*American Gothic,* U1 p. 18	U1 Portfolio Project p. 46 U3 Studio 2 p. 92 U5 Studio 5 p. 174 U5 Studio 6 p. 178 U6 Studio 5 p. 208 U6 Portfolio Project p. 216
	The World Around Us	*Helene's Florist,* U2 p. 65 *No Added Hormones,* U2 p. 79 *Central Texas Tornado,* U4 p. 147 *Migrant Mother, Nipomo, California,* U4 p. 151 *Subway (detail from Ruckus Manhattan),* U5 p. 166 *The Bus,* U5 p. 167 (Detail) *Kansas Pastoral,* U6 p. 207	U1 Studio 3 p. 28 U4 Studio 5 p. 140
	Learning and Working	*The Old Chisholm Trail,* U1 p. 36 *"In a Free Government, the security of civil rights...." (the words of James Madison),* U2 p. 50 *The Library,* U2 p. 64 *Rabbi Reading,* U2 p. 74 *Ruckus Rodeo,* U5 p. 152 *Self-Portrait as a Bus Driver,* U5 p. 153 (Detail) *Kansas Pastoral,* U6 p. 207	U1 Studio 1 p. 20
	Traditions	*Six Master Poets,* U1 p. 23 *The Centennial Quilt,* U2 p. 70 *Rabbi Reading,* U2 p. 74 *Eye-dazzler Blanket,* U5 p. 158 *Haciendo Papel Picado/Making Paper Cutouts,* U6 p. 186 *Harlem Renaissance Party: Bitter Nest, Part II,* U6 p. 188 *Mechano/Flower Fan,* U6 p. 189 *Barbacoa para Cumpleaños (Birthday Barbecue),* U6 p. 200 *Fibonacci 5,* U6 p. 202 *La Ofrenda (The Offering),* U6 p. 206 *Blanket: Map of the Four Corners Area,* U6 p. 219	U2 Studio 5 p. 72 U2 Studio 6 p. 76 U3 Studio 6 p. 110 U6 Studio 1 p. 190 U6 Studio 4 p. 204 U6 Studio 6 p. 212
	Journeys in Time and Space	*Moonwalk,* U2 p. 75	
	Creativity	*Güell Park,* U6 p. 211	U5 Portfolio Project p. 182 U6 Portfolio Project p. 216
Fine Arts	**Music**	*Violin and Sheet Music,* U4 p. 121 *Harpist,* U6 p. 193	

Art Connections

Strands/Themes/Concepts		Fine Art Images	Studios/Projects
	Theatre	*Stage Design*, U5 p. 181	
	Dance	*Nataraja: Siva as King of Dance*, U3 p. 90	
Elements of Art	**Line**	*American Gothic*, U1 p. 18 *Les joueurs de football (The Football Players)*, U1 p. 22 *Six Master Poets*, U1 p. 23 *No Added Hormones*, U2 p. 79 *Run*, U2 p. 79 *Sand Brought to an Edge to Catch the Light*, U3 p. 108 *Grey Hills*, U4 p. 133 *Neon Mural #1*, U4 p. 143 *Ribbon Glass Cup*, U5 p. 154 *Eye-dazzler Blanket*, U5 p. 158 *The Goddess Hathor and King Sethi*, U6 p. 192 *Harpist*, U6 p. 193	U1 Studio 1 p. 20 U1 Studio 2 p. 24 U1 Studio 6 p. 42 U1 Portfolio Project p. 46 U2 Studio 6 p. 76 U3 Studio 3 p. 96 U4 Portfolio Project p. 148 U5 Studio 1 p. 156 U5 Studio 2 p. 160 U5 Portfolio Project p. 182 U6 Portfolio Project p. 216
	Shape	*The Washerwomen*, U1 p. 26 *The Russian House (Das Russen-Haus)*, U1 p. 49 *Geraniums Before Blue Mountain*, U2 p. 52 *The Library*, U2 p. 64 *Dawn's Wedding Chapel 1*, U3 p. 98 *Tarot*, U3 p. 99 *The Snail*, U4 p. 120 *Violin and Sheet Music*, U4 p. 121 *Eye-dazzler Blanket*, U5 p. 158 *The Bus*, U5 p. 167 *Haciendo Papel Picado/Making Paper Cutouts*, U6 p. 186 *Harlem Renaissance Party: Bitter Nest, Part II*, U6 p. 188	U1 Studio 3 p. 28 U1 Portfolio Project p. 46 U2 Studio 5 p. 72 U2 Portfolio Project p. 80 U3 Studio 2 p. 92 U3 Studio 3 p. 96 U4 Studio 1 p. 122 U4 Portfolio Project p. 148 U5 Studio 1 p. 156 U5 Studio 2 p. 160 U5 Portfolio Project p. 182 U6 Studio 6 p. 212
	Form	*Royal Tide I*, U3 p. 84 *Antelope Headdress*, U3 p. 86 *Kifwebe Mask*, U3 p. 87 *Nataraja: Siva as King of Dance*, U3 p. 90 *Roller Skating*, U3 p. 91 *Red Ikebana Flower*, U3 p. 94 *Dawn's Wedding Chapel 1*, U3 p. 98 *Tarot*, U3 p. 99 *Pastry Case, I*, U3 p. 100 *Frog Sandwich*, U3 p. 101 *Ribbon Glass Cup*, U5 p. 154 *Pirovano Watch*, U5 p. 169 *Harpist*, U6 p. 193 *Alebreje*, U6 p. 196	U3 Studio 1 p. 88 U3 Studio 2 p. 92 U3 Studio 4 p. 102 U3 Studio 6 p. 110 U3 Portfolio Project p. 114 U4 Studio 6 p. 144 U5 Studio 1 p. 156 U5 Studio 4 p. 170 U6 Studio 2 p. 194 U6 Studio 3 p. 198
	Space	*The Old Chisholm Trail*, U1 p. 36 *Maguey de la Vida*, U1 p. 40 *Subway (detail from Ruckus Manhattan)*, U5 p. 166	U1 Studio 5 p. 38 U1 Studio 6 p. 42
	Value	*Mont Sainte-Victoire Seen from the Bibermus Quarry*, U2 p. 60 *Migrant Mother, Nipomo, California*, U4 p. 151 *Byzantine Emperor*, U6 p. 210	U4 Studio 3 p. 130
	Color	*Maguey de la Vida*, U1 p. 40 *Long Live Life (Viva la vida)*, U2 p. 56	U2 Studio 1 p. 54 U2 Studio 2 p. 58 U2 Studio 3 p. 62

Strands/Themes/Concepts	Fine Art Images	Studios/Projects
Color (continued)	*Mont Sainte-Victoire Seen from the Bibermus Quarry*, U2 p. 60 *The Library*, U2 p. 64 *Helene's Florist*, U2 p. 65 *Evening Star, III*, U2 p. 66 *Hide*, U2 p. 79 *Tropical Storm with a Tiger (Surprise)*, U2 p. 83 *Red Ikebana Flower*, U3 p. 94 *Dawn's Wedding Chapel 1*, U3 p. 98 *Tarot*, U3 p. 99 *Yellow Still LIfe*, U4 p. 118 *The Snail*, U4 p. 120 *Neon Mural #1*, U4 p. 143 *Ribbon Glass Cup*, U5 p. 154 *San Antonio Public Library Fiesta Tower*, U5 p. 155 *Eye-dazzler Blanket*, U5 p. 158	U2 Studio 4 p. 68 U2 Portfolio Project p. 80 U4 Studio 5 p. 140 U4 Portfolio Project p. 148 U6 Studio 6 p. 212
Texture	*Scamp in the Snow*, U1 p. 32 *Kifwebe Mask*, U3 p. 87 *Sand Brought to an Edge to Catch the Light*, U3 p. 108 *Ribbon Glass Cup*, U5 p. 154 *Eye-dazzler Blanket*, U5 p. 158 *The Goddess Hathor and King Sethi*, U6 p. 192 *Byzantine Emperor*, U6 p. 210	U1 Studio 4 p. 34 U3 Studio 4 p. 102 U4 Studio 3 p. 130 U6 Studio 2 p. 194
Principles of Design — **Balance**	*Evening Star, III*, U2 p. 66 *Tropical Storm with a Tiger (Surprise)*, U2 p. 83 *Nataraja: Siva as King of Dance*, U3 p. 90 *Squash Blossom Necklace*, U3 p. 95 *Cadillac Ranch*, U3 p. 117 *The Snail*, U4 p. 120 *Eye-dazzler Blanket*, U5 p. 158 *Haciendo Papel Picado/Making Paper Cutouts*, U6 p. 186 *Harlem Renaissance Party: Bitter Nest, Part II*, U6 p. 188 *Mechano/Flower Fan*, U6 p. 189	U2 Studio 4 p. 68
Emphasis	*Les joueurs de football (The Football Players)*, U1 p. 22 *Red Ikebana Flower*, U3 p. 94 *Subway (detail from Ruckus Manhattan)*, U5 p. 166 *The Bus*, U5 p. 167 *Marilyn*, U5 p. 172 *Self-Portrait*, U5 p. 173 *Harlem Renaissance Party: Bitter Nest, Part II*, U6 p. 188 *Joy Ride*, U6 p. 201 *Byzantine Emperor*, U6 p. 210	U1 Studio 6 p. 42 U3 Studio 3 p. 96
Proportion	*The Old Chisholm Trail*, U1 p. 36 *Helene's Florist*, U2 p. 65 *Subway (detail from Ruckus Manhattan)*, U5 p. 166 *Marilyn*, U5 p. 172 *Self-Portrait*, U5 p. 173 *Jonathan Buttall: The Blue Boy*, U5 p. 176	U1 Studio 1 p. 20 U2 Portfolio Project p. 80 U5 Studio 5 p. 174 U5 Studio 6 p. 178

Art Connections

Strands/Themes/Concepts	Fine Art Images	Studios/Projects
Pattern	*The Centennial Quilt*, U2 p. 70 *Sand Brought to an Edge to Catch the Light*, U3 p. 108 *Video Flag Z*, U4 p. 135 *Celebration*, U4 p. 142 *Eye-dazzler Blanket*, U5 p. 158 *Harlem Renaissance Party: Bitter Nest, Part II*, U6 p. 188 *Mechano/Flower Fan*, U6 p. 189 *Fibonacci 5*, U6 p. 202 *African Raffia Cloth*, U6 p. 203 *Güell Park*, U6 p. 211	U5 Studio 2 p. 160 U6 Studio 1 p. 190 U6 Studio 4 p. 204
Rhythm	*Nataraja: Siva as King of Dance*, U3 p. 90 *Roller Skating*, U3 p. 91 *Ruckus Rodeo*, U5 p. 152 *Ribbon Glass Cup*, U5 p. 154 *San Antonio Public Library Fiesta Tower*, U5 p. 155 *Joy Ride*, U6 p. 201	U4 Studio 4 p. 136
Unity	*Map*, U4 p. 124 *San Antonio Public Library Fiesta Tower*, U5 p. 155 *Subway (detail from Ruckus Manhattan)*, U5 p. 166 *La Ofrenda (The Offering)*, U6 p. 206 *(Detail) Kansas Pastoral*, U6 p. 207	U4 Studio 2 p. 126 U6 Studio 5 p. 208 U6 Portfolio Project p. 216
Variety	*Dawn's Wedding Chapel 1*, U3 p. 98 *Tarot*, U3 p. 99 *Map*, U4 p. 124 *La Ofrenda (The Offering)*, U6 p. 206 *(Detail) Kansas Pastoral*, U6 p. 207	U2 Portfolio Project p. 80 U4 Studio 2 p. 126 U6 Portfolio Project p. 216
Techniques/Media	**Fine Art Images**	**Studios/Projects**
Collage	*The Snail*, U4 p. 120 *Violin and Sheet Music*, U4 p. 121 *Mechano/Flower Fan*, U6 p. 189	U1 Studio 3 p. 28 U4 Studio 1 p. 122 U4 Portfolio Project p. 148
Computer Graphics **Computer-Generated Art/Design**	*Neon Mural #1*, U4 p. 143	
Drawing • **Charcoal** • **Crayon** • **Pastel** • **Pen & Ink** • **Pencil**	*PEANUTS*, U5 p. 162 *GARFIELD*, U5 p. 163	U1 Studio 1 p. 20 U1 Studio 4 p. 34 U1 Studio 5 p. 38 U1 Studio 6 p. 42 U2 Studio 2 p. 58 U4 Studio 2 p. 126 U4 Studio 4 p. 136 U4 Studio 5 p. 140 U5 Studio 3 p. 164 U5 Studio 5 p. 174
Glass	*Red Ikebana Flower*, U3 p. 94 *Ribbon Glass Cup*, U5 p. 154 *San Antonio Public Library Fiesta Tower*, U5 p. 155	
Metal	*Squash Blossom Necklace*, U3 p. 95	U5 Studio 4 p. 170

Techniques/Media	Fine Art Images	Studios/Projects

Mixed Media/ Multi-Media	*Space Kid*, U4 p. 125
	Video Flag Z, U4 p. 135
	Celebration, U4 p. 142
	Neon Mural #1, U4 p. 143
	Lowrider Bike, U5 p. 168
	Pirovano Watch, U5 p. 169
	Harlem Renaissance Party: Bitter Nest, Part II,
	   U6 p. 188
	Killingworth Image, Man on a Hog,
	   U6 p. 197
		U1 Studio 2 p. 24
		U4 Studio 6 p. 144
		U5 Studio 1 p. 156
		U5 Portfolio Project p. 182
		U6 Studio 1 p. 190
		U6 Studio 2 p. 194

Mosaic	*Byzantine Emperor*, U6 p. 210 *Güell Park*, U6 p. 211	U6 Studio 6 p. 212

Painting
• **Acrylic**
• **Oil**
• **Watercolor**
	(Detail) *Waterlilies: Green Reflections,*
	   U1 p. 16
	American Gothic, U1 p. 18
	The Washerwomen, U1 p. 26
	The Old Chisholm Trail, U1 p. 36
	"In a Free Government, the security of civil
	   rights...." (the words of James
	   Madison), U2 p. 50
	Geraniums Before Blue Mountain, U2 p. 52
	Long Live Life (Viva la vida), U2 p. 56
	The Library, U2 p. 64
	Evening Star, III, U2 p. 66
	Tropical Storm with a Tiger (Surprise),
	   U2 p. 83
	Yellow Still LIfe, U4 p. 118
	Interior Landscape, U4 p. 139
	The Bus, U5 p. 167
	Jonathan Buttall: The Blue Boy, U5 p. 176
	Barbacoa para Cumpleaños (Birthday
	   Barbecue), U6 p. 200
	Joy Ride, U6 p. 201
		U2 Studio 1 p. 54
		U2 Studio 3 p. 62
		U5 Studio 6 p. 178
		U6 Studio 5 p. 208

Paper	*Haciendo Papel Picado/Making Paper* *Cutouts*, U6 p. 186 *Alebreje*, U6 p. 196	U2 Studio 4 p. 68 U2 Studio 5 p. 72 U3 Studio 1 p. 88 U3 Studio 5 p. 106 U4 Studio 4 p. 136 U5 Studio 2 p. 160 U6 Studio 3 p. 198 U6 Studio 6 p. 212
Photography	*Louise Bourgeois, Sculptor*, U4 p. 128 *My Father at Ninety*, U4 p. 129 *Central Texas Tornado*, U4 p. 147 *Migrant Mother, Nipomo, California,* U4 p. 151	U4 Studio 3 p. 130
Printing	*Six Master Poets*, U1 p. 23 *Maguey de la Vida*, U1 p. 40 *Rabbi Reading*, U2 p. 74 *Moonwalk*, U2 p. 75 *No Added Hormones*, U2 p. 79 *Run*, U2 p. 79 *Hide*, U2 p. 79 *Self-Portrait as a Bus Driver*, U5 p. 153 *Marilyn*, U5 p. 172 *Dali Salad*, U5 p. 185	U1 Portfolio Project p. 46 U2 Studio 6 p. 76 U2 Portfolio Project p. 80

Art Connections

Techniques/Media	Fine Art Images	Studios/Projects
Sculpture • Clay • Stone • Metal • Mixed Media • Pottery/Ceramics • Industrial Design • Furniture • Installations	*Royal Tide I*, U3 p. 84 *Antelope Headdress*, U3 p. 86 *Kifwebe Mask*, U3 p. 87 *Nataraja: Siva as King of Dance*, U3 p. 90 *Roller Skating*, U3 p. 91 *Red Ikebana Flower*, U3 p. 94 *Dawn's Wedding Chapel 1*, U3 p. 98 *Tarot*, U3 p. 99 *Pastry Case, I*, U3 p. 100 *Frog Sandwich*, U3 p. 101 *Sand Brought to an Edge to Catch the Light*, U3 p. 108 *Vietnam Veterans Memorial*, U3 p. 109 *Stoneware Pitcher*, U3 p. 113 *Cadillac Ranch*, U3 p. 117 *Ruckus Rodeo*, U5 p. 152 *Subway (detail from Ruckus Manhattan)*, U5 p. 166 *The Goddess Hathor and King Sethi*, U6 p. 192 *Harpist*, U6 p. 193	U3 Studio 1 p. 88 U3 Studio 2 p. 92 U3 Studio 3 p. 96 U3 Studio 4 p. 102 U3 Studio 5 p. 106 U3 Studio 6 p. 110 U3 Portfolio Project p. 114
Textiles • cloth • yarn • clothing • costume	*The Centennial Quilt*, U2 p. 70 *Eye-dazzler Blanket*, U5 p. 158 *Fibonacci 5*, U6 p. 202 *African Raffia Cloth*, U6 p. 203 *Blanket: Map of the Four Corners Area*, U6 p. 219	U6 Portfolio Project p. 216
Wood	*Royal Tide I*, U3 p. 84 *Dawn's Wedding Chapel 1*, U3 p. 98	U6 Studio 4 p. 204
Architecture	*Rouen Cathedral*, U1 p. 30 *Ranchos Church—Taos*, U1 p. 31 *The Russian House (Das Russen-Haus)*, U1 p. 49	U1 Studio 1 p. 20

Front Matter	Art Prints	Fine Art Transparencies
Start with Art		Transparency 4-7a: *Irises* Transparency 4-7b: *Gold Stag*
Visit a Museum		Transparency 4-10: *Chalet in the Mountains*
Make a Sketchbook Journal		Transparency 4-14: *Don Quijote*

Unit/Lesson	Art Prints	Fine Art Transparencies
Unit 1 Opener	Art Print 1: (Detail) *Waterlilies: Green Reflections*	Transparency 4-16: (Detail) *Waterlilies: Green Reflections* Transparency 4-17: *Self-Portrait*
Unit 1, Lesson 1		Transparency 4-18: *American Gothic*
Unit 1, Lesson 2		Transparency 4-22: *Les joueurs de football (The Football Players)* Transparency 4-23: *Six Master Poets*
Unit 1, Lesson 3		Transparency 4-26: *The Washerwomen*
Look and Compare	Art Print 2: *Rouen Cathedral* Art Print 3: *Ranchos Church—Taos*	Transparency 4-30: *Rouen Cathedral* Transparency 4-31: *Ranchos Church—Taos*
Unit 1, Lesson 4		Transparency 4-32: *Scamp in the Snow*
Unit 1, Lesson 5		Transparency 4-36: *The Old Chisholm Trail*

Art Prints and Transparencies

Art Prints and Transparencies

Unit/Lesson	Art Prints	Fine Art Transparencies
Unit 1, Lesson 6		Transparency 4-40: *Maguey de la Vida*
Artist at Work		
Unit 1 Review	Art Print 4: *The Russian House (Das Russen-Haus)*	Transparency 4-49: *The Russian House (Das Russen-Haus)*
Unit 2 Opener	Art Print 5: *"In a Free Government, the security of civil rights...." (the words of James Madison)*	Transparency 4-50: *"In a Free Government, the security of civil rights...." (the words of James Madison)* Transparency 4-51: *Self-Portrait*
Unit 2, Lesson 1		Transparency 4-52: *Geraniums Before Blue Mountain*
Unit 2, Lesson 2		Transparency 4-56: *Long Live Life (Viva la vida)*
Unit 2, Lesson 3		Transparency 4-60: *Mont Sainte-Victoire Seen from the Bibemus Quarry*
Look and Compare	Art Print 6: *The Library* Art Print 7: *Helene's Florist*	Transparency 4-64: *The Library* Transparency 4-65: *Helene's Florist*
Unit 2, Lesson 4		Transparency 4-66: *Evening Star, III*
Unit 2, Lesson 5		Transparency 4-70: *The Centennial Quilt*
Unit 2, Lesson 6		Transparency 4-74: *Rabbi Reading* Transparency 4-75: *Moonwalk*
Artist at Work		Transparency 4-79a: *No Added Hormones* Transparency 4-79b: *Run* Transparency 4-79c: *Hide*
Unit 2 Review	Art Print 8: *Tropical Storm with a Tiger (Surprise)*	Transparency 4-83: *Tropical Storm with a Tiger (Surprise)*
Unit 3 Opener	Art Print 9: *Royal Tide I*	Transparency 4-84: *Royal Tide I*
Unit 3, Lesson 1		Transparency 4-86: *Antelope Headdress* Transparency 4-87: *Kifwebe Mask*
Unit 3, Lesson 2		Transparency 4-90: *Nataraja: Siva as King of Dance* Transparency 4-91: *Roller Skating*
Unit 3, Lesson 3		Transparency 4-94: *Red Ikebana Flower* Transparency 4-95: *Squash Blossom Necklace*
Look and Compare	Art Print 10: *Dawn's Wedding Chapel 1* Art Print 11: *Tarot*	Transparency 4-98: *Dawn's Wedding Chapel 1* Transparency 4-99: *Tarot*
Unit 3, Lesson 4		Transparency 4-100: *Pastry Case, I* Transparency 4-101: *Frog Sandwich*
Unit 3, Lesson 5		
Unit 3, Lesson 6		Transparency 4-108: *Sand Brought to an Edge to Catch the Light* Transparency 4-109: *Vietnam Veterans Memorial*
Artist at Work		Transparency 4-113: *Stoneware Pitcher*
Unit 3 Review	Art Print 12: *Cadillac Ranch*	Transparency 4-117: *Cadillac Ranch*

Art Connections

Unit/Lesson	Art Prints	Fine Art Transparencies
Unit 4 Opener	Art Print 13: *Yellow Still Life*	Transparency 4-118: *Yellow Still Life* Transparency 4-119: *Lady (Portrait of Gabriele Münter)*
Unit 4, Lesson 1		Transparency 4-120: *The Snail* Transparency 4-121: *Violin and Sheet Music*
Unit 4, Lesson 2		Transparency 4-124: *Map* Transparency 4-125: *Space Kid*
Unit 4, Lesson 3		Transparency 4-128: *Louise Bourgeois, Sculptor* Transparency 4-129: *My Father at Ninety*
Look and Compare	Art Print 14: *Cliff Portion at Bornholm* Art Print 15: *Grey Hills*	Transparency 4-132: *Cliff Portion of Bornholm* Transparency 4-133: *Grey Hills*
Unit 4, Lesson 4		Transparency 4-135: *Video Flag Z*
Unit 4, Lesson 5		Transparency 4-138: *Tahitian Landscape* Transparency 4-139: *Interior Landscape*
Unit 4, Lesson 6		Transparency 4-142: *Celebration* Transparency 4-143: *Neon Mural #1*
Artist at Work		Transparency 4-147: *Central Texas Tornado*
Unit 4 Review	Art Print 16: *Migrant Mother, Nipomo, California*	Transparency 4-151: *Migrant Mother, Nipomo, California*
Unit 5 Opener	Art Print 17: *Ruckus Rodeo*	Transparency 4-152: *Ruckus Rodeo* Transparency 4-153: *Self-Portrait as a Bus Driver*
Unit 5, Lesson 1		Transparency 4-154: *Ribbon Glass Cup* Transparency 4-155: *San Antonio Public Library Fiesta Tower*
Unit 5, Lesson 2		Transparency 4-158: *Eye-dazzler Blanket*
Unit 5, Lesson 3		Transparency 4-162: *PEANUTS* Transparency 4-163: *GARFIELD*
Look and Compare	Art Print 18: *Subway (detail from Ruckus Manhattan)* Art Print 19: *The Bus*	Transparency 4-166: *Subway (detail from Ruckus Manhattan)* Transparency 4-167: *The Bus*
Unit 5, Lesson 4		Transparency 4-168: *Lowrider Bike* Transparency 4-169: *Pirovano Watch*
Unit 5, Lesson 5		Transparency 4-172: *Marilyn* Transparency 4-173: *Self-Portrait*
Unit 5, Lesson 6		Transparency 4-176: *Jonathan Buttall: The Blue Boy*
Artist at Work		Transparency 4-181: *Stage Design*
Unit 5 Review	Art Print 20: *Dali Salad*	Transparency 4-185: *Dali Salad*
Unit 6 Opener	Art Print 21: *Haciendo Papel Picado/Making Paper Cutouts*	Transparency 4-186: *Haciendo Papel Picado/Making Paper Cutouts*
Unit 6, Lesson 1		Transparency 4-188: *Harlem Renaissance Party, Bitter Nest, Part II* Transparency 4-189: *Mechano/Flower Fan*

Unit/Lesson	Art Prints	Fine Art Transparencies
Unit 6, Lesson 2		Transparency 4-192: *The Goddess Hathor and King Sethi* Transparnecy 4-193: *Harpist*
Unit 6, Lesson 3		Transparency 4-196: *Alebreje* Transparency 4-197: *Killingworth Image, Man on a Hog*
Look and Compare	Art Print 22: *Barbacoa para Cumpleaños (Birthday Barbecue)* Art Print 23: *Joy Ride*	Transparency 4-200: *Barbacoa para Cumpleaños (Birthday Barbecue)* Transparency 4-201: *Joy Ride*
Unit 6, Lesson 4		Transparency 4-202: *Fibonacci 5* Transparency 4-203: *African Raffia Cloth*
Unit 6, Lesson 5		Transparency 4-206: *La Ofrenda (The Offering)* Transparency 4-207: (Detail) *Kansas Pastoral*
Unit 6, Lesson 6		Transparency 4-210: *Byzantine Emperor* Transparency 4-211: *Güell Park*
Artist at Work		
Unit 6 Review	Art Print 24: *Blanket: Map of the Four Corners Area*	Transparency 4-219: *Blanket: Map of the Four Corners Area*

Technique Handbook

Using Glue

 1

Have students cover the work area with newspaper. Remind them to find an arrangement that pleases them before they apply the glue.

 2

Demonstrate applying glue near the center of the object. Make available brushes or instruct students to use their fingers to spread glue to the edges. Point out that too much glue causes paper to wrinkle.

 3

Instruct students to lay paper over the object and gently rub to make sure that all edges are glued down.

Using Paper

 1

Help students notice the texture and color of different kinds of paper. Point out different uses for paper, such as cover stock or tissue paper.

 2

Students can cut paper with scissors. They can tear paper. Or they can first fold, then tear. Help students notice how the edges of the paper look.

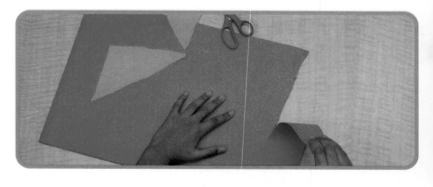

 3

Encourage students to experiment with paper. They can curl paper by wrapping a strip around a pencil, for example. They can also fold or crumple paper.

Drawing with Crayons and Oil Pastels

1

Students can use the tip of a crayon or an oil pastel to make thin lines.

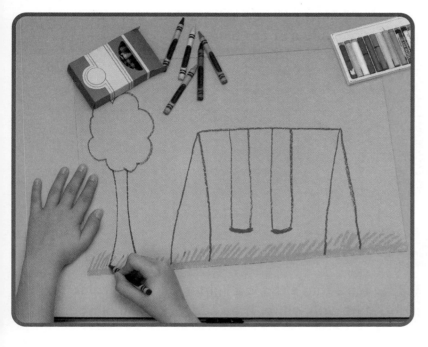

2

Show students how to make thick lines with the side of a crayon or oil pastel. Peel part or all of the paper off, depending on how thick the student wants the line to be. Then have students draw thick lines with the side.

3

Remind students that pressing firmly with a crayon or oil pastel makes a bold or bright color. Pressing lightly yields a softer color. Note that oil pastels break somewhat more easily than crayons do. Caution students about pressing *too* hard.

4

Demonstrate mixing colors by pressing lightly with one color (the lighter color), then going over it lightly with another, darker color. Show how to blend colors by rubbing over them with a tissue.

Technique Handbook

Using a Paintbrush

 Tell students to dip only the bristles into the paint. To make a thin line, use the tip of the brush. Use the side for broader lines. Advise students not to push down hard.

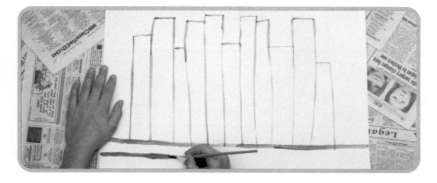

 Remind students to clean their paintbrushes before they switch colors. Make water and paper towels available.

Painters should wash each paintbrush with warm, soapy water. After a clear rinse, blot the paintbrush on a paper towel, then place in a can or jar with the bristles up.

Mixing Colors with Tempera Paints

 Demonstrate for students how to mix secondary colors. For orange, start with yellow and add a dot of red. For green, start with yellow and add a dot of blue. For violet, start with red and add a dot of blue.

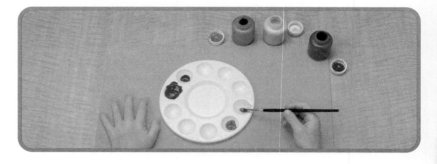

 Tell students that a tint is a lighter value of a color. To mix a tint, start with white. Then add a small amount of color to it. Remind students to add very small amounts of color until they get the tint they want.

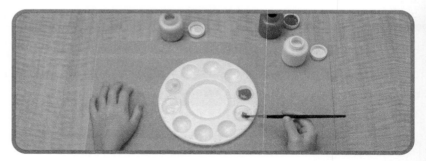

 To mix a shade, or a darker value of a color, have students begin with a color. Then add a small dot of black. Adding small amounts is important when mixing shades.

Making Prints

Point out that when students dip an object into paint, then press it on paper, they are making a print.

2

Students can also make their own stamps out of cardboard, craft foam, or clean foam plates or meat trays. After students cut a desired shape, attach a twisted piece of masking tape to the back for a handle. Remind students to press the stamp onto their paper firmly, but not to wiggle it.

3

To make a relief print, have students draw a design on a clean foam plate or meat tray. Direct them to roll water-based printer's ink evenly over the design. Have students place a sheet of paper over the inked surface and rub gently. Pull the paper off and see the print.

Making a Collage

1

Have students first decide on an idea. Will their collage show only shape and color? Will it include photographs?

2

Tell students to select shapes, colors, and pictures that go well together. For example, they can choose shapes that are all warm or cool colors. They can also choose pictures that have related subjects.

3

Encourage students to experiment with different arrangements before they begin gluing. Suggest that they cover all parts of the background paper. Remind them to glue one piece at a time.

Technique Handbook

Working with Clay

Have students cover the work area with brown paper or canvas. Make available tools for carving, found objects for pressing designs into the clay, and bowls of water. Provide cardboard on which to dry artworks.

Show students how to prepare clay by wedging it. Thump the clay down on the work surface. Press into it with the heels of your hands. Tell students to continue turning and pressing until there are no more air bubbles.

3

Demonstrate how to score clay parts, then add slip, or water-thinned clay, and stick the clay parts together.

Sculpting with Clay

Have students use a tool to carve shapes from the clay. Students can then join shapes together, or they can press tools or found objects into the clay to show texture.

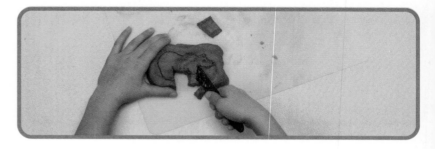

To make a clay sculpture by pinching, have students begin with a ball of clay. Tell them to press one thumb into the middle of the ball. Then they should push outward, or pinch the clay between their thumb and their fingers on the outside of the ball.

To use the coil method, instruct students to make ropes of clay. Show how to roll a lump of clay on the work surface with flat palms, starting in the middle and working outward as the rope lengthens. Students can coil ropes into forms by stacking them or by cutting and pressing pieces together.

Using Found Objects in an Artwork

1 _____

Students can use found objects in many types of artworks. Tell them to be on the lookout for usable objects that people throw away.

2 _____

Point out that found objects can also be natural objects. Remind students not to pick up anything they cannot identify. Also, students should never use living materials.

3 _____

Students can use found objects in a collage. Have them try different arrangements before gluing.

4 _____

Students can build a sculpture out of found objects. The sculpture may stand on its own, or it can be formed on a background.

5 _____

Tell students that most found objects can be used as stamps to make prints. Have students dip the surface of a found object in paint, then press it onto paper.

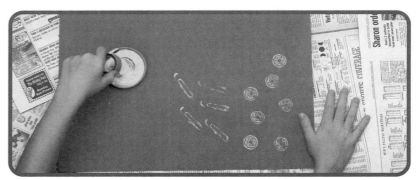

6 _____

Students can add interest to a sculpture by pressing found objects into the clay to create texture.

Technique Handbook

Weaving

Follow these steps to make looms for weaving. Cut squares or rectangles of sturdy cardboard. Keep in mind that the finished product will be roughly the size of the loom. Draw a line half an inch from the top and bottom edge of the loom. Then make a mark every quarter inch or so along the lines. Cut out a little V at each mark to make "teeth" along the top and bottom of the loom. ⚠

Now students can create a warp on the loom. Tell them to make a loop in one end of a long piece of yarn and hook it around the first "tooth" at the top of the loom. From there, the yarn goes down and around the first "tooth" at the bottom. Then it comes back up and around the next "tooth" at the top, then down, and so on. Advise students to pull snugly, but not too tightly as they create the warp. Have students continue hooking the yarn until the loom is full. At the last "tooth," students should loop the yarn around an extra time and tie a knot.

Now students can begin weaving. They can use their fingers or they may tie yarn through a hole in a narrow craft stick. Demonstrate how to go over and under, over and under, all the way across the warp. As they begin a second row, point out that it will be opposite the previous row—i.e., under and over, under and over. Tell students not to weave too close to the loom's "teeth." They will need to leave enough room to tie knots in the warp threads when they remove the weaving from the loom.

Show students how to weave each row at about a 45° angle to the previous row. Then provide plastic forks for students to use as "rakes" to pull each row tight against the others. Weaving at an angle prevents the warp threads from getting pulled in too tightly at the edges. When the weaving is complete, tell students to unhook the warp threads from the ends of the loom. Knot each pair of warp threads together and secure any loose yarn ends on the sides of the weaving.

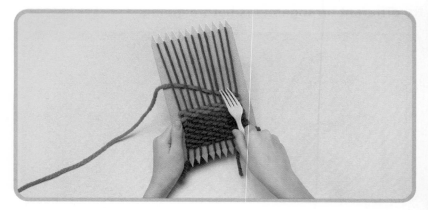

Making a Mosaic

1

Students can make mosaics out of a number of materials, depending on what you have available. Tell students that the small pieces, or tesserae, can be paper, stones, beads, or shells, for example.

2

Students can draw the shape for their mosaic on a base. The base can be heavy paper, wood, or cardboard. It can also be an item a student wants to design, such as a small box or picture frame.

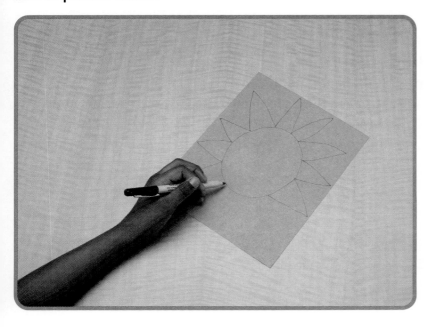

3

Instruct students to prepare their tesserae. If they are using paper, they must choose colors. Then they can decide whether to cut or tear the pieces. Help students notice the different effects the two methods create.

4

Tell students to begin gluing tesserae at the center of their mosaic's shape. They should cover a small area with glue and place their tesserae, leaving a small amount of space around each piece. Then, continuing to work outward from the center, students should apply glue in another area, place tesserae, and so on, until the shape is covered.

Technique Handbook

Stitching

1

Show students a large darning needle. Point out that the eye is large enough for thick fibers, such as yarn. WARNING: Even a blunt darning needle is somewhat sharp. Students should not use needles without the help of an adult.

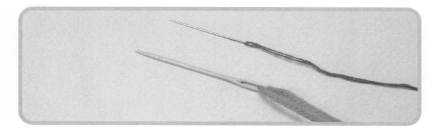

2

Provide darning needles and yarn. Instruct students to dampen their fingers, then pinch the end of the yarn. Push this flattened end of yarn through the eye of the needle, then pull it through. Tie a knot in the end of the yarn.

3

Have students push the needle through from the back of the fabric and pull until the knot stops the yarn. When students finish stitching, instruct them to push the needle through to the back of the fabric. There, they should make two small stitches right next to each other. Then they should push the needle under these two stitches, knot the yarn, and cut it off.

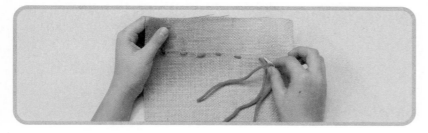

Making Armatures

1

An armature provides a basic shape for a mask, a sculpture, or other form. Materials used in an armature depend on the use or form of the final product.

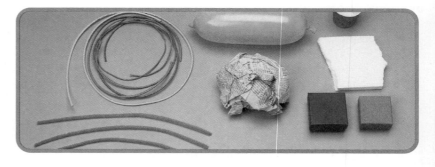

2

Show students how to cut and bend wire or pipe cleaners in whatever shape they desire.

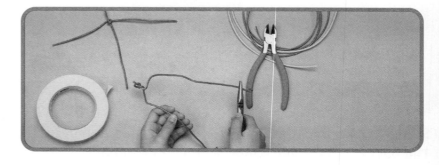

3

To form an armature for a mask or an animal sculpture, begin with an object such as an inflated balloon, a wad of newspaper, a piece of foam, or an empty box. Tell students that they can attach objects with tape or glue. Point out that the entire armature is likely to be covered with another medium such as foil, papier-mâché, or paint.

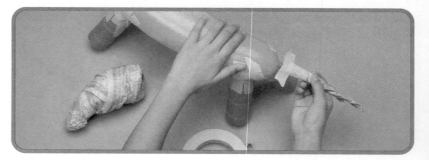

Working with Papier-Mâché

1

Once students build an armature, they can use papier-mâché to complete a mask or sculpture. Have them prepare by tearing newspaper into 1-inch-wide strips.

2

When it is time to apply the papier-mâché paste, cover all work areas with plastic or multiple layers of newspaper. You can choose to use wallpaper paste, or you can prepare your own mixture, using equal parts of flour and water. Place the paste in large, open bowls or saucers that students can easily reach.

3

Direct students to soak their newspaper strips in the paste, then apply them over their armature. They should lay the strips in various directions, criss-crossing them to build a smooth surface. Plan on having students apply at least two layers of strips. Allow for drying time between layers as well as after the final layer.

4

Students will enjoy painting their sculptures. You may also wish to make other materials available so students can add details. Yarn, raffia, beads, fabric, and found objects can add interest to sculptures.

List of Artworks

List of Artworks

Seasonal Projects

 Fall

Bark and Leaf Rubbing Tree

Materials

- white butcher paper
- brown paper lunch bags
- woven baskets (optional)
- scissors ⓢ
- assorted real or artificial leaves
- peeled crayons
- white paper
- tape
- glue

1. Have students help you cover an area of wall space with white butcher paper. Draw the outline of a large tree with branches. Tell students they will make rubbings of bark and leaves in autumn colors to bring the outdoors inside.

2. To create bark, have students crinkle brown paper bags, flatten them out, and cut them into organic shapes. Make rubbings against nearby trees to make bark texture. If no trees are available, have students make rubbings against woven baskets. Have students glue the "bark" to the trunk, working up from the bottom, overlapping the shapes as they add them.

3. As a class, gather a variety of leaves, or give each student an artificial leaf from a craft store. To make leaf rubbings, have each student arrange one leaf at a time, or a cluster of leaves, under a piece of white paper and rub over the top using the flat side of a crayon.

4. Students then cut out the leaves or leaf clusters and tape or glue them to the branches.

Autumn Pointillism

Materials

- markers
- drawing paper
- magazine or calendar photographs depicting autumn landscapes

1. Ask students to characterize autumn in the northern United States with examples from nature, such as leaves turning color, birds migrating, crops being harvested , and wildlife preparing for winter. Tell students that they will use these ideas to create an autumn landscape.

2. Display magazine or calendar photographs of autumn landscapes, or simply have students look out the classroom window for a source of inspiration. Ask students to lightly pencil a landscape.

3. Tell students they will use a technique called Pointillism. Demonstrate how to use markers to draw many tiny dots of different colors close to each other to create impressions of color. Have students experiment on a blank sheet of paper before they begin to fill in their landscapes using the technique. Point out that yellow and red dots can create an impression of orange, while yellow and blue dots can create an impression of green. Then encourage students to use a color wheel as a guide to help blend other colors.

4. Display the completed artworks for everyone to view.

Seasonal Projects

 Winter

Sparkling Snowmen

Materials

- black construction paper
- white chalk
- glue
- fabric scraps
- dry twigs
- construction paper scraps
- buttons
- coarse salt
- white tempera paint
- paintbrushes

1. Have each student use white chalk to draw a large snowman on black construction paper. Ask students to fill in the snowman shape with white.

2. Direct students to glue on fabric scraps, twigs, construction paper scraps, and buttons to decorate their snowman.

3. Add coarse salt to white tempera paint to give it a sparkly texture. Have students use the sparkly paint to paint snowflakes, snow-covered hills, and snowy ground cover around their snowman.

Winter Miniatures

Materials

- white bread
- white glue
- tablespoon
- acrylic paints
- paintbrushes

1. Have students brainstorm a variety of northern winter symbols, such as snowflakes, snowmen, sleds, mittens, ice skates, and skis. Record students' ideas on the board and explain that they will create a miniature of one of the symbols.

2. Tell students that they will create their miniatures from *migajon,* a substitute for clay that is used in Mexico and Central and South America to make ornaments.

3. To make *migajon,* have each student remove the crust from a slice of white bread, break the bread into small pieces, add a tablespoon of white glue, and mix by hand until it is like clay.

4. Have students mold a miniature symbol using the *migajon.*

5. Let the miniatures air dry. Then have students use acrylic paint to decorate them. Display the completed miniatures on a table next to cards that identify the objects and the artists.

 **Spring**

Sun Catchers

Materials

- fresh wildflowers
- leaves
- newspaper
- heavy books
- waxed paper
- cloth
- iron ⚠
- construction paper
- glue

1. Tell students that they will make sun catchers using pressed flowers and leaves. If possible, take students on a hike to gather fresh leaves and wildflowers. You may prefer to gather them beforehand, or purchase flowers.

2. Have students press the flowers and leaves by arranging them between sheets of newspaper and then placing heavy books on top.

3. When flowers and leaves are completely dry after about two weeks, have students make an arrangement between two identical waxed paper shapes.

4. When students are not present, put a towel or cloth on top and then press each arrangement with an iron set on low.

5. Have students then measure, cut, and glue a construction paper frame to both sides of the sun catcher and hang it by the window.

Thank-You Baskets

Materials

- large paper plates
- wax crayons
- tub of water
- large plastic cups
- rubber bands
- construction paper strips
- cut flowers

1. Have each student use wax crayons to decorate a large paper plate with spring designs or patterns.

2. Have students soak their plates in water until completely wet and mold them over large inverted plastic cups to form an upside down basket. Have students secure the plate with a rubber band about one inch below the basket's rim.

3. Have students roll the paper plate up to the rubber band to form a lip, or ruffle. Allow baskets to dry overnight.

4. Have students remove the baskets the next day and place them right side up. Ask each student to staple a construction paper strip onto the basket to make a handle.

5. Students can fill the baskets with cut flowers and deliver to someone special in their lives.

Seasonal Projects

 Summer

Clown Faces

Materials

- assorted photographs of clown faces
- black construction paper
- oil pastels

1. Tell students that the first week of August is National Clown Week. Explain that the art of clowning goes back thousands of years. Tell students that today, many clowns wear face make-up, and each clown has his or her own "face." No two clown faces are alike, and each clown adds something unique or personal as a way to be identified. Show students photographs of clown faces, and have them point out interesting details in each one.

2. Have students create their own clown face and draw it using oil pastels on black construction paper. Encourage students to add a personal symbol to the face, hair, or hat that they feel represents them.

3. Invite each student to show his or her clown face and explain the meaning behind the details.

Melted Crayon Painting

Materials

- white construction paper
- heavy cardboard
- black markers
- old crayons
- vegetable peelers ⚠ or hand-held pencil sharpeners ⚠
- paper plates
- rocks
- waxed paper (optional),
- iron and ironing board (optional) ⚠

1. Ask students to tape the corners of a sheet of white construction paper to heavy cardboard. Then ask them to use a black marker to draw an outline of something they associate with summer, such as a beach ball, butterfly, flower, or bird.

2. Have students work together to create crayon shavings using vegetable peelers or hand-held pencil sharpeners. Once the shavings are ready, have students generously sprinkle shavings inside the lines of the picture.

3. Have students place pictures outside in the sun, set a rock or heavy object on each corner, and then allow the sun to melt the crayon shavings. If necessary, have students place a piece of waxed paper over their designs. When the children are out of the room, place a towel over each design and iron to melt the crayon.

4. When the wax begins to cool, students can bring their pictures inside to display. If using the iron-on method, leave the waxed paper in place.

Materials

The following lists include suggested materials needed to complete all Studio activities and Portfolio Projects.

Drawing and Painting Tools

- ☐ chalk pastels (one set per student)
- ☐ colored pencils (one box per student)
- ☐ crayons (one box per student)
- ☐ markers (one set per student)
- ☐ oil pastels (one set per student)
- ☐ paintbrushes (different sizes, at least three per student)
- ☐ pencils (one box per student)
- ☐ pens (one per student)

Paint

- ☐ acrylic paint (assorted colors, two pints per student)
- ☐ tempera paint (assorted colors including neon, six pints per student)

Paper Products

- ☐ butcher paper (one roll)
- ☐ construction paper (assorted colors, six packs of 100)
- ☐ drawing paper (assorted sizes, seven reams of 500)
- ☐ heavy stock paper (three packages of 100)
- ☐ mat board (one per student)
- ☐ newsprint (two pads of 100)
- ☐ poster board (three per student)
- ☐ waxed paper (one roll)

Clay

- ☐ self-hardening clay (two pounds per student)

Materials

Classroom Materials

- [ ] glue stick (two per student)
- [ ] hole punch ⚠ (one per student)
- [ ] paper clips ⚠ (one box)
- [ ] measuring tape (one for every pair of students)
- [ ] rulers (one per student)
- [ ] scissors ⚠ (one per student)
- [ ] stapler ⚠ (several per classroom)
- [ ] tape, masking (several rolls per classroom)
- [ ] tape, transparent (several rolls per classroom)
- [ ] thumbtacks ⚠ (assortment)
- [ ] white bottle glue (two per student)

Specialty and Craft Materials

- [ ] balloons (one package of 100)
- [ ] brayer (one per student)
- [ ] burlap squares (8″ squares, one per student)
- [ ] buttons, beads, etc. (assortment)
- [ ] copper foil (one sheet per student)
- [ ] craft sticks ⚠ (two packs of 100)
- [ ] feathers (assortment)
- [ ] grass and straw (assortment)
- [ ] heavy cord (several spools)
- [ ] heavy wire ⚠ (one spool)
- [ ] meat trays ⚠ (one per student)
- [ ] narrow gauge wire, color ⚠ (one large spool)
- [ ] needles ⚠ (one per student)
- [ ] nuts, bolts, washers, etc. (assortment)
- [ ] pipe cleaners ⚠ (one package of 100)
- [ ] pliers ⚠ (one per student)
- [ ] polystyrene foam balls (3–4 per student)
- [ ] ribbon (assorted colors, several rolls)
- [ ] sponges (one per student)
- [ ] string (three spools)
- [ ] tissue paper (assorted colors, several packs)
- [ ] water containers (one per student)
- [ ] wire cutters ⚠ (one per student)
- [ ] yarn (assorted colors and weights, several bundles)

Others

- ☐ aluminum foil (two rolls)
- ☐ blender ⚠ (one)
- ☐ dish soap (one bottle)
- ☐ disposable cameras (black and white film, several per class)
- ☐ disposable drinking cups (four packs of 50)
- ☐ mirrors ⚠ (one per student)
- ☐ paper towels (two rolls)
- ☐ plastic tubs (several per classroom)
- ☐ shallow trays, large (two)
- ☐ toothpicks ⚠ (one box)
- ☐ window screen sheets (two per classroom)

Inexpensive Materials and Sources

- ☐ cardboard (retail and grocery stores, student provided)
- ☐ egg cartons (student provided)
- ☐ fabric scraps (fabric and decorating stores)
- ☐ magazines (student provided)
- ☐ newspaper (student provided)
- ☐ paint-mixing tray (clean plastic food containers, student provided)
- ☐ paper towel tubes (student provided)
- ☐ papier-mâché paste (flour, salt, and water mixture)
- ☐ plastic water bottles (student provided)

Optional

- ☐ ceramic clay (two pounds per student)
- ☐ ceramic glaze (assorted colors, five pints)
- ☐ charcoal (one piece per student)
- ☐ foam scraps (assortment)
- ☐ graph paper (one pad)
- ☐ heavy stock construction paper (one package)
- ☐ high-gloss varnish (one quart)
- ☐ plastic knives ⚠ (one per student)
- ☐ smocks (one per student)
- ☐ starch (one box)
- ☐ tape, masking (several rolls per classroom)
- ☐ water-resistant table protectors (several per classroom)
- ☐ wood scraps (assortment)

Bibliography/Additional Resources

Books for Teachers

General Reference Books

Arnason, H. H. *History of Modern Art: Painting, Sculpture, Architecture.* 3rd ed. New York: Harry N. Abrams, 1986.

Arnheim, Rudolf. *Visual Thinking.* Berkeley and Los Angeles, California: University of California Press, 1969.

Carpenter, James M. *Visual Art: A Critical Introduction.* New York: Harcourt Brace Jovanovich, 1982.

Gardner, Helen. *Art Through the Ages.* 7th ed. New York: Harcourt Brace Jovanovich, 1986.

Gombrich, E. H. *The Story of Art.* 16th ed. London: Phaidon Press, Ltd., 1995.

Hobbs, Jack A. and Robert L. Duncan. *Arts, Ideas, and Civilization.* 2nd ed. Englewood Cliffs, New Jersey: Prentice Hall, 1992.

Janson, H. W. *History of Art.* 5th ed. New York: Harry N. Abrams, 1995.

Katz, Elizabeth L., Louis E. Lankford, and Jan D. Plank. *Themes and Foundations of Art.* St. Paul, Minnesota: West Publishing Company, 1995.

Silver, Larry. *Art in History.* New York: Abbeville Press, 1993.

Art Education

Armstrong, Carmen L. *Designing Assessment in Art.* National Art Education Association, 1994.

Berk, Ellyn, Jerrold Ross. *A Framework for Multicultural Arts Education.* New York: The National Arts Education Research Center at New York University, 1989.

Berry, Nancy and Susan M. Mayer, eds. *Museum Education: History, Theory, and Practice.* Reston, Virginia: National Art Education Association, 1989.

Blandy, Douglas and Elizabeth Hoffman. "Toward an Art Education of Place," *Studies in Art Education,* 1993.

Chapman, Laura H. *Approaches to Art Education.* New York: Harcourt Brace Jovanovich, 1979.

_____. *Instant Art Instant Culture: The Unspoken Policy for American Schools.* New York: Teachers College Press, 1982.

Cohen, Elaine P. and Ruth S. Gainer. *Art: Another Language for Learning.* New York: Schocken Books, 1984.

Day, Michael and Al Hurwitz. *Children and Their Art.* 5th ed. Harcourt Brace Jovanovich, 1991.

Eisner, Elliot W. *Educating Artistic Vision.* New York: Macmillan Publishing Co., 1972.

_____. "What the Arts Taught Me About Education." *Art Education,* September 1991.

Gardner, H. *Artful Scribbles: The Significance of Children's Drawings.* New York: Basic Books, 1980.

Henry, Carole, ed. *Middle School Art: Issues of Curriculum and Instruction.* Reston, Virginia: The National Art Education Association, 1996.

Hume, Helen D. *A Survival Kit for the Secondary School Art Teacher.* West Nyack, New York. The Center for Applied Research in Education, Inc., 1990.

Hurwitz, Al and Michael Day. *Children and Their Art: Methods for the Elementary School.* 5th ed. New York: Harcourt Brace Jovanovich, 1991.

Lowenfeld, Viktor and Lambert W. Brittain. *Creative and Mental Growth.* 8th ed. New York: Macmillan Publishing Co., 1987.

_____. *Safety in the Artroom.* Reston, Virginia, 1986.

_____. Visual Standards Task Force (Jeanne Rollins, Chair). *National Visual Art Standards.* Reston, Virginia, 1994.

Ocvirk, Otto, et al. *Art Fundamentals, Theory and Practice.* 6th ed. Dubuque, Iowa: William C. Brown, 1990.

Qualley, Charles. *Safety in the Artroom.* Worcester, Massachusetts: Davis Publications, 1986.

Reynolds, Nancy Walkup. *Art Lessons for the Middle School: A DBAE Curriculum.* Portland, Maine: J. Weston Walch Publishers, 1992.

Smith, Peter. "Art and Irrelevance." *Studies in Art Education.* Winter 1995.

Smith, R. A. *Excellence in Art Education: Ideas and Initiatives.* Reston, Virginia: National Art Education Association, 1986.

Sullivan, Graeme. "Art-Based Art Education: Learning That Is Meaningful, Authentic, Critical and Pluralistic," *Studies in Art Education,* September 1993.

Texas Education Agency. *Art Education: Planning for Teaching and Learning.* Austin, TX: TEA, 1989.

Thompson, Christine, ed. *The Visual Arts and Early Childhood Learning.* Reston, VA: National Art Education Association, 1995.

Wolf, D. P. and N. Pistone. *Taking Full Measure: Rethinking Assessment Through the Arts.* New York: The College Board.

Teaching Art History

Baxandall, M. *Patterns of Intention: On the Historical Explanation of Pictures.* New Haven: Yale University Press, 1985.

Bourde, N. and M. D. Garrard. *Feminism and Art History: Questioning the Litany.* New York: Harper & Row, 1982.

Richter, H. *DaDa: Art and Anti-Art.* New York: Norton, 1985.

Art and Multiple Intelligences/ Interdisciplinary Education

Coming to Our Senses: The Significance of the Arts for American Education. New York: American Council for the Arts, 1988.

Gardner, Howard. *Frames of Mind: The Theory of Multiple Intelligences.* New York: Basic Books, Inc., 1983.

Art Criticism and Aesthetics

Arnheim, Rudolph. *Visual Thinking.* Berkeley: University of California Press, 1980.

Barrett, Terry. *Criticizing Art: Understanding the Contemporary.* Mountain View, California: Mayfield Publishing Company, 1994.

Cromer, James. *Criticism: History, Theory and Practice of Art Criticism in Art Education.* Reston, Virginia: National Art Education Association, 1990.

Day, Michael, and Elliot Eisner, et al. *Art History, Art Criticism, and Art Production.* Santa Monica: Rand Corporation, 1984.

Feldman, Edmund B. *Becoming Human Through Art: Aesthetic Experience in the School.* Englewood Cliffs, New Jersey: Prentice-Hall, 1970.

_____. "The Teacher as Model Critic." *Journal of Aesthetic Education,* January 1973.

_____. *Thinking About Art.* Englewood Cliffs, New Jersey: Prentice-Hall, 1985.

_____. *Varieties of Visual Experience.* 4th ed. New York: Harry N. Abrams, 1992.

Hamblen, Karen A. "An Art Criticism Questioning Strategy Within the Framework of Bloom's Taxonomy." *Studies in Art Education,* September 1984.

Lankford, E. L. *Aesthetics: Issues and Inquiry.* Reston, Virginia: National Art Education Association, 1992.

Werhane, P. H. *Philosophical Issues in Art.* Englewood Cliffs, New Jersey: Prentice-Hall, 1984.

Art in Cultural Traditions

Bearden, Romare and Harry Henderson. *A History of African-American Artists from 1792 to the Present.* New York: Pantheon Books, 1993.

Driskell, David C. *Hidden Heritage: Afro-American Art, 1800–1950.* San Francisco: The Art Museum of America, 1985.

_____. *Two Centuries of Black American Art.* New York: Alfred A. Knopf and the Los Angeles County Museum of Art, 1976.

Lee, S. *A History of Far Eastern Art.* New York: Harry N. Abrams, 1982.

Lewis, Samella. *African American Art and Artists.* Berkeley, California: University of California Press, 1990.

_____. *Art: African American.* Los Angeles: Hancraft Studios, 1990.

Rosenak, Chuck and Jan. *Museum of American Folk Art Encyclopedia of Twentieth-Century American Folk Art and Artists.* New York: Abbeville Press, 1991.

Studio Museum in Harlem. *Harlem Renaissance Art of Black America.* New York: Harry N. Abrams, 1987.

Sullivan, Charles, ed. *Children of Promise: African American Literature and Art for Young People.* Bergenfield, New Jersey: Harry N. Abrams, 1994.

Turner, Robyn Montana. *Texas Traditions: The Culture of the Lone Star State.* Boston: Little, Brown, 1996.

Weatherford, Jack. *Native Roots: How the Indians Enriched America.* New York: Fawcett Columbine, 1991.

Young, Bernard, ed. *Art, Culture, and Ethnicity.* Reston, Virginia: National Art Education Association, 1991.

Women and Art

Broude, Norma and Mary D. Garrard, eds. *Feminism and Art History—Questioning the Litany.* New York: Harper & Row, 1982.

Collins, Georgia and Renee Sandell, eds. *Gender Issues in Art Education: Content, Contexts, and Strategies.* Reston, Virginia: National Art Education Association, 1996.

Collins, Georgia and Renee Sandell. *Women, Art, and Education.* Reston, Virginia: National Art Education Association, 1984.

Collins, Jim and Glenn B. Opitz. *Women Artists in America: Eighteenth Century to the Present.* Poughkeepsie, New York: Apollo, 1980.

Bibliography/Additional Resources

Fine, Elsa Honig. *Women & Art: A History of Women Painters and Sculptors from the Renaissance to the 20th Century.* Montclair, New Jersey, and London: Allanheld & Schram: Prior, 1978.

Freedman, Kerry. "Interpreting Gender and Visual Culture in Art Classrooms." *Studies in Art Education,* Spring 1994.

Greer, Germaine. *The Obstacle Race: The Fortunes of Women Painters and Their Work.* New York: Farrar, Straus, & Giroux, 1979.

Harris, Ann Sutherland, and Linda Nochlin. *Women Artists: 1550–1950.* New York: Alfred A. Knopf and the Los Angeles County Museum of Art, 1984.

Hedges, Elaine and Ingrid Wendt, comps. *In Her Own Image, Women Working in the Arts.* Old Westbury, New York: Feminist Press; McGraw-Hill, 1980.

Heller, Reinhold. *Gabriele Münter: The Years of Expressionism 1903–1920.* Munich, Germany and New York, New York: Prestel-Verlag, 1997.

Lerner, Gerda. *The Majority Finds Its Past: Placing Women in History.* New York: Oxford University Press, 1979.

Munro, Eleanor. *Originals: American Women Artists.* New York: Simon & Schuster, 1979.

Nemser, Cindy. *Art Talk: Conversations with Twelve Women Artists.* New York: Scribner, 1975.

Nochlin, Linda. *The Politics of Vision: Essays on Nineteenth-Century Art and Society.* New York: Harper & Row Publishers, 1989.

Petersen, Karen and J. J. Wilson. *Women Artists: Recognition and Reappraisal, From the Early Middle Ages to the Twentieth Century.* New York: Harper Colophon Books and New York University Press, 1976.

Rubinstein, Charlotte Streifer. *American Women Artists: From Early Indian Times to the Present.* Boston: G. K. Hall, 1982.

Slatkin, Wendy. *Women Artists in History: From Antiquity to the 20th Century.* Englewood Cliffs, New Jersey: Prentice-Hall, 1985.

Tufts, Eleanor. *American Women Artists, Past and Present: A Selected Bibliographic Guide (to Works on 500 Selected Artists).* New York: Garland, 1984.

_____. *Our Hidden Heritage: Five Centuries of Women Artists.* New York and London: Paddington Press, 1974.

Art Forms and Techniques

Betti, Claudia and Teel Sale. *Drawing: A Contemporary Approach,* 2nd ed. Orlando, Florida: Holt, Rinehart and Winston, 1986.

Brooke, Sandy. *Hooked on Drawing: Illustrated Lessons & Exercises for Grades 4 and Up.* Englewood Cliffs, New Jersey: Prentice Hall, 1996.

Edwards, Betty. *Drawing on the Artist Within.* New York, New York: Simon & Schuster, Inc., 1986.

Enstice, Wayne and Melody Peters. *Drawing: Space, Form, and Expression.* Englewood Cliffs, New Jersey: Prentice-Hall, 1990.

Hurwitz, Al, Brent Wilson, and Marjorie Wilson. *Teaching Drawing from Art.* Worcester, Massachusetts: Davis Publications, Inc., 1987.

Mayer, Ralph. *The Artist's Handbook of Materials and Techniques.* 5th ed. New York: Viking-Penguin, 1991.

Mills, John. *The Encyclopedia of Sculpture Techniques.* New York: Watson-Guptill, 1990.

Nicolaides, Kimon. *The Natural Way to Draw: A Working Plan for Art Study.* Boston: Houghton Mifflin, 1990.

Patterson, Freeman. *Photography and the Art of Seeing.* San Francisco: Sierra Club Books, 1990.

Ross, John, Tim and Claire Romano. *The Complete Printmaker.* New York: The Free Press/Macmillan, 1990.

Periodicals

American Artist

Art in America

Art Education

Communication Arts

Design for Art Education

Graphic Design

Journal of Aesthetic Education

Journal of Aesthetics and Art Criticism

National Art Education Association News

School Arts

Smithsonian

Studies in Art Education

Books for Students

Davidson, Rosemary. *Take a Look: An Introduction to the Experience of Art.* New York: Viking, 1993.

Epstein, Vivien S. *History of Women Artists for Children.* Denver: V. S. Epstein, 1987.

Flower, Cedric, and Alan Fortney. *Puppets: Methods and Materials.* Worcester, Massachusetts: Davis Publications, 1983.

Franc, Helen M. *An Invitation to See: 125 Paintings from the Museum of Modern Art.* New York: Harry N. Abrams/Museum of Modern Art, 1973.

Gatto, Joseph. *Drawing Media and Techniques.* Worcester, Massachusetts: Davis Publications, 1986.

Greenberg, Jan and Sandra Jordan. *The Painter's Eye.* New York: Delacorte Press, 1991.

Janson, H. W. *History of Art for Young People.* 4th ed. New York: Harry N. Abrams, 1992.

Laybourne, Kit. *The Animation Book: A Complete Guide to Animated Film-Making—From Flip-Books to Sound Cartoons.* New York: Crown Publications, 1988.

Price, Susanna & Tim Stephens. *Click!: Fun with Photography.* New York, New York: Sterling Publishing Company, Inc., 1995.

Storr, Robert. *Chuck Close.* New York: The Museum of Modern Art, 1998.

Turner, Robyn Montana. *Portraits of Women Artists for Children (Rosa Bonheur, Georgia O'Keeffe, Mary Cassatt, Frida Kahlo, Faith Ringgold, Dorothea Lange)* (series). Boston, Massachusetts: Little, Brown, 1991–1994.

Von Oech, Roger. *A Whack on the Side of the Head: How You Can Be More Creative.* New York, New York: Warner Books, 1983.

_____. *A Kick in the Seat of the Pants: Using Your Explorer, Artist, Judge, & Warrior to be More Creative.* New York, New York: Harper & Row Publishers, Inc., 1986.

Zelanski, Paul. *Shaping Space.* Fort Worth, Texas: Holt, Rinehart & Winston, 1987.

Art on the Internet

Web sites often change. The following Web sites are examples of acceptable sources for information. Establish guidelines for your students' safe and responsible use of the Internet.

American Folk Art Museum
http://www.ny.com/museums/museum.of.american.folk.art.html/

Art Access
http://www.artic.edu/aic/artaccess/

Art Museum of the Americas
http://www.museum.oas.org/

Art Net
http://www.artnet.com/library/index.asp/

Artchive
http://www.artchive.com/core.html/

Artcyclopedia
http://www.artcyclopedia.com/

Artlex Visual Arts Dictionary
http://www.artlex.com/

ArtsConnectEd
http://artsconnected.org/

Asian Art Museum of San Francisco
http://www.asianart.org/

Ask Art
http://askart.com/

Carnegie Museum of Art
http://www.cmoa.org/

Dallas Museum of Art
http://www.dm-art.org/

Fine Arts Museums of San Francisco
http://www.famsf.org/

Guggenheim Museum
http://www.guggenheim.org/
http://www.guggenheimcollection.org/

J. Paul Getty Museum
http://www.getty.edu/museum/

Metropolitan Museum of Art, New York
http://www.metmuseum.org/

Milwaukee Art Museum
http://www.mam.org/

Museum of Fine Arts, Houston
http://www.mfah.org/

Museum of Latin American Art
http://www.molaa.com/

Museum of Modern Art
http://www.moma.org/

National Gallery of Art
http://www.nga.gov/

National Museum of African Art
Smithsonian/Washington D. C.
http://www.nmafa.si.edu/

National Museum of Women in the Arts
http://www.nmwa.org/

Smithsonian American Art Museum
http://www.nmaa.si.edu/

Web Museum
http://www.ibiblio.org/wm/

Whitney Museum of American Art
http://www.whitney.org/

Learning Styles

A Student Who Is . . .	Is Likely to Enjoy Art projects that . . .	And May Enjoy Helping Out in the Classroom by . . .
An Interpersonal Learner • interactive • communicative • group-oriented • extroverted	• are group projects • require giving/receiving feedback • require group leaders	• distributing and collecting materials • mediating
An Intrapersonal Learner • individualistic • solitary • self-reflective • introverted	• are individual projects • focus on feelings, dreams, or self • are goal-oriented	• arranging items in storage spaces • assisting the teacher before or after class
A Bodily/Kinesthetic Learner • physically active • hands-on • talkative	• involve motion such as dancing or acting • involve touching various objects, materials, and textures	• running errands • role-playing safety rules • distributing and collecting materials
A Verbal/Linguistic Learner • oriented toward language, words, reading, and writing	• involve spoken or written words • involve storytelling	• reading instructions aloud • labeling storage spaces • creating "rules" posters
A Logical/Mathematical Learner • inquisitive • experimental • oriented toward numbers, patterns, and relationships	• involve patterns, relationships, or symbols • require problem-solving	• arranging or classifying materials • counting materials for distribution • helping solve problems
A Visual/Spatial Learner • imaginative • oriented toward colors and pictures	• involve colors and designs • involve painting, drawing, or sculpture • require active imagination	• creating displays of artworks • designing charts and posters
A Musical/Rhythmic Learner • oriented toward music, rhythmic sounds, and environmental sounds	• involve rhythmic patterns, singing, humming, responding to music, keeping time, or listening for sounds	• thinking of or leading clean-up songs (primary grades) • creating displays about music or musicians
Acquiring English	• require limited word usage • involve terminology from their first language • involve simple name/word games	• creating labels and posters in their first language • creating images or icons for bulletin boards • sharing elements of their culture with other students

Safety

Art should be fun. It should also be safe. Use these guidelines to help ensure the safety of your art classroom and to help teach your students about safety.

⚠ Make your classroom safe.

- Provide water-based materials (markers, paints, clay, etc.).
- Provide nontoxic glue, clay, and other materials.
- Provide safety scissors for young children.
- Do not use glass containers. Instead, use plastic, polystyrene, or waxed-paper cups or containers.
- Do not provide sharp-edged tools such as knives or razor blades. Students can use plastic knives for cutting clay and toothpicks or paperclips for carving clay. (Remind students to be especially careful with any objects that have sharp points.)
- Keep a well-stocked first-aid kit in the classroom.
- Label and date all materials and chemicals. Store them properly. Keep solvents and powders in containers with lids. If you must store potentially hazardous materials in the classroom, do so in a place where students do *not* have access to them.
- Report unsafe or malfunctioning equipment or facilities to the administration, verbally and in writing.
- Dispose of waste materials properly.
- Clean up spills immediately.

⚠ Read labels.

- Check for age-appropriateness. The Art and Creative Materials Institute (ACMI) labels art as approved or certified when they are safe for young children, even if ingested. Look for these round ACMI labels. A product bearing the square "Health Label" is safe only for children over twelve.
- Check products' ventilation requirements. For products that do require ventilation, an open classroom door or one window is probably not adequate.

⚠ Know your students.

- Be aware of students' allergies. Children with allergies to wheat (gluten), for example, may be irritated by the wheat paste used in papier-mâché. Other art materials that may cause allergic reactions include chalk or other dusty substances, water-based clay, and any material that contains petroleum products.
- Use your knowledge of individual student's tendencies to plan art activities that are safe for all students.

A note on toxicity:

Toxic materials can enter the body in a number of ways.

Inhalation Eliminate from your classroom aerosol spray mists or paints, solvents that give off vapors (turpentine, paint thinners, etc.), and gases such as those given off by some kiln fuels. Inhalation of a toxic substance can cause allergic reactions as well as other, more dire or long-lasting conditions.

Ingestion Children frequently taste substances that are visually appealing, even though they know the substances are not edible. In particular, certain colors of paint and ceramic glazes may be tempting for children to taste. Doing so could be fatal. Be aware of the "food appeal" factor any time you offer a material to a child.

Skin contact Allergic reactions and burns may result from skin contact with some art materials, particularly solvents. Even "safe" materials such as powdered tempera paint can cause irritation if rubbed in the eyes, for example. Encourage students to minimize the splashing, spilling, and pouring of liquid or powdered art materials. Provide protective gloves or clothing if necessary.

⚠ Discuss safety.

- Teach students how to care for and safely use art materials, tools, and equipment.
- Post rules where they will be effective. For example, place a "Don't forget to wash up!" sign over the sink.
- Before each art activity, alert students to potential dangers and relevant safety procedures.
- Teach students what to do in an emergency. Practice emergency procedures such as room evacuation regularly.

Teacher Glossary

A

abstract A style of art that does not show a realistic style. Abstract art usually contains geometric shapes, bold colors, and lines.

abstraction A subject that has been simplified, stylized, or broken down into basic shapes.

actual lines Lines that are real, not imaginary.

altered proportion A technique used by an artist to change the size relationship of shapes in an artwork. See *monumental*, and *miniature*.

alternating rhythm Rhythm created in an artwork by repeating two or more elements on a regular, interchanging basis.

analogous Colors that appear next to each other on the color wheel. Analogous colors have one hue in common. For example, blue, blue-green, and blue-violet all contain blue. Also known as *related colors*.

animation The art of putting together drawings in a sequence. The pictures are recorded onto film. When the film is run at high speed, the pictures appear to be in motion.

applied art Artworks that are functional. Also known as *utilitarian art*.

aqueduct A channel or conduit built for transporting water from a distant source.

arch A semicircular or curved shape in a building. An arch can frame a doorway or it can support a wall or ceiling.

architect An artist who plans buildings and other structures.

architecture The art and science of designing buildings and other structures.

armature A skeletal framework or support for a sculpture.

art historians Those who study art history and cultural traditions that relate to art, such as forms of government, religious beliefs, and social activities.

art media The materials used by artists to create artworks.

Art Nouveau French for "new art," this style of art in the late 1800s and early 1900s, uses exaggerated asymmetrical designs and makes use of undulating forms of all kinds, most notably tendrils, plant stems, flames, waves, and flowing hair.

art teacher A specialist in the field of visual art who teaches and helps students and others understand and participate in the world of visual arts and ideas.

artificial intelligence The ability of a computer or other machine to perform those activities that are normally thought to require intelligence.

artwork Any artistic object or production.

assemblage An additive sculpture often made of recycled objects that assume new meaning within the artwork.

asymmetrical balance A type of balance in which the two sides of an artwork look equally important even though they are not alike. Also known as *informal balance*.

atmospheric perspective A technique used to create the illusion of air and space in an artwork through changes in value. Close-up objects are bright and consist of darker colors; faraway objects consist of muted colors. Also known as *aerial perspective*.

B

background The part of an artwork that seems the farthest away.

balance The way an artwork is arranged to make different parts seem equally important. Balance is a principle of design.

barrel vault A semi-cylindrical structure made up of successive arches.

Bauhaus design A twentieth-century German school of design and art. This style of art used simplified forms and unadorned functionalism. It was influenced by and derived from techniques and materials used in industrial fabrication and manufacture.

binder A material, such as wax, egg, glue, resin, or oil, that binds together the coloring grains and powder in a pigment.

blending A shading technique that changes the value of a color little by little.

block In printmaking, a piece of flat material, such as wood or metal, with a design on the surface, which is a mirror image of the composition that will appear as a print. The block is used to print the design. (See also *plate.*) In sculpture, a solid material, such as wood or stone, used for carving.

blue screen A technique used in filmmaking to create special effects. The subjects are filmed against a blue screen. Later, the blue screen is replaced by another background.

blueprint A photographic print used to copy the final drawing of a plan for building something.

bronze A metal alloy made of copper and tin and other metals, often used in cast sculpture.

C

calligraphy Ornamental writing, done mainly with a pen in the West and with a brush in China and Japan.

caricature An artwork that exaggerates the features or aspects of a person or object, usually in a way that is funny.

cartoonist An artist who draws cartoons for newspapers, magazines and other print media.

carving A subtractive method of sculpting requiring the sculptor to cut or chip away pieces from a block of material, such as wood, stone, or other hard material.

casting A sculpting process in which a liquid, such as molten bronze or liquid plaster, is poured into a heat-proof mold to create a three-dimensional form or an impression.

cathedral A church that is the official seat of a bishop.

cell One frame of an animated film that is created by hand. Before digital and computer technology, all cells that comprised a film had to be drawn and painted by hand.

ceramics The art of making objects from clay and hardening them with fire. Also, artworks made by this process.

cityscape Artwork that gives a view of a city.

Classical Style A term applied to an artwork that exhibits the characteristics of ancient Greek and Roman art, such as proportion, balance, and idealized forms and themes.

Claymation An animation process in which clay figurines are manipulated and filmed to produce an image of lifelike movement.

Teacher Glossary

collage A medium in which the artist glues bits of cut or torn paper, photographs, fabric, or other materials to a flat surface.

color The visual quality of objects caused by the amount of light they reflected. Color is an element of art. See *hue*.

color scheme A plan for combining colors in a work of art.

complementary Colors that contrast with one another. Complementary colors are opposite one another on the color wheel.

compositing A process by which combined images are burned or recorded onto a single piece of film by using either photographic or computer equipment.

composition The plan, placement, or arrangement of the elements of art in an artwork. Composition may also refer to any work of art.

Computer Aided Design (CAD) The use of computer programs and systems to design detailed two- or three-dimensional models of physical objects, such as mechanical parts or buildings.

computer arts Artworks created using computer technology as a medium.

conservator A person who works to protect artworks from damage and decay.

contrast The difference between two unlike things, such as a light color and a dark color.

converging lines Actual or implied lines that recede toward an intersecting point in space.

cool colors The family of colors that includes greens, blues, and violets. Cool colors bring to mind cool things, places, and feelings.

costume A style of dress characteristic of a particular country, historical period, or culture. An outfit or disguise worn for certain celebrations, or an outfit in dramatic productions.

creativity A state characterized by originality, imagination, and expression.

cross-hatching A shading technique using lines that cross each other.

curator A person who does research for a museum. Curators recommend artworks for the museum to consider purchasing. They also select artworks for display from the museum's permanent collection.

decorative art Handicrafts that result in beautiful, useful objects. Rug and fabric design, furniture-making, and glassblowing are all decorative arts.

depth The third dimension or the illusion of deep space on a two-dimensional plane.

detail A small part of a larger artwork enlarged for closer viewing. Also, a minute or particularly interesting part of an artwork.

diagonal line A slanted edge or line.

digital technology Technology that converts visual images into binary code through the use of items such as digital cameras, video and audio recorders, or computers.

docent A person who volunteers in an art museum. Docents give information and conduct tours.

E

earth art A type of art created with natural materials. The completed artwork often becomes a part of the environment in which it was created. Also known as *earth work.*

elements of art The basic parts and symbols of an artwork. The elements of art are line, color, value, shape, texture, form, and space.

emphasis Importance given to certain objects or areas in an artwork. Color, texture, shape, space, and size can be used to create dominance, contrast, or a focal point. Emphasis is a principle of design.

etching A printing process in which a design is drawn into a wax-covered metal plate. The plate is then bathed in acid, which eats the metal on the areas unprotected by the wax. The wax is removed and ink is applied to the etched surface. The plate is then pressed onto a surface to reveal the print. Also, a print made by this process.

exhibition A public display of artworks.

F

fantasy art Art that reflects the imagination.

fashion The prevailing style or custom, as in dress or behavior.

feature Any distinct part of the face, such as the nose, mouth, or eyes.

fiber arts Artworks created from yarn, thread, or cloth. Stitchery and weaving are examples.

fine art Artworks that are created for the sole purpose of being viewed.

focal point The center of interest in a work of art. A way to show emphasis in an artwork in which the artist sets an area or element apart from the others.

foreground The part of an artwork that seems nearest.

form A three-dimensional object, such as a cube or ball. Form is an element of art.

frame One of many pictures in a filmstrip. Also, a decorative border or support for an artwork.

function The purpose or use of an object.

G

geometric form A form such as a sphere, cube, or pyramid whose contours represent a circle, square, and triangle, respectively.

geometric shape A shape that is precise and mathematical. Circles, squares, triangles, ovals, and rectangles are geometric shapes.

gesture A motion of the limbs or body made to express or help express a thought or to emphasize speech.

gesture drawing A drawing technique in which artists move a drawing medium, such as a pencil, quickly and freely over a surface to capture the form and actions of a subject.

glaze A thin layer of transparent paint made of minerals. A glaze can be applied to a piece of pottery, which is then re-fired.

Gothic A word used to describe all medieval art from the middle of the twelfth century to the beginning of the Renaissance.

Teacher Glossary

H

hardware Computer components, such as monitors, keyboards, CPUs, and modems.

hatching A shading technique using thin parallel lines.

hieroglyphics A system of writing using symbols and pictures.

horizon line The line created in an artwork by the meeting of sky and ground. In linear perspective it also represents the viewer's eye level.

horizontal line In an artwork, a line that runs side-to-side, parallel to the horizon. Horizontal lines appear peaceful and calm.

hue Another word for color.

human form Form of the human body.

I

implied lines Lines that are not real, but suggested by the placement of other lines, shapes, and colors.

impressionism An art movement and style developed in the late 1800s by a group of French artists. Artists of the Impressionist style drew and painted their impressions of visual reality by showing the effects of light and color on everyday objects.

indoor space The space inside a house or building.

installation An artwork that is assembled for an exhibition and removed when the exhibition is over.

intensity The brightness or dullness of a hue. A hue mixed with its complement is less intense than the pure color.

intermediate color A color that is a mixture of a primary and a secondary color that are next to each other on the color wheel. Blue-green, red-orange, and red-violet are examples of intermediate colors.

L

landscape architecture The planning and design of outdoor areas.

light source A point of illumination for emphasis, contrast, unity, or dramatic effect in an artwork.

line A thin mark on a surface created by a pen, pencil, brush, or any other tool. Line is an element of art.

linear perspective A technique that makes use of actual and implied lines to create the illusion of depth on a two-dimensional surface. If the lines in an artwork created with this technique are extended, they converge at a point on an imaginary line that represents the eye level of the viewer. This point is called the vanishing point.

lithograph A type of print made by drawing a design on a metal or stone plate using a greasy substance. The plate is washed with water, and then covered with greasy ink that adheres only to the design and not the wet surface of the plate. The plate is then processed onto paper.

loom A frame or machine used to hold yarn, or other fibers, for weaving, usually at right angles to one another.

M

matte painting Scenery, such as a darkened city or a vast ocean, painted on glass or created with a computer as a background to replace the blue screen in a film shot.

medium A material used to create artworks, such as clay or paint. The plural of *medium* is *media.*

Middle Ages The period in European history between the fall of Rome in A.D. 410 to about 1450. Also known as the *Medieval period* and the *Dark Ages.*

middle ground In an artwork, the part between the foreground and the background.

miniature Artworks that are of smaller-than-life proportions.

mixed media Artworks that are created from more than one medium.

modeling A sculpture technique in which a three-dimensional form is manipulated in a soft material, such as clay.

monochromatic A color scheme that uses different values of a single hue by showing tints and shades of that hue.

monumental Artworks that are of larger-than-life proportions.

morphing Transforming an image by computer. Transforming from one shape to another.

motif An element that is repeated often enough to be an important feature of a design.

N

natural form A form of, relating to, or concerning nature.

negative space The empty space around and between forms or shapes in an artwork. See *positive space.*

neutral A word used for black, white, and tints and shades of gray. Some artists use tints and shades of brown as neutrals.

O

oil-based paints Paints made from a mixture of colored pigment and linseed oil.

one-point perspective A form of linear perspective in which all lines appear to meet at a single vanishing point on the horizon.

opaque The quality of not letting light through; the opposite of *transparent.*

Op Art A style of art in which artists create the illusion of movement or other optical illusions. Op Art flourished in the 1950s and 1960s.

optical illusion A visually perceived image that is deceptive or misleading.

organic form A "free-form" that has irregular and uneven edges and may be found in nature, such as an apple, tree, or animal.

organic shape A "free-form" shape that is irregular and uneven, such as the shape of a leaf, flower, or cloud.

outdoor space The space outside of a structure or building; space that is in the open or leading to the open.

overlapping Partly or completely covering one shape or form with another to show space and distance in an artwork.

Teacher Glossary

palette A flat board on which a painter mixes color.

parallel lines Two or more straight lines or edges on the same plane that do not intersect. Parallel lines have the same direction.

pattern Repeated colors, lines, shapes, forms, or textures in an artwork. Pattern is a principle of design. Also, a plan or model to be followed when making something.

pediment In classical architecture, a triangular space at the end of a building, formed by the ends of the sloping roof and the cornice. Also, an ornamental feature having this shape.

permanent installation Art made for a specific space, often outdoors, that is not intended to be moved.

Pharaoh A ruler of ancient Egypt.

photographer A camera artist.

pigment A coloring material made from crushed minerals and plants or chemicals, usually held together with a binder.

pixel The basic unit of the composition of an image on a television screen, computer monitor, or similar display.

placement The act of placing or arranging elements and objects in an artwork.

plaque An ornamental or informative tablet.

plate In printmaking, a piece of flat material, such as wood or metal, with a design on the surface. The plate is used to print the design, which is a mirror image of the composition. See also *block*.

portfolio A portable container used to hold and organize artworks, especially drawings and paintings. Also, the artworks collected in this container.

portrait A work of art created to show a person, animal, or group of people, usually focusing on the face.

pose The way a subject sits or stands while an artist creates a portrait.

positive space Shapes, forms, or lines that stand out from the background in a work of art. See *negative space*.

pottery Objects made of clay, which can be useful and/or decorative.

Pre-Columbian Art Artworks created in the Americas before Christopher Columbus and other Europeans arrived in the area.

primary color A color that cannot be mixed from other colors, but from which other colors are made. The primary colors are red, yellow, and blue.

principles of design Guidelines that artists use to organize the elements in a composition. Unity, variety, emphasis, balance, proportion, pattern, and rhythm are the principles of design.

printmaking The process of transferring an image from an inked surface to another surface to create an artwork.

profile The side view of a subject.

progressive rhythm Rhythm created in an artwork by showing regular changes in a repeated element, such as a series of circles that progressively increase in size from small to large. The changes may also progress from light to dark, or from bottom to top.

proportion The relation of the parts of an artwork to each other and to the whole. Proportion is a principle of design.

Q

quilt A padded bedcover made from two layers of cloth that are sewn together and stuffed. Usually, one or both layers are made from scraps of fabric that have been arranged and stitched together in a colorful design. Also, the process of creating a quilt.

R

radial balance A type of balance in which lines or shapes spread out from a center point.

regular rhythm Rhythm in an artwork created by repeating the same element, such as a shape, without variation.

relief print The technique of printing in which an image raised from a background is inked and printed.

relief sculpture A type of sculpture in which forms project from a background and are meant to be seen from one side.

Renaissance The period between the 1300s and 1600s, during which new ideas and technological advances, as well as renewed interest in the Classical styles of the Romans and Greeks, laid the foundation for modern art and society.

rhythm The repetition of elements, such as lines, shapes, or colors, that creates a feeling of visual motion in an artwork. Rhythm is a principle of design. In music, rhythm refers to the pattern of the notes.

S

scale The size of an object in relation to an ideal or standard size.

scanner A device used to transfer text or graphics into a computer.

sculpture An artwork made by modeling, carving, casting, or joining materials into a three-dimensional form. Clay, wood, stone, and metal are often used to make sculptures.

secondary color A color made by mixing two primary colors. The secondary colors are orange, violet, and green.

shade A color made by adding black to a hue. For example, adding black to green results in dark green. Also, the darkness of a color value. See *value.*

shading A way of showing gradual changes in lightness or darkness in a drawing or painting. Shading helps make a picture look more three-dimensional.

shape A flat, two-dimensional area with height and width, which might have an edge, or outline, around it. Shape is an element of art.

size relationships A technique that alters the proportions of compositions. The three categories are monumental, miniature, and exaggerated.

slip A soft, wet mixture of clay and water that acts as glue to join scored pieces of clay.

Teacher Glossary

software Computer applications used for various functions, such as drawing, editing text, creating graphics, or altering images.

solvent A liquid, such as turpentine or water, used to control the thickness or thinness of paint.

space The open or empty area around, above, between, within, or below objects. Shapes and forms are defined by the empty space surrounding them. Space is an element of art.

still photography The art and science of making a picture with a camera.

stippling A shading technique creating dark values by applying a dot pattern.

stirrup A part of a vessel shaped like an inverted U in which something is held, supported, or fixed.

stitchery A term for artwork created with a needle, thread or yarn, and cloth, such as a quilt.

stop action A technique for filming animated features in which figures are positioned into place, a frame is shot, and the figures are repositioned for the next frame. When played back, the figures appear to move naturally.

storyboard A series of drawings on small cards that represents the visual plan of a video production.

style An artist's individual way of expressing his or her ideas. Also, a technique used by a group of artists in a particular time or culture.

subject What an artwork is about. A person, animal, object, or scene can be the subject of an artwork.

Surrealism A style of art developed during the 1920s that combines realistic images and dream-like ideas. Many Surrealist artworks contain illusions.

symbol A letter, color, sign, or picture that represents words, messages, or ideas, such as thoughts and feelings. For example, a red heart is often used as a symbol for love.

symmetrical balance A type of balance in which both sides of an artwork look the same or almost the same. Also known as *formal balance*.

tactile texture A texture you can feel with your hands, such as rough or smooth. Also known as *actual texture*.

Taoism A principle philosophy and system of religion of China based on the teachings of Lao-tzu in the sixth century B.C. It advocates restoring in the mind and body the Tao, or the source of being, non-being, and change, in the universe.

technique The way an artist uses and applies art media and tools to create a certain type of artwork.

tempera paint A chalky, water-based paint that is thick and opaque. Also known as *poster paint.*

temporary installation A form of installation art that is not meant to be permanently on display.

terra cotta Fired clay with no glaze, usually reddish-brown in color, used for pottery, architectural ornament, and sculpture.

tessellation A pattern of shapes that fit together in a way that leaves no space in between, as in the artworks of M. C. Escher.

textile An artwork made from cloth or fibers, such as yarn.

texture The way something feels to the touch or how it may look. Texture is an element of art.

tint A light value of a color, such as pink, that is created by mixing a hue with white. Also, the lightness of a color value. See *value.*

transparent The quality of letting light pass through; the opposite of *opaque.*

triptych A picture or carving in three panels.

trompe l'oeil (meaning "fool the eye") A type of painting in which various illusionary devices persuade the viewer that he or she is looking at the actual objects represented.

two-point perspective A form of linear perspective in which all lines appear to meet at either of two vanishing points on the horizon.

U

unity The quality of seeming whole and complete, with all of the parts looking right together. Unity is a principle of design.

urban Of, relating to, or located in a city.

urban environment The circumstances or surroundings in a city.

utilitarian Designed for a specific purpose.

value The lightness or darkness of a color. Tints have a light value. Shades have a dark value. Value is an element of art.

vanishing point In linear perspective, the place on the horizon where parallel lines seem to meet or converge.

variety The use or combination of elements of art, such as line, shape, or color, to provide interest in an artwork. Variety is a principle of design.

vertical line In an artwork, a line that runs up and down, such as a flagpole or a giant redwood tree. Vertical lines appear strong and powerful.

vessel A functional and/or decorative container made from clay used to hold solids or liquids.

video art A medium for creating motion pictures, such as motion picture films or videotaped television programs. An artwork whose medium includes television or film images.

visual texture The way a surface appears through the sense of vision. For example, the surface of a sculpture may appear shiny or dull. Also known as *simulated texture.*

Teacher Glossary

warm colors The family of colors that includes reds, yellows, and oranges. Warm colors bring to mind warm things, places, and feelings.

warp In weaving, the threads attached to the top and bottom of a loom.

water-based paints Water-soluble paints, such as tempera, watercolor, or acrylic, that use different binders and have different qualities.

weaving A process of interlocking thread, yarn, or other fibers to create a fabric, usually on a loom.

Web design Design specializing in the development of a page or site on the World Wide Web for a person, group, or organization.

weft The threads that cross over and under the warp fibers on a loom.

Artistic Perception

Awareness and sensitivity to natural and human-made environments

Concepts

Students progressively learn that their multisensory experiences, such as hearing, touching, moving, and seeing, can help them perceive and identify the visual elements of art as well as the visual principles of design.

Legend

○ Open circles indicate the grade where aspects are introduced.

● Shaded circles indicate the grades where aspects are developed.

	Levels								
	K	1	2	3	4	5	6	7	8
Elements of Art — Line									
Explore and examine line in art	○	●	●	●	●	●	●	●	●
Identify and name types of lines such as curved, straight, thick, thin, fine, broad, dotted, wavy, zigzag, continuous, broken	○	●	●	●	●	●	●	●	●
Use a variety of art media and tools to create line	○	●	●	●	●	●	●	●	●
Recognize horizontal, vertical, and diagonal lines				○	●	●	●	●	●
Recognize actual and implied lines					○	●	●	●	●
Use line to create shape or form	○	●	●	●	●	●	●	●	●
Use line to create pattern and texture	○	●	●	●	●	●	●	●	●
Use line to create movement	○	●	●	●	●	●	●	●	●
Use line to express thoughts and emotions	○	●	●	●	●	●	●	●	●
Name, identify, and use line as an element of art	○	●	●	●	●	●	●	●	●
Color									
Explore and examine color in art	○	●	●	●	●	●	●	●	●
Name and identify warm colors and use them in a composition	○	●	●	●	●	●	●	●	●
Name and identify cool colors and use them in a composition	○	●	●	●	●	●	●	●	●
Name and identify primary and secondary colors	○	●	●	●	●	●	●	●	●
Mix primary colors to make secondary colors	○	●	●	●	●	●	●	●	●
Name and identify intermediate colors					○	●	●	●	●
Mix primary colors with secondary colors to make intermediate colors		○	●	●	●	●	●	●	●
Name, identify, and use neutrals such as white, black, gray				○	●	●	●	●	●
Name, identify, and use color schemes: harmonies			○	●	●	●	●	●	●
Recognize properties of color such as hue, value, intensity					○	●	●	●	●
Name, identify, and use color as an element of art	○	●	●	●	●	●	●	●	●

Scope and Sequence

		Levels							
	K	1	2	3	4	5	6	7	8
Value									
Explore and examine value in art		○	●	●	●	●	●	●	●
Recognize value as being the lightness or darkness of a color		○	●	●	●	●	●	●	●
Create color tints	○	●	●	●	●	●	●	●	●
Create color shades	○	●	●	●	●	●	●	●	●
Name, identify, and use value as an element of art		○	●	●	●	●	●	●	●
Shape									
Explore and examine shape in art	○	●	●	●	●	●	●	●	●
Recognize shape as being a two-dimensional flat space enclosed by actual or implied lines	○	●	●	●	●	●	●		
Identify organic shapes		○	●	●	●	●	●	●	●
Name and identify geometric shapes	○	●	●	●	●	●	●	●	●
Arrange shapes to create a work of art	○	●	●	●	●	●	●	●	●
Use shape to create pattern and texture	○	●	●	●	●	●	●	●	●
Name, identify, and use shape as an element of art		○	●	●	●	●	●	●	●
Texture									
Explore and examine texture in art	○	●	●	●	●	●	●	●	●
Recognize texture as the look and/or feel of a surface	○	●	●	●	●	●	●	●	●
Name and identify different types of textures	○	●	●	●	●	●	●	●	●
Distinguish between tactile and visual texture		○	●	●	●	●	●	●	●
Create texture in a work of art	○	●	●	●	●	●	●	●	●
Name, identify, and use texture as an element of art		○	●	●	●	●	●	●	●
Form									
Explore and examine form in art	○	●	●	●	●	●	●	●	●
Recognize form as being a three-dimensional object with height, width, and depth	○	●	●	●	●	●	●	●	●
Identify organic forms		○	●	●	●	●	●	●	●
Name and identify geometric forms	○	●	●	●	●	●	●	●	●
Arrange forms to create a work of art	○	●	●	●	●	●	●	●	●
Name, identify, and use form as an element of art	○	●	●	●	●	●	●	●	●

	Levels								
	K	1	2	3	4	5	6	7	8
Space									
Explore and examine space in art	O	●	●	●	●	●	●	●	●
Recognize that space is the actual or visual area within and around shapes and forms: foreground, middle ground, background		O	●	●	●	●	●	●	●
Recognize positive space		O	●	●	●	●	●	●	●
Recognize negative space		O	●	●	●	●	●	●	●
Work with space in a work of art	O	●	●	●	●	●	●	●	●
Name, identify, and use space as an element of art	O	●	●	●	●	●	●	●	●
Principles of Design **Unity**									
Explore and examine unity in art			O	●	●	●	●	●	●
Recognize that unity in a work of art is a quality that occurs when all its elements and principles are working together			O	●	●	●	●	●	●
Name and identify the elements and/or principles in a work of art that create unity				O	●	●	●	●	●
Understand and use unity as a principle of design			O	●	●	●	●	●	●
Variety									
Explore and examine variety in art			O	●	●	●	●	●	●
Recognize that variety in a work of art is a change in shape, form, appearance, or detail that creates interest			O	●	●	●	●	●	●
Recognize that unity and variety often work together in design			O	●	●	●	●	●	●
Understand and use variety as a principle of design			O	●	●	●	●	●	●
Emphasis									
Explore and examine emphasis in art		O	●	●	●	●	●	●	●
Recognize that emphasis implies areas in a work of art that dominate and draw attention to the main idea		O	●	●	●	●	●	●	●
Identify emphasis in works of art		O	●	●	●	●	●	●	●
Understand and use emphasis as a principle of design		O	●	●	●	●	●	●	●

Legend

O Open circles indicate the grade where aspects are introduced.

● Shaded circles indicate the grades where aspects are developed.

Scope and Sequence

	Levels								
	K	1	2	3	4	5	6	7	8
Balance									
Explore and examine balance in art	○	●	●	●	●	●	●	●	●
Recognize that balance is a way of arranging elements of design to give an artwork a sense of equality in visual weight	○	●	●	●	●	●	●	●	●
Identify symmetrical balance	○	●	●	●	●	●	●	●	●
Identify radial balance			○	●	●	●	●	●	●
Identify asymmetrical balance		○	●	●	●	●	●	●	●
Understand and use balance as a principle of design	○	●	●	●	●	●	●	●	●
Proportion									
Explore and examine proportion in art			○	●	●	●	●	●	●
Recognize that proportion is the size relationship of one part to the whole			○	●	●	●	●	●	●
Recognize that proportion can indicate distance			○	●	●	●	●	●	●
Understand and use proportion as a principle of design			○	●	●	●	●	●	●
Pattern									
Explore and examine pattern in art	○	●	●	●	●	●	●	●	●
Recognize that pattern is an arrangement of lines, shapes, colors, or forms in a regular repetition	○	●	●	●	●	●	●	●	●
Understand and use pattern as a principle of design	○	●	●	●	●	●	●	●	●
Rhythm									
Explore and examine rhythm in art			○	●	●	●	●	●	●
Recognize that rhythm is a sense of visual movement achieved by the repetition of one or more elements of art in a work of art			○	●	●	●	●	●	●
Recognize types of rhythm: random, regular, alternating, flowing, progressive							●	●	●
Understand and use rhythm as a principle of design			○	●	●	●	●	●	●

Creative Art Process

Inventive and imaginative expression through art materials and tools

Concepts

Students progressively learn to experiment with art materials in order to understand properties and develop manipulative skills and in order to express individual ideas, thoughts, and feelings in simple media.

Media and Methods		Levels								
		K	1	2	3	4	5	6	7	8
Drawing										
Express individual ideas, thoughts, and feelings through drawing		○	●	●	●	●	●	●	●	●
Draw with a variety of materials such as pencils, crayons, pastels, chalk, water-based pens		○	●	●	●	●	●	●	●	●
Draw from memory, imagination, or observation		○	●	●	●	●	●	●	●	●
Create an artwork using a variety of drawing materials, such as charcoal, pen and ink								○	●	●
Collage, Mosaic, and Mixed Media										
Express individual ideas, thoughts, and feelings through collage, mosaic, and mixed media		○	●	●	●	●	●	●	●	●
Create a collage using a variety of materials such as paper, found objects, cardboard, string, plastic, fiber		○	●	●	●	●	●	●	●	●
Create a mosaic using a variety of materials such as pieces of tile, construction-paper pieces, small stones			○	●	●	●	●	●	●	●
Create a mixed-media artwork using a variety of materials such as photographs, magazine pictures, paper, yarn, paint, crayons		○	●	●	●	●	●	●	●	●
Painting										
Express individual ideas, thoughts, and feelings through painting		○	●	●	●	●	●	●	●	●
Create an artwork using a variety of painting tools and materials such as tempera or liquid school acrylic, brushes, string, fingers, sponges, found objects, paper		○	●	●	●	●	●	●	●	●
Printmaking										
Express individual ideas, thoughts, and feelings through printmaking		○	●	●	●	●	●	●	●	●
Create an artwork using a variety of printmaking tools and materials such as tempera or liquid school acrylic, brushes, string, fingers, sponges, found objects, paper		○	●	●	●	●	●	●	●	●
Sculpture										
Express individual ideas, thoughts, and feelings through sculpture		○	●	●	●	●	●	●	●	●
Understand the differences between two-dimensional artworks and sculpture		○	●	●	●	●	●	●	●	●
Create an artwork using a variety of sculpture tools and materials for sculpture such as papier-mâché, plaster of Paris, kiln-fired clay		○	●	●	●	●	●	●	●	●
Differentiate between additive and subtractive sculpture				○	●	●	●	●	●	●

Scope and Sequence

	K	1	2	3	4	5	6	7	8
Textiles and Fibers									
Express individual ideas, thoughts, and feelings through textiles or fibers	○	●	●	●	●	●	●	●	●
Identify characteristics of fibers in textiles: heavy, light, smooth, rough, natural, synthetic, tightly woven, loosely woven			○	●	●	●	●	●	●
Create a textile artwork using a variety of fiber tools and materials such as yarn, string, plastic, synthetic fabric, natural fabric	○	●	●	●	●	●	●	●	●
Create a textile artwork using a variety of methods: weaving, knotting, batik, stichery	○	●	●	●	●	●	●	●	●
Technology and Photographic Imagery									
Express individual ideas, thoughts, and feelings through photographic imagery				○	●	●	●	●	●
Create a photographic artwork using a variety of tools and materials such as sun prints, photograms, photomontages				○	●	●	●	●	●
Understand that photographic imagery can be still or motion			○	●	●	●	●	●	●
Understand that photographic imagery can be made with a variety of tools and materials such as still cameras, video cameras, motion picture cameras	○	●	●	●	●	●	●	●	●
Explore and examine a variety of ways that computer technology is used to create works of art	○	●	●	●	●	●	●	●	●
Simple Architectural Structures and Environmental Art									
Express individual ideas, thoughts, and feelings through simple architectural structures and environmental art	○	●	●	●	●	●	●	●	●
Recognize simple architectural structures and environmental art	○	●	●	●	●	●	●	●	●
Construct simple architectural models of structures from a variety of materials such as sticks, rocks, bricks, plastic, wood, boxes, fabric	○	●	●	●	●	●	●	●	●
Differentiate among a variety of architectural styles							○	●	●
Recognize how architectural styles relate to environmental factors: cultural traditions, aesthetic values, climates, geographic locations, types of available materials, landscapes					○	●	●	●	●
Sketchbook and Portfolio **Keep a sketchbook to:**									
record own artworks	○	●	●	●	●	●	●	●	●
observe and evaluate development of creativity, originality, and individuality in style	○	●	●	●	●	●	●	●	●
Keep a portfolio to:									
organize own artworks	○	●	●	●	●	●	●	●	●
document, observe, and evaluate artistic development	○	●	●	●	●	●	●	●	●
Safety in the Creative Art Process **Safety**									
Demonstrate a cautious respect for art materials and tools	○	●	●	●	●	●	●	●	●
Demonstrate caring for and cleaning art materials and tools	○	●	●	●	●	●	●	●	●

Art History

Art appreciation through historical and cultural context

Concepts

Students progressively learn and talk about contemporary and past styles and types of artworks, to include cultural origins and functions. They study themes, relative ages of artworks, reasons for creative art, art museums, careers in art, and biographical information about individual artists.

Legend

○ Open circles indicate the grade where aspects are introduced.

● Shaded circles indicate the grades where aspects are developed.

		Levels								
	K	**1**	**2**	**3**	**4**	**5**	**6**	**7**	**8**
Artistic Traditions, Past and Present									
Recognize art as a visual record of humankind	○	●	●	●	●	●	●	●	●
Focus on cultural traditions and ethnic heritage in art by recognizing images, symbols, motifs, and themes representing the art of specific cultures, traditions, and schools of artists	○	●	●	●	●	●	●	●	●
Focus on cultural traditions and ethnic heritage in art by recognizing differences among styles of art reflecting cultural tradition and ethnic heritage				○	●	●	●	●	●
Focus on historical time frames in which art was created					○	●	●	●	●
Focus on contextual information about the art of individual artists			○	●	●	●	●	●	●
Art in the Environment and Community									
Focus on the role of art museums in the community	○	●	●	●	●	●	●	●	●
Recognize the function of visual arts in the community			○	●	●	●	●	●	●
Develop an awareness of art and its origins in natural and manufactured environments				○	●	●	●	●	●
Art Careers									
Explore careers in the field of art	○	●	●	●	●	●	●	●	●
Recognize the value of art in a variety of careers	○	●	●	●	●	●	●	●	●

Scope and Sequence

Art Criticism

Aesthetic valuing through initial response and evaluation

Concepts

Students progressively learn about looking at and exploring art—perceiving, analyzing, comparing, contrasting, evaluating, and judging their own and others' artworks. Positive attitudes are reinforced through thoughtful response, as well as through individual and group evaluations.

Legend

○ Open circles indicate the grade where aspects are introduced.

● Shaded circles indicate the grades where aspects are developed.

	Levels								
	K	1	2	3	4	5	6	7	8
Explore and Examine Artworks									
Selections from self and other students	○	●	●	●	●	●	●	●	●
Selections of major artists	○	●	●	●	●	●	●	●	●
Selections from home and community design	○	●	●	●	●	●	●	●	●
Focus on Contextual Clues									
Setting in which art is created				○	●	●	●	●	●
Manner and setting in which art is experienced				○	●	●	●	●	●
Focus on Functions and Purposes of Art	○	●	●	●	●	●	●	●	●
Develop a Knowledge of the Process of Art Criticism									
Discuss initial response to an artwork	○	●	●	●	●	●	●	●	●
Describe sensory qualities and technical aspects of an artwork by identifying elements of art and principles of design				○	●	●	●	●	●
Describe sensory qualities and technical aspects of an artwork by identifying media, techniques, and processes used to create artworks	○	●	●	●	●	●	●	●	●
Analyze an artwork by comparing and contrasting principles of design	○	●	●	●	●	●	●	●	●
Interpret an artist's meaning, mood, and symbolism and other expressive qualities of artwork	○	●	●	●	●	●	●	●	●
Judge an artwork and offer reasons	○	●	●	●	●	●	●	●	●

Index

Index

Index

N

O

P

R

S

Index

Grade 4 Art TEKS

TEKS Objective	Page Numbers
(4.1) Art. Perception. The student develops and organizes ideas from the environment. The student is expected to:	
(4.1)(A) communicate ideas about self, family, school, and community, using sensory knowledge and life experiences; and	
1. communicate ideas about self, using sensory knowledge	**6, 85, 119, 174, 175**
2. communicate ideas about self, using life experiences	**6, 50, 58–59, 85, 108, 140–141, 170,** 101
3. communicate ideas about family, using sensory knowledge	**6, 15, 102, 128, 154, 187**
4. communicate ideas about family, using life experiences	**6, 41, 118, 160**
5. communicate ideas about school, using sensory knowledge	**6, 20, 21, 60, 124**
6. communicate ideas about school, using life experiences	**6, 104, 168, 178, 179, 181,** 72
7. communicate ideas about community, using sensory knowledge	**6, 61, 65, 104**
8. communicate ideas about community, using life experiences	**6, 105, 110, 167, 206, 207,** 153
(4.1)(B) choose appropriate vocabulary to discuss the use of art elements such as color, texture, form, line, space, and value and art principles such as emphasis, pattern, rhythm, balance, proportion, and unity.	
1. choose appropriate vocabulary to discuss the use of art elements such as color, texture, form, line, space, and value	**8, 9, 17, 18, 19, 23, 24, 25, 26, 28, 32, 33, 34, 36, 37, 38, 40, 41, 42, 44, 48, 49, 52, 53, 56, 57, 60, 61, 67, 75, 82, 83, 84, 85, 86, 87, 91, 100, 104, 105, 116, 117, 119, 128, 150, 151, 154, 155, 158, 159, 169, 173, 191,** 22, 203
2. choose appropriate vocabulary to discuss the use of art principles such as emphasis pattern, rhythm, balance, proportion, and unity	**8, 9, 66, 67, 70, 71, 82, 83, 85, 90, 91, 94, 95, 116, 117, 124, 125, 129, 132, 133, 149, 150, 151, 158, 159, 169, 172, 173, 176, 177, 184, 191, 197, 219,** 17, 201

Bold numbers indicate skill emphasis.

TEKS Objective	Page Numbers
(4.2) Art. Creative expression/performance. The student expresses ideas through original artworks, using a variety of media with appropriate skill. The student is expected to:	
(4.2)(A) integrate a variety of ideas about self, life events, family, and community in original artworks;	
1. integrate a variety of ideas about self in original artworks	**92–93, 122–123, 130–131, 174–175, 216–217**
2. integrate a variety of ideas about life events in original artworks	**58–59, 110–111, 140–141,** 88–89
3. integrate a variety of ideas about family in original artworks	**15, 28–29, 102–103, 164, 187**
4. integrate a variety of ideas about community in original artworks	**20–21, 28–29, 62–63, 76–77, 106–107, 208–209**
(4.2)(B) design original artworks; and	**20–21, 24–25, 28–29, 34–35, 38–39, 42–43, 46–47, 54–55, 58–59, 62–63, 68–69, 72–73, 76–77, 80, 88–89, 92–93, 96–97, 102–103, 106–107, 110–111, 114, 122–123, 126–127, 130–131, 136–137, 140–141, 144–145, 148, 156–157, 160–161, 164–165, 170–171, 174–175, 178–179, 182, 190–191, 194–195, 198–199, 204–205, 208–209, 212–213, 216**
(4.2)(C) invent ways to produce artworks and to explore photographic imagery, using a variety of art media and materials.	
1. invent ways to produce artworks, using a variety of media	**20–21, 24–25, 28–29, 34–35, 38–39, 42–43, 46, 54–55, 58–59, 62–63, 68–69, 72–73, 76–77, 80, 88–89, 92–93, 96–97, 102–103, 106–107, 110–111, 114, 122–123, 126–127, 130–131, 136–137, 140–141, 144–145, 148, 156–157, 160–161, 164–165, 170–171, 174–175, 178–179, 182, 190–191, 194–195, 198–199, 204–205, 208–209, 212–213, 216**
2. invent ways to produce artworks, using a variety of art materials	**20–21, 24–25, 28–29, 34–35, 38–39, 42–43, 46, 54–55, 58–59, 62–63, 68–69, 72–73, 76–77, 80, 88–89, 92–93, 96–97, 102–103, 106–107, 110–111, 114, 122–123, 126–127, 130–131, 136–137, 140–141, 144–145, 148, 156–157, 160–161, 164–165, 170–171, 174–175, 178–179, 182, 190–191, 194–195, 198–199, 204–205, 208–209, 212–213, 216**
3. invent ways to explore photographic imagery, using a variety of art media	**122–123, 129, 130–131,** 164, 178
4. invent ways to explore photographic imagery, using a variety of art materials	**122–123, 129, 130–131,** 164, 178

Bold numbers indicate skill emphasis.

TEKS Objective	Page Numbers
(4.3) Art. Historical/cultural heritage. The student demonstrates an understanding of art history and culture as records of human achievement. The student is expected to:	
(4.3)(A) identify simple main ideas expressed in art;	**11, 30, 51, 64, 108, 121, 129, 135, 173, 201,** 167
(4.3)(B) compare and contrast selected artworks from a variety of cultural settings; and	
1. compare selected artworks from a variety of cultural settings	**31, 64–65, 75, 166–167, 172, 192, 193, 200, 201,** 132–133
2. contrast selected artworks from a variety of cultural settings	**31, 64–65, 75, 132–133, 166, 192, 193, 200, 201**
(4.3)(C) identify the roles of art in American society.	**37, 39, 44, 45, 61, 94, 95, 100, 109, 113, 134, 146, 158, 162, 163, 168, 169, 196, 202, 206, 215,** 18, 67, 71, 78, 112, 203
(4.4) Art. Response/evaluation. The student makes informed judgments about personal artworks and the artworks of others. The student is expected to:	
(4.4)(A) describe intent and form conclusions about personal artworks; and	
1. describe intent about personal artworks	**14, 20, 24, 29, 35, 43, 49, 54, 62, 68, 80, 83, 92, 97, 107, 126, 136, 156, 164, 170, 178, 194, 198,** 204
2. form conclusions about personal artworks	**13, 21, 29, 35, 43, 47, 49, 55, 59, 63, 69, 77, 81, 83, 89, 97, 103, 111, 115, 123, 131, 137, 139, 149, 157, 159, 161, 171, 175, 179, 183, 209, 219**

Bold numbers indicate skill emphasis.

Grade 4 Art TEKS

TEKS Objective	Page Numbers
(4.4)(B) interpret ideas and moods in original artworks, portfolios, and exhibitions by peers and others.	
1. interpret ideas in original artworks by peers	**11, 25, 29, 47, 71, 93, 101, 117, 125, 151, 169, 183**
2. interpret ideas in original artworks by others	**11, 16, 23, 33, 36, 37, 40, 41, 53, 61, 71, 75, 100, 109, 117, 121, 129, 135, 167, 173, 185, 189, 207, 211, 219,** 27, 49, 51
3. interpret ideas in portfolios by peers	**11, 47, 81, 117, 151, 183, 185, 217**
4. interpret ideas in portfolios by others	**11, 151, 163, 185**
5. interpret ideas in exhibitions by peers	**11, 149, 169, 183**
6. interpret ideas in exhibitions by others	**11, 95, 116, 120, 147, 173, 185**
7. interpret moods in original artworks by peers	**11, 99, 115, 141, 149, 151, 169, 183, 185**
8. interpret moods in original artworks by others	**11, 27, 33, 53, 57, 67, 83, 87, 91, 98, 99, 100, 101, 117, 119, 132, 133, 139, 146, 152, 153, 155, 177, 185, 193, 197,** 17
9. interpret moods in portfolios by peers	**11, 115, 149, 151, 185**
10. interpret moods in portfolios by others	**11, 151, 163, 185**
11. interpret moods in exhibitions by peers	**11, 115, 169, 183**
12. interpret moods in exhibitions by others	**11, 147, 173, 185,** 116

Bold numbers indicate skill emphasis.

Notes

Notes